CW01460790

Witchcraft and Witch Trials

WITCHCRAFT AND WITCH TRIALS:

A History of English Witchcraft and its Legal Perspectives, 1542 to 1736

by

Gregory Durston

MA, Dip.L, LL.M, of the Middle Temple and Lincoln's Inn, Barrister, Senior Lecturer in Law, Kingston University, England

Barry Rose
Law Publishers

ISBN 1 872328 73 3

Published by
Barry Rose Law Publishers
Chichester, England

For P.J.R.

What are these,
So withered, and so wild in their attire,
That look not like th'inhabitants o'th' earth,
And yet are on't?

Macbeth, Act 1, Scene iii.

Contents

Acknowledgments

I would like to acknowledge the help provided by Gentian Durston in the preparation of this manuscript. Thanks are also due to the staff at the British Library, the Public Record Office, and the libraries of Lambeth Palace, Kingston University, the LSE and Lincoln's Inn for their assistance with the collection of materials. I am indebted to the work of a large number of scholars, amongst them Sharpe, Briggs, Thomas, Larner, Levack, Rosen, Geis and Bunn, as well as many others. Their books and articles can be found in the Select Bibliography and in the footnotes. The spelling and punctuation of contemporary sources is as in the original, except where modified to facilitate comprehension. All mistakes are, needless to say, entirely the author's responsibility.

Gregory Durston

London,
All Souls' Day, 1998

Preface

In recent decades witchcraft in early modern Europe generally, and England in particular, has been fertile ground for published research. The justification for this fresh book is that the English persecution of witches was overwhelmingly a secular legal phenomenon, rather than the result of popular or ecclesiastical action. As William Perkins noted in *A Discourse on the Damned Art of Witchcraft* published in 1608: "The discovery of a witch is a matter judicial, as is also the discovery of a thief and a murderer, and belongeth not to every man." Prior to it becoming a secular crime, it appears to have been of little significance. With its decriminalisation (both *de facto* and *de jure*), it gradually died out as a topic of concern. This book is aimed at remedying a lacuna in recent scholarship by making a proper examination of the subject in its legal context, as well as providing a more general history of the phenomenon. Despite the fact that witchcraft was, by its very nature, supernatural, the English courts largely attempted to deal with it as they did any other type of felony. This proved impossible, forcing recourse to methods, and standards, of proof that were not normally acceptable in the wider system, in turn occasioning severe institutional stress. As a result, a study of the legal ramifications of witch prosecutions is not only crucial to an understanding of witchcraft in England, but is also invaluable in understanding the wider operation of the English criminal justice system of the period. The persecution of witches in England, and the attendant levels of witch trials and executions never came close to reaching the worst continental levels. There were many reasons for this: social, cultural, religious and political. However, an important role must also be ascribed to the common law, and the English criminal justice system, of the era. For all their many faults, it is clear that those charged with the administration of English justice made a major contribution to this process.

PART ONE: GENERAL HISTORY

Chapter 1

An Overview of Witch Persecution in England and Continental Europe

"When the foolisher sort of people are alwaies most mistrustfull of hurt by witchcraft, and the simplest and dotingest people mistrusted to doo the hurt: what wise man will not conceive all to be but follie?." Reginald Scot *The Discovery of Witchcraft* (1584).

The Medieval Background

In popular debate, the formal persecution of suspected witches is often referred to as "medieval", and, until the 1960s, many scholars considering the phenomenon also believed that early modern prosecutions for witchcraft were merely the continuation of an existing, and long-standing, medieval process, albeit on a larger and more intensive scale. They were assisted in this belief by a number of ingenious forgeries from the nineteenth century, many of which have only been exposed in the last few decades.

Since the 1970s, and aided by the work of scholars such as Norman Cohn, it has been appreciated that large scale witch persecutions did not occur in Europe until the very end of the medieval period.[1] Thus, what occurred in the sixteenth

---

1. Cohn, N., *Europe's Inner Demons* at pp.164 and 165.

century was not simply a survival of archaic practices, as these had been largely absent before 1450. Of course, there *had* been occasional cases involving allegations of witchcraft between 1000 and 1400. Amongst them was the sensational trial of Dame Alice Kytler, for ritual witchcraft, in Ireland, in 1324, and the prosecution for the same crime of many of the Knights Templar, after their organisation was disbanded by Philip IV of France (in 1308 to 1314). There had also been occasional allegations that sorcery had been used as the *modus operandi* for ordinary late medieval crimes (such as murder). Significantly, the early (c.1300) treatise on English law termed *Britton*, written in law French, with Royal authority, placed those who used "enchantment," to send people to sleep, in its chapter on larcenies (its only mention of the subject). It was banded with other offences of dishonesty, such as cutting purses, forgery and robbery, presumably being used to effect similar purposes.[2] In England, the number of such crimes increased slightly as the fifteenth century advanced, though their position was always ambiguous. Were they simply conventional felonies carried out by supernatural means, or also heresy? Additionally, with the passing of a statute against heresy in England, in 1401, came commissions for the arrest of sorcerers in general, in 1406, and, in 1441, special rewards were offered to all who could discover witches. Nevertheless, with a few reservations, it can be said that during the medieval period, the secular courts were little concerned with witchcraft, and even the church courts do not normally appear to have been

---

2. Nichols F.M., *Britton an English Translation and Notes*, at pp.51-52.

excessively preoccupied with it.[3] It is possible that some of the judicial mechanisms of the medieval period actively discouraged spurious allegations of witchcraft, for example, by making accusers liable to punishment themselves if they failed to establish their charges.

Large scale action against witches, in England, was particularly late in arriving, being absent before the end of the sixteenth century. Some thoughtful observers were aware, even at the time, that they were witnessing a new phenomenon in the unprecedented level of popular concern. The sceptic Reginald Scot presciently observed: "... heretofore Robin Goodfellow, and Hob goblin were as terrible, and also as credible to the people, as hags and witches be now: and in time to come, a witch will be as much derided and contemned, and as plainly perceived, as the illusion and knaverie of Robin Goodfellow."[4] Nevertheless, although the judicial persecution of witches was overwhelmingly a phenomenon of the early modern period in Europe, many of its intellectual roots can be traced far back into the medieval period, and beyond. Thus, Thomas Aquinas, the most influential medieval philosopher and theologian, though not particularly concerned about witches, had speculated on their existence and operation. His views were to become important authority in later years, as were those of St. Augustine, who had also believed in the possibility of a demonic pact.

---

3. Bellamy John, *Crime and Public Order in England in the Later Middle Ages*, at pp.61-63, and p.156.
4. Scot, Reginald, *The Discovery of Witchcraft*, at p.131.

The Onset of Persecution

By the early fifteenth century a more systematic, developed, and widespread witch-belief was emerging in parts of continental Europe. Pope Eugenius IV (Pontiff from 1431-1447) addressed the issue briefly in several of his letters. Writing to the Inquisitor, Pontus Fougeyron, in 1434, he observed that amongst many different types of heretic in Europe were "magicians, diviners, invokers of demons, bewitchers, conjurers, superstitious people, augurs, those who use nefarious and forbidden arts." In a letter to all Inquisitors of Heresy, in 1437, he further observed that the "Prince of Darkness" was ensnaring many Christians into his sect. These unfortunates reportedly made sacrifices to demons and (an early indication of the demonic pact) made a "written agreement or another kind of pact", which empowered them to perform evil deeds and sorcery. Because of this, they could summon bad weather, as well as curing diseases. He was already of the opinion that they might employ perverted forms of Christian ritual or images, such as a reversal of the Holy Cross. At much the same time, 1437, Johannes Nider, a Dominican theologian, and the author of a treatise on theology, the *Formicarius* quoted a repentant witch who described his initiation into the craft, his renunciation of Christ and his baptismal faith, and the doing of homage to "the magisterulus, that is, to the little master", as they termed the devil. This individual's wife was also allegedly a witch, but, unlike her husband, refused to confess or repent, despite being subjected to torture. Both were burnt.[5]

The emergence of this continental persecution, in the fifteenth century, is still not fully explained, and a plethora of causes has been suggested. Some have attributed it to a reaction by the Church to the Cathar doctrines that had resulted in the Albigensian crusade (1208-1213), with their Manichean emphasis on a dualistic moral order of good and evil. However, the significant gap between the defeat of these beliefs, which had gradually died out in the century after the crusade, and the onset of major witch persecution, reduces the plausibility of this theory. Others have stressed the wider manner in which the persecution of witches was merely a late manifestation of periodic campaigns that had been launched against "special" groups generally, not simply Cathars, but also Jews, Waldensians, the Knights Templar (who had been specifically accused of devil worship), Hussites, Lollards etc. Again, this explanation is not wholly satisfactory. Unlike witches, many of the above groups existed in identifiable, and largely separate, communities. However, whatever the causes, it remains the case that in the late fifteenth century, two German Dominican theologians, Jacob Sprenger and Heinrich Krämer, produced a definitive (and hugely influential) work on witchcraft, the *Malleus Maleficarum* (1486). It had gone through 14 editions by 1520 (although not translated into English until the modern period, it was well known to educated people in England, partly prompting Reginald Scot's work of 1584). It was a proselytising and campaigning book, challenging the alleged complacency of

---

5. Translation in Kors, A.C., and Peters, E. *Witchcraft in Europe* 1100-1700, at pp. 109-110, and pp.98-104.

the local ecclesiastical authorities in Germany to the existence and practise of witchcraft. Their earlier complaints had already prompted Pope Innocent VIII to issue the *Summis desiderantes*, the "Witch Bull", of 1484. This encouraged the removal of the local judicial obstacles that were (apparently) preventing men like Sprenger and Krämer from carrying out their work. Thus freed they could proceed to the "correction, imprisonment, and punishment" of witches and those dealing with the devil.[6]

The emerging concern with witchcraft in England was to be heavily influenced by such continental thought, though it developed appreciably later, retained many singular and peculiarly "English" characteristics, and was especially slow to adopt some of the more exotic continental theories. Given the general moderation of judicial activity against witches in England, one partial explanation is that it merely reflected the arrival, in a somewhat attenuated form, of a continental fashion.

The most reliable estimates suggest that, in Europe as a whole, and making allowances for failures in recording through lost documentation, the number of executions for witchcraft during the early modern period, was between 40,000 and 50,000 people (of whom 75 per cent were women).[7] Additionally many would have died in prison awaiting a determination of their cases, and some would have been "lynched" in local outbursts of popular action (as occurred, as late as 1751, in England, and on a very much

---

6. *Ibid.*, at pp. 109-110.
7. Briggs, R. *Witches and Neighbours*, at p.260. Some modern figures, still occasionally quoted, are clearly absurd, such as the 300,000 to three million advanced by *The Times* as recently as May 30 1998.

larger scale in some parts of continental Europe). Thus, given the more than 200 years involved, and despite some recent portrayals of the persecution as being of Nazi or Stalinist intensity, the average annual level was relatively modest. Large numbers of villages in Europe would not have produced a single executed witch.

England, witnessed one of the least intense "persecutions" (if it even warrants the word). During the 200 years in which witchcraft was prosecuted as a felony, between 350 and 1,000 judicial deaths took place (with c.500 being, perhaps, a realistic figure). About 90 per cent of villages would not have produced a single hanged witch, and many not a single formal allegation of witchcraft that came before the secular courts or JPs. Thus, to talk about an early modern "Witch craze", as, for example, Professor Trevor-Roper did in the 1960s, is inaccurate. For most of England, for the majority of the time, it probably did not even amount to a minor pre-occupation for the authorities. Indeed, it has been observed that without Essex (statistically the epicentre for such trials in England), there would almost have been no English "witch craze" at all. While this is a slight exaggeration (Lancashire, Kent, and some other parts of East Anglia returned relatively high figures as well), it is certainly true that Essex witnessed a quite disproportionate number of the nation's trials for the crime. A majority of indictments for the crime on the extensive Home Circuit during the two centuries that witchcraft was a felony (473 of 790) came from that county, and of the 112 individuals executed for witchcraft on the Home Circuit, 82 came from Essex.[8] (As the case of the

---

8. Sharpe, J.A., *Early Modern England: A Social History 1550-1760*, at p.311.

Coggeshall witch in 1699 indicates, a fear of witches, though not formal trials, seems to have survived vigorously there until at least the end of the seventeenth century.) The highly untypical witch-hunt associated with Mathew Hopkins, an Essex-man and the self-termed "Witch-Finder General", in the eastern counties, between 1644 and 1647, appears to have resulted in between 100 and 200 executions (and is thus itself a major component of the relatively modest English total between the sixteenth and eighteenth centuries). By contrast, in some counties, charges of witchcraft were largely absent. Thus, in East Sussex, such accusations appear to have been very rare, involved almost as many allegations against men as women, and nearly always ended in acquittal, or, where a conviction was secured, a reprieve.[9]

As a result of these fairly low totals, many of those who favoured an active persecution, both in England and on the Continent, were permanently concerned at the laxity of enforcement of the criminal law against witches. The Frenchman, Jean Bodin, was openly astonished at how low the offence stood in the European priority scale of crimes, compared to more conventional forms of deviance. He: "... marvelled at why many princes have set up inquiries and named special commissioners to conduct the trials of thieves, financiers, usurers, and highway robbers and have left unpunished the most detestable and horrible wickednesses of witches."[10] Bodin's concern was shared by some

---

9. This highly localised pattern was not unique to England. In France, those in Cambresis witnessed many trials, their neighbours in Artois saw very few. Even within Cambresis, some parts were untouched, others were very active against witches.
10. Bodin, *Demonomanie*, Book 4. Chapter 1, at p.174.

Englishmen, and was cited by Holland, who was shocked at those countries: "... where he knoweth the judges and magistrates are very sharp against ... common sinnes [conventional crimes such as theft], but pass over the most horrible sinnes of sorceries unpunished." Holland also asserted that the famous Protestant reformer, Theodore Beza favoured more vigorous enforcement and "complaineth against this negligence in magistrates."[11]

Anti-Witch Panics

Nevertheless, even in England, there were times and places where public concern about witches could reach acute levels. Although for much of the period there was a "steady state" level of individualised persecution in England, with occasional trials of isolated individuals, small groups and families as witches, under certain circumstances, this could achieve the level of a local "panic," one fanned by popular rumours and exaggerated reports. The Reverend Samuel Harsnet, wrote vividly of the general anxiety prevailing in Nottingham, at the height of such a small witch scare, at the end of the sixteenth century: "The pulpets also rang of nothing but Devils, and witches: wherewith men, and women, and children were so affrighted, as any of them durst not stir in the night, ... Fewe grew to be sicke or evil at ease, but straight way they were deemed to be possessed."[12]

11. Holland, *A Treatise Against Witchcraft* at p.23.
12. Pamphlet 1599, at p.8. Harsnet's substantial work records, in detail, the practices of John Darrel, who modelled himself, to some extent, on the Jesuit missionary William Weston (who carried out several exorcisms in

The consequences of such publicity induced hysteria were widely noted throughout Europe during the early modern period by thoughtful individuals. Thus, the sceptical Spanish inquisitor, Alonso de Salazar y Frias, believed that he had not found any evidence from which to "infer that a single act of witchcraft has really occurred", and felt that the evidence of accomplices, without proof from other parties, was insufficient to justify arrest, let alone conviction. Yet, he was well aware of the manner in which the fevered publicity surrounding such cases could be self-fulfilling. He noted that in the "diseased state of the public mind, every agitation of the matter is harmful and increases the evil. I deduce the importance of silence and reserve from the experience that there were neither witches nor bewitched until they were talked and written about." He observed that at Olague, near Pamplona, even those who confessed to witchcraft, had admitted that it only began there after one Fray Domingo de Sardo came to preach about the evil.[13] The same process undoubtedly occurred in England. Nevertheless, apart from Hopkins' East Anglian campaign in the 1640s, it is hard to find a case where such a panic went beyond a purely local level.

Although active, largescale, government inspired persecution was new, allegations of witchcraft had been

---

England in the 1580s). Darrel seems to have developed a form of Puritan exorcism. Eventually, he was exposed for fraudulent witch mongering in front of the Court of High Commission, deposed from the Ministry, and sent to prison.

13. Letter to the Supreme Court of Spain by Alonso de Salazar y Frias. Translation in Kors, A.C., & Peters, E., *Witchcraft in Europe* 1100-1700, at pp.340-1. His two fellow inquisitors at Logrono were apparently shocked by his opinions.

made for centuries. A distinction must be drawn between the witch-beliefs that constituted peasant folk-lore and superstition (beliefs that modern anthropology would suggest are fairly widespread in primitive societies), and which had presumably been present during the whole of the medieval era, and the systematic "demonology" that was constructed in the late mediaeval and early modern period. It was the development of this phenomenon that produced the threatening, and intellectually coherent, diabolical "system" that justified an officially blessed persecution.[14] Nevertheless, the existing peasant beliefs were a crucial component in the mature demonology that ultimately developed. In England, especially, given the comparatively late arrival of the complex continental thought on the subject, such superstitions became recognised as an essential, or at least widespread, component of witchcraft by many experts. It appears to have been a symbiotic process. The English yeomen and peasantry would gradually be introduced to "new" concepts of witchcraft, these originally emanating from other parts of Europe, and would progressively absorb them into their own popular counter-witchcraft practices. In exchange, their existing practices and beliefs were adopted by theorists writing on the subject as normal ingredients of the phenomenon. Thus, the "swimming" of witches, unheard of in early sixteenth century England, was being conducted on an informal, widespread and popular local basis well before the middle of the following century, and persisted long after witchcraft had been abolished as a felony.

---

14. *See on this* Trevor-Roper, H.R. *The European Witch-Craze of the Sixteenth and Seventeenth Centuries*, at pp.9 and 12.

Conversely, the almost unique English emphasis on animal familiars appears to have been a long-standing popular belief, yet one that became a recognised indicator for "experts" such as Mathew Hopkins.

Throughout western Europe, as witchcraft became a secular crime, levels of persecution increased. By contrast, in the late sixteenth and seventeenth centuries, Spain and Italy, where the religious courts of the Inquisition had kept control of witchcraft prosecutions, witnessed relatively modest levels of both prosecutions and executions. (In the case of Spain, they were arguably too preoccupied with other forms of religious deviance to concentrate their energies on witches.) However, even where secularisation occurred, it appears to have taken some time for people to become accustomed to the novel idea of processing witches through the secular courts. This partly explains the dearth of cases under the short lived Act of 1542, and the fact that after recriminalisation in 1563, the number of such trials gradually increased over the following 20 years.

In Scotland, witchcraft (which had been little mentioned before the Reformation) was included in the business previously dealt with by the ecclesiastical courts, which was subsumed into the jurisdiction of the State in 1563. Although there were some early persecutions there shortly after criminalisation, such as Erskine of Dun's campaign in Angus and the Mearns in 1568-9, a major initiative awaited a strong impetus from above. This was duly provided by James VI. Already familiar with the advanced continental theories of demonology, he had visited Denmark in 1589, witnessing a country in the throes of a major witch persecution. When a group of witches allegedly claimed to have raised storms to destroy him, at the command of Satan, a large-scale persecution ensued. King James took an active part, torture was extensively used (unlike England) and features of continental beliefs, such as the witches' Sabbath were elicited (these still being largely absent in England). This campaign lasted until 1597, when James wrote his great work on *Daemonologie,* expressly to rebut sceptics such as the Kentishman, Reginald Scot. At much the same time, however, and probably influenced by growing personal doubts about individual cases, he revoked the standing commissions on witchcraft, to the consternation of the Kirk. In retrospect, it can be seen to signify his first questioning of the witch-hunting process, doubts that were to become more overt after his move to England in the following decade.[15]

The secularisation of the crime did not necessarily reduce clerical involvement in its prosecution. In Scotland, Ministers of the Kirk took an active role in interrogating witches and, after 1563, in exhorting their persecution. Significantly, where the grip of the established Church was weak in that country, as in the Highlands, the persecution of witches was largely absent.[16] Clerical "enthusiasts" were also often heavily involved in the investigation of witches in both England and New England (in the latter case, most obviously, at Salem).[17]

Witchcraft trials in England reached a peak in the late Elizabethan and early Jacobean period (ie, around the turn of the sixteenth century), before gradually declining, especially after 1620. The timing of this peak is, perhaps, not insignificant. Witchcraft was recriminalised at a time when

---

15. Wormald, Jenny, *Court, Kirk, and Community: Scotland 1470-1625,* at pp.168-169.
16. *Ibid,* at pp.168-169.
17. Levack, Brian *The Witch-Hunt in Early Modern Europe,* at p.89.

the State was set to encourage a greater real enforcement of the whole of the substantive criminal law, and eager to establish a higher level of general order and conformity. Directives went out regularly from the Privy Council exhorting JPs to this effect. The courts became more efficient, better supervised, and, consequently, more used. As a result, although the potentially harsh Act of 1542 had been largely an empty letter (more a public condemnation of witchcraft than the prelude to a major persecution), that of 1563 was to be actively invoked. Like prosecutions for conventional types of felony, witchcraft trials burgeoned. Significantly, the exposure of the Lancashire witches, in 1612, closely followed a "crackdown" that April on non-communicants in the local Anglican Churches of that largely Catholic county. This had been carried out at the behest of the Privy Council, which had sent requests to the local JPs urging that attendance be vigorously enforced. A short time afterwards, Roger Nowell, the JP at the centre of the case, also took action over the simmering local rumours of witchcraft in the Forest of Pendle and the "complaint of the Kinges subjects for the losse of their Children, Friendes, goodes, and cattle." Nowell, apparently, investigated and discovered a large local coven. He appears to have been a prime mover in the ensuing prosecutions (conducted on an unprecedented scale), fulfilling the role taken by the JP Brian Darcy in Essex almost 30 years earlier. His task was facilitated by having made the early acquaintance of an 80-year-old woman called "Demdike" (her real name was Elizabeth Sowtherns), who, it was claimed, had been a witch for up to 50 years in the forest. In April, 1612, she apparently made a "voluntarie confession" to Nowell of her involvement in witchcraft, incriminating others, and started the ensuing chain of events moving.

Witches, thieves and non-communicants were all being increasingly "regulated."

One of the most obvious (and consequently overlooked) explanations for the spread of a developed and complex demonology in the early modern period, can be found in the advent of the printing press. Johann Gutenberg's first printed book was only published in 1455, his press being introduced to England by William Caxton in 1476. The dozens of relatively cheap tracts on witchcraft that later became available were to be a highly popular form of reading matter in sixteenth and seventeenth century England (and much of the rest of Europe). These, together with the major works discussing witches and demonology, allowed new ideas about the subject to disseminate relatively swiftly. Also indicative of the widespread interest in witchcraft is the manner in which it was to be a recurring theme in popular drama for the early decades of the sixteenth century. Thus, Shakespeare's *Macbeth* was produced in 1613, Thomas Middleton's play *The Witches* came out at about the same time, and eight years later, 1621, *The Witch of Edmonton*, a collaborative work by William Rowley, Thomas Dekker and John Ford was staged. This play was produced following the trial and execution, of Elizabeth Sawyer of Edmonton on whose career it was loosely based. (It drew heavily on the moralistic tract, written by Henry Goodcole the same year, titled *The Wonderfull Discoverie of Elizabeth Sawyer a Witch, late of Edmonton ...*). These literary works provide a valuable insight into the popular understanding of the phenomenon of witchcraft.

From available records (and it must be remembered that before 1650 these are often very incomplete), by the late 1630s witch cases were comparatively rare, having fallen away over the previous 20 years. Indicative of the change after 1620, can be considered the markedly different treatment accorded to a number of people accused of witchcraft in Lancashire in 1633, when compared with the similar case, some 21 years earlier, which had resulted in the multiple executions of the Pendle witches in 1612. In the 1633 case, an 11-year-old boy, called Edmund Robins, who lived in the same Pendle Forest with his wood-cutter father, claimed to have stumbled onto a witches' Sabbath or feast, with about 60 local people present, these eating roast meat and drinking wine (such choice victuals being a common feature of their Sabbaths). This happened after he had encountered one Mother Dickinson, already locally reputed to be a witch, who appeared to him in the form of a greyhound, on All Saints Day (perhaps significantly, given witches' recognised desire to invert traditional Christian festivals). He managed to escape, albeit hotly pursued by cloven hoofed fiends, and later reported the matter to the local justices. Mother Dickinson and 17 others were arrested and thrown into jail. The boy and his father appear to have earned money by identifying other witches in the nearby parishes. At the subsequent Lancashire Assizes, 17 of the accused were found guilty. However, judicial attitudes appear to have softened by this time, and the trial Judge, finding the story unsatisfactory, obtained a reprieve for the accused before referring the matter for further investigation (though some later died while in prison, of disease). Four of them were sent to London, where they were personally examined by the King (Charles I) and by his court physicians (amongst them the eminent William Harvey, discoverer of the circulation of blood). Deciding that the matter was a fraud, the King pardoned those accused. In the meantime, Dr John Bridgemans, the Bishop of Chester, had also conducted an inquiry into the case, separating the boy from his father, lodging him on his own, and then questioning him closely. Eventually, the youth confessed that he had fabricated the whole story, with paternal assistance. The incident became the basis for Heywood and Brome's farcical play *The Late Lancashire Witches*.[18] Without the good sense of the trial Judge and authorities, this incident could, potentially, have attained the proportions of those reached in East Anglia, under the instigation of Mathew Hopkins, in the following decade, or at Salem 60 years later. Fascinatingly, and linking generations of witch allegations, it seems that one reason that young Edmund's story had not been dismissed summarily, was that one of the two examining JPs, was John Starkie of Huntroyde. He appears to have been the same individual, who, as a young boy, in 1596, had been the victim of alleged demonic possession at the hands of the infamous Edmund Hartlay (hanged for witchcraft at Lancaster Assizes). Perhaps in the circumstances, Starkie's credulity can be forgiven.[19]

Another indication of the new level of judicial hostility to witchcraft prosecutions came in March 1636, at the Chard Assizes in Somerset, on the Western Circuit. There, Lord Chief Justice Finch assigned four experienced junior barristers and an attorney to act in forma pauperis for a poor widow, Elizabeth Stile, who had been acquitted earlier in the Session of a charge of witchcraft. Her free counsel, given at her own request, was granted to enable her to bring an action for malicious prosecution against Nicholas Hobbes, the

---

18. Summers, M., *The History of Witchcraft*, at pp.294-295.
19. Catlow, C., *The Pendle* Witches, at p.24. On the original incident with Hartlay, *See* below, at p.49.

principal complainant against her, and any others from amongst her accusers that she wished to sue.[20]

However, in the unusual and disturbed circumstances of the English civil war, witchcraft accusations revived strongly, so that the 1640s were to witness Mathew Hopkins's campaign in East Anglia, and his notoriety as the self styled "Witch-finder General" (Hopkins did not purely limit himself to East Anglia, as he is reported to have attended Rebecca West in prison in Worcester, where she allegedly confessed to him in 1647). Hopkins's witch persecution lasted from 1645 to 1647, its end can be linked to his death that year from consumption, and to growing interference by the restored Assizes Judges. The exact number executed during it is uncertain. It appears that it was over a hundred, though probably significantly less than 200. Thomas Ady, referring to Hopkins, in 1656, as a "wicked inquisitor" felt that his work had resulted in the "cutting off" of 14 alleged witches at Chelmsford and 100 at Bury St Edmunds alone (though the latter figure is probably very exaggerated).[21] Other East Anglian towns would have seen smaller clusters of executions. Interestingly, decades later, John Hale firmly equated what had happened at Salem in 1692 with Hopkins's East Anglian campaign almost 50 years earlier: "It sways much with me that I have since heard and read of the like mistakes in other places. As in Suffolk in England about the year 1645 was such a prosecution, until they saw that unless they put a stop it would bring all into

---

20. Cockburn, J.S. (Ed.), *Western Circuit Assizes Orders 1629-1648: A Calendar,* at p.99.
21. Ady, *Candle,* at p.100.

blood and confusion."[22] There were lesser, but still significant, outbreaks in places as diverse as Kent and Newcastle during the civil war and its immediate aftermath (until the early 1650s). A lack of records might hide other, smaller outbreaks, at about the same time, as well as the normal isolated "steady state" prosecutions of previous years. These were possibly linked to the disruption caused by years of warfare, and, in particular, to the effects of institutional breakdown engendered by the fighting. These were especially manifest in the failure of Assizes Judges to properly ride their circuits at the peak of the fighting, and in the widespread national feeling of impending doom and destruction, something perhaps necessarily attendant on such a fratricidal conflict. As one tract from 1645 observed, anyone who witnessed such sad times, in which fathers fought sons and brothers fought brothers, must necessarily believe that: "...he liveth now in the evening of time, and in the last age of the world, wherein all things do begin to suffer a change." In such an environment, strange happenings could be expected, and were duly reported. Thus there were bizarre reports of incidents such as that of a "great stone clambering up the staires." One of the most remarkable of these incidents occurred at Garraton, near Loughborough, in Leicestershire, in 1645. There, a small lake, a little above an acre in size, which had been used for generations to water cattle, suddenly became repellant to the cows. When it was examined, it was seen that the water had begun to appear red in colour, and that the "substance thereof, was thicker than before." This transformation became more marked over four

22. Hale, John, *A Modest Inquiry into the Nature of Witchcraft,* at p.424.

days, until it became clear that the "water turned into blood." It was felt to be symbolic of the "bleeding times", in an era when "Every day almost bringeth forth some new miracle" and "wonders were never more frequent", as God's wrath was "poured forth on the face of the whole earth." In this strained psychological atmosphere, it is not surprising that allegations of witchcraft should also greatly increase in number.[23]

Significantly, most modern research suggests that the East Anglian witch finders of 1645 were not the instigators of the persecution of local witch suspects, even if they eventually shaped the manner in which it was carried out. Released from some of the traditional institutional controls by the unusual events of the civil war, local people seem to have been at the forefront of the process, taking independent action against neighbours who had probably been suspected for some time, and later calling in the "professionals" to confirm their suspicions. Significantly, when Stearne stressed that neither he nor Hopkins had used "extremity" on suspects, he qualified this by noting that: "... at first, before he or I ever went, many Townes used extremity of themselves, which after was laid on us."[24] It is clear that municipal authorities were willingly prepared to pay significant amounts of money to eliminate local witches during the East Anglian persecution. Aldeburgh in Suffolk, not a rich town, spent almost £20 on such local trials and their attendant expenses, between the autumn of 1645 and early 1647. These resulted in seven executions for witchcraft.

---

23. Pamphlet 1645(1) at pp.1-5.
24. Stearne, *Confirmation* at p.61.

However, Mathew Hopkins's modest share of this total, based on his two visits to the town, was the sum of £4, probably little more than his expenses. Mary Phillips, his assistant, a recognised expert in finding the witches' mark, received £1, 5s. for her work and testimony at trial. (Other expenses included: £4, 7s. to a local woman for looking after the detained witches and providing victuals to the visiting witch-finders; 11s. to the hangman for executing the seven convicted witches; £1 to the man who erected the gallows; 8s. to a local roper for providing the nooses with appropriate knots; and 6s. for the burial of the witches and the marking of their grave with an appropriate post.)[25]

America

Although a belief in witchcraft was carried to America from England (and other countries), the American colonies appear to have been free of the high levels of persecution that characterised much of Europe. Despite the infamous Salem trials in 1692, they experienced, perhaps, only 40 executions (half of these at Salem). Given this, and considering the scale, and late date of occurrence (at a time when the witch "craze" was clearly well on the decline in most of western Europe) the events at Salem seem all the more remarkable. The trials there began after two young girls in the household of the Reverend Samuel Parris started to show strange patterns of behaviour. They admitted to taking part in meetings, conducted by a Caribbean slave called Tituba, at which, it

---

25. Sharpe, James, *Instruments of Darkness*, at p.145.

was alleged, spells had been cast and fortunes told. These were probably little more than children's games. Nevertheless, on being examined by a local doctor, ministers, and magistrates, it was concluded that the children were bewitched. Panic developed swiftly. By mid-May of that year a hundred people were in prison awaiting trial. By late September, at its peak, an improvised court had tried and convicted 27 people, 19 of whom were hanged, and another pressed to death by heavy stones for refusing to enter a plea. In addition, dozens more had "confessed," and were in custody. Accusations, in some form, had touched 200 people. A variety of explanations have been advanced for these unprecedented (in America) events, usually stressing aspects of the social, political, governmental and religious structures of the colony, and their interaction on the interpersonal relationships of the Salem villagers. Nevertheless, Salem was an aberration, quite unique in American history.

Decline in England and America

After the Restoration in 1660, witch trials declined rapidly in England as élite attitudes changed (though Scotland experienced a major outbreak in 1660-1661, producing about 400 trials). By the time witchcraft was abolished as a felony in 1736, they had been a rarity for two generations, and absent for one. However, although in the period following 1660, there was a general popular awareness that prosecutions for witchcraft were declining, the reasons for this were not always clear to contemporary observers. Not all attributed it simply to the growth of scepticism; some believed it was because witches themselves had become rarer. There was also a general awareness that England had seen fewer such trials than most other European countries, even at its peak, though this was again sometimes linked to national incidence, rather than differing levels of prosecution. Thus, one book from 1665, declared that "Yet we have not one witch to one hundred that be in other Countreys, and fewer than formerly; and therefore the fewer are bewitched." (Though the same writer believed that some ongoing cases of bewitchment were being overlooked.)[26]

One, very practical, factor behind the diminution of witch cases after the Restoration was probably an increased reluctance, on the part of the political élite, after the traumatic and iconoclastic events of the Interregnum, to allow previous levels of expression to popular beliefs within the legal process. In the unusual political environment of the civil war, men of relatively marginal social status (Mathew Hopkins, for example, was a prosperous yeoman), just on the fringes of the political nation, had gained an unprecedented degree of power in many diverse fields, whether in the parliamentary army, as expounders of radical religion, or, in Hopkins's case, by harnessing popular anxieties about witches.

The last certain executions for the crime in England appear to have taken place in 1682, with the last death sentence that may have been carried out, being that of Alice Molland, at Exeter, in 1684. The last Assize trial that produced a conviction (albeit swiftly followed by a reprieve), was that of Jane Wenham, in 1712. In 1717 Jane Clerk was indicted for witchcraft but the case was dismissed before trial. Perhaps

26. *Daimonomageia* at p.4.

appropriately, given the significantly greater number of executions for witchcraft North of the border, the last witch to be executed on British soil was Janet Horne, at Dornoch in Scotland, in the June of 1727. By the 1690s most such cases were producing acquittals. Thus, in 1698, at the Lent Assizes in Maidstone, Mary Clerk of Ashford in Kent was found not guilty of bewitching 13-year-old Phillip Howard so that he "languished." This followed a string of cases over the previous 20 years on the Home Circuit, virtually all of which had been found "ingnoramus" by the Grand Jury, or, if there had been a trial, produced a not guilty verdict, with indictment after indictment being marked "Po se non cul."

By the early 1700s, the judiciary were willing to take active steps to discourage further prosecutions for the crime, and to attempt to bring such trials to a de facto end. In 1702 Sarah Morduck was tried for witchcraft at the Assizes in Surrey after an allegation was made against her by Richard Hathaway, an apprentice, to the effect that he had been bewitched. Although his account, to modern eyes appears highly dubious, it was widely believed, and prompted her trial under the 1604 Act. Whether he was motivated by a plan for blackmail, personal malice or genuine belief is not precisely known. However, one possibility is that he intended to sell his story in pamphlet form, hoping to make a handsome profit by it (perhaps an early illustration of "tabloid journalism"). Morduck was acquitted. By then it would have been very surprising if she had not been.

However, despite Morduck's legal vindication, there was widespread popular hostility manifest towards her afterwards, and a constant threat of violence to her person. It was widely represented that the accuser (Hathaway) had had "hard measure," and as a result, a magistrate had refused to protect her from attacks by the rabble. So many attacks were made on her that it eventually became necessary to prosecute Hathaway, as a deterrent to others, as she was likely to be "torn to pieces" in her own house by the "unruly proceedings of unthinking people." An institutional response to this was required. It appears likely that the prosecution was deliberately aimed at ending such wasteful cases on the circuit, though as the Wenham case was to show, it was not entirely successful in this. Hathaway was tried for being a cheat and an imposter in making his accusations against Morduck. He and several others, were also tried separately, for riot during the disturbances occasioned by Morduck being at liberty. The indictment for this trial stated that he had "assaulted the said Sarah and beat, scratched and wounded her, in contempt of the King, and against the peace."[27] The case was presided over by Lord Chief Justice Holt, one of the most eminent Judges of the early eighteenth century.[28] A noted sceptic, no case of witchcraft over which he presided (there were as many as 11 of them) appears to have resulted in a conviction, largely, it seems, because of his overtly hostile attitude to such cases, something that he successfully conveyed to the jury. The prosecution of Hathaway was conducted by counsel. Extremely unusually, and contrary to most normal non-treason practice at the time,

---

27. Pamphlet 1702, a p.691.
28. Sir John Holt was born in 1642, the son of a Serjeant at law. He was educated at Winchester and then Oriel College in Oxford, before progressing to Grays Inn. As a student he appears to have followed a very much more relaxed regime than Mathew Hale, before being called to the Bar in 1663. Although in no sense a "liberal" lawyer, Holt was a firm believer in the need for due process. Thus, at his hearings he discontinued the practice of bringing prisoners into court wearing irons.

the defendant Hathaway was himself represented by a well known lawyer, Serjeant Thomas Jenner, a former (albeit disgraced) Judge.[29] This was some 30 years before defence representation became relatively common in criminal trials, other than to argue points of law. It appears that Jenner's conduct of the defence went well beyond this.

The importance placed by the authorities on this prosecution (for what was not, at least technically, a very serious crime) can be seen in the fact that it was led by the outstanding lawyer Robert Raymond (1673-1733; ironically, he was the son of a timid Judge who had presided over the conviction and execution of the witches in Exeter in 1682, amongst the last in England, though whether this influenced him is impossible to say).[30] The prosecution was intended to set an

---

29. Thomas Jenner was a fairly successful, if star-crossed, lawyer. Born in Sussex in 1637 he was educated at Cambridge and the Inner Temple, where he was called to the Bar in 1663. Despite being called an "obscure lawyer" by the diarist John Evelyn, he was made Recorder of London in 1683. He became a Knight and King's Serjeant in 1684, an M.P. the following year, Baron of the Exchequer in 1686, and Justice of the Common Pleas in the same year. However, he was arrested while trying to escape to France with James II, the monarch under whom he had gained preferment. He was later expelled from the Bench, but continued to practice as a Serjeant, until his death in 1707. (The Hathaway trial appears to have ben his last noted case.) Although described by Edward Foss, as having "very small pretensions to law," and despised by other lawyers, his defence of Hathaway was not obviously lacking in ability. How he was funded is unknown, Hathaway could not have afforded his normal fees.

30. Raymond was educated at Eton and Cambridgeshire, and was always intended for the law, apparently being admitted to Gray's Inn at the tender age of nine, in 1682, though called to the Bar at a more conventional age, in 1697. Raymond is still known for his detailed legal reports, which he appears to have begun when he was only 21, and which provided an early indication of the learned and very thorough Judge that he would later become. Later, he was made a Justice of the King's Bench in 1723, and became Chief Justice of that court the following year.

example and a warning to other fraudulent "witch-mongers." However, the factual background to the trials also casts an important light on the state of popular belief in witchcraft. It is apparent from the case that although "scepticism" might have been close to triumph in its struggle with such beliefs amongst the educated and the judiciary, there was still a widespread popular faith in witchcraft, even in London and suburban Surrey (areas which might have been expected to be more sophisticated than the more remote rural communities). This belief was clearly not only confined to the "rabble". Raymond, noted that many had asserted that Hathaway"s trial was a: "...great affront to the public justice of the nation." They had put up bills in several churches asking people to pray for him against the trial, and gathered money to support him (perhaps also paying Jenner's brief fee).

A case from Coggeshall in Essex, at the very end of the seventeenth century, provides a fascinating illustration of the conflicting intellectual and popular currents in such cases, as they moved towards their close. When the Reverend Boys visited an elderly widow named Coman, in June 1699, shortly after her husband was drowned in a well, he was well aware of the "Common report representing her as a witch," and was clearly curious.[31] She admitted to him that she had seen the Devil (describing him as having "broad goggle eyes and very rough hands") conceded that she believed in the reality of God, but confessed she "did not know Jesus." When the vicar asked her if she had made a covenant with the devil (by this period a well-established doctrine) she was initially "loth to

31. Pamphlet 1712 (1) at p.3.

speak," but eventually acknowledged that she had made an "agreement" with him. She stated that she thought she would go directly to hell on death, as the devil was her master, and claimed she had made a local man, one Cox, lame by sticking pins into a wax chicken. Her behaviour was extremely eccentric, and today might be diagnosed as schizophrenic. Even the vicar, who prayed with her, thought she might have a fever in the brain that needed medication and "desiring two or three of her relations, to give her a Clyster, and somewhat to cause sleep," sent out to an apothecary for laudanum.[32] Despite his initial confusion as to the degree to which her symptoms were a product of the devil or mental illness, he noted that she repeatedly failed a well acknowledged test for witches, by mistaking the petition to the Lord's prayer. Her immediate neighbours also questioned her about any imps (familiars) she might have and whether she was suckling them at her "fundament," to which she gave an affirmative answer. Finally, persuaded of her being a witch, and clearly concerned at the growing national climate of scepticism about the subject, the vicar brought in more villagers as witnesses, in the hope that: "... the sparks of the age might entertain more easily a beliefe that there may be that which we call witchcraft." The woman refused to denounce the devil and her imps, and declined the vicar's attempt to make her touch Cox's thigh while saying "I pray God that Mr. Cox's thigh may be well" (thus refusing to withdraw her spell, a well-accepted cure for bewitchment). At this, Cox decided to have recourse to traditional and well tried remedies. He desired to know of the vicar whether he might "force some

---

32. Pamphlet 1712 (1), at pp. 5-11.

blood from her." The Reverend Boys, showing remarkable, and Byzantine, hypocrisy (as well as clerical collusion with popular magic), stated that he could do so, but only if it was "natural," not if it itself was magic! He then tactfully withdrew. At this, Cox effected his purpose, by holding her hand and scratching her arm with his nails, then: "... dipped his handkerchiefe in the blood and carried it to his father's house, and there burnt it." When the vicar visited her later she looked strangely red in the face, was in a great sweat and appeared uneasy. He asked if she was suckling her imps, and she admitted that she was. Coggeshall seems to have sustained a strong tradition of witchcraft; as late as 1755, the parish register recorded the burial of a local man, noting that he was a "reputed witch."

In America, allegations of witchcraft appear to have gradually fallen into desuetude after the extent of the mistakes committed at Salem became apparent. Nevertheless, 1692 did not mark the end of such trials in America, which continued on an occasional basis over the next 15 years. Only five years after Salem, in August 1697, the Superior Court sat at Hartford, in the colony of Connecticut, to try one mistress Benom for witchcraft. She had been accused by some children that: "... pretended to the spectral sight; [as a result] they searched her several times for teats; they tried the experiment of casting her into the water, and after this she was excommunicated by the Minister of Wallingford." However, there was little other evidence against her: "Upon her trial nothing material appeared against her, save spectral evidence." Even at Salem, this, on its own, had not been enough to convict. As a result, she was acquitted, as was her daughter, a girl of 12 or 13 years old, who had also been accused. Nevertheless, many local people appear to have been convinced of their guilt, because they subsequently fled to the State of New York after there had been "renewed complaints against them."[33]

33. Calef, Robert, *More Wonders of the Invisible World*, at p.339, drawing its title from Cotton Mather's work, and apparently written in 1697, it could not find a publisher in Boston and was first published in England in 1700.

Chapter 2

Magic in Early Modern England

Who were the witches of early modern England? Various answers to this question have been provided in the twentieth century. In Margaret Murray's early, and influential *The Witch Cult in Western Europe* (1921), it was suggested that they were the adherents of a surviving pagan cult, one stretching back into history. Although this view has been totally discredited, it is, undoubtedly, the case that to the medieval and early modern mindset, magic was widespread. Behind the visible and tangible world, were great reserves of supernatural power. These could be tapped, for good or ill, by anyone who knew how to set about it.

Magic in Everyday Life

Magic was inextricably interwoven into the fabric of medieval rural life. There were saints' shrines, such as that of St Thomas Beckett at Canterbury, which provided miracles and cures. Effigies of St Christopher were believed to attribute protection for a day to those who looked upon them in church. Fasting on St Mark's day could provide protection from fire. From the dark ages, many pagan practices and beliefs had been assimilated into those of the church. For example, magical wells were converted to saint's wells, while retaining their healing powers etc. The Mass, in particular, was widely associated with quasi-magical power, something that had been enhanced by the practice of reserving the sacrament at the altar (adopted in the thirteenth century).

Communicants at mass might not swallow all of the host, but secrete and carry away a portion. This would be used as a valuable source of power, one that could be carried to provide protection, or, alternatively, might even be ground into a powder to deal with pests on the vegetable patch. As a consequence, it has been observed that the medieval church was a "vast reservoir of magical power" which could be used for secular purposes.[34] Magic pervaded society, and many of its practitioners would never be considered as "witches," though the distinction was often hopelessly fine. To an extent, rural life required magic. Thus, until the late eighteenth century, some parts of Wales, Herefordshire and Shropshire, still retained a village "sin-eater." This person, usually an old man, would attend funerals, in return for a fee, and consume a portion of bread and a bowl of beer over the coffin, symbolically taking upon himself the deceased person's sins.

Definition of Witchcraft

One major problem in making witchcraft a crime was its definition. Indeed, so great was this, that Anglican divines and writers on the subject, both sceptics and enthusiasts, were often surprisingly willing to adopt "Romish" definitions, or those of other Reformed churches. George Gifford a preacher from Maldon in Essex (almost at the heart of witch-hunting in England), produced two major works on witchcraft, *A discourse of the subtill practices of devilles by witches and sorcerers* in 1587, and, six years later, and aimed at a more

---

34. Thomas, Keith, *Religion and the Decline of Magic,* at p.51.

general audience, *A dialogue concerning witches and witchcraftes*, in 1593.[35] In his 1587 work he attempted to produce an encompassing definition for all types of witch, whether they were conjurers, necromancers, enchanters, sorcerers or diviners. He believed that: "A witch is one who worketh by the Devil or by some curious art either healing or revealing things secret, or foretelling things to come which the Devil hath devised to ensnare men's souls withal unto damnation." Witches were witches, however their differing specialities were defined "yet have they all but one familiar tearme with us in English called witches." He allowed only one exception, some of those who purported to deal in some forms of minor magic, who were merely cheats: "As for the conceit of wisemen or wisewomen, they are all meerely cozeners and deceivers; so that if they make you believe that by their means you shall hear of things lost or stolen, it is either done by Confederacy, or put off by protraction to deceive you of your money."[36]

Cunning Men, Wise Women and Benign Magic

Despite such robust clerical attitudes, the pervasiveness of magic in society meant that there were many practitioners of the art who would never be considered as "witches." Most people drew one firm distinction, that between malign witchcraft, practised by witches, and "helpful" magic, the latter being the province of wise women and cunning men.

---

35. Gifford was an Oxford graduate who had become an Anglican priest and subsequently a non-conformist preacher.
36. Pamphlet 1618 at p.B12.

It has been observed that the basic dichotomy of witchcraft into "white" or the craft of healing, and "black" or maleficium goes back thousands of years, and was known to Roman law. The distinction is one still found in modern primitive societies. (To this essential bifurcation, in much of early modern Europe was added a refinement entailing the idea of the demonic pact, in which the witch became the servant of the devil and was granted power and material goods in exchange for renouncing his/her baptism. Services on earth being given in return for the forfeiture of the soul at death.)[37]

This division of magic into "good" and "bad" can be observed in many contemporary accounts. "M.B.", the schoolmaster in Gifford's 1593 work, noted that: "We doe count them witches which have their spirits, we doe not take them to be witches which doe but use those things that the cunning men have taught." Similarly, when the (relatively obscure) writer and former Oxford university student, Richard Bovet wrote a book on witchcraft, *Paendaemonium, or, The Devil's Cloyster,* in 1684, he noted, sadly, that practitioners of magic were distinguished, in the popular mind, into "black" and "white" ones: "The black of those which are looked upon to do the most Mischief, because they commonly Torment mens bodies, or Injure them in their Estates; and the White are reckoned to be such as restore people to health, and to goods lost." In the same vein, John Gaule was to note: "According to the vulgar conceit, distinction is usually made betwixt the White and the Blacke Witch: the Good and the Bad witch. The Bad witch they are

---

37. Larner, Christina, *Whitchcraft and Religion: The Politics of Popular Belief,* at p.3.

want to call him or her, that works Malefice or Mischiefe to the bodies of Men or Beasts: the good Witch they count him or her, that helps to reveale, prevent, or remove the same."[38] Perhaps the most bizarre accreditation of the power of white witches came from Bovet, who, although accepting that it was diabolical in origin, nevertheless felt that it was real, and could even effect the cures of those afflicted by black witches. He felt that its existence may have stemmed from a form of diabolical apathy, or a rare show of common decency by Satan; as a result "... by a Diabolical Complaisance, or goodnature, [they] are to uncharm and give ease to those the other [black witches] have afflicted."[39]

Cunning people provided a wide range of services, the most important being: healing, establishing if someone had been the victim of bewitchment and identifying who the witch was, identifying a thief or arsonist, recovering lost or stolen goods, and locating buried treasure. The recurrence of this last request may appear odd (it was even specifically covered by the witchcraft statutes). However, in an era when banking was almost non-existent, and domestic security poor, there really were many such caches hidden around the country. Inevitably, the numbers and sizes of these treasure hordes would become exaggerated in popular conversation. Cunning people used a variety of techniques, depending on the type of personal problem they were confronted with. These could range from herbal remedies for sickness (some of them on the fringes of mainstream medicine), to divination using the "sieve and shears" or the "key and book" for lost or

38. Pamphlet 1646 at p.4.
39. Bovet, *Pandaemonium* at p.22.

stolen goods, and the identification of thieves. Such wise women and men could also use quite esoteric cures for sickness; these were often not dissimilar to the incantations of their malign cousins, occasioning further confusion. According to one tract, from 1665: "One white witch is recorded to Cure by the heads of Crows and Braines of Cats."[40] Others, such as Anne Bodenham in Wiltshire in 1652, used a crystal glass for divination (something that has survived in popular mythology, as the crystal ball used by gypsies). Others provided charms to protect the user from illness, thieves and murderers, or offered love charms, and potions, to encourage romance or to put off fellow (and rival) suitors for a woman's hand (to the spurned party this could easily appear as malefic witchcraft, rather than benign magic). Importantly, they would also make recommendations for dealing with any "black" witches that might have bewitched their clients. So frequent was this last service that Ady attributed much of the country's preoccupation with malign witches to the work of such cunning people. "Another abominable cause is the suffering of imposters to live, such as silly people call cunning men, who will undertake to tell them who hath bewitched them, who, and which of their neighbours it was." These "imposters" labelled many poor, innocent people as witches, and, because this type of evidence first came from another witch (the cunning man or wise woman) the victims were "... in process of time, suspected, accused, arraigned and hanged."[41]

The examination of several witches in Manningtree,

40. *Daimonomageia* at p.23.

41. Ady, *Discovery* at p.169. This book was essentially a re-edition of his *Candle in the Dark* 1656.

including that of Elizabeth Clark in 1645, by Hopkins and Stearne provide a classic illustration of this phenomenon. Several women were identified by John Rivet, a tailor from the town who was questioned on March 21, 1645 by the local JPs. His wife had been taken ill with such violent fits that he decided that her sickness was "something more than meerly naturall." As a result, he had gone to a well respected "Cunning woman" in the neighbouring county of Suffolk, who told him that his wife was bewitched by two women, who were living close to his house. He immediately suspected Clark because of her ancestry and associations with witches (a common diagnostic indicator): "... for that the said Elizabeth's mother and some other of her kinsfolke did suffer death for witchcraft and murther."[42] Rivet was not unusual in suspecting malign magic as the cause of his wife's illness. An indication as to how widespread such beliefs were comes from the casebooks of Richard Napier, who was (perhaps significantly) both a Buckinghamshire clergyman, and an astrological physician, in the early seventeenth century. Over 500 of his patients and those who consulted him, believed that they were suffering from the effects of bewitchment.

The level of involvement in the "craft" of such cunning men and women, and their social backgrounds, would vary. For most it would be a money earning side line to another, more conventional occupation, such as that of shoemaker, labourer or carpenter, rather than their principal form of remunerative employment. A few, probably only a small minority, came from a more educated strata of society, such as minor clerics. A small number gained considerable

42. Pamphlet 1645 (2) at pp.1-6.

reputations for their abilities, with potential clients coming from many miles around, and could make a reasonable living from their earnings for such services alone. Thus, in 1593, Gifford's fictional "Samuel," suspecting that a spell had been cast on him and his animals, is urged to "take helpe at the hands of some cunning man, before I have any further harme." He notes that there was such a cunning man at a distance of 20 miles from his home, to whom a friend had gone when he, too, suspected that he was bewitched. This man had used a glass to show his friend the guilty woman and her familiars. At an even greater distance was: "... a woman at R.H. five and twenty miles hence, that hath a great name, and great resort there is daily unto her."[43] For most white witches, however, their reputation would have been confined to their native parishes, and those immediately adjacent to them. Such practitioners were numerous. John Cotta, writing in 1616, felt that the country "swarmed" with such wise men and women, resulting in the "uncontrolled liberty and licence of open and ordinary resort in all places unto wise-men, & wise women, so vulgarly termed for their reputed knowledge concerning such diseased persons as are supposed to be bewitched."[44] Their exact numbers are necessarily imprecise, if only because at the lowest level there must have been a considerable number of low grade cunning people, with basic skills, and a purely parish reputation. Those who had a county wide reputation were probably quite few in number, perhaps not more than half a dozen (in each shire). Between these two strata would have been many

43. Gifford, *Dialogue* at p.B1.
44. Potts, Thomas, *The Arraignment And Triall of Jennet Preston, of Gisborne in Craven* at p.60.

with differing degrees of influence. They would normally charge only a few shillings for their services, and might even vary the price according to the supplicants' ability to pay, perhaps only demanding pennies from their poorer clients. Recourse to white witches was not confined to the peasantry, as Edward Fairfax regretfully noted of the people in Yorkshire, who were allegedly afflicted by the many witches living in the Forest of Knaresborough: "... the inhabitants complain much by secret murmerings of great losses sustained in their goods." A typical example of this was that their cows' milk yield was reduced. Fairfax noted that, to deal with such problems: "... their usual remedy is to go to those fools whom they call Wise-men." These would propose drastic remedies, such as burning young calves alive: "... whereof I know that experiments have been made by the best sort of my neighbours."[45] (He felt that this was profoundly un-Christian.) Shakespeare's foolish Gloucestershire magistrate, Justice Shallow, was willing to send to the "wise woman of Brainford" to determine whether an individual had a stolen chain.[46] Theoretically, the clients of cunning-folk were sometimes committing a criminal offence in having recourse to such people at all, but there are very few records of secular prosecution for this (though presentations in the ecclesiastical courts were more common). In most cases, it seems that when the secular authorities did intervene, a blind eye was turned to the client, whose evidence might, in any case, be needed to effect a successful prosecution of the cunning person. This was probably a practical necessity for

---

45. Pamphlet 1621(1) at p.11.
46. *The Merry Wives of Windsor*, Act 4, Scene v.

other reasons; when it came to prosecuting the popular recourse to benign magic, in front of secular courts with a jury, it is likely that there would have been several jurors who had done very similar things themselves. Shakespeare's comment that: "The jury, passing on the prisoner's life, May have in the sworn twelve a thief or two, Guiltier than him they try," would certainly have applied with even greater force to such cases.[47] The reality of this probably explains why periodic demands by some Puritans that there be more vigorous action against both the purveyors of, and those who had recourse to, white magic, did not meet success. Nevertheless, under the Rump Parliament it was proposed (unsuccessfully) to make recourse to a cunning man or woman, to find lost property or relatives, a specific criminal offence in its own right, something that was considered especially important given that the church courts had temporarily ceased operating.[48]

Inevitably, some of the "cunning people" were out and out tricksters, or "coseners", as was well appreciated by the sceptics. In an age that was, in some ways, more credulous than the present media dominated era, fraud could be more easily perpetrated. Thus, when the monasteries were dissolved in 1540 a number of ingenious devices were discovered. One, for example, was used to make the eyes of holy statues move. It is likely that cunning people and witches sometimes had recourse to such tricks in prompting a satisfactory estimation of their abilities (Scot identified at least a dozen). However, many probably genuinely believed

---

47. *Measure for Measure,* Act 2, Scene I.
48. Thomas, Keith, *Religion and the Decline of Magic,* at p.309.

that they had been gifted with special powers at birth, or, alternatively, had learnt such techniques from their mothers or another relative.

In a society with a widespread belief in magic it was difficult to draw firm lines of demarcation between cunning people and ordinary villagers. Ordinary people would often have recourse to self-divination, using different, and widespread, techniques. The immediate origins of the Salem witch trials were in the magic games initiated by the Caribbean slave Tituba. Others would learn about such practices from friends and acquaintances when they needed to. It was from a traveller, staying in her hostlery, that an innkeeper's wife learnt the technique which was used to implicate Joan Cason of Faversham in 1586.

Cunning people, like many modern fortune tellers, would probably have had an intuitive grasp of human psychology, something that allowed them to give the answers that were required in most cases. Others could probably learn what was troubling their clients simply by listening to popular gossip in the locality. Many, however, appear to have been quite overt, especially in witchcraft cases, in asking those who came to them what they suspected was wrong, and, if it was malicious magic, who they thought was behind it, leaving the wise man/woman merely to confirm their suspicions. This was not a difficult task. Such white witches appear to have survived into the Victorian period in some rural areas.

The phenomenon of benign or white magic was not confined to England, being found everywhere else in Europe. Indeed, Carlo Ginzburg's portrayal of a sect of peasants in Friuli, known as the benanditi (good walkers), and chosen from those born with a caul (part of the membane enclosing the foetus), is an extreme illustration of this phenomenon. This group believed that, on certain nights of the year, their souls left their bodies and did battle with malefic witches to save the area's crops. They also provided healing and other types of benevolent magic. Such people would certainly not have seen themselves as using the devil's power (they viewed themselves as his mortal enemy).[49]

However, many early modern writers of a religious bent, whether avowedly Protestant or Catholic, waged a relentless literary campaign to destroy what they felt to be a mistaken and highly dangerous distinction. In England and Scotland this was to be a constant refrain of Protestant writers. Typically, Gifford viewed all practitioners of magic as being of a similar vein, people who "dealt altogether by the power and direction of the devill," even if, in reality, many of their powers did not truly exist.[50] In some respects Bernard felt they were even worse than their openly evil colleagues. James VI was another who believed that recourse to white witchcraft was in "No waies lawfull," even in cases of bewitchment, which could only be lawfully cured by "earnest prayer to God."[51] Bovet too, felt that they were really the same, being "both alike guilty in compounding with the devil." Both types of witches dealt with the same "forbiden Acts," and lead their clients to damnation.[52] Gaule felt that if the power of white witches did not come from God (as was

---

49. *See* generally Ginzburg, C., *The Night Battles, Witchcraft and Agrarian Cults in the Sixteenth & Seventeenth Centuries.*
50. Gifford, *Dialogue,* at p.G.1.
51. James VI and I, *Daemonologie,* at p.48.
52. Bovet, *Pandaemonium,* in Kors, A.C., and Peters, E., *Witchcraft in Europe 1100-1700.* at p.285.

clearly not the case), it could necessarily only have come from the devil. Gifford, too, felt that the: "... greatest part of those which cry out that they are bewitched, that run unto witches for help, that use their charmes, & seeke so many waies to unwitch, are even as ignorant, as far from zeale & Love of ye gospel, & as full of vices as the very witches themselves."[53] To those who believed in witchcraft, cunning men and women provided a slippery slope, an easy and gradual entrée to more clear cut examples of maleficium. By attempting to defend themselves against other witches, through recourse to such people, they would "arm themselves with the devils shield against the devils sword," having recourse to charms and spells until they were "Devil-fenc'd." As a result, in Bovet's words, what had started as a "league Defensive" with Satan inevitably became "Offensive."[54] This issue also exercised minds across Europe, among them that of Jean Bodin. He concluded that majority of the "soundest" theologians believed that it was: "... idolatry and apostasy to employ the aid of devils and witches to prevent or drive away evil spells." He noted, approvingly, the case of one Barbe Dorée, who in 1577 had invoked the Holy Trinity when exorcising a bewitched person, but had combined this with depositing the innards of a dead pigeon on the patient, an idea she admitted (at her trial) that she had got from Satan. She was convicted and executed. Bodin was convinced that man could never do good by using evil, something he believed that the Faculty of the Sorbonne had

---

53. Gifford, *Discourse,* at p.L2.
54. Bovet, *Pandaemonium,* in Kors, A.C., and Peters, E. *Witchcraft in Europe 1100-1700,* at p.286.

condemned as far back as 1398.[55]

Nevertheless, the publicly stated views of such clerics on the indivisibility of witchcraft, had little effect on the belief of ordinary people that there was a very important dividing line between wise women and witches, between good and bad magic. According to John Walsh, a Dorset cunning-man examined by the ecclesiastical authorities in 1566, the two categories of hurting and curing witch were distinct and mutually incompatible. Thus, when asked if those who "do good to such as are bewitched cannot also do hurt if they list" he was adamant that a hurting witch could never do good. A man or woman with the "gift of healing" could do harm, but if they did so they would never be able to do good again.[56] As a result of this popular distinction, as Bernard noted, although: "Bad witches many prosecute with all eagernesse ... the curing witch, commonly called the good witch, all sorts can let alone." He lamented that even church-wardens often failed to present both white witches and "such as resort to them" to the ecclesiastical courts (which normally dealt with such cases).[57] Although those who had recourse to white magic were theoretically open to such punishment, they were probably too numerous to make it feasible to prosecute them, and there was very little inclination to do so.

However, real though the division was, the line between good and bad magic could easily be crossed. The fragility of this division was something that was stressed by many Anglican clergymen, such as John Gaule. This was to be a

---

55. Bodin, *Demonomanie*, Bk. 3, Ch. 5 at p.158.
56. Rosen, Barbara (Ed.), *Witchcraft in England* 1558-1618, at p.70.
57. Bernard, Richard, *A Guide to Grand-Jury Men*, Second Ed., at p.A5.

near universal view, as Reginald Scot noted (albeit with some exaggeration), in 1584, the divisions were inherently prone to obfuscation: "... at this daie it is indifferent to saie in the English tongue; She is a witch; or, She is a wise woman. Sometimes observers of dreames, sometimes soothsaiers, sometimes the observers of the flieng of foules, of the meeting of todes, the falling of salt, &c: are called witches." Indeed, unlike Walsh, Scot asserted that some overtly provided both services, good and bad, resulting in a more correct sub-division into "three sorts of witches," namely: "One sort (they say) can hurt and not helpe, the second can helpe and not hurt, the third can both helpe and hurt."[58] Such a complicated trichotemy appears to have been unsatisfactory to most, who preferred a neat division.

As a result of the fineness of the distinction, several individuals appear to have made the journey from good to bad witch. This can be seen clearly in the case of Anne Bodenham, who was executed after trial at the Salisbury Assizes presided over by Lord Chief Baron Wilde (a Serjeant appointed to the Bench in 1648 by Parliament to fill vacancies occasioned by the civil war; Whitelock described him as lacking "depth of judgment," perhaps because of this, a common fault in such appointments, his tenure of the position was fairly brief). Bodenham had allegedly bewitched a woman called Anne Styles, who was in domestic service. Styles had originally had recourse to her to effect the finding of a lost silver spoon, something that was within the traditional province of such "white" witchcraft. After she went to the "aforesaid Witch, to discover the person that had

58. Scot, Reginald, *The Discovery of Witchcraft*, at p.110.

stolen it," this "cunning woman put on her spectacles" (the mixing of the titles, and the possession of eye-glasses at this time are both significant), and asked for a fee of 12d. She then opened a book in which there appeared to be a picture of the devil, and used a "green glass" (as a type of crystal ball) which showed the "shape" of many people in Styles' master's house. Styles was subsequently sent again, by her mistress, to see Bodenham, as she was afraid of being poisoned and wanted to know if there was "any such thing intended" (another typical white-witch service). However, as she walked towards Bodenham's house, a dog seemed to lead the way, and the doors to it opened automatically. The witch told her that there was such a plot against her mistress, and, rather strangely, subsequently gave her a potion made of a mixture of parings from her nails and dill "to rot their [the plotters] guts in their bellies," and to make their teeth fall out. However, apparently keen for an apprentice, later, the "Witch [Bodenham] desired the maid to live with her, and [promised that] she would teach her a more stranger art." She also appeared to Styles in the form of a great black cat, and invoked the devil, at which appeared "two spirits in the likeness of great boys, with long shagged black hair." The maid was made to seal a compact by writing in a book (the devil's book) and then saying "amen," this apparently being duly witnessed by the two spirits who also said "amen" (the devil was always a stickler for legal niceties). Styles touched the Spirits' hands which, typically, "did feel cold to the maid." However, this having been done, Bodenham swiftly "changed her tune," became nasty, and told her that: "I will now vex thee far worse than ever I did the man in Clarington Park, which I made walk about with a bundle of pales on [his] back all night in a pond of water." As a result she suffered "inward torments" and was visited with five days of fits and convulsions, until a "spirit in the likeness of a great black man," without a head, came for her soul. At this, however, instead of succumbing, Styles strongly averred that she was still a Christian, and eventually the devil desisted and she was restored to her "former state and condition." At her trial, it was claimed that Bodenham could propel "either man or woman [at] 40 miles an hour in the Air," and would also "undertake to cure almost any diseases" as well as finding lost objects.[59] The last two were normal cunning woman occupations. She was subsequently executed for witchcraft.

Similarly, Joan Peterson, the celebrated, suburban, Witch of Wapping, who was executed at Tyburn in 1652, appears to have had a foot in both camps (white and black). The author of the tract describing her case agreed with Scot, when he observed that: "... there are two sorts of Witches, which the Vulgar people distinguish by the names of the Good Witch, (I wonder how that can be), and the bad; by reason, when one bewitcheth a party, the other unwitcheth him again: Now this Joan Peterson, it should seem was both." Although it was proved that she had done "much mischief" in her life, many local people were willing to speak in her support, and there were "divers others that came to witnesse that she had cured them of several diseases." Thus, one man had been afflicted by severe headaches for five weeks, until, despairing of conventional doctors, he had visited Peterson, who gave him a special drink to take, on three occasions. After doing this, he was "as well as ever he was." This drink

---

59. Pamphlet 1653(1) at pp.3-8.

appears to have worked through magical means, as he specifically denied that it had "purged" him, and thus possibly removed the malignant "humours" that lay behind his affliction in a natural manner. Another woman, a cow-keeper's wife, had a cow that "lay in such a condition" that she was persuaded that it must be bewitched. As a result, she visited Peterson, and promised her a reward if she would cure the animal. Peterson asked her to collect some of the cow's urine (a common diagnostic tool), which she then set on the fire and brought to the boil. From the bubbles she confirmed the existing suspicion (as white witches so often did) and "shewed her the face of the woman which the Cow-keeper's wife suspected to have bewitched it." She then prescribed a cure for the beast.

Despite these good works, Peterson's malefic side was also clearly evidenced by her "evil actions." These included afflicting one Christopher Wilson, whom she had earlier cured of a disease for the promise of a sum of money, which he had subsequently refused to pay. As a result, she warned him that: "... you had been better you had given me my money for you shall be ten times worse than ever you were." Shortly afterwards, he fell into fits and would rage and "slabber" like a mad man. He then fell sick so that he "languisheth away, and rots as he lies." Even worse than this (Wilson had, after all, provoked her), a local child had also fallen sick, and, while being watched by two women, was visited by a great black cat which started to rock its cradle. It was believed that it had been sent by Peterson. Peterson was evidently not devoid of money, as she appears to have been able to afford a maid-servant who claimed that she had witnessed her talking to a familiar that appeared in the form of a squirrel. Peterson's son, aged seven or eight, also apparently told his school fellows about the squirrel. One of her terrified neighbours claimed to have seen a "black dog" visit her and "put his head under her armpits" as though searching for a witch's teat. Peterson was convicted and condemned to hang on Monday April 12, 1652.[60]

Although some cunning men and women could take considerable financial advantage of their position, if this went too far, they, too, risked being identified as "diabolical." In 1594, the children of Nicholas Starchie, apparently a Northcountry "gentleman" (though probably only a prosperous yeoman), became sick. Having an unusually small family for one in his position, only two children, Starchie was greatly alarmed when they started having fits, and had swift recourse to a local cunning man: "... one Edmund Hartlay a conjurer to whom he repaired, made knowne his greife, & with large profers craved his help." Hartlay agreed to come to his assistance, and after he had apparently used "certain popish charmes and hearbs, by degrees, the children were at quiet." He helped in this way for several years, but eventually threatened to leave Starchie's employment to go to another county. At this point the son started to have more fits, which prompted Starchie to offer Hartlay a pension of 40s. a year, and a place at his family table if he remained. However, eventually, even this was not enough for the greedy Hartlay who: "... not being satisfied desired more, [and wanted] an house and ground." The father finally "waxed wearie of him" and his ever increasing demands. He took his son's urine to a physician in Manchester, who "sawe no signe of [natural] sickness" in it.

60. Pamphlet 1652(1) at pp.3-7.

It became apparent that the children were actually bewitched, and as they began to "bark and howle," suspicion fell on Hartlay himself (his breath being the instrument of enchantment). In due course he was formally indicted at the Assizes and executed, a germane illustration of the journey from helpful wiseman to malefic witch.[61]

This potential confusion between good and bad witchcraft was certainly not unique to England, and was probably found all over Europe. In November 1643, John Burgh from Perthshire was tried, executed and burnt in Edinburgh for acts carried out during a 36-year career as a witch. Apparently, he had been responsible for the "laying of seikness and diseassis" on people and animals, as well as frequenting the "ungodlie and damnable meitings of witches." However, the vast majority of the counts in his indictment (termed the "articles" in Scotland), did not refer to conventional cases of malefic witchcraft, but rather dealt with his claims, made to the local people, that he could cure them of their illnesses, and give them "health of bodie," as a result of his "knowledge of dyverse sortis of seiknessis and diseissis learned by him from a widow woman." More seriously, he claimed that these cures were effected through an immediate pact with the devil, though this claim may simply have been attributed to him retrospectively. It would appear that, as much as anything else, the high price of the esoteric cures he offered (they involved cold water bathing in Highland streams), and the "great soumes of money, victuall, butter, cheise, and other commodeteis," that he demanded of the impoverished local people, may have been

61. Pamphlet 1660 at pp.1-7.

significant factors in bringing about his prosecution.[62]

Bewitchment was obviously outside the scope of most (though not all) normal doctors' professional competence, and more properly the domain of a wise woman or cunning man. Thus, when Thomas Sawdie, the Cornish youth who was bewitched in 1663, fell ill, he was taken first to "Mr. Cary a Physician at Liskeard," who examined his urine (a common test, as can be seen in the case of the Throckmorton children in Warboys, and the Hartlay case over 80 years earlier). The sample was, apparently, "very full of black dust." Fearing that the glass vessel had not been properly cleaned, Cary ordered a fresh sample to be taken. This produced the same result, and he concluded that it was a sign of bewitchment. Hearing this, the boy "confessed" to (or fabricated) having congress with the devil (the latter in canine form). A concerned uncle (he held property in which the boy's life was of "main concernment") stepped in at this point and seeking the services of a cunning man: "... took him and carryed him to one Condy's of Stoke-Clymland in the said County, who said that the Boy was overlookt. He gave him a Plaister, a Powder, and a little Bag to hang about his neck, and doubted not to cure him," though his confidence was to be misplaced.[63]

Some cunning folk specialised purely in witchcraft diagnosis. Thus, Durrant feeling "exceedingly troubled" at her child's continuing fits, in 1657, eventually went to a "Dr Jacob" in Yarmouth. This man "... had the reputation in the country, to help children that were bewitch'd" and after

---

62. Irvine Smith, J. (Ed.) *Selected Judiciary Cases 1624-1650*, Vol.3, at pp.597-599.
63. Pamphlet 1664 at p.3.

having diagnosed witchcraft, proposed the test that was to implicate Amy Duny. Jacob suggested hanging up a blanket for a day, and seeing what was drawn to it. This produced a toad, which fell out of the blanket, when it was shaken. When the toad was thrown into a fire, it apparently made a particularly loud pop. Subsequently, Duny was seen to have a burn on her face, although she had allegedly not lit a fire that day, but rather worn a shawl to keep warm. This man (Dr Jacob) has left no firm record. However, he may have been a tailor by the name of Jacob Travers, a man much given to alcohol abuse, but apparently with the local reputation of being able to deal with the machinations of witches.[64]

Continental Influences on England

It has been remarked that English witch cases and the trials that arose from them were mundane compared to those spawned by the more "scientific" (or at least elaborate) demonology of the continent. Indeed, for many years they were considered by academics to be a "class apart" from mainstream Europe. This uniqueness has been increasingly challenged by historians, such as Larner, as it has become apparent that European currents of thought on witchcraft significantly influenced proceedings in England. Many parallels are evident, especially in the seventeenth century (it appears to have taken a considerable time for them to permeate from the continent). The Hopkins campaign in East Anglia shows marked similarities to many continental

---

64. Geis, Gilbert and Bunn, Ivan, *A Trial of Witches: A Sixteenth-Century Witchcraft Prosecution,* at p.48

witch-hunts, in its scale, intensity and many of its details. These include the higher proportion of men tried compared to "normal" times in England (but not dissimilar to the percentage in Lorraine) and the demonology that was cited and attributed to the accused. Hopkins's witches reputedly made pacts with the devil, attended communal meetings and even, on occasion, had sexual intercourse with the devil. All of these were, more commonly, features of the continental and Scottish tradition, rather than the often solitary, and even anti-social, English witch. Of course, "traditional" English characteristics were also widely present. These included the regular attendance on those accused, of familiars in a variety of animal forms. The typical English pattern of allegations against poor women who had been refused charity and reportedly sought revenge, through maleficium involving attacks on children, animals etc. afterwards was also present. Thus, while England was not necessarily a case apart, it does remain the case that English witchcraft did have special and singular characteristics, some of them unknown or rare on the continent and that England was late in developing many continental aspects of witchcraft, and did so much less completely. This was something that was facilitated by the country's unique legal system.

Chapter 3

Special Characteristics of English Witch Cases

"O world, how apt the poor are to be proud!"
Twelfth Night, Act 3, Scene I.

Given the variety of origins and perspectives on English witchcraft it might be expected that there would be few, or no, unifying factors present. This, is something that makes the sameness of so many contemporary English pamphlets describing incidents of witchcraft hard to explain. The answer is that the homogeneity in the process was enforced by factors which were cultural, rather than situational. However an allegation came to be made, it occurred against a backdrop of village lore, theological speculation, custom and belief that shaped it into certain common forms.

The Devil's Inducements

People did not usually have recourse to Satan for the prospect of communication with evil for its own sake. The devil tempted mankind by working on human weaknesses and desires, and his inducements were extremely practical. He could claim to satisfy basic human needs by having recourse to his own powers. As George Gifford succinctly observed in 1587: "For this is man's nature, that where he is persuaded that there is the power to bring prosperity and adversity, there will he worship."[65] Almost invariably, the motivations inducing congress with the devil were personal material advancement, or the power to be revenged on enemies.

The devil could provide material advancement and even tangible wealth to his followers. However, the gifts that his supplicants requested were usually petty and unimaginative, a little money or perhaps small amounts of choice food, especially meat or wine. They were virtually never donations of great riches, and were often for the smallest amounts, a few shillings or even pennies, or a single animal. These were, perhaps, the most that the poor women to whom such inducements were supposedly offered, could dream of obtaining. When the devil appeared to Susan Edwards, in Devon, in 1682, he merely promised her that: "... she should neither want for meat, drink or clothes." Similarly, when Joane Williford, in Faversham, in 1645, confessed that the devil had appeared to her several years earlier (in the "shape of a little dog"), and "bid her to forsake God and lean to him", she admitted that as well as offering her revenge upon one Thomas Letherland and his fiancé Mary Woodrufe (she may have been "jilted" by Letherland) the devil had: "... promised her, that she should not lack, and that she had money sometimes brought her she knew not whence, sometime one shilling, sometimes eight pence, never more at once."[66] One of the most extreme (and untypical) examples of diabolical material gain that was recorded, appears to have been that of Elizabeth Francis of

65. Gifford, *Disclosure,* at p.B4.
66. Pamphlet 1645(3) at p.3.

Hatfield Peverel in Essex, in 1566 (it was also one of the earliest cases). Francis was initiated into witchcraft by her grandmother, who also gave her a familiar, in this case a "white spotted cat", that she called, perhaps rather unimaginatively, "Satan." She had swiftly asked the cat that she might be rich and "have goods", and when asked what she would like in particular (the cat apparently spoke in a "strange hollow voice"), had requested sheep. As a result the cat "forthwith brought sheep into her pasture to the number of 18, black and white." However, as with most diabolical gifts (and, conveniently for witchmongers), they swiftly turned to dust and disappeared. The devil was believed to be notoriously fickle and unreliable in meeting his contractual obligations (Edgar's comment in *King Lear* that "The Prince of Darkness is a gentleman", did not correspond with reality). Thus, Francis noted, after a time all the sheep did "wear away, she knew not how."[67] Exceptional human physical abilities could also be attributed to diabolical power, rather than to a blessing by God. According to Reginald Scot, in West Malling, in Kent, a local JP (one apparently appointed during Catholic Queen Mary's reign), had had a village archer put in the stocks because of his extraordinary accuracy with the bow, something that meant that he consistently shot "neere the white at buts." An informer had said that he used a "devil or familiar", in the form of a fly, to achieve his expert degree of marksmanship. Because the JP had never heard of such good shooting, he decided that it could not be done in "God's name, but by enchantment." It appears that the archer had won a prize of

67. Rosen, Barbara (Ed.), *Witchcraft in England 1558-1618*, at p.74.

a few shillings for his accuracy, and was consequently punished not for witchcraft (something that was not a secular offence in Queen Mary's reign due to the repeal of the Act of 1542) but rather for cheating, as well as to encourage "the overthrow of witchcraft" by example.[68] It was, perhaps, fortunate for the archer that the allegation was not made 50 years later. Similarly, over a century later, in 1692, when the Reverend George Burroughs was accused of witchcraft at Salem, part of his examination focused on his reputation for enormous personal strength, which was again attributed to supernatural powers. The reports of his undoubted muscularity became exaggerated, several soldiers, who had fought with him on an earlier campaign against the Indians, were called to give evidence that he had lifted a heavy barrel of molasses with one finger, and raised a large musket in the same manner. Yet, as Robert Calef was to point out, those who had known him at school could have testified that even then his strength was "much superior" to their own, and something that needed no diabolical pact to achieve.[69]

The other great diabolical enticement was the ability to be revenged against an enemy. This clearly exceeded material advancement in significance and frequency as a motive, undoubtedly because it was all too obvious that the marginalized women accused of being witches, were usually very poor. As Thomas Ady observed, although it was sometimes suggested that they could procure food through diabolical means, it was strange to note: "... how

---

68. *Ibid.*, at p.65.
69. Hill, Francis, *A Delusion of Satan*, at p.135.

many poor lean starved people have been executed in several places for witches."[70] One witch even ruefully told John Stearne in 1645, that although the devil had promised her both material advantage and revenge, he was rather better at providing the latter than the former. Witches were believed to be hyper-sensitive to personal slights and affronts and to have an insatiable appetite for revenge. Thus, the author of a tract on a Leicestershire witch in 1619, felt that their motivation was frequently: "... a heart burning desire of revenge, having entertained some impression of displeasure, and unkindness."[71] It was said of Elizabeth Southerns, one of the Lancashire witches from the Forest of Pendle (who was executed in 1613) "no man escaped her or her furies that ever gave them any occasion of offence, or denied them anything they stood need of." Even if such a hunger for revenge was not initially present in a witch, their familiars might cultivate it in them. A tract from 1665 noted: "The first and movent cause is, the Witch some way offended, and she doth ill by Revenging her self; but sometimes their imps force and persuade them."[72]

The scores that witches were believed to wish to "pay off", were probably often imagined, and nearly always decidedly petty, usually "parish" pump type grievances. Time and again they can be seen to have arisen out of the normal frictions of rural life. Thus, it was a desire for revenge that prompted Mary Smith to become a witch. In her case, it seems to have arisen out of economic competition in the cheese dealing trade, and a number of perceived

---

70. Ady, *Candle,* at p.141.
71. Pamphlet 1618 at p.C2.
72. *Daimonomageia,* at p.12.

minor slights: "Marie wife of Henrie Smith, glover, possessed with a wrathful indignation against some of her neighbours, in regard that they made gain of their buying and selling cheese, which she (using the same trade) could not doe, or they did better (at the least in her opinion)." The devil was always alert for the opportunity provided by this sort of discord, as he well knew how "to stir up the evil affected humours of corrupt minds", and appeared to her in the traditional form of a black man. She duly renounced God and became his servant, and then proceeded to vent her spleen on local people who had roused her ire. Amongst them was a sailor called John Orkton who had apparently struck her son (albeit with good cause). She cursed him and asked that his fingers rot off, he duly became ill and his "fingers did corrupt" in what sounds very much like a case of gangrene. She then bewitched Elizabeth Hancocke, a local woman whom she mistakenly accused of stealing her prized hen. In this case, although the victim was publicly cursed by Smith she initially made light of it, presumably attributing it to the normal social intercourse of a foul mouthed harridan: "... which speech also she made no great reckoning of, supposing them to be but words of course, and might bee uttered in jest." She, too, duly fell ill. With Cicely Bayle she "began to pick a quarrel" about the manner in which Bayle swept the front of her house. Edmund Newton was a rival cheese trader, as a result of whose operations in an evidently competitive market: "She thought her benefit to be somewhat impaired, using the like kind of trading." He fell sick and developed signs of "madness."[73] Similarly, 30 years

73. Pamphlet 1616, at pp.1049 & 1054.

later, Elizabeth Harris, when examined for her motives in becoming involved in witchcraft, at Faversham, in 1645, declared that she had a "desire to be revenged, and the devil told her that she should be revenged." Apparently one Goodman Chilman from the village of Nuenham had publicly accused her of stealing a pig, so that "she desired that God [a strange plea for a witch] would revenge her of him, and the man pined away and dyed, and she saw it apparent that her impe was the cause of that mans death."[74] There was nothing new (i.e. post 1563) in such scenarios. At Castle Cary, in about 1530, when Christian Shirston was denied a quart of ale, a barrel of the brew, of about 12 gallons, started to "boil as fast as a crock on the fire." When Joan Vicars also refused Shirston milk, her cow swiftly passed only blood and water. One Henry Russe made the same mistake, and could not make cheese until Michaelmas.[75] This background to allegations was not confined to England, also being found on the continent and in America. The perceived "thin skins" of witches allowed the most innocuous situations to acquire enormous significance. Thus, the *Malleus Maleficarum* described a case in which an honest man had been bargaining with a woman over a purchase, without coming to terms, the disappointed woman was heard to call after him "You will soon wish you had agreed." However, instead of considering this to be a normal reaction to a failed deal in the market place, it attributed sinister meaning to the words, and conveniently noted that "witches generally use this manner of speaking,

---

74. Pamphlet 1645 (3) at p.5.
75. Thomas, Keith, *Religion and the Decline of Magic*, at p.661.

or something like it, when they wish to bewitch a person by looking at him." The man subsequently became ill, or rather, within these terms of reference, was "bewitched."[76]

Acts of witchcraft were carried out against those who were seen to have shown hostility to witches. Witchcraft was used to revenge insults, a lack of respect, or, very significantly, a refusal of charity. In particular, an "unreasonable" refusal of charity, was at the back of many such accusations. To understand this it must be remembered that charity had a significance far transcending its role in the modern welfare era, or even that of the increasingly sophisticated eighteenth century poor law. It was an essential part of rural life, and provided a potentially vital insurance system for the majority of villagers, as disaster could strike almost anyone at anytime. However, there were no clear guidelines as to what was a legitimate request and what was not. Throughout Europe, at this time, there were economic and demographic changes that were putting the existing social system under enormous pressure, voluntary poor relief was set to give way to compulsory parish based schemes (first introduced in England in the Elizabethan period). Times were often harsh, and aspects of village solidarity may also have been breaking down. Small groups of richer peasants were emerging from the mass, others were falling below the average level. As a result of these factors, requests might have been refused, and yet still have inspired guilt at the refusal, a guilt that was then projected onto the spurned party. As a general theory this appears to

---

76. Sprenger, Jacob and Kramer, Heinrich, *Malleus Maleficarum* (1486), Translated by Montague Summers at p.223.

be particularly apposite in England, where the strains in the early modern system were most acute (and evidenced by the enormous fear of idle vagabonds). Numerous accusations of witchcraft appear to have been premised on a refusal of alms to a poor old woman, as a result of which she had gone off muttering. When this was closely followed by a natural disaster, it was attributed to the refused witch exacting revenge. This was something that Reginald Scot observed in 1584. The type of woman who was likely to gain the title of witch was: "... so odious, and so feared, as few dare offend them or deny them anything they ask ... go from house to house and from door to door for a pot full of milk, yeast, drink, pottage, or some other relief, without which they could hardly live." Such fears and superstitions were not confined to the lowest strata of society. Edward Fairfax noted that one of the alleged witches who afflicted his daughters had "so powerful a hand over the wealthiest neighbours about her, that none of them refused to do anything she required."[77] Sometimes, however, they were refused in their requests, and would go off cursing: "Thus in the process of time they have all displeased her, and she hath wished evil luck unto them all ... Doubtless at length some of her neighbours die or fall sick, or some of their children are visited with diseases that vex them strangely ... which by ignorant parents are supposed to be the vengeance of witches."[78] It was the coincidence of refused charity, towards a woman who already had a "reputation" and was the object of local gossip, with subsequent misfortune, that

77. Pamphlet 1621(1) at p.7.

78. Briggs, R. *Witches and Neighbours,* at pp.137-146.

prompted many allegations. A typical illustration was Ann Foster, in 1674. She was an old woman, who had long been observed to be in the habit of "muttering to herself", who asked a farmer with a large flock of sheep for mutton. Unfortunately, he was not willing to freely "spare it or she to pay for it." She went off mumbling that he should have given it to her. This was probably an everyday incident in country life, and the farmer thought nothing more about it, until a few days later when he found 30 of his sheep dead, from an unidentifiable disease, when he suspected bewitchment.[79] Another case, from Windsor, concerned an ostler, who was in the habit of giving to one Mother Stile food that was left over from his master's house. However, one day, arriving late, when there was little food remaining, she was only given a modest allotment of provisions: "... she therewith not contented went her ways in some anger and, as it seemed, offended with the said ostler for that she had no better alms." When he developed a "great ache" in his limbs shortly afterwards it would not have needed a great leap of the imagination to attribute it to Mother Stile. In any event, imagination was not needed as he sought the assistance of a local wiseman who confirmed it. (Wisemen and cunning women often appear to have simply supported existing suspicions and expressly asked those who sought their advice to name likely suspects.) The same scenario can be found in Gifford's dialogue; a man who thought a local witch: "... was once angry with him because she came to beg a few pot-herbs and he denied her; and presently after he heard a thing, as he thought, to whisper in his ear "thou

---

79. Pamphlet 1674 at p.4.

shalt be bewitched!" The next day he had such a pain in his back that he could not sit upright." Obviously, it was witchcraft.[80]

Scot's contemporary analysis of the background to many such cases of witchcraft was convincingly used as a model, at least in Essex, in the modern academic work of Alan Macfarlane. Macfarlane established that a refusal of charity, perhaps producing what Robin Briggs has termed a "refusal-guilt" syndrome, was behind many accusations in that county, at least. Such a pattern clearly persisted to the end of the witch trial era, and beyond. Thus Ruth Osborne, who was lynched at Tring in 1751, had been refused buttermilk by a farmer, whose subsequent illness spawned the allegations against her. This was not a uniquely English phenomenon. In France the same scenarios involving begging and poverty appear to have been well to the fore. The model identified by Macfarlane applies well in Essex, and probably has considerable application on a nationwide basis. However, it is important not to raise it to the status of a universal paradigm. Even within Essex there were many exceptions, and in other parts of England, especially in certain periods, the background to cases that came to trial was often very different. In some cases of witchcraft, both main inducements (revenge and personal gain) would be combined, as the background to the crime. Rebecca West, while imprisoned in Worcester, prior to her trial and execution in 1647, allegedly told Mathew Hopkins that the devil had come to her in the "likeness of a young man", promising her that she would be both "revenged on all her

---

80. Gifford, *Dialogue* at p.D1.

Enemies, and have what she desired", provided she denied God and wholly trusted in him. West promptly requested that she be revenged on one John Start who lived in the same house as she did; he "quickly after Sickened and Dyed."[81] Similarly, a widow named Clark, clearly a highly marginal member of Essex society, when examined by the JPs, said that she had been "put on" to the devil by another widow called Anne Waste, who: "... seemed much to pity this examinant for her lameness (having but one leg) and her poverty." Waste had offered her the ways and means to do something about it. Clark, in turn, incriminated a married woman, Elizabeth Gooding, whose motivation was apparently revenge, not gain, an allegation that was backed up by the alleged victim, Robert Taylor. Taylor ran a shop in the same town (Manningtree) and had received a visit from Gooding, who "desired to be trusted for half a pound of cheese, which being denied, she went away, muttering and mumbling to herself." Given that she subsequently returned with money and purchased a full pound of cheese, little might be attributed to her upset. However, that night the shopkeeper's horse took ill, and died a few days later. This appears to have been enough to back up Clark's accusation.[82]

The devil was believed to be constantly alert to human weaknesses that might give him an opening (such as a desire for revenge or wealth). Thus, Dorothy Ellis, from the Isle of Ely, noted, in 1647, that the devil first appeared to her, in the form of a cat, 30 years earlier, when she was "much troubled in her mind." This process of diabolical

81. Pamphlet 1670 at p.4.
82. Pamphlet 1645 (2) at pp.1-6.

intervention was commonly portrayed in literary portrayals. In *The Witch of Edmonton* (1621) it is Elizabeth Sawyer's desire to be revenged on "Banks", and the manner in which she curses him, that results in the arrival of the devil, in the form of a familiar shaped as a dog. She mutters aloud: "Would some power, good or bad, Instruct me which way I might be reveng'd Upon this churl." At this point the "dog" enters declaring: "Ho! Have I found thee cursing? Now thou art Mine own." Similarly, in a supposedly factual case involving material gain rather than revenge, in June 1663, one Thomas Sawdie, a youth of twelve years, went to a fair in Cornwall with his mother. He asked her for some extra spending money, although he already had some coins in his pockets, but she was short of cash herself and could not oblige him. Later, the boy "having seen many, and bought some toys", returned home alone. As he walked, doubtless ruing his missed purchases, he met a spectral woman in a field who was "very gaudy, all in white." She asked him if he would like some money, and offered it, but he cautiously refused to accept it, at which she "vanished away, rushing by him with some muttering, discontented words, which he did not understand, and suddenly a great Black Dog, with very great and fiery eyes stood before him; on which he fell to the ground as dead." When he recovered from his faint it had gone. However, that night he could not sleep, and the "dog" appeared to him again, and told him to keep quiet about his visit. The dog came once more the next night and "made him some tempting proffer and went off." Ominously, by this point, the boy had ceased to be afraid of the creature, even though the dog spoke like a man. The next night he entered a compact and received eight pieces of money, he was also told that the dog would take him to the next fair, where he would "have all his desires." Like so many gifts from the devil, the money turned to dust, and had disappeared by the next day, although he was told that he would get more. Swiftly afterwards, however, the "boy fell sick, swelling in his stomach and belly."[83]

For a few, it was an unhealthy thirst for knowledge that drove them to witchcraft. This was especially true for the handful of adherents who could be described as "educated", particularly where they were male. Faust was not entirely without a foundation of real-life examples. Richard Bovet felt that it was indisputable that spirits had special knowledge of things that were naturally "above the reach of Humane Capacities", especially the power to foresee the future. This encouraged some men to seek knowledge of matters of which they were, quite properly, ignorant.[84] Lése-majesté was a common theme in these cases, people aspiring to discover "such things as God would have kept secret."[85] As Richard Bernard observed, it was a certain type of person, "Those that are given to curiosities, to seek after vain knowledge, in pride of heart to go beyond others, to understand secrets and hidden things", that were likely to become involved with the devil for this reason.[86] An English illustration of this breed, might be the elderly Parson John Lowes, who had been the Vicar of Brandeston in Suffolk for 40 years before his exposure as a witch. He had the misfortune to fall foul of Mathew Hopkins's

83. Pamphlet 1664 at pp. 2 and 3.

84. Bovet, *Pandemonium,* at p.22.

85. Perkins, William, *A Disclosure of the Damned Art of Witchcraft* (1608) at p.591.

86. Bernard, Richard, *A Guide to Grand-Jury Men,* Second Edn. at p.94.

campaign in 1645, when it was reported that he delighted in making ships, sailing along the local coast, sink. Although rare, he was not unique. Henry Carre, also from Suffolk, a "scholar fit for Cambridge", and, if not actually a Cambridge man, certainly "well educated", also "fell into this grievous sin." He died in the gaol at Bury St Edmunds before trial.[87]

Despite its attraction, it was widely recognised that witches were fools to become involved with the devil. Sooner or later, not only did his gifts turn to dust, but he failed to aid them in their hour of need. They were women "whom their Grandmaster the devil, at one time or other leaves in the lurch."[88] Similarly, the witch of Edmonton cautioned: "All take heed How they believe the devil; at last he'll cheat you."[89] The devil could never be trusted, even (or especially) by his minions. Occasionally, he might positively revel in their exposure. Jane Hott, a witch executed at Faversham in 1645, was to testify to his deception. When she was first committed to gaol she advised other detained witches to confess if they were guilty, and maintained that she herself was: "... cleared of any such thing, and that if they should put her into the water to try her, she should certainly sink. But when she was put into the Water and it was apparent that she did flote upon the water, being taken forth, a Gentleman to who before she had so confidently spoke, and with whom she offered to lay twenty shillings to one that she could not swim, asked her how it was possible that she could be so impudent as not to confess herself,

---

87. Stearne, *Confirmation,* at p.25.
88. Pamphlet 1652 (2) at p.9.
89. Act 5, Scene iii.

when she had so much persuaded the other to confesses: to whom she answered that the Devil went with her all the way, and told her that she should sink; but when she was in the Water he sat upon a Crosse-beame, and laughed at her."[90] In the same way, at the gallows, a Worcester witch, in 1647, lamented that the devil had tricked her and her three colleagues, and "told them to the last, that he would secure them from public punishment, but now too late they found him a Lyer."[91] Indeed, those who worked for the devil would very often not even have to wait for a natural death to receive their just deserts (the forfeit of their souls to Satan). It was alleged that his vassals usually came to a premature demise as a result of the: "... execution of justice for their demerits, or by laying violent hands upon themselves, or else God powreth upon them some strange and extraordinary vengeance, or their Grand-master whom they have served, dispatcheth them in such manner, as they become dreadful and terrible spectacles to the beholders."[92] Suicide was commonly associated with witchcraft, being committed both by its victims and perpetrators. It was thought that witches in gaol might be cajoled by the devil into self-destruction, so that they could not make admissions.

Familiars

Witches' familiars were an especially English phenomenon (though not quite uniquely so, being found on an occasional

---

90. Pamphlet 1645 (3) at p.7.
91. Pamphlet 1670 at p.7.
92. Roberts, Alexander, *A Treatise of Witchcraft*, at p.15.

basis elsewhere, especially in the Basque country). They were sometimes called imps and were a cross between demonic spirits and domestic pets, being granted to witches after they had entered the service of the devil. Witches would get diabolical counsel and sometimes tangible gifts from them (such as money or food) and could send them abroad, where they would effect diabolical services at the witches' behest. In exchange, they would be cared for by their mistresses. Familiars came in many differing animal guises; rats, cats, dogs, mice, squirrels, polecats, insects, even farm animals. Elizabeth Harris, who was examined on September 26, 1645 by the Mayor of Faversham, observed that 19 years earlier, the devil had appeared to her "in the form of a Mule."[93] Nevertheless, as the canine familiar in the Witch of Edmonton (1621) noted, although they could assume any shape, they tended to confine themselves to a few specific types of animal "chiefly those coarse creatures, dog, or cat, hare, ferret, frog, toad." Some witches only had one familiar, others several. They were given personal names like any other type of English pet. Amongst them were Lucifer, Smacke, Little Lord, Lunch, Litefoote, Pluck, Blu, Hardname, Swart, Dick, Jack and Prettie. These names were sometimes believed to have been given in a grotesque parody of baptism: "... they meet together to christen the spirits (as they speak) when they give the spirit a name."[94] It was the need for familiars to receive nourishment that produced the witches' "teat", something that was gradually perceived to be a classic indicator of a witch.

---

93. Pamphlet 1645 (3) at p.7.
94. Bernard, Richard, *A Guide to Grand-Jury Men*, Second Edn. at p.109.

The Method of Enchantment

Familiars could be sent to effect bewitchment, while sometimes it was done by the use of sympathetic magic. The Flowers, smarting from a grievance at the hands of the Earl of Rutland took their revenge in this manner: "Margaret, was put out of the Ladies service of Laundry, and exempted from other services about the house, whereupon her said sister, by the commandment of her mother, brought from the castle the right hand glove of the Lord Henry Roffe, which she delivered to her mother; who presently rubbed it on the back of her Spirit Rutterkin, and then put it into hot boiling water, afterwards she pricked it often, and buried it in the yard, wishing the Lord Roffe might never thrive."

Several decades earlier, Reginald Scot had noted that a "charme touching how to hurt whom you list with images of wax", could be constructed by making "an image in his name, whom you would hurt or kill", appending a swallow's heart and liver to it, and then having recourse to "a new needle pricked into the member which you would have hurt." According to James VI, in 1597, the devil would instruct his acolytes directly in these techniques: "To some others at these times he teacheth, how to make Pictures of wax or clay: That by the rotting thereof, the persons that they bear the name of may be continually melted or dyed away by continual sickness."[95] The construction of such images might be accompanied by special spells and incantations. Abraham Chad, when giving evidence against Susan Cock and Rose Hallbread, at Worcester Assizes in

95. James VI and I, *Daemonologie,* at p.44.

1647, stated that: "... the two prisoners made a great Fire, they made the shape of the deceased children in Wax, and putting them both on a spit, one of the prisoners turn'd it, while the other stuck pins and needles in their Bellies, Heads, and Eyes, and told him that as them Figures wasted, the children wou'd waste and as the spit went round, they both muttered to themselves strange kind of words which he did not understand." During this incantation, imps in the shape of mice were seen to run out (perhaps unsurprisingly given the often vermin infested cottages of the time).[96] Thirty-five years earlier, in 1612, in the Lancashire Forest of Pendle, the octogenarian witch Elizabeth Southerns had claimed that "... the speediest way to take a man's life away by Witchcraft, is to make a picture of Clay, like unto the shape of the person whom they mean to kill, & dry it thoroughly: and when they would have them to be ill in any one place more than an other; then take a Thorne or Pinne, and prick it in that part of the picture you would so have to be ill; and when you would have any part of the Body to consume away, then take that part of the picture and burn it. And when they would have the whole body to consume away, then take the remnant of the sayd Picture and burne it: and so thereupon by that means, the body shall die."[97]

Many of these themes were well known to the general populace, and thus feature in both the specialist literature and the popular drama of the period. In *The Witch*, by Thomas Middleton (c.1570-1627), apparently written about 1613, and probably connected to the earlier events in Lancashire, "Hecate" and five of her fellow witches, discuss

---

96. Pamphlet 1670 at p.6.
97. Pamphlet 1613 (1) at p.B3.

their planned vengeance on a neighbouring farmer and his family for their repeated refusal of flour and milk. The witches decide to use sympathetic magic consisting of wax figures "Stuck full of magic needles", and burning pictures, to make the man and his wife ill. Additionally, their cows will run dry of milk and their other animals fall sick: "Seven of their young pigs I have bewitch'd already ... Nine ducklings, thirteen goslings, and a hog Fell lame last Sunday after Evensong." Anthropologists suggest that such sympathetic magic is widely found throughout the world.

Aside from images, some witches were believed to use potions or formal spells to produce their evil. Margaret Flower confessed, that she often heard her mother: "... curse the earl and his Lady, and thereupon would boyle feathers and blood together, using many devilish speeches and strange gestures." Base animals, such as rodents and reptiles, and the blood of babies and infants, were thought to be particularly efficacious in casting such spells. Thus, too, in Middleton's play, the witches discuss the ingredients of one of their potions:

> First Witch: Here's the blood of a bat.
> Hecate: Put in that, oh, put in that.
> Second Witch: Here's libbard's bane.
> Hecate: Put in again.
> First Witch: The juice of toad, the oil of adder.
> Second Witch: Those will make the younker madder.
> Hecate: Put in; there's all, and rid the stench.
> Firestone: Nay, here's three ounces of the red-hair'd wench [a girl murdered by the witches the previous day].
> All: Round, around, around, about, about, All ill come

running in, all good keep out.[98]

Although some *soi disant* witches may well have used animals like toads in their practices, the abduction of children probably existed more in the popular imagination than reality, though there may have been occasional cases. Certainly, in the apparent upsurge of witchcraft in the mid-1990s in South Africa, a number of children, abducted in parts of the country such as the Orange Farm township near Johannesburg, appear to have been murdered to provide parts for magical practices and potions by local sangomas (witchdoctors).[99] However, in England, such cases must have been exceptionally rare, leaving very few traces in the records. By contrast, simple spells, unaccompanied by any brews, appear to have been quite common. The canine familiar in the *Witch Of Edmonton*, instructs his mistress, Elizabeth Sawyer, to bewitch by merely repeating a short incantation, directed at the object of her spite, one which invoked the devil and which ran: "If thou to death or shame pursue 'em, Sanctibecetur nomen tuum [hallowed be thy name]."[100]

Even more frequently, however, a witch does not appear to have used any material aids or formal words, but rather to have simply cursed her victim, so that he or she was said to be "forspoken." Other cases appear to have been effected by a simple use of the "evil eye." The witch's power over the object of her malice being effected by physical contact, or

---

98. Middleton, Thomas, *The Witch,* Act V. Scene. ii.

99. See *"Witchcraft returns to haunt new South Africa," The Independent,* January 21, 1998 at p.13.

100. Lawrence, R.G. (Ed.) *Jacobean and Caroline Comedies,* at p.100.

simply by an invisible power given out by her eyes, so that the victim was said to be "overlooked" or "fascinated."[101] Thus, William Drage, a doctor writing in 1668, felt that by their "voyce and eyes some dǒ bewitch ... some have two Pupils, and look crosse." A few years later, the Scotsman, George Sinclair, was also convinced that they could harm: "By their looks ... as when a witch sendeth forth from her heart throw her eyes venemous and poysonful Spirits as Rayes, which lighting upon a man will kill him."[102]

However effected, the results of bewitchment were fairly standard throughout the country. For humans it could be death (usually after a lingering illness), or sickness. Dead, sick and lamed animals feature heavily, together with crops failing, houses falling or, less drastically, cows and goats not milking, beer not brewing properly, butter not curdling, or cheese refusing to set.

Witchcraft and Disease

The most serious forms of witchcraft were directed against the person, and would usually manifest themselves in the form of a disease or other illness. All diseases were potentially the result of witchcraft, rather than a natural cause. As one treatise on the subject from 1665 put it, when attempting a definition: "... disease of Witchcraft is a sickness that arises from strange and preternatural causes, and from Diabolical Power in the use of strange and ridiculous ceremonies by Witches or Necromancers,

101. Thomas, Keith, *Religion and the Decline of Magic*, at p.519.

102. Mather, William, Preface to *Satan's Invisible World Discovered*, at p.1325.

afflicting with strange and unaccustomed symptoms, and commonly preternaturally violent, very seldom or not at all curable by Ordinary and Natural remedies." However, although easy to describe in general terms, at the heart of the problem of medical diagnosis of bewitchment was the difficulty that: "All that are bewitched, are handled after some extreme or strange way, or both; but all that are handled after some extreme and strange way are not bewitched."[103] It could be exceptionally difficult, if not impossible, to separate the effects of a severe, but natural, disease from enchantment or possession.

Any form of illness that followed an unusual path was especially likely to receive such a diagnosis. Thus, when the Earl of Rutland's sick children suddenly deteriorated, he changed his opinion from natural illness to witchcraft. The eldest son (and heir), Henry, apparently "sickened very strangely" and after a while died, his other children fell ill, and Francis was "most barbarously and inhumanely tortured by a strange sickness", before dying as well.[104] Some symptoms, however, were particularly associated with witchcraft induced illnesses. Among them were unnatural forms of vomiting. These might include situations whereby some "void 1200 worms at a time", or where "the Sick Vomits gallons of blood." Even more indicative would be the regurgitation of non-natural objects, especially pins and needles (a regular feature of such cases). Thus, in one case a maid who had been bewitched: "vomited Wool, hair, Needles, Pins ... One vomited Thorns of the Sloe-tree, and

103. *Daimonomageia* at pp.1-3.
104. Pamphlet 1619 at p.D2.

hooks ... another vomited Cloth, pieces of Iron, Stones and bones." However, even in this context, as the author appreciated, there would be some (such as tricksters "who swallow pebbles") who pretended to such affliction by ingesting these items and then expelling them (the roughness and size of the articles were a useful indication that this had not occurred). Naturally, in such situations, a careful doctor must enquire what was eaten previously, and also "if a suspected witch was offenced."[105]

As Scot noted in 1584, to ignorant people, even the normal symptoms of illness "apoplexies, epilepsies, convulsions, hot fevers, worms &c." could readily be supposed to be the vengeance of witches. He felt that this process was aided by "ignorant physicians" who might attribute their own failings to witches. This observation was to become a regular theme, even amongst believers. Richard Bernard was similarly explicit, in 1627, in emphasising how false allegations could be made as a result of the mis-attribution to witchcraft of what was actually the symptom of a natural, albeit unusual, disease: "It is the general madness of people to ascribe unto witchcraft, whatever falleth out unknowne, or strange to vulgar sense." He cited several rare illnesses that produced symptoms normally felt to be consistent with bewitchment. One gentleman's daughter apparently experienced: "... divers tortures of her mouth and face, with staring and owling of her eyes, sprawling and tumbling upon the ground, gristing and gnashing of her teeth", but the cause was "naturall." Purely natural means, including baths, were used to cure

105. *Daimonomageia* at pp.3-5 and 42.

her by a doctor. He also observed that in some cases, people recovering from an illness were told by a white witch that they had actually been bewitched, leading them to make accusations, and thus prompting trials and executions. A few years later, exactly the same symptoms would recur, indicating a natural provenance for their sickness.[106] A century after Scot first made the point, John Brinley, a late believer in witchcraft, who, nevertheless, wished to "undeceive" the people about erroneous popular beliefs on the subject, also specifically identified a number of strange diseases that were occasioned by natural causes, but whose symptoms were commonly ascribed by "countrey people" to witchcraft. These were unlike those afflictions, such as measles and small-pox, with which they were readily familiar, and which were thus usually accepted as "normal." Thus, in "catalepsies", the body was suddenly frozen rigid, so that no movement was possible for a time. Similarly, rabies, with its attendant strange terror of water, might appear to be the work of a witch. (He also noted that such illnesses could prompt simple people to cut off some of the victim's hair, for diagnosis by the local wiseman.)[107] In their turn, such cautionary tales prompted some believers, such as Edward Fairfax in 1622, to worry that magistrates were becoming "incredulous" of witchcraft, because they were excessively influenced: "By such as attribute too much to natural causes." These people, he complained (amongst them divines and doctors), always argued that fits and convulsions caused by witchcraft were "merely natural

106. Bernard, Richard, *A Guide to Grand-Jury Men*, Second Edn., at pp. 11-18.

107. Anon. (John Brinley) *A Disclosure Proving by Scripture and Reason And the Best Authors, Ancient and Modern, That there are Witches*, at p.16.

infirmity."[108]

Nevertheless, by the late sixteenth century, there were signs that the devil was gradually being pushed out of the physical world, and increasingly confined to the spiritual one. It was a very slow process, one that would take many years to complete. However, indicative of this development was that even for most Elizabethan doctors, identifying the work of the devil was very much a "last resort" in medical diagnosis, albeit that there were exponents of such a prescription, such as Thomas Brown, who continued to trigger or encourage witch persecutions late into the following century. Many doctors never had recourse to a diagnosis of witchcraft at all, even if totally perplexed by an illness. To others, satanic influence, though conceded as possible, was increasingly considered to be "very rare nowadays," though those dealing with psychological, rather than physical, disturbances were slower in reaching this position.[109]

The Devil's Pact

Although a relatively late arrival in the English speaking world (at least in its sophisticated continental form) the idea of the "devil's pact", a formal agreement between Satan and acolyte, was well established by the early 1600s, and continued to the end of the witch trial period. William Perkins's work on witchcraft, published in 1608, but based on earlier sermons dating back to the 1590s, opined that the

---

108. Pamphlet 1621(1) at p.13.
109. Kocher, Paul, *Science and Religion in Elizabethan England*, at p.138.

ground of all witchcraft practices was a "league or covenant" made between the witch and devil, in which they bound themselves to each other.[110]

Thus, according to "Old Demdike", one of the Lancashire witches of 1612, 20 years earlier, she had met "a spirit or devil in the shape of a Boy, the one half of his coat black, and the other brown, who bade this examinant stay, saying to her, that if she would give him her soul, she should have any thing that she would request." Rather strangely, she had agreed to enter this fairly standard demonic agreement. Strangely, because she apparently wanted, and asked, nothing from him for many years, but nevertheless, saw the devil periodically, during this time, sometimes in the form of a dog.[111] As the century advanced, the formality of Satan's agreement with his disciples frequently became more developed and complex. Thus, after Joan Flower and her daughters became embittered at their misfortunes in the world generally, and their treatment by the Countess of Rutland in particular (especially the dismissal of Margaret for some "indecencies both in her life and neglect of her business") the devil, ever watchful for such an opportunity, appeared and offered them his service. He proposed to visit them "in such pretty formes of dog, cat, or Rat." It appears that in this particular case the "deal" was accompanied by certain solemnities, they agreed to: "... give away their souls for the service of such spirits, as he had promised them; which filthy conditions were ratified with abominable kisses, and an odious sacrifice of blood, not leaving out

---

110. Perkins, W., *A Disclosure of the Damned Art of Witchcraft*, at p.593.
111. Pamphlet 1613(1) at p.B2.

certain charms and conjurations with which the devil deceived them, as though nothing could bee done without ceremony, and a solemnity of orderly ratification."[112] The devil/acolyte formalities reached a peak in the 1640s, when they amounted at times to a "wedding." Thus, Matthew Hopkins gave evidence that Rebecca West, had admitted to him (while in prison in Worcester for witchcraft) that the devil came to her one night and told her they would be married, that he then kissed her but, as always in his physical relations with people (by the early seventeenth century the devil was sometimes even having full conjugal relations with his followers), was as "cold as clay." He then led her about the room a few times and said that they were "thus married."[113] In some cases the "marriage" services were more formal, akin to Christian ones. More common were the circumstances surrounding the induction of an old woman from Yarmouth, one of a group of 15 tried and executed there (the number may be an exaggeration). She gave extensive details about her enrolment as one of Satan's disciples, after being refused charity by a local man's servant. She was an almost classic illustration of the witch who was refused expected gifts. For some time, she had been "relieved twice a week at Mr.Whitfield's Door", however, when she came one week, the master of the house was away, and his servant felt that he did not have the authority to provide food to her. The maid of the house also refused her paid employment (doing some piecework

---

112. Pamphlet 1619 at p.D12.

113. Pamphlet 1670 at p.4. In 1645 an alleged Suffolk witch, a widow from Barton, said that the devil had appeared to her as a dark swarthy youth who was "colder than man."

knitting). As a result, the devil sensed her dissatisfaction and a "tall black man" (a by then classic description of Satan) knocked at her door one night: "He told her that he understood that she was discontented, because she could not get work as expected." Later, having reached a mutually acceptable agreement, he "wrote her name in his book."[114] The devil appears to have become assiduous about keeping such records, commonly carrying a special book containing the names of his disciples, and evidencing his agreements with properly written contracts (it was a highly litigious age). Sometimes, names would be signed in blood, and special language might be used to record the agreement. Thus, in 1663, in Cornwall, Thomas Sawdie in his "contract" with the devil had to refer to the Lord's day as the "Ugly day." A similar situation developed in America. In 1671, an alleged case of witchcraft occurred at Groton in Massachusetts, and the local minister (the Reverend Samuel Willard), who employed the "victim" as his servant, examined it in detail, subsequently writing a long letter to Cotton Mather providing details of the case. The victim, Elizabeth Knapp, was about 16 years of age. It initially manifested itself in the apparently hysterical conduct commonly associated with such cases, so that she gave "sudden shrieks." Subsequently, she claimed that the devil appeared to her encouraging her to make a pact with him and had shewn her: "... a booke written with blood of covenants made by others with him, & told her such & such (of some whereof we hope better things) had a name there."

---

114. *A Relation of a Yarmouth Witch, who with Fifteen more Convicted upon their own Confession, was executed in 1644,* at pp.46-48.

Later, the devil urged her to murder her parents and neighbours, even suggesting that she put Willard's youngest child in the oven. Knapp appears to have been well versed in the mature demonology of the devil's pact, whether from her own reading, or as a result of leading questioning by Willard. Indeed, at times Satan sounds almost like a cross between a door to door salesman and a corporate lawyer. Thus, on one occasion she saw the devil dressed as an old man, coming over a meadow lying near the house. Suspecting his "designe", she considered leaving before he got there but eventually decided to wait and "heard what he had to say to her." On arrival, he promptly: "... demanded of her some of her blood, which she forthwith consented to, & with a knife cut her finger, he caught the blood in his hand, & then told her she must write her name in his booke, she answered, she could not Write, but he told her he would direct her hand, & then took a little sharpened stick, & dipt in the blood, & put it into her hand, & guided it, & she wrote her name with his help: what was the matter she set her hand to, I could not learn from her; but thus much she confessed, that the term of time agreed upon with him was for 7 years; one year she was to be faithful in his service, & then the other six he would serve her, & make her a witch." Nevertheless, Elizabeth regularly changed the details of her story, and contradicted herself, encouraging strong doubts about the reality of her case. She eventually recovered her mental equilibrium without trial or imprisonment, and ceased her strange behaviour. This was something that sceptics, such as Thomas Brattle, were later to contrast favourably with what occurred, on apparently much thinner evidence, after the panic at Salem in 1692.[115]

115. Letter of Willard, *A brief account of a strange & unusual Providence of God befallen to Elizabeth Knap of Groton,* Printed in the Collections of the Massachusetts Historical Society, Volume viii, fourth series, at pages 555-570.

Chapter 4

Perspectives on Witchcraft

"Some call me witch,
And being ignorant of myself, they go
About to teach me how to be one; urging
That my bad tongue, by their bad usage made so,
Forespeaks their cattle, doth bewitch their corn,
Themselves, their servants, and their babes at nurse,
This they enforce upon me, and in part
Make me to credit it."
The Witch of Edmonton, Act 2, Scene I.

To understand the legal process in which witches were tried, some understanding of the crime itself is necessary. Any plausible explanation for accusations of witchcraft necessarily has to be multifaceted, "sole cause" accounts must be treated with extreme caution. There has been a plethora of these in recent years, ranging from medical explanations invoking the hallucinogenic effects of "magic mushrooms" and the results of syphilis, to social ones, attributing the phenomenon to the presence of heretics and covert pagans, and, more plausibly, the exigencies of early modern "State-building.". Others have stressed geographical explanations. Professor Trevor-Roper observed that the great European witch hunts would centre on mountain areas, such as the Vosges, the Alps and Pyrenees. (However, in Scotland, the Highlands were largely free of such cases, unlike the Central and Eastern Lowlands.) Many feminists have seen witch trials as the organised persecution of women by men, often greatly exaggerating the numbers of women involved.[116] Nevertheless, many of these explanations have some value, if not taken in isolation. Combined with others, they can be seen as providing useful perspectives on the phenomenon. Some of these will be considered in this chapter.

Social, Economic and Religious Change in the Early Modern Period

For most of the period that witchcraft was a secular crime, England was experiencing religious, social and political turmoil. That such periods of social tension and transformation can produce an increase in concern about, and attacks on, alleged witches and witchcraft, is something that can be confined neither to England, nor to the early modern period in general. The phenomenon recurred in the early 1990s in South Africa, when there was a marked increase in levels of local "witch purging."[117]

Witchcraft had first become a felony during the tumultuous reign of Henry VIII (King from 1509 to 1547), whose unsuccessful efforts to secure an annulment from his marriage to Catherine of Aragon, prompted a break with the papacy. As a result, in 1533 the Church of England, an independent national church, was established, the English religious houses being dissolved, and their property seized

---

116. *See* on this Briggs, R, *Many Reasons Why: Witchcraft and the problem of multiple explanation,* at pp.51-52.

117. *See "Witchcraft returns to haunt new south Africa," The Independent,* January 21, 1998 at p.13.

by the Crown. Despite the innate religious conservatism of Henry VIII it gradually fell under Protestant influence (both continental, and from the native Lollard tradition), although most changes were relatively small until his death. After Henry's reign, England was to witness wild religious fluctuations, as Protestantism flourished during the brief reign of the juvenile Edward VI, only to be replaced by Catholic Restoration under Queen Mary, but to witness eventual triumph, in a unique but fairly unstable, national form, under Elizabeth I. At times, especially in the early days of the crime, the dividing line between witchcraft and other forms of religious deviance could become obfuscated. Thus, Mother Waterhouse, who was executed in 1566, and who admitted to having been a witch for 15 years, stated that she had still been accustomed to going to church to attend divine service (interestingly, absence from church, though a matter regularly dealt with by the church courts, was not commonly associated with witches). There, however, when making the Lord's Prayer, amongst others, she always said them in Latin, rather than the vernacular, despite it being set out by public authority that it should be said in English. She allegedly declared that it was because Satan (perhaps a Papist at heart) would "at no time suffer her to say it in English." Given her age, Waterhouse would have grown up with Latin prayers, and, considering the relatively recent ending of Queen Mary's reign, her persisting with the old customs were, perhaps, not surprising. [118]

---

118. Rosen, Barbara (Ed.), *Witchcraft in England 1558-1618,* at p.82.

Religion and the Decline of Magic

One argument, made with great persuasiveness in the 1970s, is that Medieval Catholicism had accommodated a popular need for magic in many of its practices, in a way that the reformed religion of the mid-sixteenth century onwards, with its uncompromising attitude to popular "superstition", was unable to do. According to this (beguiling) analysis, the distinction between religion and magic had been obscured by the medieval church, but was strongly re-established by the Protestant Reformation, which vigorously rejected many former Catholic practices, outlawing them, and thus forcing the populace to have recourse to magic from other sources (in particular from witches). There may be some truth in this. Certainly, illustrations can readily be found which give limited support to the paradigm. Thus, when the English priest, William Wey, went on a pilgrimage to Santiago, in 1456, keeping a record of his journey, he observed how a fellow traveller on his ship had his purse stolen, losing valuable jewels and money. The victim immediately promised St James that he would visit his shrine if he recovered it. The thief, a Breton, was subsequently detected trying to steal from another passenger, and the stolen purse found. It was clear to Wey, and the victim, that he had only: "... regained the purse with the help of St James and [he] immediately made his way to his shrine as he had promised."[119] In post-Reformation England, this very

119. Manuscript account by Wey reproduced in Englander, D. *et al.* (Eds.) *Culture and Belief in Europe 1450-1600: An Anthology of Sources*, at p.20. On the magic/witchcraft thesis see generally: Thomas, Keith, *Religion and the Decline of Magic.*

practical service might well have been rendered by a cunning woman or wise man.

However, the argument also has a number of major flaws. Many English "sceptics" were convinced that it was residual Catholics in the population who were most prone to believing in witches. (Of course, it can be argued that it was the earlier obfuscation between popular Catholicism and magic that led many sceptics, such as Scot and Ady, to attribute a belief in witchcraft to "Romish" error.) Thus, in 1584, Scot observed: "I have dealt and conferred with manie (marrie I must confesse papists for the most part) that mainteine every point of these absurdities [witchcraft]."[120] It was an allegation that would be made by most other major English "doubters", though likening any practice to Catholicism in a Protestant country beset by papist foes was always a useful debating point. Assuming that it was even partially accurate (by no means certain), it invites the question as to why, if traditional Catholicism accommodated a desire for magic, its adherents should have greater recourse to witchcraft than their Protestant neighbours? In any event, much of the evidence is inconclusive one way or the other. In Essex, at least, the distribution of prosecutions does not show a clear correlation with either Puritanism or that county's (very few) strongholds of recusancy.[121] There may have been some correlation between areas of recusancy and witchcraft in Lancashire, in the early 1600s, as the Pendle witch trials of 1612 might indicate (the area was still producing witches

120. Scot, Reginald *The Discovery of Witchcraft,* at p.484.
121. Macfarlane, Alan, *Witchcraft in Tudor and Stuart Essex,* in Cockburn, J.S., (Ed.), *Crime in England 1550-1800,* at p.81.

over 20 years later). Equally, however, it might have been Protestant Millenarianism that contributed to the upsurge in witchcraft allegations at the turn of the sixteenth century. James VI was one of many who felt that the devil was in a hurry, knowing that the time available to him was short: "And on the other part, the consummation of the worlde, and our deliverance drawing neare, makes Sathan to rage the more in his instruments, knowing his kingdome to be so neare an ende." Internationally, the picture is equally cloudy when it comes to drawing denominational significance from witchcraft accusations. Just as in Catholic Spain persecution was relatively moderate, so it was in largely Calvinist Holland, at least after 1600. The last witch was burnt there in 1597, and witch trials were totally abolished in 1610. In Germany, Friedrich Spee, a sceptical Jesuit, was (to his admitted embarrassment) driven to the view that belief in witchcraft was especially common amongst Catholics, yet the Calvinist lowlands of Scotland were also hotbeds of persecution. Presbyterian Scotland, despite having a significantly smaller population, produced perhaps three times as many executions for witchcraft (possibly c.1,350) as Anglican England (the Scottish use of torture in such cases also facilitated this). Thus, Professor Trevor-Roper was probably right in believing that, when it came to the persecution of witches, "honours remained even" between Catholicism and Protestantism to the very end of the period.[122] As a result, more recent paradigms linking witchcraft to wider religious currents have tended to stress the role of religious strife, and the pressures occasioned by

---

122. *Ibid.*, at p.98.

a conflict of denominations (of whatever type), in producing witch hunts.

There was an international quality to the debate about witches, which often transcended issues of denomination or nationality, and in which arguments and techniques might be transmitted and approved by different parts of Europe, even if they had radically different religious alignments. This sometimes came close to making it an "ecumenical" subject, at a time of otherwise bitter religious conflict. Thus, the French scholar and witch-hunting enthusiast, Jean Bodin noted with approval that the Calvinist Scottish custom of having chests in their Kirks into which anonymous allegations of witchcraft could be made was also found in parts of Italy, being: "... the praiseworthy custom of Scotland, [also] practiced at Milan, which is called 'indict'."[123] The JP and hammer of Essex witches, Brian Darcy, referred to Bodin's work, and several other foreign treatises, while the *Malleus Maleficarum* could cross religious frontiers despite its Dominican provenance.

Biblical Authority for the Existence of Witchcraft

In a largely Protestant country like England, it was vital that a belief in witchcraft be founded in scripture. There was a limited amount of Biblical (especially Old Testament), authority for the existence and persecution of witches and their familiars. However, there was also considerable academic debate about their significance, and also the

---

123. Bodin, *Daimonomageia*, Book 4, Chapter 4, at p.176.

quality of translation of these passages from the original Greek and Hebrew into the vernacular (especially in the King James Version of the Bible). As Bishop Hutchinson was to observe in 1718, the Authorized version of the Bible had "received some phrases that savour the vulgar Notions more than the old Translation did."[124] Nevertheless, given a sympathetic interpretation, there was enough evidence for a zealot or "witchmonger", to deny allegations that their pre-occupation was completely without scriptural foundation. Certainly, many important Protestant theologians were firmly in the believers' camp. Thus, Martin Luther was convinced of the reality of witchcraft, and freely recounted how his mother had herself been the victim of a witch. Several major writers on demonology, such as William Perkins, placed great importance on the scriptural authority for the subject, as the extended title of his work suggests. In the 1640s, John Stearne was to demonstrate a detailed knowledge of the Bible, citing it as justification for his witch-hunting in East Anglia. Men of his ilk tended to focus on a few recurring passages. Most importantly, Chapter 18 of the book of Exodus, "Thou shalt not suffer a witch to live", was regularly cited, appearing in the preface to numerous books and tracts on the subject (amongst them that of Mathew Hopkins). There were a few others. Thus, Chapter 18 of Deuteronomy required that: "There shall not be found among you ... an enchanter, or a witch. Or a charmer, or a consulter with familiar spirits, or a wizard, or a necromancer." The books of Samuel, Chronicles, Jeremiah, Malachi, and, in the New Testament, Acts, *inter alia*, also

---

124. Hutchinson, Francis, *Historical Essay on Witchcraft*, at p.225.

contained short mentions of the subject.

Such Biblical authority on the issue was, however, extremely limited, often being mixed in with other religious injunctions that were widely, and freely, ignored in the early modern period. Clearly, witchcraft was not a particularly significant issue to either the Jews or the early Christians, something that many theologians in the sceptical camp were to stress. Additionally, Scripture did not provide precise details as to what constituted a witch, and how such people could be identified. There was a lingering doubt, in many educated people's minds, as to whether Biblical witches, in so far as they had existed, bore much resemblance to the marginalised women so often accused in the early modern era. As one of Holland's protagonists ("Myfodaemon") in his fictional debate on witchcraft, observed: "But shall we imagine that our poore doting old women (which are commonly called witches) at this day, are like in any point unto those which are mentioned in scripture."[125] The sceptic Sir Robert Filmer was especially eager to distinguish biblical witches from those alleged to exist in his own time. Even Stearne accepted that the sort of ferocious witches that were active "nowadays" were almost absent from the Bible[126].

Nor did the Bible ascribe many of the powers to witches that were attributed to them in the early modern period in Europe, and certainly did not give any support for the numerous popular methods of detecting witchcraft that developed (such as "swimming"). As Reginald Scot was to

125. Holland, *A Treatise Against Witchcraft*, at p.E1.
126. Stearne, *Confirmation*, at p.56.

note, in 1584: "But as for our old women, that are said to hurt children with their eies, or lambs with their lookes, or that pull down the moone out of heaven, or make so foolish a bargaine, or doo such homage to the divell; you shall not read in the Bible of any such witches, or of any such actions imputed to them."[127] Similarly, "Myfodaemon", Holland's imaginary interlocutor, opined that: "There are many things which are said to be in the witches of our time, which were never heard of in these old witches, mentioned in scripture, as namely these points: there transportations, there bargaine with the devill, there sathanicall Sabaoths, their oyntments of the fatte of young children, theur transformations and such like miracles and wonders."[128] Seventy years later, Thomas Ady was still pointing out that there was no scriptural authority for the belief that the devil "Setteth privy marks upon witches", or even that they had the magical power to kill others on their own initiative.[129] Similarly, he wished to know where in the Bible: "... is it written, that the tryall of a witch should be by sinking or swimming in the water? or by biggs or privy marks."[130] Some "witchmongers" got round this problem by conceding that many of the popular beliefs about witchcraft were misconceived, but arguing that this did not alter the reality or malign nature of witches. Thus, Holland's "Theophilus"

---

127. Scot, Reginald *The Discovery of Witchcraft,* Book v, Chapter 9, at p.109.
128. Holland, *A Treatise Against Witchcraft,* at p.E3. A belief in the efficacy of the "fatte" of infants appears to have been widespread. In Middleton's *The Witch* (1613) one of Hecate's colleagues hands over a dead child's body with the words "Here, take this unbaptised brat," and the enjoinder to "Boil it well, preserve the fat."
129. Ady, *Discovery,* at p.6.
130. Ady, *Candle,* at p.6.

admitted that many "fabulous" pamphlets were published on the subject, and that the devil might be deluding their authors. He also conceded that: "... the ignorant people, [were] carried away in deede with many fonde opinions concerning witches." Nevertheless, with some ingenuity, he found sufficient scriptural authority for the validity of a belief in witchcraft.[131] He was not alone. Another (pamphlet) writer in the "pro-persecution" lobby, angrily noted that: "... many have taken very great pains to confute, by reason of the opinion so long held in the world, that there have been and are witches." These sceptics, he felt, tried to make the Biblical witch of Endor into a conjurer that was equipped with "some few tricks of legerdemain." He also expressly rejected the argument that a belief in witchcraft was either a popish myth (fundamental to writers such as Gifford or Ady) or one based on heathen fables.[132]

Economic and Social Change

Early modern England saw considerable economic and social dislocation, separate to its religious problems, with patterns of migration from the poorer areas to the more prosperous ones, and from the countryside to the towns (especially London), these being accelerated by population increase. From the late medieval period, England had ceased to be the static society that it had been in the fourteenth century, with considerable movement between villages and large numbers of travellers on the roads, and

---

131. Holland, *A Treatise Against Witchcraft*, at p.E2.
132. Pamphlet 1674 at pp. 2 and 3.

consequently the increased presence of strangers. In London, the problems this engendered reached crisis proportions. In a letter to the Council in 1594 the Lord Mayor, Sir John Spencer, asserted that many places South of the river were "very nurseries and breeding-places of the begging poor", who swarmed the streets of the City. There was a widespread belief among the literate, that a new and swiftly expanding class of semi-criminal vagrants abounded in the Kingdom, and that felonies such as the theft of cattle, sheep and horses were becoming more common.[133] In 1596, an Order by the Privy Council to the Justices of the Peace of urban Middlesex complained of the great number of "dissolute, loose and insolent people."[134]

The countryside also had very serious problems. Another theme, not directly linked to religious changes (though perhaps indirectly associated with some of them), has been that of the consequences of the breakdown in social cohesion within rural villages in the early modern period. Indicative of this process, was a change in patterns of charitable giving in the late fifteenth century. Thus, for example, bequests in the wills of prosperous yeomen providing bread for the poor, became much rarer in Leicestershire after 1600. The poor were increasingly dealt with not by personal charity, but rather by institutionalised obligations imposed on the community by statute. Pursuant to this, the helpless poor were provided for, the idle set to work or whipped. This process occurred in the advanced counties faster than in more remote ones. In Essex, in the

---

133. Dean, M., *Law-Making and Society in Late Elizabethan England* at p.189.
134. Quoted *ibid* at p.35.

1630s, even elderly vagrants were whipped, while in Westmoreland they still received charity.[135] It has been argued that as social and economic differences increased between villagers, with some outstripping their neighbours, and some falling well behind, they may have engendered feelings of guilt and fear on the part of those who refused charity to their poorer fellows. In the correct circumstances (for example after a natural disaster) these feelings might prompt allegations of witchcraft. It does appear that, in many cases, those accused of the crime were significantly inferior in social or economic status to their accusers. The stereotype of the witch established by Macfarlane and Thomas in the early 1970s, female, elderly, widowed, poor and often dependent on alms is a generally valid one for much of England. She was normally accused as a result of misfortune (sickness etc.) coming to someone with whom she had had recent dealings, and for which she received the blame. In a classic contemporary analysis of this process, Reginald Scot was to observe that: "It falleth out many times, that neither their necessities, nor their expectation is answered or served, in those places where they beg or borrowe; but rather their lewdnesse is by their neighbors reprooved. And further, in tract of time the witch waxeth odious and tedious to hir neighbors; and they againe are despised and despited of hir: so as sometimes she curseth one, and sometimes another; and that from the maister of the house, his wife, children, cattell, & c. To the little pig that lieth in the stie. Thus in processe of time they have all displeased her, and she hath wished evill lucke unto them

---

135. Underdown, David, *Revel, Riot & Rebellion,* at p.36.

all; perhaps with curses and imprecations made in forme. Doubtlesse (at length) some of hir neighbors die, or fall sicke; or some of their children are visited with diseases that vex them stranglie ..." This was then readily ascribed to the work of the witch, though in reality, it was mere coincidence. However, there were many exceptions and regional variations to this pattern. Thus, in Kent, although Reginald Scot could describe them as "lame, bearie-eied, pale, fowle, and full of wrinkles", a significant proportion of those accused of witchcraft in the late sixteenth and early seventeenth centuries were neither old, poor or widows. Between 1640 and 1660 only 30 per cent of those accused of the crime before the secular courts were recorded as widowed, though some others were described as spinsters. The social background to many of these cases was also different to the Macfarlane model, many of the women being quite well integrated into their communities. Considerable numbers who were accused and acquitted subsequently took legal action for libel against their attackers. It is also possible that "neighbourliness" was emphasized there as a social ideal simply because so many village relations were characterised by personal malice and hostility, something that could be channelled into allegations of witchcraft.[136] Of course, the Macfarlane model is more accurate for those who were actually tried, convicted and executed in the county rather than merely accused. The social implications and background of many witchcraft cases, in particular, the evident differences

---

136. *See* on this Gaskill, M., *Witchcraft in Early Modern Kent: Stereotypoes and the Background to Accusations,* in Barry, J. *et al., Witchcraft in Early Modern Europe,* at pp.257-277.

between perpetrators and victims, the refusal of charity or work so often being the cassus belli, were not lost on contemporaries. Thus, it was stressed that the Flowers' victim, Sir Francis Manners, the Earl of Rutland, was a generous pillar of his local community, especially kind to the impoverished and "neither displacing Tenants, discharging Servants, denying the accesse of the poore."

Economic conditions did, apparently, affect contemporary levels of conventional crime. Many in the 1580s accepted that there was a link between crime and the deteriorating economy of the period (suffering, as it was under the combined effects of harvest failure, war, plague and an apparent industrial stagnation).[137] Mathew Hale, a strong believer in, and scourge of, witchcraft, was certainly not lacking in concern for the poor. Motivated in part by his religious faith, he appears to have had an unusually strong social conscience, and a belief in the need for the state to make adequate provision for the disadvantaged. Thus, he believed that the prevention of poverty, idleness, and a "loose and disorderly Education", even of poor children, would do more good to the country than: "... all the Gibbets, and Cauterization, and Whipping Posts, and Jayls in this Kingdom, and would render these kinds of Disciplines less necessary and less frequent."[138] This analysis has been supported by some modern academics, who find evidence to suggest that the patterns of prosecution described by the records of the Elizabethan and Jacobean courts reflect real changes in the level of property crime, and that these

---

137. *See* on this Lawson, P., *Property Crime and Hard Times in England*, 1559-1624, at p.96.
138. Hale, Mathew, Preface to *A Disclosure touching Provision for the Poor.*

changes were themselves rooted in economic conditions.[139] J.S. Cockburn has noted a fairly firm correlation between the incidence of crime and high prices in the sixteenth century, and some correlation, albeit much less uniform, between them in the early seventeenth century. This led him to conclude that a significant amount of theft was motivated by economic necessity.[140]

However, the extent to which contemporary social and economic problems might also have influenced the incidence of witchcraft allegations is much harder to assess, and requires an obviously more complicated paradigm to explain. Nevertheless, in Scotland, it appears to have been the case that the onset of witch persecution, and the times of greatest persecutions, coincided with times of economic trouble in the State, and the undermining of "traditional" notions of charity. This was most especially present in the 1590s, but also, it appears, in the 1620s and 1640s.[141] Might the upsurge of cases in England in the 1590s have been linked in some way to the poor harvests of that decade?

Faced with these unprecedented changes in their society, the Tudors had stressed the importance of obedience, even issuing a homily on the subject in 1547, to be read out regularly from parish pulpits. The authorities also stressed the need for social cohesion. Indeed, disrupting neighbourhood peace could be a crime in its own right,

---

139. Lawson, P., *Property Crime and Hard Times in England, 1559-1624,* at p.127.

140. *The Nature and Incidence of Crime in England 1559-1625,* in Cockburn J.S. (Ed.), *Crime in England 1550-1800,* at p.70.

141. Wormald, Jenny, *Court, Kirk, and Community:Scotland 1470-1625,* at pp.168-169.

barratry, constituting one of the "Offences against Justice in general." Thus, according to Sergeant Thorpe, "If any be a common stirrer, and procurer of law-suits, or a common brabbler or quarreller; among his neighbours; this is barratry."[142] It has been widely observed that a model of "neighbourliness" was a critically important social ideal in early modern England. Nevertheless, this ideal may have been stressed simply because normal village society was so riddled with faction and division. It was a complex social relationship, based on a mixture of propinquity and shared mores and obligations. Ideally, it produced a situation in which neighbours could live in harmony and "in charity", pursuing agreement in their dealings and a wider concensus in their communities. Nevertheless, in this process, some were marginalized, and excluded, in particular, the poorest inhabitants, a social strata from whence witches often came.[143] Just as pertinently, witches were often considered to be extreme cases of un-neighbourly people, even if they were not poor. Illustrative of this was the experience of Anne Taylor, accused of witchcraft at Rye in the early 1600s. According to many of her fellow citizens, she was a sharp tongued, insensitive woman whose opposition to certain local dignitaries had threatened to revive the factional infighting that had characterised local politics in Rye in the

---

142. Oldys, William, *The Harleian, miscellany ...*, Vol.2 at pp. 1-13; *Serjeant Thorpe, judge of the assize for the northern circuit, his charge; as if it was delivered to the Grand Jury at York Assizes, the twentieth of march 1648*, at p.10.

143. Wrighton, Keith, *The Politics of the Parish in Early Modern England*, in Griffiths, P., *et al.* (Eds.). *The Experience of Authority in Early Modern England*, at p.19.

1570s and early 1580s.[144]

Witch trials may have served a number of potentially functional ends in society. Arguably, they promoted community solidarity by drawing communities together to purge the evil in their midst. Clerics, doctors and lawyers could display expertise in their respective areas. The efforts of the new nation states of the early modern period to demonstrate their power and to promote social control could be facilitated, and thus state-building promoted.[145] In many ways, witchcraft is intellectually comprehensible only within the framework of which it was the inversion. In a rigidly hierarchical, Christian, and patriarchal society, the attacks by Satan's, largely female, and often very lowly, minions were the very antithesis of "accepted" values, both social and religious. As such, it lay well within a wider tradition of late medieval and early modern concern about inversion generally, with a fear of a "world turned upside down." This was a preoccupation that was also manifest in other ways, such as the "Lords of Misrule", who presided over traditional winter festivities; the "barring out" out of masters in English grammar schools of the period; the student dominance of the Christmas revels in the Inns of Court; and various other forms of "topsy-turvyism." These were all based on a temporary but full reversal of the normal social priorities of status, gender, hierarchy and other values. It was not by chance that in Thomas Heywood and Richard Brome's comedy *The Late Lancashire Witches* of

---

144. Gregory, Annabel, *Witchcraft, Politics And `Good Neighbourhood'*, at pp.62-63.

145. *See* on this Briggs, R, *Many Reasons Why: Witchcraft and the problem of multiple explanation*, at p.56.

1634, the previously well ordered household was so afflicted by sorcery that the father and mother obeyed their children, and the children, in their turn, were overawed by the family servants. Fundamental to witches was their perceived desire to invert the moral (and social) order, caught well by Shakespeare's hags in *Macbeth* chanting "Fair is foul, and foul is fair." In a Catholic country, this could find a practical form in the Black Mass, an ornate and grotesque parody of the Eucharist, that they were supposed to practise. This avenue of expression was not open in a Protestant nation, however, equivalents, if slightly less eye-catching, could be readily found. Thus, to the witch finder John Stearne, in the 1640s, it was obvious that "... the devil imitates God in all things as he can, much after the book of Common-prayer, then in his outward Worship."[146] Similarly, Cotton Mather, writing in Massachusetts after the events at Salem in 1693 was struck that: ""Tis very Remarkable to See what impious and impudent Imitation of Divine Things, is apishly affected by the devil, in Several of those Matters, whereof the Confessions of our Witches, and the Afflictions of our Sufferers have informed us."[147] In 1664, Margaret Johnson of Marsden was to note that her group of witches made a point of meeting on All Saints Day, and that "Good Friday is one constant day for a yearly general meeting of witches."[148] The essayist William Cornwallis observed in 1604 that men

146. Stearne, *Confirmation* at p.38. This also probably reflects a Puritan prejudice against the liturgy of the established church. Mathew Hopkins was another who believed that the devil married his acolytes according to the rites of the Church of England.

147. Mather, Cotton, *The wonders of the invisible World,* at p.431.

148. Catlow, R., *The Pendle witches* at p.22.

"cannot judge singlie, but by coupling contrarieties."[149] As such, arguably, notions of witchcraft made their own contribution to reinforcing the predominant values of the wider society, during a period of change which appeared to threaten them.

Nevertheless, social, religious and economic explanations must be treated with caution. One limitation to functionalist explanations for the secular crime of witchcraft is that some areas of Europe were virtually untouched by such campaigns. Within England, in many counties, accusations were sufficiently rare that it is hard to see what, if any, necessary function they could have been fulfilling. Additionally, to consider two epicentres of early modern English witch trials, the counties of Essex and Lancashire, is to view two radically different societies. Essex was Puritan, heavily governed and regulated, adjacent to London and socially and economically advanced. Its economy was based on rich farmland, with expanding manufacturing industries, both increasingly orientated towards the London market. By contrast, much of Lancashire was poor, recusant, remote and backward. In the early seventeenth century, it was a relatively lawless county, possibly, in part, due to its isolation. It was also a centre of Catholicism. So alarming was this situation to some Puritans that, in 1590, a group of clergymen from the county had complained to the Privy Council about the religious and personal laxity prevalent in the region: "... most of the people refraine theire Parishe Church, ... many of them grow into utter Atheisme and Barbarisme, manie enjoy full security in Poperie and all

149. *Cf.*, Clark, Stuart, *Inversion, Misrule and Witchcraft* at pp. 98-127.

Popishe practices." London responded with various initiatives to counter this situation. The Forest of Pendle area (despite the name, it was not actually woodland), a suspected hotbed of witchcraft, was especially bleak, an extensive area of waste, with a few poor farms hugging the valley bottoms. Catholic priests continued to operate covertly in the area, though many of the local people were probably totally unchurched. In such an environment superstition was likely to flourish. In 1628 a Westminster MP might have had the area in mind when he spoke of the "utmost skirts of the north, where the prayers of the common people are more like spells and charms than devotions."

At a very practical level, witchcraft allegations could also be used to "cover up" other, conventional, crimes. Thus, in Kent, in 1651, 25 people testified against one Helen Dadd of Hougham for bewitching children and animals. Most of the allegations were thrown out by the Grand Jury, nevertheless, she was convicted on the testimony of one Thomas Hogbin, a local yeoman, for killing his three year old son. She was duly executed for this crime. However, six weeks later others came forward to say that Hogbin had murdered his son. One witness claimed to have seen him kick his son in a manner which "shee [the witness] wold have bine loath to have given to a dogg." Hogbin, it appears, also tried to conceal the corpse after death, possibly to prevent others seeing the child's injuries. In light of this it seems likely that Hogbin was using an unpopular local woman to hide his own crimes.[150] Alternatively, such accusations could be levelled at local nuisances. In a blatant example of this, the Lincolnshire JP Sir Nicholas Sanderson accused a poor Tetney widow of witchcraft, from the Bench, at the Quarter Sessions. His motivation appears to have been annoyance at her willingness to sue his own servants for an attack on her property, after she had stood in the way of an enclosure scheme that he had proposed.[151]

An Absence of Stoicism

Life in the early modern era was often harsh, painful, and unpredictable. Misfortune could strike unexpectedly against anyone, Lord or commoner alike, piety and prosperity being no protection. It was impossible to inure oneself to such risks. Many people accepted such disasters relatively stoically, as a manifestation of the hand of providence, an inscrutable act of God. To devout men, in an age where piety was relatively common, divine disfavour might manifest itself in draconian forms, even over matters that to modern observers might be considered mere pecadillos. Thus, in 1648, the Essex clergyman, Ralph Josselin, considering, in his diary, the death of his baby son, at the age of only 10 days, considered that the aim of God, in inflicting this "correction of his upon me", might have been linked to his excessive fondness for playing chess. He

---

150. *See* on this Gaskill, G., *Witchcraft in early modern Kent: stereotypes and the background to accusations,* at p.283.

151. Heal, F. and Holmes, C., *The Gentry in England and Wales, 1500-1700* at p.176.

resolved, as a result, that in future, he would be "very sparing in the use of that recreation and that at more convenient seasons."

To many, however, even in the early modern period, such fortitude cannot have come easily. For these, witches provided a ready explanation for apparently undeserved catastrophe. Reginald Scot, amongst many others, felt that one of the reasons for the increase in witchcraft allegations in his age was a decline of stoicism in the face of natural disaster. The "fables" about witchcraft had taken such a hold on people that few could patiently "indure the hand and correction of God", but, rather, attributed any "adversitie, greefe, sicknesse, losse of children, corne, [or] cattel" to witches. This was to be a recurring theme amongst both sceptics and the more cautious believers in witchcraft. As Bernard was to observe, God allowed the devil to afflict the good directly, "for their tryall", and the bad "for their punishment" yet this occurred "without any association of witches." Theologians, in particular, were concerned at the implications of attributing too much power to the devil. Such an attitude risked falling into the error of postulating a dualistic, or Manichean, analysis of the universe, one fought over by a God and devil that were of almost comparable strength. Nevertheless, such an analysis could be intellectually satisfying. Thus, in the preface to his work *A Treatise Against Witchcraft* (1590) Holland observed that: "... there are two spiritual kingdomes in this world, which have continual hatred and bloody wars, without hope of truce for ever." Bernard, who firmly believed in the existence of witchcraft, though not in all the alleged instances of it, thought that an excessive popular belief in witches as the cause of all affliction, made people forget

God's role in creation, and act as though the witch was the "onely commander or ruler in this action."[152] In particular, it was argued that attributing great power to witches was religiously unsound, and even smacked of Romish practices.

For many Protestants, however, including those who believed in witchcraft, reconciling the devil's ability to strike at the Godly through witches, something that would necessarily have to be permitted by God, was inherently quite difficult. To some, witchcraft was simply one manifestation of the normal vicissitudes of life. James VI explained, at least to his own satisfaction, why anyone, however virtuous, could be afflicted by witchcraft. The wicked, not surprisingly, were afflicted for their "horrible sinnes, to punish them in the like measure." The apparently Godly that were secretly "sleeping in anie great sinnes or infirmities and weaknesse in faith" might also be troubled, so as to "waken them up the faster." For the truly virtuous, even "some of the best", it was allowed so that their patience and faith might be "tryed before the world, as Job's was." More generally, God could allow "extraordinarie punishment" such as that effected by witchcraft, to take place on earth, in exactly the same way as he allowed natural disasters, the "ordinarie roddes of sicknesse or other adversities", to vex mankind.[153] Not everyone found King James's analysis totally satisfactory. There was a widespread English belief, in the early stages of the witch trial period, that devout and good men could not be subject to such attacks on their person. Although this view had been

---

152. Bernard, Richard, *A Guide to Grand-Jury Men*, Second Edn., at pp.52 and 76.

153. James VI & I, *Daimonomageia*, at p.47.

rejected by many with an academic interest in the subject by the early seventeenth century, it lingered on in the popular mind, in some cases until the end of the era. Thus, in *The Witch of Edmonton* of 1621 the devil informed Elizabeth Sawyer that she could not be directly revenged against her antagonist "Banks" because:

> "Though he be cursd to thee, yet of himself he is loving
> to the world, and charitable to the poor. Now men
> That, as he, love goodness, though in smallest measure,
> Live without compass of our reach. His cattle
> And corn I'll kill and mildew, but his life,
> Until I take him, as I late found thee,
> Cursing and swearing, I have no power to touch."[153a]

Numerous popular accounts of other incidents supported this proposition. Thus, when one witch attempted, in 1644, to exact diabolical revenge on two servants who had offended her, she was unable to do this, as both went "constantly to church ... and said [their] prayers Morning and evening." Strangely, however, this immunity did not extend to their children, and he (the devil) was able to injure the baby of one of the men. This was effected using sympathetic magic. The "black man" brought: "... an image of wax, and told her they must go and Bury that in the Church-yard, and then the child which he had put into great pain already shoulde waste and consume away as that image wasted." The child sickened for 18 months and was close to death when the witch confessed, at which point it

153a. Act 2, Scene 1.

immediately recovered. However, when they tried to dig up the wax image in the church yard, though directed to the right spot by the witch: "... tho they dug and fought for it as well as they could, they could find nothing." It was believed that it had been destroyed either by digging or by the devil.[154]

Concern at the decline of fortitude and stoicism was not just confined to English or Protestant writers. In the German State of Würzburg, in the late 1620s, the Jesuit Friedrich Spee deplored the manner in which divine judgments, even when threatened by Holy Writ, were attributed to witches: "No longer do God or nature do aught but witches everything."[155] However, this begs the question as to why this phenomenon should occur in the early modern, rather than the medieval, period in Europe. At first sight, the advent of the Reformation might seem to provide fertile ground for an explanation. Protestantism, especially in its Calvinist form, appeared to suggest that a sign of God's favour towards the elect might often (though not always) be manifest in this world, as well as the next. If it was not, it might be easy to view it as the result of some malign, or diabolical interference. This might potentially explain why there were more accusations in Presbyterian Scotland, than, for example, in Anglican England. However, as Spee's comment indicates, some of the worst European persecutions were in the Prince Bishoprics in Germany, and

---

154. *A Relation of a Yarmouth Witch, who with Fifteen more Convicted upon their own Confession, was executed in 1644,* published in *A collection of Modern Relations of Matter of Fact, Concerning Witches and Witchcraft Upon The Persons of People.* Part 1, Printed for John Harris 1693. At pp. 46-48.

155. Kors, A.C., & Peters, E., *Witchcraft in Europe 1100-1700,* at p.351.

other distinctly Catholic areas; thus, the paradigm is unsatisfactory. Nevertheless, it may still have some value if stripped of its denominational label, and attributed to the general development of a less fatalistic, yet still not secular, attitude towards the world. Harsh though life was, by modern standards, in early modern England, it was better than it had been two centuries before; mortality rates had declined and living conditions somewhat improved. Later, as society became more secularised at the turn of the seventeenth century, security could increasingly be sought in mechanisms other than those that provided protection against witches. Thus, a parallel (of very limited value) can probably be drawn between the growth of insurance and a decline in a belief in witchcraft.

Feminist Critiques

Women were, overwhelmingly, the majority of those accused under the Witchcraft Acts, constituting between 80 per cent and 90 per cent in England, and with similar (if slightly less extreme), patterns being present in many parts of continental Europe, such as Denmark, Germany, and also in Scotland. Additionally, of those men who actually were accused of witchcraft, significant numbers were married to women who were also alleged to be witches, or, alternatively, were the subject of other charges, such as treason, a situation in which an allegation of witchcraft may have been added to bolster the case against them on the substantive charge. In England, witchcraft was the only serious felony which could be described as a primarily female offence. Commentators in the early modern period were as aware of this as modern feminists. Numerous sixteenth and seventeenth century demonologists, including James VI and I, spent a considerable amount of time attempting to explain why women should be so much more prone to committing witchcraft than men. Most explanations for the disproportionate distribution of witches amongst the sexes were fairly standardised. Women were, at this time, considered the weaker sex or vessel, and, inevitably, this influenced male explanations, some of which were almost sympathetic to the demonic entanglements that women's feebleness could lead them into. Even the sceptic, Reginald Scot, believed that superstition and the feminine nature went together, so that it was often the province of "women, and effeminate men." Similarly, the question did not trouble King James unduly, being simply resolved, in his mind at least: "The reason is easie, for as that sexe is frailer then man is, so it is easier to be intrapped in these grosse snares of the devill." This was manifest by the example of Eve; obviously, the devil was more comfortable and "homelier with that sex."[156] Like many writers, James VI and I linked this to the inherent peculiarities of the female sex. In particular, he identified the operation, much stronger, he felt, in women than men, of three ruling passions: curiosity, a greedy appetite caused by acute poverty, and a burning desire for revenge for perceived, and deeply felt, wrongs inflicted against them.[157]

---

156. James VI and I, *Daemonologie,* at p.44.
157. James I, was the son of Mary, Queen of Scots, and the first king to rule both England and Scotland (as James VI in that country). Born in 1566, he succeeded to the Scottish throne when still a baby. In 1603, following the death of Queen Elizabeth, he became King of England, and remained there for most of the remainder of his life; he died in 1625.

When Richard Bernard writing his *A guide to Grand-jury men* in 1629, also addressed his mind to the disproportionate number of women in the ranks of alleged witches, he produced a number of similar explanations. Amongst them, he noted, that Satan had been heartened early on by his success with Eve, encouraging him to focus on women, adding that their naturally more "credulous nature" meant they were "apt to be misled and deceived." His view that the devil's early success with Eve in the Garden of Eden had encouraged him to specifically target her sex was widely held. Indeed, some convicted witches (probably with clerical encouragement) even confirmed this diagnosis. Thus, of four witches convicted and executed together at Worcester in 1647, two (Cock and Margaret Landis) died "penitent", telling spectators "that as Satan in the first Infancy of the World prevailed on woman to bring his hellish attempts to pass, so he still strives with that sex as the weaker Vessels to work their destructions" (the other two women, apparently, died "very stuburn and refractory without any remorse").[158] Bernard, too, felt that when "displeased" women were prone to be more malicious than men, and thus more eager for revenge. Certainly, in a patriarchal society, their avenues for non-demonic retribution were far more limited than those open to men.

Such stock explanations for women appearing as the accused in witchcraft cases continued in circulation for

---

Although a well educated man, his intellectual pretensions exceeded, perhaps, his abilities. Nevertheless, he wrote several books, on a variety of matters, including theology, and, most pertinently, witchcraft, in particular his *Daemonologie* of 1597.

158. Pamphlet 1670 at p.8.

decades. Typically, the un-original Richard Bovet, writing as late as 1684, and seeking reasons as to why it was "Observable that Witches are commonly of the Female Sex", felt that this was not really surprising, as the devil, since he had first tempted Eve, was likely to: "... offer his Baits to such palats as are most desirous to taste Fruits forbidden; and more negligent in Enquiring into the Nature of what they Swallow."[159] Bovet appears to have been in possession of an almost classic Madonna/whore complex, believing that few could excel women who inclined to virtue, but that if they followed evil "none surpass them in Heights of Wickedness and mischief." Despite the widespread nature of such aspersions against women, they did not go totally unchallenged. In his work of 1604, *A Confutation of Astrologicall Demonologie,* John Chamber, the Canon of Windsor, opined that "no imputation of witchery or sorcery ought more to lie upon women than upon men." Nevertheless, it is not difficult to find instances of overt misogyny in some witch tracts, especially those from continental Europe. An obvious (and extreme) example is provided by the classic early witchcraft text, the *Malleus Maleficarum,* of 1486, which felt that women spurned by their lovers having: "... immodestly copulated with them in the hope and promise of marriage with them, and have found themselves disappointed in all their hopes and everywhere despised, they turn to the help and protection of devils; either for the sake of vengeance by bewitching those lovers or the wives they have married, or for the sake of giving themselves up to every sort of lechery. Alas!

---

159. Kors, A.C., and Peters, E., *Witchcraft in Europe 1100-1700,* at p.285.

experience tells us that there is no number to such girls, and consequently the witches that spring from this class are innumerable." Its two German Dominican authors were convinced that women were inherently more carnal and insatiably lustful than men, and were intellectually childlike, being both credulous and deceptive.[160]

Because of this concentration of cases against one sex, and the often misogynistic language used, it is not surprising that witchcraft should loom large in modern feminist critiques of the Criminal Justice system of the period. At first sight it does appear to be tailor-made to support assertions that the law was an instrument of the male domination of women. Some features particularly, such as the widespread concern that midwives might be given to diabolical practices, make such an analysis appear especially plausible. When James VI and I was faced with the Millenary Petition, a plea for reform in the Church of England, on his trip south from Scotland in 1604, he convened a conference at Hampton Court to debate it. There, while demonstrating his own learning he dismissed the custom of allowing midwives to baptise dying babies. The reason for his strong views (he stated that he would rather that any child of his be "baptised by an ape as by a woman") was a fear that it was being used as a cover by witches intent on taking infants for Satanic rituals.[161] As a result of incidents like this, the theme that witch hunts constituted calculated and systematic violence by men against women has surfaced periodically in the post-war

160. Sprenger, Jacob and Kramer, Heinrich, *Malleus Maleficarum* (1486), Translated by Montague Summers, at pp.43-44.

161. Kishlansky, M., *A Monarchy Transformed: Britain 1603-1714*, at p.72.

era, most recently in work by Anne Llewellyn Barstow.[162]

However, seeing witchcraft trials purely as an instrument of male domination is simplistic, and must be qualified by a number of major reservations. The English predominance of women was not invariably the case in other parts of Europe. In some remote areas, such as Iceland and Estonia, men formed the majority of those accused of witchcraft (90 per cent and 60 per cent respectively). Russia was probably the same. In other places, although women made up the bulk of the accused, there were significant numbers of men implicated as well. Thus, in the Saarland and Lorraine, they made up 28 per cent of those accused. Even in England, there were times, such as Hopkins's East Anglian campaign in the 1640s, when considerable numbers of men were drawn into the net of accusations. Contemporary commentators themselves sometimes exaggerated the proportion of women to men involved, something that in turn has encouraged a number of modern "myths." Jean Bodin, for example, thought that it was a ratio of 50 women for every one male witch.[163] In reality, in France at least, it was much smaller. James VI and I, in his celebrated work on witchcraft, *Daemonologie* (1597) was slightly more conservative (and statistically more accurate for the British Isles), in his gender distribution, when asking himself: "What can be the cause that there are twentie women given to that craft, where there is one man?"

It is also the case that women played a major role in

---

162. Llewelleyn Barstow, A., *Witch-Craze: A New History of the European Witch Hunts* (1994).

163. Briggs, R., *Many Reasons Why: Witchcraft and the problem of multiple explanation*, at pp. 259-262.

witchcraft trials, other than as defendants; a much greater one, it appears, than they did in any other type of felony trial. A much higher proportion of women appeared as witnesses for the prosecution than for any other crime. In witchcraft trials on the Home Circuit, between 1600 and 1702, of the 1207 witnesses called, 576 or 48 per cent were women. In some cases, nearly all of the prosecution witnesses were female. This can be contrasted with typical felony cases in Hertfordshire in the years 1610 to 1619, when, of the 608 witnesses called to give evidence at the Assizes, only 36, one in 12, were women.[164] Women were also given great importance in the process by being entrusted with the search for the witches' mark. This would be carried out by a team or "jury" of "matrons", allowing searches to be conducted in the most intimate places without violating accepted standards of decency. The size of this group of women would vary, though at least three was preferred, and often more. Anne Bodenham, the Salisbury witch, was found to have a witches' teat on her left shoulder and in her "secret place" (genitalia), evidence of which was given in court by the three women who had examined her, Molier Damely, Alice Cleverly and Grace Stokes.[165] In this process, there was a marked parallel with another traditional female province in the criminal system, the jury of matrons to determine whether a temporary reprieve from the death sentence should be given to a pregnant woman who was "pleading her belly." Significantly, Mathew Hopkins was heavily assisted in his work by a woman,

---

164. *See* on this Sharpe, J., *Women, crime and the Courts, Women Witchcraft and the Legal Process,* at p.112.
165. Pamphlet 1653(1) at p.8.

Mary Phillips, who proved highly adept at locating the witches' mark on those accused.

It must also be noted that although women were more commonly accused of witchcraft than men, this does not necessarily indicate discrimination on a gender basis. It is possible that women were disproportionately prone to this form of crime, or (more likely) fell in greater numbers into those categories of people of whom witchcraft might be suspected. By instinct women appear, in general, to be more overtly religious than men (something that seems to supported by modern figures for church attendance). As William Alexander, the Earl of Stirling observed in 1637: "The weaker sex, to piety more prone." It is possible that this tendency might have been as manifest in adherence to alternative belief systems as to mainstream ones, even in the early modern period.

In most of Europe, once they were within the criminal justice system, the treatment of those being processed for witchcraft does not show extensive differential bias between men and women. Thus, in Scotland, roughly the same numbers of women as men were executed (55.8 per cent and 52.3 per cent), and acquitted (21.7 per cent and 19.8 per cent). Significantly more men accused of witchcraft were executed, and fewer acquitted, than women in Geneva. In England however, on the Home Circuit at least, men were in a more favourable position. There, between 1559 and 1736, 70 per cent of men and only 53.4 per cent of women were acquitted, while 25.1 per cent of women were executed after conviction, compared to only 14 per cent of men. Nevertheless, though statistically significant, given the relatively low numbers of men put on trial, the differences are modest enough to encourage caution before ascribing systemised bias in the criminal justice system against women at this time.[166]

This last observation must be qualified by the apparent lack of uniformity in the distribution of women amongst those accused for different types of magical practice. In Essex, at least, a much higher proportion of allegations of minor provision of, or recourse to, magic (usually involving "white" magic, and heard in front of the ecclesiastical courts), appear to have involved men, when compared to the mainly female "black" witches tried at the secular Assizes. In large part this appears to have been because a high proportion of "cunning" folk, perhaps over half, were male. As John Stearne observed, the female predominance was especially marked amongst malefic witches: "yet of Witches there be commonly more women than men: this is evident ... especially of hurting witches."[167]

In a society where female subordination to men was taken largely for granted, all women living independently from men were likely to pose some form of social and psychological threat, though it is possible to exaggerate this. Certainly, women who did not accept their "proper" role in society might be the subject of a number of informal methods of social control. Thus, in some parts of England, there occurred the ritual shaming of the "skimmington ride", a procession in which a local woman who was thought to have usurped the authority of her husband was paraded

166. McLachlan H., and Swales J., *Lord Hale, Witches and Rape: A Note,* in *British Journal of Law and Society,* 1978 Vol.5 at pp.251-261. Such a pattern was not unique to England, in Franche Comte, 33.3 per cent of men were executed compared to 41.9 per cent of women, with a similar bias in favour of male acquittals.

167. Stearne, *Confirmation,* at p.87.

through the streets. Her neighbours, dressed up as the couple, would re-enact an incident in which the wife had violated accepted gender roles and caused local offence, while she would be mounted backwards on a horse, or a man-borne pole. The display might end with the offending woman being seized and ducked in a local pond, or thrown into a dung heap. It has been asserted that late Tudor and Jacobean writers were often pre-occupied with scolding, domineering and unfaithful women; something typified by Shakespeare's *Taming of the Shrew*. This does not necessarily mean that women were increasingly independent and assertive at this time; however, it does appear that this was perceived to have been the case, prompting a torrent of literature that has been termed, perhaps a little harshly, as misogenystic. Perhaps significantly, in Thomas Heywood's *The Lancashire Witches* when a community is turned upside down by bewitchment one manifestation of the enchantment is women ruling men. Although it seems strange to include witches amongst the ranks of independent women, being so often old and apparently helpless, witchcraft could be seen as one response of such people to their inherent powerlessness. A possible conclusion is that such concerns might be manifest in allegations of witchcraft.

It has been asserted that there is a correlation between action against scolds, that is women who used verbal abuse against others, and accusations of witchcraft. Both reached their peak in the late sixteenth century and had declined to insignificance a century later. This has led one commentator to suggest that the evidence supports a perceived threat to patriarchal authority in the years around 1600, and was an important feature in the general crisis of order of that time. That order changed after the Restoration, and especially after 1688, as patriarchy lost much of its credibility as a theory of government, under the influence of writers such as John Locke. Others have questioned this argument, pointing out that action against scolds had taken place on a similar scale in the fifteenth century, though accepting that the punishments for the offence, became more draconian in the 1500s. Formerly, they had been fined, later there was recourse to the ducking stool (in which scolds were dipped in rivers and ponds) and, in some Northern areas, the scold's bridle (probably an importation from Scotland). However, the imposition of these punishments does not appear to have been largescale; therefore, caution is needed before too exact a parallel with witchcraft is drawn.[168]

Malicious Allegations of Witchcraft

Many accusations of witchcraft do appear to have been motivated by deliberate spite. Of course, by its very nature, witchcraft was an ideal allegation to be made maliciously, without any belief in its truth. Even if an accused person were ultimately acquitted, there was the possibility that they might have spent months in a squalid prison, and their reputation would be severely damaged. An indication of the seriousness with which witchcraft was taken in the latter part of the sixteenth and the early part of the seventeenth century can be seen in frequency with which it formed the basis of libel actions. An allegation of witchcraft, even if not made seriously, was a grave matter. Those on the receiving

---

168. Underdown, David, *Revel, Riot & Rebellion*, pp.38-40, and 287.

end of such an insult, would often not only find it highly offensive, but would worry lest inactivity on their part allowed the slander to gain currency. Vigorous action, by those who had the substance to use the courts, might be necessary to clear a reputation. The commonest, cheapest and most convenient courts for determining these cases, were the religious ones, in particularly the local consistory courts, though they could also be heard in the Royal Courts at Westminster, such as that of King's Bench (a much more expensive proposition). Typical, was the case of *Kingwell v. Taylor*, heard before John Bloxton B.Ch.L., at the consistory court of the diocese of Exeter, in 1559. John Kingwell accused Robert Taylor of saying, "falsely, wickedly, maliciously and for the sake of hatred", in front of other witnesses ("before neighbours"), on numerous occasions the previous year, "John Kingwell is a witch." As a result, the reputation of Kingwell was apparently "grievously injured and diminished."[169] In 1578 William Netlingham sued Ralph Ode in the Court of King's Bench, alleging that he had said to him (Netlingham), in front of a number of people in Camberwell, that: "If there ever were any witch, thou art one." He claimed £100 in damages for the harm done to his character, which had, apparently, previously been: "... unspotted and untainted by any stain of theft, felony, sorcery, falsity or whatsoever other magic or noxious art"; he stressed that he had never in his life used any "sorcery or magic art." Netlingham evidently took witches seriously, as, in his aversions, he stated that there were many witches in

---

169. *See* on this Helmholz, R.H. (Ed.), *Select Cases on Defamation to 1600,* at p.16.

England, and that their activity was a "monstrous transgression and offence against the word of God and the laws and statutes of this realm of England." The defence offered by Ode was not very strong. He suggested that the plaintiff had mistaken his words; he had actually said: "I will not say that thou art a witch, but if there is any witch on earth, as some say there are, I think in my conscience that thou art one." Perhaps not surprisingly, the jury preferred the plaintiff's version, though not his estimate of his loss, and awarded £11 and 5s. in damages and costs.[170] The Star Chamber was also a forum in which victims who had felt themselves to be the victims of malicious or unfounded allegations could take proceedings against their attackers.

Psychological Explanations

Several psychological explanations can be advanced as to why people should accuse their neighbours of being witches, and also why some of these neighbours might admit to such powers even without duress. According to Karl Menninger, criminals often represent people's alter egos, their submerged hates and aggressions, their "bad" selves, rejected and projected in a process of displacement: "They do for us the forbidden, illegal things we wish to do and, like scapegoats of old, they bear the burdens of our displaced guilt and punishment."[171] For the "innocent", to see criminals punished, eases individual guilt at wanting to do these things themselves, and, at the same time, rewards their

---

170. *Ibid.*, at p.61.
171. Menninger, Karl, *The Crime of Punishment*, at p.153.

own virtue. Witches certainly provided simple (and not so simple) people with the opportunity to project and externalise evil on to a small number of marginalized individuals.

Other contemporary writers also appreciated the process whereby a "labelled" woman might adopt the identity that had been ascribed to her, especially if she was of low intelligence: "... the parish having lodged that name over her for some years, the poor Simple Creature owne'd herself to be what they had stigmatiz'd her for, without either knowing the Hazard of Confession, or the Properties of a witch."[172] This is something that has been well attested to by modern psychology.

---

172. Pamphlet 1712(2) at p.23.

Chapter 5

The Triumph of Scepticism

Scepticism about the existence of witches, or at least the reality of their power, was a constant factor, amongst many educated people, throughout the 200 years that it was a crime. Significant numbers (albeit, a minority in the early years of the period) of Judges, JPs and Grand-Jurymen, would have subscribed to such views. Others would have been influenced by them, even if not fully agreeing with them. This widespread scepticism must have contributed to the situation, in England, in which many accused witches failed to come to trial, or to be indicted and convicted if they did. Its growth was ultimately to result in such prosecutions dying a natural death long before the crime was formally abolished, and is thus deserving of special examination.

Even in 1616, around the peak of the witch-hunting period in England, when men such as Alexander Roberts believed that there were "no small multitude swarming in the world," he could still lament that they were "yet supposed of many, rather worthy pity than punishment, as deluded by fantasises, and mis-led, not effecting those harmes wherewith they bee charged, or themselves acknowledge."[173] Similarly, a few years earlier, at the turn of the sixteenth century, William Perkins had regretted that there were "sundry men who receive it for a truth that witchcraft is nothing else but a mere illusion."[174]

---

173. Roberts, Alexander, *A Treatise of Witchcraft*, at p.15.
174. Perkins, William, *A Disclosure of the Damned Art of Witchcraft*, at pp.587-609.

In the same way, in midst of the activities of the self appointed East Anglian "Witch-Finder General," Matthew Hopkins, during the highly unusual circumstances of the English civil war and Interregnum (possibly as close as England came to witnessing a continental type of "witch mania"), there were many, such as John Gaule, the Vicar of Great Staughton in Huntingdonshire, who spoke out fearlessly against witch-hunting. Gaule, though a believer in the reality of the "dreadful sin" of witchcraft, had extreme doubts about the manner in which witches were being identified, and doubted the validity of most attributions. He felt that the situation had been reached, in parts of East Anglia, in which: "... every old woman with a wrinkled face, a furr'd brow, a hairy lip, a gobbertooth, a squint eye, a squeaking voice, or a scolding tongue, having a rugged coate on her back, a skull cap on her head, and a dog or cat by her side; is not only suspected, but pronounced for a witch." He complained that every new disease, or "notable accident" that occurred was being attributed to witchcraft.[175] John Stearne, Hopkins's associate, considered that there were many men like Gaule, and complained that those opposed to the prosecutions were "enemies to the Church of God." Nevertheless, his fear of being sued for libel induced personal timidity when it came to naming them: "I dare not instance, not only for fear of offence, but also for suits of law."[176] This is not the reaction of a man used to unquestioning acceptance of his views. So often do the writings of "enthusiasts" begin in this way, that it is

175. Gaule, John, *Select Cases of Conscience Touching Witches and Witchcraftes*, at pp.4-6.

176. Stearne, *Confirmation*, at p.58.

impossible to believe that there was not at any time a vigorous level of public criticism of the very idea of witches having magical powers. The defensive language so commonly employed is not that of writers who feel that they have a mastery of the intellectual debate. This scepticism on the part of many of those in authority, especially elements of the judiciary, was alluded to by "Theo," one of the protagonists in the sceptic/believer dialogue in Holland's classic work against witchcraft of 1590. He observed that it was to be: "... wondered, and in a manner incredible, that as yet there are found among Christians, and especially among magistrates and Judges, which doe suppose all these things to be but vaine and fabulous."[177]

A number of major figures in the "sceptical" tradition can be identified. Foremost amongst them, in the sixteenth century, was Reginald Scot, a Kentish Squire who produced a highly influential work, *The Discovery of Witchcraft*, in 1584, a book that assumed European wide significance (it was translated into Dutch). Scot's great tome on witchcraft (over 500 pages with numerous illustrations) was aimed at counteracting and explaining popular belief in witchcraft. In particular, he hoped to refute the work of Jean Bodin's *De la Demonomanie des Sorciers* (1580), and Krämer and Sprenger's *Malleus Maleficarum*, books which were referred to and cited throughout the text. It was a well researched book, quoting dozens of authorities and authors, ranging from the ancient

---

177. Holland, *A Treatise Against Witchcraft*, at p.G.3. Such a dialogue was to become a common literary device in the witchcraft debate. It was later employed by Gifford and by Increase Mather in America.

classics to more contemporary works.[178]

Scot had attended Oxford University, but not graduated, before returning to his native county. He appears to have been particularly interested in horticulture, and his first book, was, appropriately for a Kentishman, on the correct cultivation of a hop garden, *A Perfect Platform of a Hop-garden ...* (published in 1576). Exactly what prompted him to write on witchcraft is unclear. However, it may have been connected to an upsurge of such cases in Kent in the 1570s and 1580s. In turn, this seems to have been linked to commissions sent by the government of Queen Elizabeth to the nation's JPs, urging them to act against the menace from witches. These were referred to explicitly by the witch-hunting enthusiast, and Essex JP, Brian Darcie, in 1582. Darcie asserted that, the Queen having been alerted to the number of witches in England, he and: "... other of her Justices have received Commission for apprehending as many as are within these limits."

In many ways a highly conventional gentleman, Scot was a JP in Kent, and a vehement anti-Catholic, attributing much of the popular belief in witchcraft to the survival of papist superstition and the influence of continental Catholic writers. His book was an insightful combination of logic, personal knowledge and commonsense. Witchcraft and witches were exhaustively explained as the products of charlatans, coincidence, trickery, imposters, superstition,

---

178. So incensed was James 1 by Scot's work that it prompted him to produce his own, much slimmer, volume in rebuttal, *Daemonologie,* in 1597 (though his own work, and sources, were heavily derivative of Scot's). He is alleged to have had all copies of Scot's book, that he could secure, burnt.

misfortune and psychological disturbance. Arguably, he ranked second only to the Flemish Physician Johan Weyer in the roll of witchcraft sceptics. Weyer had published an earlier work condemning witch persecution, *De Praestigiis Daemonum*, in 1563, and asserting that alleged witches were merely melancholic, unhappy and deluded women (it went through numerous editions over many years). Weyer and Scot, together, were to be the primary targets of James I.

Such prominent sceptics were not confined to Protestants. The German Friedrich Spee was also to be an important, and Catholic, doubter. As a result of his experiences as a witch-confessor during the persecution at Würzburg (an experience that apparently turned his hair white, though he was still in his 30s) he became convinced that virtually all witch confessions were worthless. Consequently, he wrote a book, intending it to be privately circulated in manuscript form, condemning the whole process. This anonymous work was secretly taken by a friend to the (Protestant) city of Rinteln, where it was published in 1631 as *Cautio Criminalis*, a book that was to be highly influential in moderating such persecutions in Germany later in the century (though it did not bring a quick end to the process).

A quarter century later, in England, in a deliberate (and freely admitted) seventeenth century echo of Scot's work, Thomas Ady published *A Candle in the Dark*, 1656 (it was reissued under a different title in 1661). His stated ambition was to expose the fact that: "The Grand Errour of these Latter ages is ascribing power to Witches, and by foolish imagination of mens brains, without grounds in the Scriptures, wrongful killing of the innocent under the name of witches." Ady felt this had become necessary because

Scot's work, published relatively early in Queen Elizabeth's reign for the "instruction of the Judges and justices of those times," although successful in its day, and making a "great impression in the magistracy, and also in the Clergy," had been neglected of late years (the civil war and Interregnum). Since that time, he felt that England had "shamefully fallen from the Truth which they began to receive" about the subject (it was certainly true that the period had witnessed a sudden upsurge in such prosecutions). In reality, Ady overstated the extent to which Scot's work had ceased to be influential. Even in 1667 Samuel Pepys was to record purchasing it in his diary (12th August): "To my bookseller's and did buy Scot's Discourse of Witches." What Ady did achieve, however, was to produce a potted summary of the common objections to witchcraft, one that was both cheaper and easier to digest than Scot's much larger work. Ady, like Scot, did not categorically deny that witches existed, but rather denied their powers, and argued that "witches are not such as are commonly executed for witches."

At about the same period as Ady was writing, Sir Robert Filmer (c.1590-1653), also addressed his mind to a literary work on the subject, being a strenuous opponent of witch persecution. Shortly before his death in 1653, and motivated by recent executions in Kent following the summer Assizes there, he produced a highly sceptical work on witch trials. In particular, he ridiculed Perkins's earlier book on the evidence that could be used to establish that an accused person was guilty, especially the belief that there were 18 sure signs to indicate a witch.[179] Filmer wanted to influence those, especially potential jurors, who: "... have not deliberately thought upon the great difficulty in discovering, what, or who a witch is."[180]

Nevertheless, few of the great sceptics, Weyer, Scot and Spee amongst them, rejected the very possibility of attempts being made at effecting witchcraft, in the sense that they believed that there were some, deluded individuals, who had recourse to it. The devil was central to early modern thought, and there were bound to be some who tried to consort with him. What they doubted was the reality of the powers that were attributed to such witches, or the threat that they posed to their neighbours and the wider society. Similarly Gifford's character, "Daniel," believed that although witches were few in number, and could not kill people, except for those "witches which kill by poyson," they should, nevertheless, be punished for dealing with the devil.[181]

Although the best known of the English sceptics prior to 1660, Scot, Ady and Filmer were supported by a host of less celebrated writers. The debate, between sceptics and believers, waged via tracts, pamphlets and books, was deliberate and continuous. Each side would refer to the others' published works and arguments, sometimes publishing specifically to rebut them. Sceptics came in all descriptions of political belief. The "enthusiast" Jean Bodin

---

179. He was not alone in this. According to Ady (*A Candle in the Dark*), Perkins's work was only published after his death, to maintain his wife as she "had but small meanes for her maintenance," and was not even very accurately reproduced as a result.

180. Pamphlet 1653(3) at pp.A1-3.

181. Gifford, *Dialogue*, at p.B1.

was generally an exponent of toleration (except where witches were involved). The Judge Sir John Kelyng combined extreme political and judicial conservatism with profound doubt as to the existence of witchcraft. This was manifest in his attempt to discourage the conviction of two witches tried at Bury St Edmunds in 1662. Although he diplomatically accepted Mathew Hale's view that the two girls thought to be victims in this case were bewitched, he expressed grave doubts about the cause and attribution of their symptoms: "Mr. Sergeant Keeling seemed much unsatisfied with it, and thought it not sufficient to convict the prisoners."[182] Yet, despite this, as a Judge, Kelyng is best remembered for a number of reactionary decisions which had major constitutional implications, and has been described as a judicial bully. When still a Sergeant, he presided over John Bunyan's famous trial at the Bedfordshire County Sessions in 1661, prompting Bunyan's description of the hectoring "Lord Hategood" in the *Pilgrim's Progress* . Later, in Hood's Case (1666), he fined a jury five pounds each after they brought in a manslaughter verdict against his direction.[183] The following year, 1667, he was called before the Bar of the House of Commons to answer allegations of oppressing jurors.[184] Clearly, he was not a

---

182. *A Trial of Witches, at the Assizes held at Bury St Edmund's, for the County of Suffolk ... Taken by a Person then attending the Court,* London: Printed for William Shrewsbery, at the Bible in Duck-Lane' in *Cobbett's State Trials* Vol.6 at p.699.

183. Reference to case taken from Kaye, J.M., *The Early History of Murder and Manslaughter* (part 2), at p.601.

184. Stockdale, Eric, *A Study of Bedford Prison,* at p.5. The career of Sergeant Kelyng (or Keeling), is not fully documented. However, he seems to have been a man of high (if bigoted) personal principles. Unlike Mathew Hale, who, although apparently a "firm Royalist" decided,

"liberal," even in seventeenth century terms. Similarly, while staunchly opposing witch trials, Sir Robert Filmer was a firm and vociferous believer in the unmitigated divine right of kings to rule (and the author of books promoting both causes).

Scot, Filmer and Ady all based their arguments on a robust mixture of their own interpretations of Protestant theology and biblical exegesis, combined with very practical, commonsense observations. They felt that the matters alleged in such cases were quite simply too fantastic to be believed. As Scot observed: "All wisemen understand that witches miraculous enterprises, being contrarie to nature, probabilitie and reason, are void of truth or possibilitie." In addition, Scot believed that if witchcraft allegations really were true, there should have been far more cases than actually occurred. Butter would never set,

---

discreetly, during the Interregnum, not to involve himself in controversy, even taking judicial office in 1654, Kelyng (if Clarendon is to be believed) spent much of that period in gaol. He was rewarded on the Restoration by being raised to the Order of Serjeants in the first batch created in the new reign (1660). Thus, unlike Hale, who was made a Serjeant simply as a formality, prior to being raised to the Bench (as was common by that period), he practised in the position before receiving judicial office, and this explains his title in the trial reports. Sergeant Kelyng only became a Justice of the King's Bench in 1663, whereafter he rose swiftly to become Lord Chief Justice of that Court in 1665 (he was replaced by Hale on his death in 1671). Thus, at the time of the trial he was not a Royal Judge (Serjeants were employed in a judicial capacity, on an occasional basis, to bolster the numbers available for Assizes hearings). Nevertheless, he was not without legal ability, and not everyone had a low opinion of him. On July 4, 1667, Samuel Pepys went to the Sessions-house in London to watch trials presided over by Kelying, and later lunched with him. He left feeling that: "The Judge seems to be a worthy man, and able," a view that he restated when Kelying was called before Parliament.

the corn would always fail, the weather would be permanently bad. As he noted, if the examples set out in "the pamphlets late set forth in English, of witches executions" were genuine, "what creature could live in securitie?"[185] In turn, Scot's ideas heavily influenced a group of Anglican clergymen, including Samuel Harsnet, John Deacon and John Walker, who were preoccupied with possession and exorcism, or rather its absence. In particular, they denied that devils could be "cast out" of possessed people, either by Catholic ritual or by Puritan prayer and fasting. In his *A Discovery of the Fraudulent Practices of John Darrel* (1599) Harsnet argued that many Puritans such as Darrel and More who engaged in such exorcisms were imposters, and their supposed cases shams, the biblical era of miracles being over, such acts were no longer possible. Although not concerned directly with the existence of witchcraft, Harsnet alluded to it, making his views clear: "Whether witches can send devils into men or women (as many do pretende) is a question amongst those that write of such matters & the learneder and sounder sort doe hold the negative."[186] The implications of this were not lost on Darrel, who replied to Harsnet by exposing it in: *A Detection Of Samuel Harshnet* (1600), pointing out that his approach was: "... not plainly denying any such to be, but secretly insinuatinge as much to the reader."[187] It should be remembered that Harsnet was no obscure cleric, but the private chaplain to Bancroft, the Bishop of London.

---

185. Scot, Reginald *The Discovery of Witchcraft*, at pp.50 and 483.
186. Kocher, Paul, *Science and Religion in Elizabethan England*, at pp.129-132.
187. *Ibid.*, at pp.129-132.

Until the 1620s, some "believers," while acknowledging the existence of the debate, still felt able to dismiss it without serious consideration. Thus, in 1613, the author of a tract on the Flower family of witches began by saying that he did not intend to make any "contentious Arguments" about witchcraft, despite the doubters, as he felt that its existence had already been proved satisfactorily, by both scripture and authoritative writers, such as King James I.[188] Such confidence became progressively rarer as the century advanced, the number of sceptics becoming steadily larger after the early seventeenth century. As with normal religious belief, for all but the most committed, attitudes were flexible; people could simultaneously both believe in witchcraft, and yet have doubts about it; or, conversely, not believe in it, and yet harbour a residual fear of it. Both doubts and fears might be situational. The sight of a condemned witch going to the scaffold might prompt reservations about the whole process of accusal and trial, even in a believer (as appears to have occurred at some of the Salem hangings). Seeing someone fall ill or suffer misfortune shortly after being cursed by the local hag might engender suspicion, even in a sceptic. The debate was fluid, individuals could change their minds on the subject. An obvious (though undeclared, and only partial) example of this was James I himself. As the initially witch-hunting enthusiast James VI of Scotland became exposed to English witch trials, and a more sophisticated Court, doubts (the seeds of which were probably present well before his journey south) began to develop in his mind about the

---

188. Pamphlet 1619, at p.B12.

validity of many cases. Increasingly, his position became one of accepting the theoretical possibility of witchcraft, but not the individual cases that came before him. (It appears clear now that he was not, as once thought, the prime mover in the large-scale Lancashire witch trials of 1612.) Ultimately, he even supervised some ingenious empirical tests for disproving the presence of witchcraft.

By the early seventeenth century, despite the occasional judicial enthusiast, an awareness of the "sceptical" school was also increasingly widespread amongst lawyers. Reconciling this with the continued existence of witchcraft as a felony vexed some of the finest legal minds of the time. An illustration of this is provided by John Selden (1584-1654), who practised as a lawyer and became, in due course, a Bencher of his Inn (on his death being buried in the Temple church). He was intimately associated with the world of scholarship in England, writing on many diverse subjects, both legal and non-legal. Selden produced an ingenious rationale to justify punishment for a crime which many educated men, probably himself included, believed to be non-existent. He focused on the inchoate offence of attempt (albeit that it was an attempt to effect the impossible): "The law ag[ains]t witches does not prove that there bee any [witches], but it punishes the malice of those people, that use such meanes to take away mens lives."[189] Interestingly, this view was to be shared by the political philosopher Thomas Hobbes, in 1651. Although he felt that a belief in witchcraft was largely confined to simple, or "rude," people, and, hardly surprisingly, did not believe in

189. Pollock, Sir Frederick, (Ed.), *The Table Talk of John Selden*, Fo. 74, at p.133.

it himself, he accepted that those who did, and practised it, were deserving of punishment: "I think not that their witchcraft is any real power, but yet that they are justly punished for the false belief they have that they can do such mischief, joined with their purpose to do it if they can."[190] Of course, this was no justification for the punishment of the many accused who had never believed in, nor attempted to exercise, such power.

Gradually, especially after 1660, the proponents of witch trials were pushed onto the defensive, though as late as the 1720s, serious defences were still being made. By the time of the Restoration, scepticism was in the ascendant. The persecution of witches, other than in the decade around the turn of the sixteenth century and (for a few) in the mid-1640s had never taken a very vigorous hold on the English political nation. It probably did not need very much to tip the balance towards de facto suspension, followed by abolition. Legal "enthusiasts" would have come to see their views considered unsophisticated and to have modified them (or at last concealed them) if they sought judicial advancement. Jurors would have been outvoted by increasing numbers of sceptics. Influentially, the larger part of the clergy gradually came to accept a rational form of Protestant theology, finding it intellectually more attractive, and believing it to be more defensible, than what had gone before. Indeed, some Anglican clerics were to be especially active in attempting to suppress "superstition," even though it opened them to popular disapproval, as *The Tatler* noted in 1709, it could prompt cries of: "Shame! That one of his

---

190. Hobbes, Thomas, *Leviathan*, Chapter II.

coat should be such an atheist."[191]

Increasingly, a general resistance to the active prosecution of witchcraft developed. When, in 1664, a Somerset JP, Robert Hunt, believed that he had discovered two active local covens of witches, he was unable to see them successfully prosecuted because of the "cynical attitude" of his fellow justices.[192] This move towards cynicism placed practical limitations on the potential for further witch trials, and accounts, in part, for their rapid decline after 1660. Even where JPs were still enthusiastic about pursuing witches, they might be apprehensive about the reaction of the superior authorities. Significantly, according to Francis Hutchinson, Hunt's "searches and Discoveries were opposed by a higher Authority."[193] Thus also, as late as January 1686, after one Thomas Webb of Malmesbury fell ill, 14 people (11 of them women) were initially questioned by a group of three local magistrates in the presence of an Alderman from that town. Satisfied that there was a case to answer for all of them, the justices' clerks were in the process of drawing up the appropriate mittimus to commit them to the county gaol, when a fourth JP arrived. He was clearly less credulous about the matter, and asked that the room where they were sitting be cleared of casual observers, so that he could speak to his colleagues with a degree of privacy. He informed them that he was extremely concerned at the precipitate nature of the

191. *The Tatler,* No.21, May 28, 1709, Reproduced in Bond, D.F., (Ed.), *The Tatler,* Vol.1 at p.589.

192. Geis, Gilbert and Bunn, Ivan, *A Trial of Witches: A Seventeenth-Century Witchcraft Prosecution,* at p.6.

193. Hutchinson, Francis *Historical Essay on Witchcraft,* at p.40.

proceedings, pointed out that Malmesbury was remote from the Assizes town (being 40 miles from Salisbury) and expressed a fear that they would be "severely censured" by the authorities for sending so many for trial on such a charge. As a result of his robust advice, the others moderated their decision, and restricted themselves to committing three of the accused to gaol and releasing the others, with a strong warning that those committed should not be mistreated, or that: "... any tryals [be] made on their persons, as had been so usual in the lately passed times."[194]

The judiciary (by definition highly educated men), although usually accepting the theoretical possibility of witchcraft, were becoming reluctant to accept its reality in practice. By 1662, Mathew Hale's views, though not seen as ridiculous, were no longer firmly within the mainstream. Nevertheless, because of his great (and justified) prestige as a Judge, Hale's conduct of the trial at Bury St Edmunds in that year was probably instrumental in prolonging witchcraft trials in England, at a time when the growth of rationalism may have tended towards their de facto, if not de jure abolition. It is possible that, if he had taken an overtly sceptical approach to the evidence, the small number of women who died in the remaining period that it was legally prescribed, might have avoided their fates. Because of his judicial reputation, sound Puritan antecedents and obvious piety (something which struck a chord amongst many New Englanders), Hale's views on witchcraft were also to be cited with approval in support of the proceedings held at Salem 30 years later. According to Cotton Mather,

---

194. Reproduced in *The Gentleman's Magazine* Vol. 102, 1832 at p.490.

the hearing at Bury St Edmunds was "a Tryal much considered by the Judges of New-England."[195] Immediately after the 1662 trial, Hale penned his thoughts on the proceedings. Writing at Cambridge the "next Lord's day" afterwards, he opined that the reality of such "evil Angels", was unquestionable. Drawing authority from the Bible and human experience he concluded that witches had a "great measure of Power, and a greater measure of malice," possessing both the ability and the motivation to "mischief" people.[196] Hale's apparent need to justify his actions (if only to himself) was, perhaps, not totally surprising. He was well aware that, even then, the trend was against such trials ("he well knew the notion and sentiments of the age") and had known in advance, from his Judge's calendar, the nature of the trial that he would have to deal with in Suffolk.

The Rise of the Rational Spirit

A belief in witchcraft was firmly consistent with the sixteenth, and early seventeenth century, world picture. As a result, significant numbers of educated and intelligent men could subscribe to it. Jean Bodin (1530-1596), the eminent French jurist and political philosopher is, a prime illustration of the manner in which the intellectual currents of the era could entrance the very best minds. He was, to modern eyes, a bizarre mixture of wisdom and apparent

---

195. Mather, *The wonders of the Invisible World,* at p.419.
196. Hale, Sir Mathew, late Lord Chief Justice of the Kings-Bench, *A Discourse concerning the Great Mercy of God, in Preserving us from the Power and Malice of Evil Angels,* at pp.1-4.

superstition. His sophisticated legal works, amongst them *Les Six Livres de la République* (1576) discussing, in liberal terms, the desirability of a limited monarchy, and his famous Colloquiam Heptaplomeres, asserting the need for a degree of religious toleration between different faiths, make a strange contrast with his *Demonomanie des Sorciers* (1580) with its tirades against the menace of witchcraft, and a willingness to entertain draconian systems of proof in such cases. Significantly, perhaps, Reginald Scot was no "intellectual." Despite his impressive citation of academic authority, he belongs to a long tradition of English pragmatism, rather than one that subscribes to abstract intellectual systems. This encouraged him to rely on personal observation of the reality of witchcraft cases (in his native Kent), and his own shrewd appreciation of human nature, rather than on the demonological theories that were fashionable, and which led better minds astray. Once these abstract theories were accepted, evidence to support them was readily forthcoming. In the words of the philosopher and statesman, Francis Bacon: "What a man had rather were true, that he more readily believes."[197] As Francis Hutchinson appreciated, once such theories were abandoned, so was a belief in witchcraft, and attendant prosecutions for the crime. He saw that "witchcraft follows principles," especially those sanctioned by the legislature, and that the number of accusations would increase or decrease as these principles "prevail or are exploded."[198] As a new intellectual spirit, one rooted in the new philosophy,

197. Bacon, Francis, *Novum Organum*, 1, 49.
198. Hutchinson, Francis *Historical Essay on Witchcraft*, at p.49.

triumphed in the latter seventeenth century, educated belief in witchcraft became progressively rarer, until, by the early 1700s, it was largely the province of eccentrics.

After 1660, the existing century old "sceptical" school, couched largely in the religious terms of Protestant biblical criticism allied with "commonsense" empirical observation, received a massive fillip from this advance of scientific rationalism. The post-1660 decline in witchcraft trials was closely linked to an increasing unwillingness to give credence to such occult practices amongst the educated people who made up the bulk of personelle involved in the trial process. As educated beliefs about the nature of the world became progressively more sophisticated and "rational," élite "high culture," and popular "low culture," became increasingly distinctive.[199] It is hard to imagine the barristers of Lincoln's Inn burying magical charms in their grounds in the 1660s; yet a century before, a lead tablet had been interred there to invoke the spirit of the moon, containing a charm from an earlier published work of 1533, and asking that "nothing maye prosper [that] ... Ralph Scrope takes in hande." Scrope was Treasurer of the Inn in 1564-65.[200] Equally, their post-Restoration cousins in the Middle Temple would probably not have spent three weeks recording the ramblings of an allegedly demonically possessed member of the Inn, one who had earlier attempted suicide, as their predecessors had in 1574.[201]

---

199. Hay, D., and Rogers, N., *Eighteenth-Century English Society,* at p.35.
200. Discovered by workmen digging drains in 1899; currenty on display in the Inn.
201. *See Mr Brigg's Visitation,* unpublished manuscript discovered in Lambeth Palace Library in 1996 by Jeremy Maule. Briggs recovered to become an MP.

The new rational spirit was itself grounded in the emerging philosophy of the era. In particular, materialists, like Thomas Hobbes, by rejecting the notion of incorporeal substances, forced demons out of the natural world. To many people, it became evermore implausible that Satan, or his servants, could assume a physical form. As a result, the devil was increasingly relegated to the spiritual realm, if he had an existence at all. Thus, devout though he was, Sir Isaac Newton believed that evil spirits were merely desires of the mind. Others even questioned the physical existence of Hell itself, at least as a real place of torment, rather than a state of mind. Educated believers in witchcraft, in the latter seventeenth century, were well aware of this process even as it occurred. They resisted it, seeing in these changes a menacing fifth column that would eventually go far beyond simply abandoning witches and devils, and which had the potential to become a threat to all forms of revealed religion. These men continued to produce serious works encouraging the prosecution of witches until the early 1700s.

The 1680s saw a flurry of works aimed against men whom Richard Bovet (clearly appreciating that he was on the losing side in the intellectual debate) termed "witty and (otherwise) Ingenious" people who were openly, and with "great zeal," doubting the existence of witches.[202] George Sinclair, in his major work *Satan's Invisible World Discovered,* published in 1685 in Edinburgh, claimed that the new philosophy was a primary cause for the regrettable decline in witchcraft. Sinclair's views are significant, if only because

202. Bovet, *Pandaemonium,* at p.59.

he was himself a man of science, being an accomplished mathematician, and a professor at the University of Glasgow, who had also worked as a mining engineer. In particular, he attributed the advance of scepticism to the spread of the doctrines of Hobbes, Spinoza and Descartes. Despite his scientific background, he continued to be a firm believer in the reality of witchcraft, though he accepted that: "... it is commonly believed that many innocent persons have suffered as witches," especially those who had been tortured to confess (as was not uncommon in Scotland). His response to this, however, was robust. Even if it were the case that some innocent people had been wrongly convicted "will it follow that all suffer after that manner?" While Sinclair accepted that some popular accounts of witches transforming themselves into cats and dogs were absurd, he remained confident that witches could harm by touch of hand, by their breath and by their glances.[203] He was not alone in fearing the inroads that the new philosophy of the late seventeenth century was having on belief in witchcraft.

In England, Joseph Glanvil also attempted to alert people to an awareness that the issue as to whether witches existed was not a matter of "vain speculation," but rather one of "very great and weighty importance." He hoped thus to defend against the advance of "atheism and infidelity" and similar doctrines that he felt were the fellow-travellers of scepticism about witchcraft. Aware of the (to him) insidious process of retreat from active prosecution of witchcraft, Glanvil had published *Some Philosophical Considerations Touching Witches and Witchcraft*, in 1666,

203. Sinclair, George, Preface to *Satan's Invisible World Discovered*, at p.1325.

defending the reality of witchcraft, placing it on a more "scientific" basis, and founding it firmly in mainstream theology. It was a relatively sophisticated and quite widely read book. Samuel Pepys purchased it shortly after its first publication, and took it to bed to read, declaring that it was "well writ in good style," but still concluding "methinks not very convincing."[204] Glanvil's book prompted the sceptical John Webster to reply with his own *Displaying of Supposed Witchcraft* in 1677, in which he distinguished the validity of a belief in angels from that in witches. Glanvil's work was re-issued in a much expanded version entitled *Sadducismus Triumphatus*, in 1681. Like Sinclair, Glanvil identified some of the philosophers behind this process of secularisation, freely lumping "Atheists, Sadducees and Hobbists" together. Nevertheless, to an even greater extent than Sinclair, he was forced to advance a more sophisticated defence against those who ridiculed belief in witchcraft as "silly credulity," and to dispense with much of the popular baggage of witch belief. In particular, he readily accepted that "Melancholy and Imagination" or unusual diseases could lead some women to believe, mistakenly, that they were witches. Like Sinclair, Glanvil readily accepted that many had been wrongly accused by "Witch-finders," and that a lot of the "silly lying Stories of Witchcraft and Apparitions among the vulgar" were ridiculous. He was also willing to accept that some who denied the existence of witches, albeit mistakenly, were also sincere Christians (they were merely "anti scripturalists").[205]

---

204. *Diary of Samuel Pepys*, November 24, at p.382.
205. Reproduced in Kors, A.C., and Peters, E., *Witchcraft in Europe 1100-1700*, at p.304.

The final salvoes in the debate came after the publication of Bishop Francis Hutchinson's major (and much delayed) work of 1718, a book that for many spelt the end of an intelligent belief in witches. Hutchinson's personal interest in witch trials is not surprising; he had become Vicar of St James's Church, in the old Assizes town of Bury St Edmunds, in 1692. The town had witnessed the celebrated trial presided over by Mathew Hale in 1662, as well as many other major trials for witchcraft over the previous century, including one of the largest ever in 1645. The book was many years in its gestation, so that although it was only published in 1718, it contained research that Hutchinson had been able do much earlier in his life, including oral testimony from many elderly individuals with a personal recollection of events from the 1640s. Nevertheless, Hutchinson's book did not totally conclude the matter. As late as 1722, Reginald Boulton, a physician and graduate of Brasenose College Oxford, launched a vigorous (and well argued) attack on scepticism generally, and the work of Dr. Hutchinson in particular. Boulton felt that there was no need to apologise for, or be defensive about, the criminalisation of witchcraft. Indeed, misinterpreting cause and effect, he believed that the very reason that witchcraft had apparently declined in England (as evidenced by the number of trials) was because punishment, and the fear of prosecution, had engendered such a result.[206]

However, though an articulate writer, Boulton's views were viewed as decidedly strange, and such intellectual

206. Boulton, Reginald, *The Possibility and Reality of Magick, Sorcery and Witchcraft, demonstrated. Or a vindication of a complete History of Magic, sorcery and Witchcraft. In Answer to Dr. Hutchinson's Historical Essay.* at p.3.

justifications for the existence of witchcraft were widely ridiculed in print. At the beginning of the 1700s, there had still been some influential individuals, such as Daniel Defoe, who, for a variety of reasons (not all of them based on genuine belief), were opposed to overt scepticism. Most of these (including Defoe) appear to have changed their minds between 1710 and 1730.

In Scotland, resistance to abolition in 1736 was stronger than South of the Border, but there, it was as much linked to local fears of encroachment by "English" intellectual currents, as to a continuing fear of witches. Partly because of this, the belief in the need for legislation against the activity of witches survived the Act of Union (1707) by many years. Indeed, Francis Hutchinson's work was apparently delayed by the English ecclesiastical hierarchy in its publication (1718), by a decade, to avoid upsetting Scottish sensibilities. Such modest parliamentary resistance as there was to abolition, in 1735-6, came largely from Scots. Thus, James Erskine, Lord Grange, a former Scottish advocate, a Judge of the Court of Session, and personally highly learned on the more arcane aspects of daemonologie (he had a major library on the subject), made his maiden parliamentary speech opposing the Witches' Bill (apparently to considerable hilarity).

To an extent, England was behind some other European jurisdictions in the process of *de jure* abolition. In France (then a much smaller political entity than today) concern about procedural irregularities in witch cases led the Paris Parlement to install an automatic appeal procedure in 1624, whereby anyone convicted of witchcraft was sent to Paris for a rehearing (it was followed by several regional Parlements). The conduct of Judges was strictly regulated in such cases, something, which, when combined with the expense of sending those convicted to the capital, and the regular manner in which such appeals were either allowed, or, at least, the sentences reduced, greatly moderated the enthusiasm of inferior courts for dealing with this kind of case. As a result, by 1640, for half of the French population, it was effectively impossible to be sentenced to death for witchcraft. Interestingly, the Jurist William Blackstone believed that the French example had been significant in the eventual abolition of this "dubious crime," in England, in 1736, noting that: "... our legislature having at length followed the wise example of Louis XIV in France, who thought proper by an edict to restrain the tribunals of justice from receiving informations of witchcraft."[207] Certainly, there was a popular awareness in England of the French reforms. One pamphlet writer, in 1712, observed that it was "amongst the few good Things that Lewis XIV has done." It was also noted that he had ordered the release of witches from the gaols in Normandy (not then subject to the same law as the rest of France) in 1672, following a spate of prosecutions there in the years 1670 to 1672.[208] This series of trials subsequently prompted the French King, aided by his minister Colbert, to enforce the Parisian system throughout the country.[209] Nevertheless, several European countries, such as Switzerland, preserved the crime long after abolition in Britain.

---

207. Blackstone, William, *Commentaries on the Laws of England,* Vol. iv, *Of Public Wrongs* (1769) at p.69.
208. *See* Pamphlet 1712(2) at p.43.
209. *See* on this Briggs, R., *Witches and Neighbours,* at pp. 333-335.

Qualified Scepticism, and Doubts about Individual Cases

Along with what might be termed a "general" doubt about the very possibility of witchcraft, and as important in its practical effects on the level of witch trials, were the mounting reservations of those who, although accepting the theoretical possibility of witchcraft, found the individual cases actually brought for trial implausible, or, at the very least, impossible to prove to any reasonable standard of proof. Significantly, although Blackstone, writing in 1769 (long after abolition) found classifying witchcraft as a crime extremely difficult (it was a crime of which "one knows not well what account to give"), he was still not prepared to deny its existence. He readily accepted that: "... to deny the possibility, nay, actual existence, of witchcraft and sorcery, is at once flatly to contradict the revealed word of God, in various passages both of the old and new testament." However, he also agreed with the views of Joseph Addison, as expressed in the *Spectator* in 1711 (in his opinion "a most ingenious writer") that: "... in general there has been such a thing as witchcraft; though one cannot give credit to any particular modern instance of it."[210]

To "full-blooded" sceptics, such a qualified reluctance to pursue witches was inadequate, and Thomas Ady included a critical survey of "moderate" sceptics in his work. Thus, he felt that although the Gaule was "much inclining to the truth," and had done good work to prevent the persecution of the poor and innocent, he had also made major mistakes

210. Blackstone, William, *Commentaries on the Laws of England*, Vol. iv, *Of Public Wrongs* (1769) at p.78, and *The Spectator*, no.117, July 14, 1711.

about the Biblical evidence for the very possibility of witches. Gifford, he felt, had "more of the spirit of truth in him than many of his profession [clergymen]," but still fell into error by believing that imps existed, even if they could not hurt anyone.[211] Nevertheless, it was the attitude encapsulated by Addison's influential article, as much as outright scepticism, that was behind much of the initial decline, if not the final end, of witch trials. It was an acknowledgment of the near impossibility of proving the presence of witchcraft in any given case, and of distinguishing it from mania, misfortune, malice or an unfortunate co-incidence. Significantly, believers in the need for judicial action against witchcraft focused almost as much of their attention on such arguments as on those of outright sceptics. Boulton, for example, vigorously rejected the opinions of those who believed that it was impossible to prove individual cases, even while accepting the theoretical possibility of witchcraft. He readily accepted that there were risks in convicting in such cases, and that there might well have been some mistakes committed in the past. However, he felt that these risks were present in all felony trials, being an inherent part of the litigation process. Errors were periodically made even in capital cases involving "conventional" crimes, with the innocent being executed as result. Nevertheless, as Boulton pointed out, no-one argued that such trials should be abolished: "Because Cases and Circumstances may sometime be misrepresented must all Judgement be condemend? And because injustice may be

---

211. Ady, *Candle,* at pp.153-161.

done, must no justice take place?"[212]

Doubts about individual cases stemmed from a growing awareness of alternative explanations for events previously attributed to bewitchment. It was always accepted, even by the most fervent believers in sorcery, that terrible misfortunes in life might occur for other reasons (than bewitchment), such as an "Act of God." It had long been admitted, by doctors, that it was very difficult to distinguish between a natural disease and one induced by the devil. Typically, when the Earl of Rutland, his wife and children, were first assailed by the Flower family of witches, they took their bouts of sickness and misfortune to be part of the ordinary vicissitudes of life. In an age when disease could strike at any time, it was reasonable to view them, like any other disaster, as: "... gentle corrections from the hand of God."[213]

Alternatively, even if the devil was involved in instances of human misfortune, it was accepted that he might be operating in a direct capacity, without the assistance of a human intermediary. As John Cotta observed: "It is not destitute of easie proofe, that there are many supernatural workes of the divell manifest to sense, wherein man doth not participate in knowledge, or consent with him." Cotta felt that an obvious Biblical example of this, was the manner in which the devil had come to Eve, in the form of a serpent.[214] Furthermore, although admissions

---

212. Boulton, Reginald, *The Possibility and Reality of Magick, Sorcery and Witchcraft, demonstrated. Or a vindication of a complete History of Magic, sorcery and Witchcraft. In Answer to Dr Hutchinson's Historical Essay,* at p.33.
213. Pamphlet 1619 at p.D2.
214. Cotta, John, *The Triall of Witch-Craft,*at p.26.

of guilt were sometimes made, without any untoward pressure, there was a growing concern that some at least of these might be the product of mental disturbance. This growing caution about individual trials was greatly facilitated by the large body of cases that had been indisputably proven to be fraudulent. Significantly, the Judge Francis North, on circuit in the 1680s, was to stress that exposing an instance of fraud in a case was far more effective in securing a jury acquittal than "denying authoritatively such power to be given old women."[215]

Counterfeit and Fraud

Almost from the beginning, it had been appreciated, by all but the most blinkered, that there were fraudulent allegations of bewitchment, though there might be debate as to their numbers. As early as 1575, two fake pin vomiters (something that was believed to be a sure sign of witchcraft in England) had been tried in London for pretending to be bewitched, and had been forced to make a public penance. In 1605, when Anne Gunter, a 14-year-old girl had allegedly vomited pins, and accused several women of bewitching her, she was placed under the close supervision of Henry Cotton, the Bishop of Salisbury. He discovered a hoax by leaving carefully marked pins about his house, which Gunter later pretended to regurgitate. An early judicial example was made of Anne Gunter's father (at whose behest she had carried out the pretence), in the Court of Star

215. North, Roger *The Lives of the Right Hon. Francis North ...* at p.268.

Chamber, in 1606. In such prerogative courts, the normal common law formalities of Petty and Grand juries were dispensed with, and the matter determined by Judges from the Westminster courts (along with other Privy Councillors).[216] It is safe to assume that this first Government Prosecution (one in which Edward Coke was involved), had a salutary effect in curbing excessive judicial enthusiasm for such cases when on circuit.

Instances of fraud became increasingly better recognised as time passed. A particularly celebrated example was the notorious case of the "Bilston boy," in Staffordshire, in 1620. Thirteen-year-old William Perry started to have "fits," and accused one Jane Clarke of bewitching him. He, too, began to vomit bent pins, pieces of straw and bits of rag, as well as demonstrating other symptoms of enchantment. He was apparently the subject of unsuccessful religious ministrations by both Catholics and Protestants to deal with the problem. The accused woman was brought before the Judges at the local Assizes. However, they turned the boy over to Bishop Morton, who was present at court, for further investigation. This cleric, with the assistance of his secretary, set out to test the youth, their suspicions being aroused when he failed to recognise St John's gospel (the recitation of which in English had induced fits) in the original Greek. He was secretly watched, and the careful preparations for his deceptions exposed (a similar technique was to be used in the case of Richard Hathaway over 80 years later). He was then persuaded to admit that he was a cheat, in court,

---

216. Levack, Brian, *Possession, Witchcraft, and the Law in Jacobean England,* at pp.1630-1632.

in front of Sir Peter Warburton and Sir Humphrey Winch, and to beg the forgiveness of Clarke.[217]

The caution shown by Winch (1545-1625), a Judge of the Court of Common Pleas, in the Clarke case, was not surprising. Even contemporary observers had been appalled at the manner in which, in a similar case in 1616, he had condemned nine women to death at the summer Assizes in Leicester, on the totally unsupported evidence of one boy, who claimed that they had bewitched and tormented him. This youth was personally exposed as an impostor by an increasingly "sceptical" James I, when the Monarch visited the town only a month after the trials (but, sadly, too late to save the unfortunate women from the gallows). At the time, Winch fell into considerable disgrace for his conduct of the trial, though not enough to be removed from the bench. Even for a Judge noted by Francis Bacon for his "quickness, industry and dispatch," a grievous error had clearly been made.[218]

Nevertheless, fraudulent allegations of vomiting as a result of bewitchment continued long after abolition of the felony. In Kent, in 1762, a 13-year-old youth, named Ladd, "pretended to void needles and pins from his body, and his father upheld the deceit, and collected large sums of money of those whose compassion was excited by so melancholy a situation."[219] Other cheats abounded. If John Aubrey is correct, James I was personally behind the exposure of

---

217. Notestein, W., *A History of Witchcraft in England from 1558* to 1718, at pp.141-142.
218. Cockburn, J.S., *A History of English Assizes, 1558-1714,* at p.120 and Edward Foss, *Biographica Juridica,* at p.748.
219. *Gentleman's Magazine,* Vol.32(1762) at p.346.

Katharine Waldron, who, although a lady of quality, pretended to be bewitched by another woman. She mimicked having fits, during which she could endure "exquisite torments" such as having "pinnes thrust into her flesh." She was visited by the King during one of these supposed fits. However, suddenly, and in front of many people, he gave a "pluck to her Coates, and topt them over her head, and discovered All to the standers by." At this, the woman, preserving some "innate modesty," did "immediately start, and [so] detected the Cheat."[220]

As a result of such cases, even the more thoughtful "enthusiasts" attempted to establish techniques to identify fraudsters. Thus, although a strong believer in witchcraft, Bernard was sufficiently alarmed at the risk posed by such "counterfeits," to devote a whole chapter of his book to their existence, and the best means of their exposure. Typical of these frauds was a "lewd girl" at Wells, who apparently counterfeited bewitchment so that she could be revenged on a poor woman who had complained to her mistress about her. He also cited a case from Westwell in 1574 (it appears that Scot's work was the source of this illustration, he had obviously studied his "opposition"). Bernard recognised that such dissemblers might have various motives for their frauds, such as gaining revenge, the advancement of Popery, and, perhaps more pertinently, a desire to please others "which would have it so." As a result, he enjoined members of the Grand Jury, before they returned a finding of billa vera on the indictment: "... with all serious attention to looke upon the seeming bewitched and to ponder all the

220. Dick, O.L., (Ed.), *Aubrey's Brief Lives,* at p.53.

circumstances lest they be deceived by a counterfeit." Amongst the techniques he suggested for exposing counterfeits, was the by then almost stock tactic of trying ancient languages, in which they had had no education, on them. If pretending, they would not recognise religious passages, while cases in which people were truly bewitched often allowed the "unlearned to speak Greeke and Latine." He may have got the idea for this test from Reginald Scot, who had noted, of one witch supposedly possessed by the devil, that although she: "... answered men of all questions, marie hir divell could understand no Latine, and so was she (and by such meanes all the rest may be) betraied."[221] James I also had personal recourse to this method of detecting cheats.

By the 1620s, sufficient well publicised cases of fraud had occurred to prompt greatly increased levels of caution in the judicial authorities, especially with regard to allegations by juveniles. An early indication of such a new and robust degree of judicial scepticism can be seen in the handling of the case of the six women accused by Edward Fairfax of bewitching his daughters, and the child of a neighbour (one Jeffray). This case was heard at the York Assizes in August 1622. When the matter came for trial: "... first the little one, and then both the others, fell in a trance before the Judge." They were carried out of the court. However some "justices of the bench" (presumably the Assizes Judges) followed, and "made experiments to prove if they counterfeited or not." Although Fairfax did not witness the experiments they carried out on the children,

221. Scot, Reginald, *The Discovery of Witchcraft*, at p.476.

they were clearly robust: "Report said it was not so civil as I expected from such men." As a result of these tests, the Justices apparently found "nothing but sincerity" in Fairfax's two children (prudently influenced, perhaps, by his high social status), while the Yeoman Jeffray's daughter was persuaded to admit to dissembling, at the behest of her parents. It was suggested that the Fairfax daughters may have been influenced by this girl. Fairfax himself was accused "not of dishonesty, but of simplicity," and of being made a fool of by Jeffray. All the defendants were, needless to say, acquitted.[222] This was a judicial attitude that could usefully have been followed at Salem 70 years later, when the girls involved there also began having fits in court.

Awareness of potential fraud can be seen in the treatment of the evidence against the two women accused at Bury St Edmunds in 1662. The case against them was heavily based on juvenile testimony and the experiences, in particular, of two girls aged 11 and 9. These juveniles had apparently vomited pins and small nails, though the genuineness of this had not been immediately accepted. The children had initially been sent to an aunt, who suspecting deliberate fraud on their part, had removed the pins from their clothes and hidden them so that they could not be ingested. Despite this, they continued to throw up "at least" thirty pins in her presence, and had "most fierce and violent fits upon them." This prompted her to accept the truth of their allegations. Nevertheless, the aunt's precautions against such fraud appear to have been relatively minimal (no doubt other pins were readily available, or could be

222. *Ibid.*, at p.228.

secreted about the person). It can be argued that Hale failed to follow the known examples of much stronger judicial caution when accepting this evidence without enhanced scrutiny.

In a situation not dissimilar to that at Salem, the girls at Bury would also fly into fits that left them "wholly deprived of all sense and understanding," in which they clenched their fists together so that even strong men could not open them. When touched by the two alleged witches, they would immediately fall quiet. Several senior lawyers present in the court were suspicious at this feature of the case, among them Serjeant John Kelyng, Hale's coadjutor on the Assizes. They (or perhaps Kelyng alone) proposed a test in which one of the girls was removed from the court and an apron put over her face; when she had a fit, another person (than the accused women) touched her, and she fell quiet. It was this technique that would be employed successfully to expose Richard Hathaway, 40 years later in Surrey.[223] It should have dealt a fatal blow to the prosecution in Bury St Edmunds. However, the court (i.e. Hale) got round this problem, by following a suggestion from the child's father, and arguing that it was itself a devilish trick. Thus, ironically, and quite unanswerably, it was held to be "rather a confirmation that the parties were really bewitched than otherwise." Part of the explanation for Mathew Hale's reluctance to accept Keyling's test, and his willingness to accept the bizarre sophistry of the alternative explanation, may have lain in the fierce rivalry of the two men. Both were leading candidates for the position of Chief Justice of

---

223. *See* below at p.160.

the King's Bench, and had regularly disagreed over previous cases.

Much more successful were the pre-trial attempts to expose the impostor Richard Hathaway, for fraudulently alleging that Sarah Morduck, an "honest and pious" woman, had bewitched him in 1701. These were far more concerted than those conducted at many earlier trials. Hathaway, too, claimed that as an effect of her witchery, he had "vomited up nails and pins," as well as not being able to speak or open his eyes.[224] The prosecution's attitude to the regurgitation of pins and needles in this case showed a scepticism that had been sorely missing in 1662: "And as to vomiting pins, it will appear to you, that he carried papers of pins in his pocket, to make use of on occasion. But when he vomited in a bason, and his hands were kept down, and he not permitted to carry them up to the bason, there was not one pin in the bason." (This did not totally end courtroom allegations of the vomiting of bizarre objects, a decade later, in 1712, Jane Wenham was also alleged to have regurgitated bent pins.) A close parallel to the experiment conducted by Kelyng in 1662, was conducted by one Dr.Martin, a local Minister of religion. Hearing that Hathaway had tried to scratch Morduck, and yet was still unable to open his eyes, and was eager to have another attempt at drawing her blood, he brought a different woman, a Mrs.Johnson, to his (Hathaway's) bedside. Martin asked the "dumb" Hathaway (his eyes still firmly closed), before he tried to draw blood: "Do you believe you shall be relieved by scratching her? ... [at which] he did hold up his

---

224. Cobbett, William, *Cobbett's State Trial* Vol.14, at p.642.

hand." Sarah Morduck was also present and said she agreed to be scratched, but instead of proffering her arm, Martin held up Mrs. Johnson's, who had agreed to be scratched, in lieu of Morduck, on promise of compensation for any injury she received in the process. Hathaway appears to have "smelt a rat," and took precautions to establish that the proffered arm was at least female: "... two or three times he felt from her wrist to her elbow." When satisfied, he drew blood, and then opened his eyes (having been "released" from Morduck's spell). When told of his mistake he "seemed very much cast down."

Despite this, Hathaway did not immediately abandon his allegations, claiming he could not eat, because she (Morduck) was still a witch. As a result he was committed to the "care" of a surgeon, one Mr. Kensey, who was also very suspicious of his claims. Special steps were taken to keep him under covert observation, and: "... it was contrived that [peep] holes were made in the room where he was." The house-maid was instructed to tell him, privately, that she would bring him victuals in secret, which, it was observed, "he did constantly eat every day, though he pretended he fasted all that time." Hathaway was eventually tried for fraud at the Surrey Assizes of 1702.

Tests for fraud were also employed in America. In Massachusetts, in 1671, one Elizabeth Knapp implicated a seemingly pious neighbour as being involved in bewitching her. This unfortunate woman was placed next to the blindfolded Knapp, who, apparently, although: "... her eyes were (as it were) sealed up ... shee yet knew her very touch from any other, though no voice were uttered." Nevertheless, a degree of overt scepticism about this on the part of the observers seems to have influenced Knapp, for she subsequently retracted her allegation against this woman and admitted that "Satan had deluded her" over it.[225]

To sceptics, the recognised categories of imposter could simply be expanded (by acknowledging greater sophistication, even if undetected) to cover most cases that were not attributable to mental disturbance. This was something that greatly alarmed many believers in witchcraft, among them Mathew Hale's friend, and spiritual adviser, Richard Baxter. In 1691 he freely conceeded that false allegations could be made, and lamented their impact on informed opinion: "And I confess very many cheats of pretended possession have been discovered which have made some weak injudicious men think that all are such."[226]

Mental Illness and Confessions

Reginald Scot appreciated that psychological disturbance could account for many women convincing themselves that they actually were witches. "Melancholie," as he termed it (it was a common generic name for mental illness), could effect the most incredible results in those who suffered from it, many of which were well documented even in the 1580s. As Scot observed, given that some people so afflicted could believe themselves to be Kings, and others brute beasts or even urinal pots, it was not surprising that a few women might genuinely convince themselves that they were

---

225. *Letter of Willard, A briefe account of a strange & unusual Providence of God befallen to Elizabeth Knap of Groton*, volume viii, fourth series, at pp. 555-570.
226. Baxter, Richard, *The Certainty of the World of Spirits*, at p.79.

witches, or confess to committing impossibilities that "none, having their right wits, will believe." Nevertheless, people often did believe their absurd claims. He cited the case of a witch who at the time of her death had admitted to raising the storms and cold weather of the bitter winter of 1565.[227]

To Scot, a classic illustration of the way in which "voluntarie confessions may be untrulie made, to the undoing of the confessors," as a result of such "melancholy," could be seen in a case from Sellenge in his native Kent. The wife of one Simon Davie, a husbandman there, apparently became pensive (exhibiting what might be considered today as the classic signs of the onset of depression), and then agitated. She eventually announced that she had "bargained and given her soule to the devil," and also bewitched her husband and children. Her sympathetic husband counselled her that such evil could not happen to those that feared God, and then prayed with her. By sheer co-incidence, at the time the devil was supposed to come for his wife (according to her own account), a stray dog devoured a sheep that had been killed and hung up nearby, making a great noise in the process. As Scot wryly observed, in the light of this occurrence, had Jean Bodin presided over her trial, he would have decided that the evidence conclusively

---

227. Scot, Reginald, *The Discovery of Witchcraft,* at pp.52-55. This type of claim was fairly unusual in England, where allegations of witchcraft were normally highly individualised and parochial in nature (unlike some parts of continental Europe), being based on acts of maleficium against specific people, rather than more general claims to have produced environmental disasters, harvest failures, etc. Nevertheless, John Aubrey records that "Raysing Tempests" and "throwing down steeples" were amongst the powers sometimes attributed to them. *See* Dick, O.L, (Ed.) *Aubrey's Brief Lives,* at p.54.

established her guilt. Instead, with the understanding support of her husband, she made a full recovery from her fantasies and returned to being "far from such impietie, and ashamed of hir imaginations, which she perceievth to have growne through melancholie."[228]

In an era of faith, when Christianity was the main intellectual reference point for most people, and where there was a widespread fear of witchcraft, psychiatric disturbance was likely to manifest itself in such delusions, in the same way that fantasies about aliens are not uncommon in the mentally ill today. Scot was not unique in providing such a diagnosis for claims to witchcraft, it was addressed even by "believers." Thus, one of Holland's literary characters observed "... some men (as they say) of learning and reputation, affirme, that this art being rightly discovered, containeth nothing but cousenage and secret practices of wicked men, and foolish women which are full of restless melancholick."[229] A hundred years later, the Judge, Sir Francis North, noted of two witches at Exeter, who had made extensive admissions to the crime, that they had clearly developed a "sort of melancholy madness" of the type commonly associated with "lunatics." Academic authority for such delusions was increasingly available by the seventeenth century. They were widely acknowledged by proto-psychologists, such as Timothy Bright (in his *A Treatise of Melancholie* of 1586), and, a few decades later, by Robert Burton in his *Anatomy of Melancholy* (1621), a major study of psychological illness. Some sceptics, addressing the

---

228. Scot, Reginald, *The Discovery of Witchcraft*, at pp.56-57.
229. Holland, *A Treatise Against Witchcraft*, at p.B2.

fact that most witches were female, attributed claims to witchcraft specifically to psychological disturbance caused by organic disease in the womb and the female reproductive system. This analysis gained support over time, so that it has been observed that a gradual process of "hysteriazation" of witches took place in the seventeenth and early eighteenth centuries. Under the influence of men like Edward Jorden, in particular, claims to witchcraft came increasingly to be seen as an indication of the presence of mental disturbance rather than devilment. Jorden appreciated that fits, apparently set-off by the presence of alleged witches, might actually have a hysterical provenance, being the result of the "stirring of the affections of the mind." This was especially the case, given that humans were not fully masters of their "owne affections," and so could easily produce fantasies. This could readily be seen from the way in which those who felt that they were bewitched might recover if given a placebo of (for example) crows' gall and oil and told it had great curative powers for those in their condition.[230] As a result, it can be said that the subject made an important contribution to the emergence and development of modern psychiatry.[231]

It became increasingly accepted that "melancholy" induced cases could not be reliably, consistently, and safely distinguished from genuine instances of witchcraft, even allowing that the latter occurred. As this process developed, it was also recognised that it might be the principal prosecution witnesses who were deranged, or mad. Thus in

---

230. Jorden, Ed., *A Brief Disclosure of a Disease Called The Suffocation of the Mother,* at pp. 14-15.

231. Porter, Roy, *A Social History of Madness, Stories of the Insane,* at p.142.

the Wenham case from 1712, some thought that her principal accuser, Anne Thorn, was more properly to be listed amongst the: "Number of Maniacks, than Demoniacks ... Her frequent Ravings, her lucid intervals, her strong Imagination, her more than Ordinary strength, are symptoms which agree well enough with Mad people; her frequent Calling out upon Jane Wenham, as the Source of all her woe, no doubt, was owing to an idea strongly impress'd upon her Brain."

Doubts about the Extent of Witches' Powers

Even holding a belief in witches did not require an acceptance of all the powers commonly attributed to them, the use of which formed the basis of most prosecutions. Men, such as the Puritan Gifford, could believe in the reality of the devil and his powers to influence people without subscribing to many popular notions about the capabilities of witches. Although he thought it "grosse" to suggest (as he knew some did) that the power apparently wrought by the witches recorded in the Bible was actually cheatery, he appreciated that the ignorant were tempted to: "... ascribe unto them very foolishly, such power and efficacie in working, as in deede the devill is not able to perfourme." As a result of superstition, simple people often believed that witches were the "common plague of the earth" and effected their schemes at will, "worked at their pleasure."[232] Gifford had probably attended the witch trials at St.Osyth in 1582

232. Gifford, *Disclosure*, at p.A2.

and been made painfully aware of the inadequacy of the evidence on which many of the witches there had been convicted. As a result, he was keen to show how, in many cases, the devil could deceive not only witches but others (such as jurors), leading them into "many great errours" in such cases, and producing unsafe convictions so that "much innocent blood is shed," something that would itself delight Satan.[233] Significantly, his work of 1593, *A dialogue concerning Witches and Witchcraftes* was dedicated to Robert Clarke, a Baron of the Court of Exchequer. This book took the form of a dialogue between, a countryman, Samuel, who believed he was afflicted by a witch, and a sceptic, Daniel, who doubted it. Using this dialogue, and aided by conversations with a schoolmaster and Samuel's wife, Gifford explored a number of themes which he felt accounted for much of the misplaced belief in witches in his era.

Post-Repeal Witchcraft and the Law

Even after 1736, there continued to be an interaction between witchcraft, magic and the law, as a popular belief in magic remained widespread, especially amongst the poor. The authorities remained concerned at the extent of witch belief well into the eighteenth century. Although decriminalised, village mobs continued to identify and inflict summary punishment on witches. In 1751 there was a major outbreak of witch-hunting in Hertfordshire. At Tring, in that county, a man named Osborne and his wife

233. Gifford, *Dialogue,* at p.A3.

were widely reputed among their neighbours to be witches, and believed to have committed various acts of maleficium, including the killing of cattle belonging to a local farmer. One man from the area organised a local persecution, forcing the couple to seek refuge in a workhouse. A mob, which broke down the walls of this building, seized the pair, and dragged them to Marlston mere, where they were enclosed in a sheet, before being thrown in. The ringleader of the riot, a man by the name of Thomas Colley, apparently then waded in and turned them over with a stick so that the woman drowned. He was subsequently convicted of murder and hanged.[234] Colley, whose body was hung in chains as a public example after execution, had to be escorted to his death by over 100 cavalrymen. Unlike most executions, the general populace were unwilling to approach the scaffold and watch his death, in some cases, probably, because they had formed part of the lynch mob that Colley led. Instead, many thousands stood at a distance from the scaffold muttering that it was a: "... hard case to hang a man for destroying an old wicked woman who had done so much harm by her witchcraft."[235] Cases of witches being "swum" continued for decades after abolition. In the latter part of the eighteenth century, there was even a revival of concern on the part of some educated people at the way in which a popular belief in witchcraft had survived, and, according to some, grown, amongst the poorer people in the countryside. As a result, William Hogarth, in his engraving A medley-Credulity, Superstition,

---

234. Hay, D., and Rogers, N., *Eighteenth-Century English Society,* at pp.35 and 169; and Parry, L.A., *The History of Torture in England,* at p.184.

235. *The Gentleman's Magazine* Vol.21 (1751) at p.378.

and Fanaticism of 1762, was moved to feature notorious instances of popular credulity in the supernatural, such as the Bilston Boy vomiting pins.

Some elements in the increasingly rational Established Church, attributed this continuing belief to the growth of Methodism, with its attendant emphasis on the supernatural, stressed in its journals, such as the *Arminian Magazine*. Certainly, John Wesley openly lamented the fact that: "The English in general, and indeed most of the men of learning in Europe, have given up all account of witches and apparitions, as mere old wives' fables. I am sorry for it, and I willingly take this opportunity of entering my solemn protest against this violent compliment which so many that believe in the Bible pay to those who do not believe it ... the giving up of witchcraft is in effect giving up the Bible."[236] As a result of his movement, M.J.Naylor, the lecturer at the Parish Church in Wakefield in 1795, felt that the general trend towards disbelief had been reversed. A belief which had been gradually yielding to the: "... powerful progress of science, ... [had been] nourished and revived, in no inconsiderable degree, by the many extraordinary revelations, which the late venerable Mr.Wesley inserted in his Arminian Magazine."[237] By the mid-eighteenth century, the established Church was taking a robust approach to such beliefs, with straightforward denial being common. Colley was apparently cajoled by his attendant chaplain (and possibly other clerics) to sign a declaration, prior to his execution, in which he asked all to take heed from his

---

236. Wesley, John, *Journal*, May 25, 1768.
237. *See* on this Davies, Owen, *Methodism, the Clergy, and the Popular Belief in Witchcraft and Magic*, at pp. 252.257.

suffering and not be: "... deluded into so absurd and wicked a conceit, as to believe that there are any such things upon the earth as witches."[238]

Apparently conventional crimes, committed after abolition, also sometimes had a belief in magic at their root. For example, in 1848, in a Bedfordshire village, three women were brought before the local petty sessions for torturing a cat. They had had the "barbarous cruelty" to open up the body of the living animal in the belief that by sticking pins into its heart, and then burying it, they could bring back their former lovers. A belief in witches survived in many remote villages through much of the 1800s. At Cromer, in Norfolk, in 1847, a gang of boys were brought before the local magistrates for throwing stones at an old lady. They were motivated by a desire to "draw her blood," believing that she was a witch, and that it would break her power.[239] Similarly, in 1875, a magistrate at Colne in Lancashire determined a case in which an elderly woman was accused of assaulting another elderly woman, called Mary "R", by stabbing her in the face with a corking pin, because she feared that Mary was bewitching her family. As she did so, the defendant was alleged to have exclaimed: "Now I've drawn thy blood I can sleep o'nights."(The magistrate, though surprised at the survival of such a custom in the "enlightened 19th century" was convinced of the defendant's sincerity, and merely fined her a shilling.)[240] Even at the end of the Victorian period, vicars in remote

---

238. *The Gentleman's Magazine* Vol. 21 (1751) at p.378.
239. Emsley, C., *Crime and Society in England: 1750-1900,* at pp. 82 and 83.
240. Catlow, C., *The Pendle witches,* at p.24. As Shakespeare observes: "Blood will I draw on thee, thou art a witch." *King Henry VI,* at Act 1, Scene v.

parts of the country might sometimes be summoned to remove spells supposedly effected by local witches. The Reverend Francis Kilvert observed that in rural areas, people sometimes continued to visit, and pay fees, to local "cunning men," when they were the victims of theft, so that they could locate stolen goods, or carry out magical tests to identify the thief.

What this continued popular belief in witchcraft (long after it ceased to be a crime) clearly indicates, is that in England, at least, persecution was not a phenomenon that was primarily imposed from above. Nevertheless, making witchcraft a secular crime probably did have considerable ramifications on the gravity with which it was viewed at the general populace. Criminalisation did not merely give a legal avenue of expression to an already strongly held popular belief, channelling a force that would otherwise find an informal outlet in extra-legal activities (such as witch lynchings). It may also have actively encouraged such a belief by giving it an official sanction. Thus, it has been noted that the unofficial torturing of witches in Scotland, and their public lynching, appear to have been relatively rare (except during the period in which such trials were being "run down" by the State). North of the Border, there is only one recorded instance of such popular action producing death, that of Janet Cornfoot, who, when she returned home to Pittenweem in Fife in 1704, after being acquitted by the High Court in Edinburgh, was stoned to death by the harbour pier. Despite periodic cases to the contrary, even after abolition in 1736, much the same situation appears to have applied in England. Perhaps significantly, the Widow Coman in Coggeshall was left to die in her bed in 1699. A similar situation appears to have occurred where people were specially reluctant to have recourse to law for other reasons. Ireland had long been steeped in a belief in witchcraft. However, the alienation of most of its Gaelic inhabitants from English law and its attendant court system, meant that despite the introduction of a secular witchcraft statute in 1586 (similar to the English one), almost no cases came for trial, people rarely being willing to make allegations in that forum. Even so (although the evidence is not totally clear), it appears that there were few cases of informal vigilantism against witches. Instead, the countryfolk had recourse to ritual to guard themselves, with houses and barns being protected by horseshoes etc.[241] This phenomenon led Larner to observe that the "labelled" witch, in a community where the control of witchcraft is not backed up by the state, appears to be a less frightening character, one no longer needing to be permanently eliminated, but merely requiring social-marginalisation. This applies as much to the period before prescription as that following it. By making witches guilty of a serious secular crime, the state also made them more potent in popular perception. As Francis Hutchinson incisively observed in 1718, the number of witches: "... increase or decrease, according to the laws, and notions, and principles of the several times." Like many others, he noted that since France had abandoned prosecution for the offence, the French were much less troubled by such accusations, even those made informally.[242]

241. Lapoint, E, *Irish Immunity to Witch-Hunting,* at p.90.
242. Hutchinson, Francis *Historical Essay on Witchcraft,* at p.49.

PART TWO: WITCHCRAFT AND THE LAW

Chapter 6

The Substantive Law

The Felony Acts

Outline

There had been secular statutes against witchcraft before 1542. In the Saxon period, under the laws of Athelstan (925 or 939), it was ordered that men who were accused of offences of mortal witchcraft or sorcery were to be imprisoned for 120 days, and only released when they had paid compensation and given pledges for the future.[243] However, from the period of the Norman Conquest onwards, witchcraft was primarily the preserve of the ecclesiastical courts. The secular courts were not concerned with witchcraft per se until 1542, when, possibly as a result of a fear of plots against Henry VIII, a Statute made witchcraft, sorcery and enchantment subject to the death penalty. This was repealed in 1547, but witchcraft became a felony once more in 1563 (an earlier Bill to prescribe it failed to pass Parliament for procedural reasons in 1559). This was probably in response to the demands of returning Protestant exiles. These were men who had gone abroad, especially to Geneva, during the reign of the Catholic Queen Mary, had absorbed continental theories of witchcraft and who felt that such a law was necessary to protect the realm from the devil

---

243. Pugh, Brian B., *Imprisonment in Medieval England,* at p.2.

and his minions. This act was replaced and slightly strengthened in 1604.[244]

English statutes, and their judicial interpretation, were, by European standards, conservative as to what would justify prosecution for the crime. Unlike many continental jurisdictions, there was, at least at first, a heavy emphasis on the use of witchcraft to effect damage to people or property ("maleficium"), rather than the criminalising of simple devil worship or pacts with Satan. The crime was finally abolished in 1736, making witchcraft a secular and statutory felony for slightly under 200 years.

Act of 1542

The first Act was passed during the reign of Henry VIII. As William Blackstone noted: "Our forefathers were stronger believers, when they enacted by statute 33 Hen.VIII. c.8., all witchcraft and sorcery to be felony without benefit of clergy." This first, short-lived, statute of 1542, was aimed at both conventional fraud, that is the earning of money by people who claimed magical powers pretending by such means to know "for their own lucre in what place treasure of gold and silver should or might be found or had", and (listed secondly), those who: "... also have used and occupied witchcrafts, enchantments and sorceries to the destruction of their neighbours' persons and goods." It made such acts a felony, and thus liable to the death penalty. Not surprisingly, this was unmitigated by the doctrine of benefit

244. Sharpe, J.A., *Early Modern England: A Social History 1550-1760,* at pp. 309 and 310.

of clergy (something that allowed most literate defendants a first conviction for felony without death). In some ways the juxtaposition of the two clauses captures (albeit unintentionally) the intellectual ambiguity of the crime at this time. Was it real or imaginary? There were very few, if any, prosecutions under this Statute, and the State survived without a statute against witchcraft at all during Queen Mary's reign. However, shortly after the accession of Elizabeth I there was mounting concern at the lack of secular powers to combat witches.

Act of 1563

This new Elizabethan concern may have been linked to the return of influential divines from abroad. Edmund Grindal had been an exile during the reign of Queen Mary from 1553 to 1558, in his case in Strasbourg and Frankfurt, and he appears to have absorbed continental notions of demonology. On his return to England, he became, successively, Bishop of London and Archbishop of Canterbury. On 17th April 17, 1561, Grindal wrote to the Queen's Secretary, Sir William Cecil, urging reform of the law and action against a priest who was guilty not only of popery but also, apparently, of "magic and Conjuration." In the letter, Grindal lamented the fact that secular law lacked jurisdiction to deal with such matters (as had been the case since the repeal of the 1542 Act, in 1547). He urged the Privy Council to offer "some extraordinary punishment" as an example in the case, and deplored the fact that: "My Lord Chief Justice sayeth the temporal law will not meddle with them. Our ecclesiastical punishment is too slender for so grievous offences." Bishop John Jewel (1522-1571) also pressed for draconian action against witches (he, too, had been an exile in Germany). His opinions may well have been strengthened by the fact that one of his first tasks, after his return to England as the newly appointed Bishop of Salisbury, was to discipline Leonard Bilson, who had been prebendary of Teynton Regis since 1552. Bilson was accused, in December 1560, of being involved in witchcraft. He was found guilty by Jewel, in the ecclesiastical court, and ordered to be pilloried (later, Bilson was to die in prison in London when accused of a similar offence).[245] Jewel's concern about the subject was also manifest in a sermon he preached before Queen Elizabeth, in 1571; he feared that: "... witches and sorcerers, within these last few yeeres, are marvellously increased within this your Grace's realme. These eies have seen most evident and manifest marks of their wickednesse. Your Grace's subjects pine away even unto the death, their colour fadeth, their flesh rotteth." As a result, he asked the Queen that the new laws against witches should be strictly executed. Jewel and Grindal were by no means lone voices, many others pressed for action.

Despite the fact that it was not a secular criminal offence between 1547 and 1563, cases involving allegations of witchcraft did occasionally come before the criminal courts in these years. They were often dealt with ambiguously, perhaps reflecting doubts about their status. Theoretically, there was no reason why a conventional felony, such as murder, could not be committed by witchcraft (as opposed to, for example, a dagger). Arguably there would not have

245. Bilson, C.B. *The Jewel of Salisbury*, at p.12.

been an obvious reason for not prosecuting such a crime, like any other murder, as, very occasionally, occurred during the medieval period. However, in practice this does not appear to have happened.

Nonetheless, two cases involving witchcraft did come before the Chelmsford Assizes in July 1560. Joan Haddon, a spinster, from Witham in Essex, was indicted, accused of "cozening money" and bewitching people early in the same year. (The mixture of offences possibly revealing long-standing confusion as to whether the principal objection was that the witchcraft facilitated dishonesty, or that it involved diabolical dealing.) The allegation was that she had "fraudulently received divers sums of money" from people that she had either bewitched or threatened with enchantment. Conveniently, she was found not guilty of witchcraft (which was not, in any event, a crime at this time), but guilty of the conventional offence of fraudulently receiving money (she was ordered to be pilloried). Rather more doubtful, was the case of John Samond, who appeared at the same Assizes hearing, accused of bewitching someone to death in the previous year (1559) in the course of being a "common wizard." It appears that the jury initially found him guilty of this heinous crime, at which point, he entered legal argument "pleaded" on the basis of his conviction. At the very next Assizes, that conducted at Chelmsford the following March (1561), the court received a writ directed to the Assizes Judges for Essex stating that the verdict was certified from the Queens Bench court (by virtue of the Act 6 Henry VIII c.6). Samond was subsequently found Not Guilty of the crime for which he had been convicted six months earlier.[246] The court of King's/Queen's Bench (its name obviously depending on the reigning sovereign's gender) was the only one of the three Westminster courts that had a criminal jurisdiction. Since the fourteenth century, its Crown (criminal) side had had an unlimited jurisdiction for criminal matters in England as a court into which indictments could be removed from other courts for the discussion of a point of law. It is most likely that in the Samond case the court had quashed the finding of the jury the previous year as being without legal foundation, there being no statute against witchcraft.[247]

Cases like these would, in part, explain Grindal's eagerness to see witchcraft properly recriminalised by a fresh Act. There had been an attempt to pass such a statute as early as 1559, it being widely thought that the repeal of 1547 had been effected largely through inadvertence (the Act of 1542 being lumped in with other repealed Henrician statutes). The Bill of 1559 appears to have failed for procedural reasons. However, Grindal's efforts came to fruition four years later, with the Act of 1563. This made causing another's death and conjuring spirits (whether or not harm was involved in the latter case) a crime punishable by death. Other, lesser, forms of witchcraft, such as injuring people or their property, using magic to find buried treasure etc., could result in a year's imprisonment and being pilloried for a first offence, with death for a second one. Although the punishment for a first conviction for the lesser offence might appear relatively lenient, the consequences

---

246. Cockburn, J.S (Ed.) *Essex Indictments: Elizabeth 1*, at p.16.
247. Baker, J.H., in *Crime in England 1550-1800*, at p.27.

were still severe. As Gifford noted in his work of 1593, even "where the Jurie having but likelihoods both find a man or a woman guilty but for killing a beast, it casteth them into prison, setteth them up on the pillorie, and not only diffameth them for ever, but also if suspicion follow again and arraignment, it is death."[248]

By the 1580s, the dynastic uncertainties created by an ageing, unmarried and childless Queen, had prompted a further specialised Statute against witchcraft. This Act of 1581 (23 Eliz. Cap. II) provided that anyone who: "... by setting or erecting any figure or by casting of nativities or by calculation or by any prophesying, witchcraft, conjurations, or other unlawful means whatsoever, seek to know ... how long her Majesty shall live", or who would suceed her, would commit felony, for which the penalty would be death without benefit of clergy.[249] It would appear that many of these prohibited acts would not have been covered by the general statute against witchcraft of 1563.

Act of 1604

The third major Act against witchcraft, shows even clearer continental influences, and was passed in the first year of James I's reign, at a time when he was still enthusiastic about persecuting witches. Sir Edmund Anderson (1530-1605), the Lord Chief Justice of the Court of Common Pleas (from 1582 to his death), and the eminent jurist, and

---

248. Gifford, *Dialogue,* 1 t p. L1.
249. Reproduced in Prothero, G.W. (Ed.), *Select Statutes and Other Constitutional Documents illustrative of the reigns of Elizabeth I and James 1,* at pp. 77-79.

then attorney-general, Sir Edward Coke (1552-1634), were influential in drafting the bill that became the more far-reaching and draconian Witchcraft statute of 1604.[250] Like that of 1563, it divided the crime. As Mathew Hale was to observe, the Statute of 1604 (1 Jac. c.12., the only Law "now in force against it", replacing previous statutes and any common law decisions) separated it into "two degrees." First degree Witchcraft included the conjuration of an evil spirit, charm or sorcery. Second degree witchcraft, passed with a view to ensuring that any use of witchcraft should be "utterly avoided", made offering to find buried treasure or stolen goods, and providing potions or charms that might "provoke any person to unlawful Love" an offence.[251]

For this lesser form of witchcraft, a first offence would result in a year's imprisonment and being placed in the public pillory every three months, at a marketplace or its equivalent, where the offender would "openly confess his or her error and offence." Repeat offenders would be treated as felons and suffer death. Thus, Margaret Pearson, though convicted as one of the Lancashire witches in 1612, received the lesser sentence, prescribed under the 1604 Act, for those who had been found guilty of the minor offence: "You shall stand upon the Pillarie in open Market, at Clitheroe,

---

250. Edward Coke (1552-1634) was one of the most important English common law jurists and Judges of the era. In a glittering career, he became Attorney General in 1593 (gaining a reputation as a harsh prosecutor), and, successively, Chief Justice of Common Pleas in 1606 and of the King's Bench in 1613, until conflict with James I led to his dismissal in 1616. His writings included Reports on common law, and the famous *Institutes*.

251. Hale, Mathew, *Pleas of The Crown: Or a Methodical Summary of the principal Matters relating to that Subject*, at p.6.

Paddiham, Whalley, and Lancaster, foure Market days, with a paper upon your head, in great Letters, declaring your offence, and there you shall confesse your offence, and after to remaine in Prison for one yeare without Baile, and after to be bound with good Sureties, to be of good behaviour."[252] This definition of second degree witchcraft, which does not, in reality, appear to have resulted in many (if any) death sentences, was potentially a powerful weapon against the magic used by cunning women and wise men. However, the main significance of the new Act lay in its penal provision for, and definition of, "first degree" witchcraft.

The preamble to the 1604 Act made it quite explicit that it was aimed at "better restraining" witchcraft, and at its "more severe punishing." It provided death without benefit of clergy for anybody who should: "... use, practice or exercise any invocation or conjuration of any evil and wicked spirit, or shall consult, covenant with, entertain, employ, feed, or reward any evil and wicked spirit to or for any intent or purpose; or take up any dead man, woman, or child out of his, her, or their grave, or any other place where the dead body resteth, or the skin, bone, or any other part of any dead person, to be employed or used in any manner of witchcraft, sorcery, charm, or enchantment; or shall use, practice, or exercise any witchcraft, enchantment, charm, or sorcery, whereby any person shall be killed, destroyed, wasted, consumed, pined, or lamed in his or her body, or any part thereof."

Effectively, its major innovation was to make communing with familiars and spirits a capital offence *per*

252. Potts, 1612, at p.V4.

se, one no longer requiring evidence of maleficium, and thus more in keeping with the continental legal practice. The theoretical strictness of this interpretation was often to be matched in the Americas in equivalent colonial penal codes. For example, the Laws and Liberties of Massachusetts, of 1648, noted that: "If any man or woman be a WITCH, that is, hath or consulteth with a familiar spirit, they shall be put to death."

Nevertheless, despite the theory, wording and potentially much wider scope of the 1604 Act, English judicial practice continued to be extremely conservative in this regard. This was something that Sir Robert Filmer specifically alluded to when he observed that: "Although the Statute runs altogether in the disjunctive Or, and So makes every Single crime capitall, yet the Judges usually by a favourable interpretation take the disjunctive Or for the Copulative And; and therefore ordinarily they condemne none for Witches, unless they be charged with the Murdering of Some person."[253] Most (though certainly not all) witches executed were found guilty of causing death. Of the remainder, few were not accused of inflicting some form of maleficium or injury to humans, such as disease or sickness, though there were cases where a literal application of the law appears to have produced a death sentence where the only damage was to animals and property. Thus, Ann Foster, who was executed in August 1674 at Northampton, had caused neither death nor injury to man, though she had allegedly done so (on a large scale) to beast. She was accused of employing her "malice and witchcraft" to set fire

253. Pamphlet, 1653 at p.A3.

to barns and corn, and to have killed, by bewitchment, sheep and animals, belonging to a local farmer who had offended her.[254]

Such judicial pragmatism was probably, in part, a reflection of the very practical common law legal training provided by the Inns of court. Learning their law from working Judges, Barristers, Attorneys and Sergeants in London, English lawyers often lacked an interest in, and preoccupation with, the detailed "systems" (demonological or otherwise) that were naturally incalcated in their civil law, university trained, continental cousins, educated in the Codes of Justinian and other facets of Roman law. Furthermore, by the 1620s, English lawyers were becoming more impervious, generally, to continental legal influences. In the late sixteenth century, practitioners of the common law were still relatively flexible, and open to ideas from the civil law countries of Europe, something that changed in the following century. In part this change was the result of Coke's eulogising of the merits and antiquity of their native system, something that was itself linked to the domestic English political agenda of the era.

Witchcraft was considered a very serious crime, and so was specifically exempted, along with murder and rape, from an Order of the Privy Council, passed in 1617 that provided that criminals who had committed offences which "though heynous in themselves, yet [are] not of the highest nature" might be reprieved from execution if they were also people who from "strength of bodye or other abilityes shall be thought fitt to be imployed in forreine discoveryes or

254. Pamphlet 1674 at p.2.

Services beyond the seas."

Once witchcraft became a secular crime, one which would have to be interpreted according to normal tenets of common law by the courts, serious problems of legal definition arose. What exactly was a witch, and precisely what kinds of magic had been made felony? Though quite full, the wording of the statutes was never to be enough, though this also meant that witchcraft was a flexible crime, one that could be substantially reinterpreted in the court room by various social actors. Nevertheless, some potentially highly technical defences were rejected from the outset. Absurdly, Thomas Cooper, in 1617, took great care to rebut any suggestion that witches, who inflicted hurt via diabolical power, were not "Principall[s]" in the crime. He (accurately) pointed out that they were still parties to the offence and "by the Laws of Accessories" were subject to the same punishment as the principal (a fundamental principle of English law to this day).[255]

Repeal

After falling largely into desuetude for two generations, and after very limited (largely Scottish) parliamentary opposition, the Act of 1604 was repealed in 1736. Thus, at a time when capital offences were proliferating under the "Bloody Code", witchcraft went against the trend, and was decriminalised. Nevertheless, the Act (9 Geo., 2, c.5), introduced in 1735 and effective from June 24, 1736, constituted a discreet triumph for those who argued that the

255. Cooper, Thomas, *The Mystery of Witch-Craft*, at p.313.

main mischief occasioned by claims to witchcraft was the manner in which it facilitated the defrauding of the gullible. The repealing statute also expressly created an offence to deter this "for the more effectual preventing and punishing of any Pretences to such Arts or Powers as are before mentioned, whereby ignorant persons are frequently delude and defrauded." This was to remain in force until 1951. As Blackstone observed: "But the misdemeanour of persons pretending to use witchcraft, tell fortunes, or discover stolen goods by skill in the occult sciences, is still deservedly punished with a years imprisonment, and standing four times in the pillory." As recently as 1944, a Scottish spiritualist-medium, Helen Duncan, practising in Portsmouth, was arrested during a séance and subsequently convicted under the 1735 Act, for "pretending to raise the spirits of the dead." She was sentenced to nine months' imprisonment at Holloway, despite Winston Churchill asking for a report on her case and referring to the law as "obsolete tomfoolery." Nevertheless, subsequent repeal of the provision left a potential void in the law, which was dealt with by the 1951 Fraudulent Mediums Act. Prosecutions under this Act are brought directly by the Director of Public Prosecutions. It carries a potential sentence of a £500 fine, or two years' imprisonment. Between 1980 and 1996, there were seven prosecutions, resulting in six convictions.[256]

---

256. A campaign was launched in 1997 to secure a posthumous pardon for her, arguing that the trial had been held under the initial "assumption that she was a fraud." *Sunday Telegraph,* October 5, 1997, at p.19. Prior to 1944, fortune tellers had normally been prosecuted under the 1824 Vagrancy Act.

Chapter 7

The Ecclesiastical and Common Law Criminal Courts Dealing with Witchcraft

The Ecclesiastical Courts

Until 1542 the church courts had had virtually sole responsibility for punishing witchcraft (unless it was used to effect a secular felony). It was merely one of a wide range of matters, amongst them probate and slander, that the church courts had had jurisdiction over for centuries. The basic church court for hearings was that of the Archdeacon (decisions could be appealed to higher ecclesiastical courts). Thus, when Chaucer's Friar (c.1400) lists such a church official's assorted legal responsibilities, amongst them, though clearly of no special significance, is witchcraft:

> An erchedeken, a man of high degree,
> That boldly dide execucioun,
> In punisshige of fornicacioun,
> Of wicchecraft, and eek of bauderye,
> Of diffamacioun, and avoutrye,
> Of chicrche-reves, and of terstaments,
> Of contractes, and of lakke of sacraments,
> And eek of many another maner of cryme
> Which nedeth nat rehercen at this tyme.[257]

The ecclesiastical courts continued to play a major role in

257. Chaucer, Geoffrey, *The Canterbury Tales,* at p.325. They were apparently written in the late 1380s and 1390s.

combating those who had recourse to witchcraft even after it became a felony. Although there were over 1,200 prosecutions or presentments for witchcraft in Essex alone, in the period between 1560 and 1700, a high proportion of these (certainly the majority) were in the ecclesiastical courts. A typical example might be the case in 1599, of one Thomas Ward, from Purleigh (in Essex), who was presented for seeking help from a sorcerer: "He confessed that he having lost certain cattle & suspecting that they were bewitched, he went to one Tayler in Thaxted, a wizard to know whether they were bewitched or not, and to have his help."[258] Witchcraft continued to feature in the Visitation Articles of many archbishops, bishops and archdeacons in the 100 years after it became a secular crime. Thus, Bishop Sandys in the London diocese, asked, in 1571, for the presentment of any people: "... that useth sorcery, witchcraft, enchantments, incantations, charms, unlawful prayers or invocations in Latin". In many archdeaconries, church-wardens, the lay officials with responsibility for presenting offenders to the Church courts, were expressly enjoined, in their Articles of Visitation, to consider whether any in their parishes used "sorcery or witchcraft, or be vehemently suspected for the same, or that use soothsaying, charmes ... [or] resort to such for helpe and counselle."[259] However, although they saw many more cases involving magic than the secular courts (albeit of a lesser type) even the church

---

258. Briggs, J. et al., *Crime and Punishment in England,* at p.37.

259. *Articles to be Enquired of by the Churchwardens and Sworne-men within the Archdeaconrie of Execester in the visitation of the Right Worshifull Thomas Barret, Archdeacon of the said Archdeaconrie of Execester.* Printed by William Stansby London (1612) at p.A3.

courts do not appear to have been greatly concerned about witchcraft, in most of the country. The episcopal visitation to Wiltshire in 1587 produced 686 Presentments, but only seven of them related to witchcraft or sorcery (about the same number as for working on the Sabbath).[260]

After secular criminalisation, there appears to have been a fairly swift recognition by the church courts, that they should deal only with those offences not covered by the witchcraft statutes. These were usually minor manifestations of witchcraft, such as recourse to a wise woman or cunning man, though they had formerly dealt with some cases of maleficium. Given the modest penalties normally available to these courts, this was logical. Punishment was imposed by the collection of fees from those accused, fines, penances and excommunication. If a person admitted an offence, or could not produce the requisite number of neighbours to support their denial, a public penance would normally be ordered, often combined with the payment of a substantial court fee. The sentence would usually be carried out in the parish church on a Sunday, with the accused person (whether man or woman), wearing a white sheet and carrying a white wand. The guilty person would ask forgiveness of God and his or her neighbours, something that would, at least in theory, effect their re-integration into society.[261] Typically, in the 1560s, Alice Swan, who, at the behest of some other women, had used the "Turninge of the Rulle and Sheeres" to find lost property (even worse it was done after church), was required to confess in the church of

---

260. Ingram, M. *Church Courts, Sex and Marriage in England 1570-1640* at p.68.
261. Macfarlane, Alan, *Witchcraft in Tudor and Stuart Essex,* at p.72.

St Nicholas in Newcastle. Interestingly, even the public admission that she was forced to recite conceded that although instigated by the devil, such things "seeme to some to be but a trifling matter." Her confession also acknowledges that such behaviour was contrary both to the law of God and to the (secular) law of Queen Elizabeth.[262]

It is, perhaps, fortunate that they did not determine more serious matters. Much of the hearing in a church court was conducted in Latin, and their procedures were contrary to those accepted at English common law. In particular, there was the use of inquisition, with defendants often having to answer questions on oath without knowing properly what the allegations against them were, or a prima facie case being established. (This also occurred in the prerogative courts, such as that of Star Chamber.) In addition, church courts had a very formal (indeed "mechanical") system of proof. Charges would be defended by producing a number of "compurgators", people of a similar gender and social background to the accused, to swear that they found the charges against him/her implausible. If the requisite number of witnesses were adduced, and, after examination, they were found to be satisfactory, the charge would be dismissed.[263] Despite unsuccessful parliamentary attempts to reform them in the 1580s, the church courts continued to operate until the civil war and Interregnum. They were restored after 1660, but did not fully recover from their enforced absence, and

262. Raine, J. (Ed.) , *Depositions and Other Ecclesiastical Proceedings from the Courts of Durham*, at p.117.

263. Ingram, M., *Church Courts, Sex and Marriage in England 1570-1640*, at pp.51-52.

gradually died out over the following 50 years.[264]

The two systems, secular common law and ecclesiastical civil law, were not hermetically sealed. There was considerable liaison between their respective personnel, especially in cases, such as witchcraft, where jurisdictions might overlap, or where the ecclesiastical courts felt that their available penalties might be too limited for the gravity of any given offence, compared to those open to the secular courts. Thus, in Essex, in the early 1600s, officials from the Archdeaconry court would correspond regularly with their local JPs, especially those with legal experience or training, such as Sir Nicholas Coote. Also perhaps significantly, Richard Bernard, dedicated his work *A Guide to Grand Jury Men ... In Cases of Witchcraft* (1627) to both common and civil lawyers.[265]

Quarter Sessions

The lower criminal courts administering the common law, were those of Quarter Sessions. They were held, as the name suggests, at least four times a year (usually at Epiphany, Easter, Michaelmas and the Feast of St Thomas), though more frequently if necessary. Some counties, regularly exceeded this number (Sussex normally had seven sittings). In these courts, groups of JPs (those of the Quorum, who could sit on the bench at Quarter Sessions), some of whom would normally be either legally qualified, or at least

264. Dean, M., *Law-Making and Society in Late Elizabethan England,* at pp.116-120.

265. See generally, Levack, Brian, *The Civil Lawyers in England 1603-1641: a political study.*

extremely experienced, conducted the jury trials of misdemeanours and lesser felonies. Some JPs were fully admitted barristers, and many others had at least been students at the Inns of court. As a result, in nearly all Quarter Sessions, there were one or two (if not more) barrister JPs. These might be the Chairmen of the Bench, and in any event could provide expertise. For example, between January 1614 and July 1620, there were never less than three barrister JPs attending the Quarter Sessions in Somerset, and sometimes as many as six. It appears reasonable to infer from available records that there was a deliberate, if only informal, policy to ensure that there was always one man present who had been called to the bar, though there were occasional exceptions to this pattern.[266] The presence of such men was important, as originally (and still at least theoretically) they had had a more extensive jurisdiction, being able to try any case other than treason. However, this had been steadily reduced in the sixteenth century. As a result, the bulk of their judicial work in the early 1600s (they also had a major administrative function in county society) would be a mixture of prosecutions arising out of interpersonal disputes, such as petty theft, assault, poaching and trespass; regulative prosecutions, such as drunkenness, vagrancy, swearing, gaming, non-attendance at church, Sabbath-breaking, harbouring rogues etc.; and prosecutions relating to the enforcement of obligations on those who had abused or neglected an appointed office (such as constables).

---

266. Gleason, J.H., *The Justices of The Peace in England: 1558 to 1640*, at pp.107 and 112.

Although the Commission of 1590 continued to allow JPs sitting at Quarter Sessions to determine felonies, it qualified this with the provision that difficult cases should be reserved for the Royal Judges sitting at the Assizes. This was normally taken as meaning that potential death penalty cases (ie, the more serious felonies, including witchcraft) should be left for these courts to determine (according to Lambard(e) there was a degree of concern at the legal competence and understanding of many JPs, something that regularly led the Privy Council to reiterate to them the importance of reserving serious criminal cases for the Assizes). Indeed, this had been the normal practice well before 1590, which was partly why the JPs were ordered to examine suspects under the 1555 Act (1 and 2 Philip and Mary c. 13). In practice, the 1590 directive had the effect of giving the Assizes a near monopoly on serious crime (where their writ ran). As a result, in the latter part of the Seventeenth century, Mathew Hale could observe of Quarter Sessions: "... in point of discretion they do forbear to determine great felonies". Nevertheless, the continuing theoretical extent of their jurisdiction did sometimes mean that Quarter Sessions might impinge on witchcraft cases, other than in a purely procedural manner (the latter included, for example, determining appeals for bail from those kept in custody for the crime pending an Assizes hearing). This could have mixed results, encouraging either harshness or moderation, depending on the precise circumstances. JPs lacked the legal expertise of the Royal Judges, could be more closely wrapped up in local affairs, and perhaps influenced by local prejudices (including those against witches). However, in normal times they were also very much less likely to pass a death sentence, and would be more aware of allegations that were made maliciously. Thus, when, under the strains of the civil war in the mid-1640s, the system of itinerant Royal Judges broke down to a significant extent (though certainly not totally), and the JPs at Quarter Sessions were given a relatively free hand, it produced, at least in part, the results seen in Hopkins's extensive East Anglian campaign of witch persecution. Conversely, the theoretical ability to reserve cases of witchcraft to themselves, by treating them as lesser felonies, explains why these matters could be regularly withheld from the Assizes in Sussex, with the opposite effect, and partly explains why there were few convictions and only one execution for the crime in that county (outside the special jurisdictions).

Quarter Sessions hearings for witchcraft were much rarer in other counties, during normal times, though not unheard of. In some counties, those witchcraft cases which were felt to be of doubtful validity, perhaps because of the type of people accused (or making the accusation), were occasionally reserved for trial in front of the local Quarter Sessions. This would allow the case to be disposed of more expeditiously (normally by an acquittal). In 1674, in Yorkshire, a married couple and another woman, were accused of witchcraft by a teenage girl, one Mary Moor. Moor was considered a notoriously unreliable person by many of the local people, who produced a petition in support of the accused from their own parish of Denbigh, declaring the allegation against the three to be "gross and malicious". The local justices were obviously influenced by this and appear to have planned to try it locally, rather than sending it up to the Assizes. Tragically, however, the stigma of the allegation seems to have been too much for the husband, Joseph Hinchcliffe, who hanged himself, his wife apparently dying at almost the same time of natural causes (perhaps occasioned by shock).[267] Normally, however, witchcraft carrying a potential death sentence would be heard with other serious felonies at the twice yearly Assizes.

The Assizes

Witchcraft was overwhelmingly the province of the Assizes courts. These were bi-annual, temporary courts, held with great pomp, in Lent and the Long Vacation (July and August), this being termed the Summer Assizes. From the reign of Henry II England had been divided into six circuits, each of these being made up of groups of adjoining counties. The only exceptions to this system were London and Middlesex (which had the special provision of the Old Bailey), the Palatinates (Chester, Durham and Lancaster), and a few other special jurisdictions such as the Cinque Ports and a number of designated boroughs, which had the special power to try major felonies without recourse to the Royal Judges.

Although the Assizes also had a civil jurisdiction (that of *nisi prius*), their work, by the sixteenth century, was predominantly criminal. Nevertheless, the pairs of Judges sent on each circuit would still normally be allocated between the Crown (criminal) side, and the civil cases. These would usually be heard in two courts, sitting simultaneously. Thus, it was noted that the six witches arraigned at Maidstone in 1652, had their trial heard before

---

267. Sharpe, J., *Early Modern England: A Social History 1550-1760*, at p.167.

Peter Warburton, one of the Justices of Common Pleas (another civil war appointment), who "sate Judge over criminal offendors".[268] Of course, on difficult questions, Judges might consult their colleagues. Sergeant Kelyng, who gave a "sceptical" opinion at Bury St Edmunds, in 1662, was probably Hale's co-adjutor, taking the civil cases. Occasionally, if the amount of judicial work was light, both Judges might be present on the Bench at a trial, though one would normally be in a presiding role. Thus, in the trial of two alleged witches at Abington, in March 1605, both Judges then on circuit (Sir David Williams and Sir Christopher Yelverton, from the court of King's Bench) would appear, from the testimony of one of the witnesses, to have been present in court. [269]

After 1558, the home circuit constituted the counties of Essex, Hertfordshire, Kent, Sussex and Surrey. Interestingly, although the closest circuit to London, it appears to have been the least popular amongst the judiciary (partly because of significantly lower allowance scales). This perhaps explains why it was only served by two Chief Justices in the period from 1590 to 1640. The rather misleadingly named Norfolk circuit included Bedfordshire, Buckinghamshire, Cambridgeshire, Huntingdonshire, Suffolk and, of course, Norfolk. The other circuits were the Midland (Rutland, Leicestershire etc.), the Oxford (Monmouthshire, Oxfordshire etc.), the Northern (Cumberland, Northumberland etc.) and the Western (Devon, Cornwall etc.). Cases in Wales were determined by the Great Sessions after 1543. Within

---

268. Pamphlet 1652 (2) at p.4.

269. Levack, Brian, *Possession, Witchcraft, and the Law, in Jacobean England* at p.1625.

each county there would be at least one, and usually two or more, Assize towns, where the Judges would sit to determine local cases. These were normally the major towns of each county within the circuit, or those most accessible to travel. Some of these were impermanent venues, the courts only sitting there occasionally, while others were long-standing traditional locations. Thus, in Essex they were held, at various times, in Braintree, Brentwood, Colchester, Chelmsford (a regular venue) and Witham; in Kent, at Dartford, Maidstone (also a regular venue) or Rochester.

Assizes Judges were mostly Judges of the courts in Westminster, where they sat for most of the year. As Mathew Hale noted, each pair was normally: "Two of those Twelve ordinary Justices who are appointed for the Common Dispensation of Justice in the Three great courts". These were the courts of Common Pleas, King's Bench, and the court of Exchequer. As a result, they would include amongst their number the holders of the three highest judicial offices, in order of seniority, the Chief Justice of the King's Bench, that of Common Pleas, in turn followed by the Lord Chief Baron of the Exchequer. The work and travelling was arduous (especially on the Northern and Western circuits), and Judges at Westminster who were infirm, or otherwise engaged, could not attempt it. However, six pairs of Judges were needed to accommodate the demands of the circuits. As a result, their numbers would be supplemented, on an *ad hoc* basis, by senior members of the order of Serjeants at Law, these being experienced lawyers and advocates, from England's premier legal profession, but men who had yet to be raised to the Royal courts at

Westminster.[270] Mathew Hale believed that there were several advantages to this system of itinerant Royal Judges. It prevented "Factions and Parties" developing in the conduct of legal business. This was something which he believed would inevitably appear: "... in every Cause of Moment, were the Trial only before Men residing in the Counties, as Justices of the Peace, or the like, or before Men of little or no Place, Countenance or Preheminence above others". Indeed, it was to prevent exactly this sort of partiality that Assizes Judges were normally forbidden (by the statute of 33 Henry VIII c.24.), from holding their Sessions in counties where they had been born or lived (Sir Thomas Gente, an Elizabethan Judge of the Exchequer, had the rare privilege of being granted permission to sit as an Assize Judge in his own county). Additionally, Hale felt, it kept the administration of English law relatively uniform throughout the country. Judges received a common legal education, and, during legal term-time could "converse and consult" with one another, and "acquaint one another with their Judgments", when they sat in the courts at Westminster Hall.[271]

The Assizes Judges would ride their circuits together in pairs, during vacations when the Royal courts at Westminster were not sitting, swiftly moving from one Assizes town to another, and dispensing criminal justice as they went. They were empowered to do this by two commissions, that of oyer and terminer and that of gaol delivery (the itinerant Royal Judges would "deliver" the local jail by presiding over the jury trials of those in

---

270. Cockburn, J.S., *A History of English Assizes, 1558-1714,* at pp.120-127.
271. Hale, Matthew, *The History of the Common Law of England ... Written by a Learned Hand,* at p.255.

custody). These "circuits" were not without risks for both the lawyers (who often accompanied the judiciary) and the Judges making them. Bandits and highwaymen might be encountered on the roads, especially on the Northern and Western circuits. Other less violent thieves abounded. Thus, Isaac Atkinson was hanged at Tyburn in 1640 after stealing from dozens of lawyers moving around the Norfolk circuit, including, it appears, the Attorney-General to Charles I, William Noy.

The Assizes were held with great solemnity and ceremony, something that reinforced both the majesty of the law, and the authority of central government. As the Judges reached the borders of the county where they were to preside over the gaol delivery, they would be met and escorted to its Assizes town, which they would enter with an escort comprising the sheriff of the county, the under-sheriff, Bailiffs, Livery-men and major local gentry. Before beginning their lists, the Judges would attend the local parish church or Cathedral, and listen to a special Assize sermon, delivered by an important local clergyman. This might emphasise the divine nature of punishment and the judgment that all men would eventually be subject to, or the need for due obedience to the law.[272] Typically, on the 5th of August 1646, the clergyman and diarist Ralph Josselin, of Earls Colne in Essex, was in Chelmsford, his local Assize town for the Summer Sessions. He noted that he preached before Judge Bacon, and Sargeant Turner: "... on Rom: 12:3.4: wherein God was good to me, for voyce, and memory, and spirit, I dined with the Judges who used me

---

272. Beattie, J.M., *Crime and the Courts in England 1660-1800*, at p.316.

with respect".[273] The law was riddled with quasi-religious imagery and religious rituals, something that must have seemed especially pertinent in witch cases.

A normal Assize period might be about 17 days in length, with the Judges progressing round the circuit, from town to town, spending two or three days in each location. They would leave as soon as their business there was concluded. Thus, it was noted that at first light the very day after the trial of the two witches from Yarmouth, held at Bury St Edmunds, in 1662, Mathew Hale left for Cambridge (also on the Norfolk circuit). A typical home circuit might mean visiting five Assizes centres in a peregrination of 170 miles over the two-and-a-half weeks. Distances on the other circuits were similar. Given the exigencies of time, and the number of trials, hearings necessarily had to be brief.

London and Middlesex

Criminal courts in the Metropolis differed markedly from those outside London and Middlesex. In the City of London, the Old Bailey sat eight times a year (and roughly approximated to an Assize court in status). It dealt with felony trials (and occasionally serious misdemeanours) for the City and the county of Middlesex (it was a joint court). Elizabeth Sawyer, the Witch of Edmonton was tried there in 1621. In Westminster, the court of King's Bench sometimes also sat to hear criminal cases from Middlesex, or cases with political overtones, such as treason, from the nation generally. As a court with the power to transfer criminal

273. Macfarlane, A., (Ed.), *The Diary of Ralph Josselin 1616-1683*, at p.66.

cases to its jurisdiction from inferior courts, it could hear felonies from the provinces, but this was rarely exercised unless there were special reasons.

Independent Courts

The potential significance of the judicial service provided by the Royal Judges on circuit can be seen most clearly by examining those cases where it was absent, and which were tried in a number of special jurisdictions. Amongst these were the Palatinates of Durham and Lancaster, and the Cinque Ports and their subsidiaries (in Kent and Sussex). These had their own courts which were able to try all felonies, including witchcraft. Additionally, some borough courts throughout the country, such as those at Harwich and Aldeburgh had power of gaol delivery, and thus jurisdiction to determine such serious criminal cases. The practical effect of such exclusions from the Assizes system, was to reduce the level of personal independence and legal expertise amongst those presiding over the conduct of felony trials, something that was potentially very important in cases involving witchcraft. The local dignitaries and JPs who normally conducted these courts (though sometimes, there would also be a legally qualified Recorder on the Bench), would not be immune from local pressure, or detached and experienced in their conduct of such cases, in the way that an Assizes Judge normally would be (and even they could be susceptible to pressure). Sometimes, they would share the prejudices of the accusers, and would also have heard much of the local gossip about the accused. Indeed, it was the "localisation" of felony trials, in the early years of the civil war, that probably explains, at least in part, the upsurge of executions for witchcraft in the mid-1640s, a period when the normal Assizes system partially broke down. The Essex Assizes of 1645, at which so many witches from the Hopkins campaign were convicted, was presided over by the Earl of Warwick, in his capacity as a representative of military authority, and JPs, in the absence of any of the Westminster judiciary.[274] This analysis would also appear to fit the wider European pattern for the more intense type of continental persecution. These were often found in small states (such as the Prince Bishoprics in Germany), that retained independent legal jurisdictions, without any element of external involvement and supervision in their trial process. Ironically, Spain's generally modest level of witch persecution has been partly attributed to the central supervisory role over such trials of the otherwise notorious Spanish Inquisition in Madrid.

In England, a significant number of convictions and subsequent executions for witchcraft appear to have been secured in front of these independent local courts. Thus, at Harwich in 1603 the borough sessions, which had special jurisdiction to determine such matters, conducted the trials and executions of several women as witches. Similarly, the absence of the experience of an Assizes Judge from London may have been vitally important in a case from 1586, one which resulted in what many, even then, felt to have been a clear miscarriage of justice. The accused woman, Joan Cason, was tried at a "great session", held in Faversham in Kent, which town was a "limb or member of Dover", and

---

274. *See* on this, Levack, B.P. *State Building and Witch Hunting* in Barry, J., et all. (Eds.), *Witchcraft in Early Modern Europe,* at p.109. See also Pamphlet 1645(5) at pp.1-2.

thus, like all Cinque Ports, outside the normal Assizes system. She was accused of bewitching one Jane Cook, a three year old girl, who was sick for 13 days, "languished" and then died. Because of the court's special status, the trial was presided over by the local Mayor (rather than a professional Judge), who, of course, had no formal legal training. He was advised, as was common in such cases, by a gentleman of the town who was also a lawyer (probably a barrister): "... sitting upon the bench to assist, or rather to direct him in the course of the law and justice". The case against Cason was thin even for a witchcraft allegation. She was only accused of killing the child because a passing traveller had suggested the test that implicated her (burning a tile), to the infant's mother. At trial, she vigorously denied her guilt. All eight people, seven of them women, most of them her "near neighbours", who gave evidence against her, were noted as being from the town's lower social strata (and thus not inherently reliable). In her defence, Cason brought up the history of personal animosity and hostility between herself and the prosecution witnesses, adducing "malicious dealings" and "certain controversies" between them in the past. The jury were obviously persuaded on this point and predisposed to acquit. However, independently of this, Cason, perhaps foolishly, admitted to having had a squirrel like rodent about her house, which she sometimes imagined to be reminding her (or her conscience) to do her duty towards her master. As a result, although the jury acquitted her of killing the child "being loath to condemn her of witchcraft, which they knew to be felony", they felt able to convict her of what they believed to be the lesser offence of invoking wicked spirits (the rodent), thinking thereby to have "procured her punishment by pillory or imprisonment" rather than execution. In opting for this, they may well have been returning a verdict that reflected the widespread knowledge in the town that Cason had led a notoriously immoral life, and a feeling that for this alone she was deserving of some punishment, the squirrel providing a ready pretext. (While her husband was still alive, Cason had been the mistress of a man for whom she worked, and led a "lewd life", something she quite freely admitted at trial.) After she had been convicted of this, apparently lesser, offence (invoking spirits), the Mayor moved to discharge her, with an admonition that she attend church more often and listen carefully to the sermons preached there. However, at this point, the attendant lawyer intervened to draw the Mayor's attention to the letter of the substantive law (the Act of 1563), and informed him that the offence for which she had been convicted should have led to a death sentence: "... because invocation of wicked spirits was made felony by the statute whereupon she was arraigned". At this, in a grotesque volte face, the Mayor promptly felt obliged to change his sentence to one of execution. His wording appears to have been the standard one for passing such sentences, and remained so for centuries: "Goodwife Cason you must be conveyed from hence to the Whitehouse [a local prison] from whence you came, and from thence to the place of execution, where you must be hanged until you be dead, and so God have mercy on you". She was detained for three days before being hanged, when she made a penitent end, denying her guilt of witchcraft, but admitting her previous dissolute and immoral life. Faversham was later to see the conviction and execution of several women for witchcraft during the civil war and Interregnum.[275]

Similarly, Rye, which witnessed several witch trials at the start of the seventeenth century (and provided a high proportion of the generally very modest Sussex total), was another of the ancient Cinque Ports with special powers to try felonies in its own court. Like that at Faversham, this court was presided over by the Mayor and Aldermen. It was over a Rye witchcraft case that, in 1607, Henry Howard, the Earl of Northampton, and also the Lord Warden of the Cinque Ports, tried to challenge the ancient privileges of these historic towns, and to further the power of the central government. He attempted to prevent the Mayor and Jurats from trying a local woman, Anne Taylor, for witchcraft. Howard argued that they did not have the full powers of proper county magistrates to try such a matter, even in theory (as previously noted, in Sussex, unusually, many witch cases appear to have been heard at Quarter Sessions), as they derived their authority only from the town's historic charter. Nevertheless, the Judges of the court of King's Bench at Westminster upheld the town's right to carry out the trial, which was eventually heard in 1609 (it resulted in an acquittal).[276]

Across the Atlantic, a lack of professional judicial experience also appears to have contributed significantly to the events at Salem. Although each American colony had its own system and court structure, the influence of English

275. Pamphlet reproduced in Rosen, Barbara (Ed.), *Witchcraft in England 1558-1618*, at pp.163-167.

276. Gregory, Annabel, *Witchcraft, Politics And "Good Neighbourhood" in Early Seventeenth-Century Rye*, at p.37.

legal precedent was clearly evident.[277] However, the thinness of the population, and the enormous size of the country, made following the English Assizes system closely almost impossible, especially in appointing the judiciary. As a contemporary pamphlet noted, American Judges, often being merchants and planters by occupation, lacked the extensive legal education of their English counterparts.[278] At Salem, when, faced with the events of 1692, the newly arrived Royal governor, Sir William Phips, set up a special ad hoc seven-member court to try the cases. The jurors were drawn from the local church membership lists, and the Judges were local magistrates, most without any formal legal training.

As most of the participants themselves belatedly appreciated, something went seriously wrong in 1692. The reasons for this are still not totally clear, and the tangled web of interpersonal malice and local grievances that underpinned the accusations has yet to be fully established. However, it is clear that the system of protective barriers that should have been raised by a variety of officials in the colony broke down for a period of several months. Problems with the colonial supervision in the aftermath of the Glorious Revolution may well have contributed to the result, just as the breakdown in the proper functioning of the normal Assizes system may have been behind the extent of Mathew Hopkins campaign in East Anglia during the English civil war.

---

277. Report on Court Procedures in the Colonies (1700), from the reports of Six colonies as a result of a request from the Lord Justices and Privy Council in England. Reproduced in *American Journal of Legal History*, Vol.9 (1965).
278. Anon, *The Present State of Justice in the American Plantations.*

Chapter 8

From Suspicion to Formal Allegation

"Reverance Once
Had wont to wait on age; now an old woman,
Ill-favour'd grown with years, if she be poor,
Must be call'd bawd or witch."
The Witch of Edmonton, Act 4, Scene I

Candidates For "Witch-Hood"

It is possible to take two approaches towards alleged cases of witchcraft. One is to examine the phenomenon from the perspective of the accuser, and to attribute allegations of witchcraft to preoccupations and concerns on their part. The other is to examine it from the perspective of the accused, and to stress the qualities and characteristics of these individuals. Both are necessary to produce an accurate portrait of the subject.

Most prosecuted witches were unfortunate individuals, mainly older women, who had the misfortune to be unpopular amongst, and to be perceived as malign by, their immediate neighbours. Although to an extent, they were often the unlucky tip of a much larger group, these women were not selected at random. One of the reasons that the events at Salem in Massachusetts in 1692 were remembered as being so unusual, was that, along with a small number of prime contenders for the appellation of "witch", appreciable numbers of "respectable" people, not drawn from the ranks of the traditional English type of "witch fodder", were swept into the net. Indeed, when, after the magnitude of the mistake at Salem came to be understood, and John Hale tried to ask himself why "there was a going too far in this affair" (despite the "conscientious endeavour [by the judges] to do the right thing" and their willingness to consult authorities on the subject such as Hale, Bernard, Baxter etc.), it was this aspect that he focused on. It was clear to him, in retrospect, that the number and status of those being accused should have made it apparent that something was amiss. There were simply too many cases, in too small an area, involving people of quite the wrong social profile. It was inconceivable that the devil could have inveigled so many people, especially as "the quality of several of the accused was such as did bespeak better things."[279] However, Salem was highly untypical. In England, most of those selected for the label of witch, had been obvious candidates for the title for years.

To complicate matters, some of those accused undoubtedly did believe themselves, for whatever reason, to be possessed of magical power, if not always in the form attributed to them. Others held themselves out to be possessed of such powers even if not crediting them personally. In their own terms they were witches, and thus were correctly (if not "justly") punished. This has sometimes been overlooked by modern historians who seek to focus on the minds of those making the allegations, and determining the defendant's guilt, rather than that of the accused person. Apparently unforced, and probably sincere, admissions of

---

279. Jameson, Franklin, *Narratives of the Witchcraft cases 1648-1706.* Hale, John, *A Modest Inquiry into the Nature of Witchcraft,* at p.411.

guilt to judges at trial, and to examining justices and other villagers before trial, were made. A number of explanations can be advanced as to why someone might voluntarily wish to take on the mantle of a witch. For some, it might have provided a degree of power, self-respect, status, and, fundamentally, the possibility to earn a living. This was something that would be crucially important to some of the economically marginalised people, such as the poor, elderly and widowed women, who were so often identified as witches. These apparently pitiful people could engender very real fear, something which they might use to their advantage. Gifford's character "Samuel", captured this when noting that there was an old woman in his town, whom he suspected of being a witch, and who despite his efforts to placate her he still felt "frownes at me now and then." This was something that he immediately called to mind when he discovered that his pig had sickened and his hens died.[280]

Accusations of witchcraft did not usually come "out of the blue." There would normally have been a history of several years (occasionally even decades) of mounting rumour and suspicion, possibly allied with personal animosity, towards the accused person. Local memory of such gossip could be exceptionally long lived. John Lowes, Vicar of Brandeston in Suffolk for many years before his exposure as a witch by Hopkins and Stearne (he was one of 18 witches hanged at Bury St Edmunds in August 1645), had been indicted for witchcraft 30 years earlier (in c. 1615) but the charge had been thrown out by the Grand Jury. In the same year, he had gained further notoriety, by attempting

280. Gifford, *Dialogue,* at p.B1.

to protect a suspected witch, who was subsequently convicted and executed for the crime, even hiding her for a period in his own house and threatening a local constable who tried to interfere. The memory of these incidents evidently lingered on (as did the unpopularity, and ill feeling, occasioned by his legal suits against several parishioners), to be revived in the unusual circumstances of the 1640s.

Similarly, it was felt that the accusations made against Jane Wenham in 1712, were easily believed because the "whole parish" in which she lived, had been of a: "... prepossession, of Jane Wenham's being a witch for many years, [and] could not fail of believing any Thing against her, even in Opposition to their Senses."[281] Even at Salem, the first woman to be executed, Bridget Bishop, had been widely rumoured to be a witch for well over a decade, and had been formally accused and acquitted of the crime 12 years earlier. In the same way, long before Joan Flower was formally accused of bewitching the Earl of Rutland and his family the: "... whole course of her life gave great suspicion that she was a notorious Witch."[282] Nevertheless, statistically, Flower was very unlucky; there must have been numerous cases of suspected witches who went to their graves without being formally accused, albeit that occasionally a suspicious villager might pluck up the courage to scratch them, and thus "draw their blood." As Christina Larner has observed, there was a spectrum of social interactions ranging from occasional pointing finger to the identification of the fully

---

281. *See* pamphlet 1712(2) at p.11. It was allegedly written by a local physician in Hertfordshire.
282. Pamphlet 1619, at p.C2.

stigmatised witch, one who would be subject to formal sanctions.[283] Between these two extremes would have been numerous fine gradations.

Such suspicions did not fasten on individuals by chance. Certain women fitted the contemporary picture of a witch. Joan Flower was suspected because she was considered by her neighbours to be a: "monstrous malicious woman", noted for cursing and swearing, being irreligious, if not a "plaine atheist", with a strange appearance: "... her very countenance was estranged, her eyes were fiery and hollow." Additionally, some of them believed that she dealt with familiars and also terrified them with: "... threatening of revenge, if there were never so little cause of displeasure and unkindnesse."[284] This process of "natural selection" was appreciated by many perceptive individuals, even at the time. In Ford and Dekker's play, *The Witch of Edmonton* (1621), long before Elizabeth Sawyer meets or makes a pact with the devil, she has been identified as a witch, simply, as she observes: "Cause I am poor, deform'd, and ignorant." As this remark indicates, witches usually were poor, generally uncouth and even physically ugly (they were also mainly female, and frequently widowed or single). Reginald Scot was another who subscribed to this analysis, believing that one type of woman, frequently identified as a witch, were those who were: "... old, lame, bleare-eied, fowle and full of wrinkles; poore, sullen, superstitious."[285] This description is repeated so often, almost *ad nauseam*, in the accounts of

283. Larner, Christine, *Crimen Exceptum? The Crime of Witchcraft in Europe*, at p.50.
284. Pamphlet 1619, at p.C2.
285. Scot, Reginald, *The Discovery of Witchcraft*, at p.6.

executed witches, that it must have corresponded, to some degree, to the reality. A selection of cases can be taken as examples. Agnes Brown, a Northamptonshire witch, executed in 1612, was of poor parentage, education and: "... ever noted to be of an ill nature and wicked disposition, spiteful and malicious, and for many years before she died both hated and feared among her neighbours, being long suspected in the town where she dwelt of that crime which afterwards proved true." Her daughter was, not surprisingly, of equally bad repute. They were discovered, after a local gentlewoman, one Mistress Belcher, enraged by an obscene gesture made at her by the daughter, while walking in the street, was foolish enough to strike the girl. Although not hurt, she swore revenge. The two witches allegedly waited three or four days to avoid suspicion, before bewitching Belcher so that she fell ill. Similarly, Helen Jenkinson, who was executed with her, had been long suspected as a witch, and observed to be of an "evil life." With them was executed the wizard, Arthur Bill, also publicly known to be of an "evil life and reputation", and the son of parents that were both witches.[286] In the same way, according to Edward Fairfax's account of the bewitching of his two daughters in Yorkshire in 1621, nearly all the six women tried (and ultimately acquitted) carried local reputations for witchcraft, and for wider forms of deviance generally. Among them, Margaret Waite and her husband, new arrivals in the area some years earlier, had "brought with them an evil report for witchcraft and theft." Indeed, Waite's husband was subsequently executed for theft rather

286. Rosen, Barbara (Ed.), *Witchcraft in England 1558-1616*, at p.351.

than sorcery. Waite also had a slatternly daughter who was of "impudent and lewd behaviour", and kept a house that was a "receptacle for some of the worst sort", amongst them petty thieves.[287] These existing reputations were crucial in determining the making of formal allegations, which might be triggered by misfortune or coincidence.

Any misfortune that occurred in proximity to the accused woman could be attributed to her, something that the sceptics of the time were to stress. One, commenting on a hypothetical case, observed that: "Thomas Adam ... has 3 or 4 fat sheep die of the Megrim, by feeding it too rank pasture; and because this poor old creature was seen in his Turnip-Field, ergo she bewitch'd his Sheep. Fair Conseqences, and which, if made use of, might serve to condemn all the innocent People of a Parish, as well as the guilty, in the space of a Year."[288] Again, this was appreciated by the dramatists: "My horse this morning runs most piteously of the glanders [disease] ... I"ll take my death upon't, is long of this jadish witch, Mother Sawyer."[289]

Nevertheless, this did not embarrass the enthusiasts. Indeed, Jean Bodin thought that such a coincidence, for example illness or death occurring after an argument, where one of the parties already had a reputation for witchcraft, was sufficient evidence on which to convict: "If one sees a witch threaten her enemy who is hale and hearty, or she touches him, and instantly he falls dead, or he becomes a leper, or suddenly he becomes deformed or crippled or struck by a sudden illness, as we have shown by many

---

287. *Miscellanies of the Philobiblon Society,* Vol. v., at p.7.
288. Pamphlet 1712(2) at p.21.
289. *Witch of Edmonton* Act 4, Scene I, at p.122.

examples - it is a clear and concrete fact, if as well it is rumoured that she is a witch."[290] This also appears to have been the case in England, although to intelligent and thoughtful men, such reputations were not conclusive. Bernard felt that there was some value in popular reputations for witchcraft, the "common report" of neighbours, especially if the suspect was related to another proven witch. However, he was also well aware of its limitations as a diagnostic tool, and the fact that many such reputations were unfounded: "... common report may arise, though not upon no grounds, yet upon very weake grounds, being duely examined." This comment suggests that the title of "witch" was common currency in many villages, at least for a certain type of woman. As a result, Bernard felt that a prior reputation merely created a rebuttable "presumption." Even the robust witch persecuting enthusiast, William Perkins, stressed that magistrates must be "wary" of receiving such reports, as it often happened that the innocent were suspected, and even some of the "better sort" defamed. In particular, he felt that JPs should check carefully whether such "reports" came from honest and creditworthy sources.[291]

As some of these accounts indicate, it was also widely believed that witchcraft could run in families, passing from generation to generation. Some observers openly speculated that it might be a hereditary phenomenon. The third woman accused of bewitching the Fairfax child, an elderly widow called Jennit Dibble, had been reputed to be a witch for

---

290. Bodin, *Demonomanie*, Book 4, at p.182.

291. Perkins, William, *A Disclosure of the Damned Art of Witchcraft*, at p.601.

many years, and Fairfax thought that "It seemeth hereditary to her family", as her children, mother, two aunts, husband and two sisters were all believed to have been witches.[292] Ellen Smith of Maldon, executed for witchcraft at Chelmsford in 1579, had had a mother hanged many years earlier for the same crime. There were also several cases of mothers and daughters being jointly accused and tried. As a result, where someone accused of witchcraft had a relative suspected to have been a witch, it was believed by experts such as Bernard, to be salient to their guilt in any present case. This was true as late as the 1680s, as the witch "sceptic", and judge, Sir Francis North witnessed (Roger North, the author of the account, also being present). Leaving the Assizes trial at Taunton, of an alleged male witch or wizard (wizard was not a title automatically given to male witches), in which his judicial conduct had produced, as intended, an acquittal, a "hideous" old woman cried out, "God bless your Lordship." When he asked her what was amiss, she replied: "My Lord ... 40 years ago, they would have hanged me for a witch, and they could not; and, now, they would have hanged my poor son."[293] Although heredity was widely thought to play a significant role in determining who became witches, a blood relationship was not conclusive. As Bernard noted, it was possible to attribute too much significance to the accused's kith and kin: "When mothers have been executed for witchery, some of their children have not only been no witcherly miscreants, but by God's mercy have become religious and zealous

292. *Miscellanies of the Philobiblon Society,* Vol. v., at p.9.
293. North, Roger, *The Lives of the Right Hon. Francis North ...,* at p.269.

Christians."[294]

In other cases, those accused had been personally touched by formal allegations on an earlier occasion. It is clear that anyone fortunate enough to survive an accusation of witchcraft, whether through the Grand Jury finding the bill ignoramus, an acquittal by the trial jury, or being convicted for a non capital form of the crime, was marked, and a prime candidate for fresh allegations in the future. Elizabeth Francis, executed at Chelmsford in 1579, having been tried at the Easter Assizes, had previously been convicted and sentenced to a year's imprisonment and the pillory for bewitching a child in 1566. In 1572 she had again received a similar sentence for making a woman ill with witchcraft (though, for a second offence, death should more properly have been the sentence). Amy Duny had been pilloried for witchcraft only months before her trial and subsequent execution at Bury St Edmunds, in 1662. Duny's trial was presided over by Mathew Hale, who had also presided over that of Judith Sawkins of Aylesford, in Kent, in March 1658. Sawkins, too, had been accused (and acquitted) of a similar offence only two years earlier. At her second trial, she was convicted and executed (being the penultimate witch to be executed on the home circuit). In one of the most extreme illustrations of this phenomenon, Jennet Preston was acquitted before Sir Edward Bromley, at the Lent Assizes of 1612 in York, of murdering a child by witchcraft, only to be retried before his close colleague (and Assizes partner), Sir James Altham at the summer Assizes there, having allegedly "revive[d] her practices and

294. Bernard, Richard, *A Guide to Grand Jury Men, Second Edn.*, at p.207.

returne[d] to her former course of life." On this second occasion, she was convicted and executed.[295]

Nevertheless, few of these indicators were conclusive. Uncouthness amongst witches was not universal, and did not necessarily cover all aspects of their lives. In many areas, there was no apparent correlation between levels of church attendance and allegations of witchcraft (either one way or the other). Of the 10 women who were presented for non-attendance at church, between 1584 and 1600, in witch troubled Hatfield Peverel, in Essex, none were subsequently prosecuted as suspected witches.[296] Indeed, some commentators stressed that witches could be overtly devout. Mother Lakeland, executed for witchcraft at Ipswich in 1645, had been an apparent "professour of Religion" and a "constant hearer of the word [of God]", for many years before her exposure, despite being a witch throughout that period.[297] The overwhelming majority of petty criminals were not suspected of witchcraft, and the majority of witches were not accused of conventional crimes. Additionally, there were some notable exceptions to the generally low social profile. A few prosperous and even powerful people were accused of witchcraft. At the very highest level, Dr. John Lambe, who had been a private tutor before studying medicine and sorcery, was convicted twice in 1608 for witchcraft, being imprisoned in the King's Bench prison, where he carried on his medical practice as well as offering advice on magic to the Earl of Buckingham. It was

---

295. Potts, Thomas, *The Arraignment And Triall of Jennet Preston, of Gisborne in Cravan*, at p.164.
296. Macfarlane, Alan, *Witchcraft in Tudor and Stuart Essex*, at p.81.
297. Pamphlet 1645(4) at p.7.

the latter's extreme unpopularity that brought about Lambe's death at the hands of an enraged London mob in 1628. At a less exalted and political level, Alice Nutter, unlike the other witches convicted in Lancashire in 1612 (who were both very poor and uncouth) appears to have been the daughter of a fairly wealthy minor gentleman. According to Thomas Potts she was "a rich woman; had a great estate and children of good hope." (The intriguing question arises as to how she got mixed up in the affair in the first place; her own children could not "move her to confess any particular offence or declare anything even when about to die".)

One reason that such accusations of witchcraft as did occur in Sussex were so often dismissed, is probably to be found in the generally higher status, and relative social equality, of the parties involved in that singular county. In a typical case, one David Fairman, who had newly settled in the parish of Dallington, accused three neighbours (two of them men) of poisoning his animals via witchcraft, after they started to die without obvious cause. The background to the affair was a long history of animosity between the parties. This was motivated, in part, by a territorial dispute between Fairman and two of the neighbours over property boundaries, and by a conflict with the third over a trespassing pig and overcharging for the loan of a horse. Not surprisingly, the allegations were swiftly dismissed at Quarter Sessions.[298] Nevertheless, generally, the numbers of

298. Herrup, Cynthia B., *The Common Peace: Participation and the Criminal Law in Seventeenth-Century England*, at pp.32-33. This pattern was not unique to England. In France, those in Cambresis witnessed many trials, the neighbouring inhabitants of Artois saw very few. Even within

"well to do" people accused as witches were extremely small.

Some of those who were formally accused did not believe themselves to be witches, but had, nevertheless, done something to bring such an accusation on their own heads. There was considerable scope for fraudulent people to pose as witches, and for others with a facility for conjuring to be termed witches by casual observers. Reginald Scot noted, the title "witch" was given to those that "take upon them either for gaine or glorie, to do miracles", and that even common "jugglers" might be called witches. Scot went to great lengths in his book to expose their ingenious conjuring tricks, and the specialist gadgets they used to effect them. Similarly, he felt that a murderer who used poison, and alchemists (those that studied "curious and vaine arts"), might also be mistakenly considered to be practitioners of witchcraft.[299]

The Discovery of Witches

There was a large stock of popular beliefs, many of them quasi-magical, as to how a witch might be discovered or rendered powerless. These were part of the common currency of rural life. Some of these beliefs were almost universal within England, such as the notion that drawing a witch's blood destroyed her power over the bewitched. Unlike swimming, this appears to have been a long-

---

Cambresis, some parts were untouched, others were very active against witches.

299. Scot, Reginald, *The Discovery of Witchcraft*, Book v, Chapter 9, at p.110.

standing folk remedy against malign enchantment, one that probably long preceded the secular recriminalisation of witchcraft in 1563. Reginald Scot observed that it was a widespread custom, in his work of 1584, and "Samuel", in Gifford's work of 1593, noted that other villagers urged him to "claw the witch until I fetch blood on her". Typically, the aggrieved farmer in Ann Foster's case, in 1674, used a knife to cut her: "... led perhaps by that general opinion that fetching Blood of the Witch takes away her power of doing any harm."[300]

Tests to identify witches were even more numerous than "cures". Gaule attempted to summarise and list some of these popular indicators or "signes of a witch". Many of them were already centuries old, and some comparatively new, though he thought they were altogether unwarrantable, being founded on "ignorance, humor, [and] superstition". (Gaule was loath to speak out in case he taught people these techniques "in reproving them".) Amongst those listed were (in no order of importance) "The old Paganish sign" of alleged witches having "long eyes", the tradition that witches were not capable of weeping; their making "ill favored faces and mumbling", burning the thing bewitched or some of the thatch of the Witches' house to see if it affected her, or prompted her arrival. There were numerous other techniques, amongst them were those termed/described as: "heating of the horseshoe", the "scalding water", the "sticking of knives across", "putting of such and such things under the Threshold, and in the Bedstraw & c.", the "seive and the Sheares", "Casting the

300. Pamphlet 1674 at p.5.

Witch into the Water with thumbes and toes tyed across [the 'swimming test']", and the "tying of knots".[301] Some of these tests were highly esoteric. Others were based on popular stereotypes. Thus the sort of socially marginalised women on whom suspicion fell were inherently prone to mumbling to themselves, one of the supposed signs of a witch. Similarly the witches' traditional inability to cry, even in extremis, her "want of tears", was also easily explained by Francis Hutchinson: "Old age, Sorrow, and Want of Sleep under such afflictions, dry it up."[302]

Pre-trial tests for witchcraft continued in a highly idiosyncratic fashion to the end. The final witch to be tried and convicted at Assizes, Jane Wenham, agreed: "... to be search'd, and [was] willing to undergo all those Trials that never fail of discovering a Witch, according to the Countrey Probations." These were not carried out until late in the process, most of them with negative results. However, despite her ready co-operation, one longstanding test that she was subjected to, eventually produced a satisfactory result for the two local zealots, the Reverend Mr Strut, the "Chief Champion in the Lists, and his Fellow Labourer Mrs. Gardiner", who carried out an initial investigation of Wenham. In this "famous trial of skill", the suspected witch had to repeat the Lord's Prayer; Wenham, possibly nervous at her considerable audience, obligingly made a (common) mistake: "... great stress is laid upon her repeating Lead us not into Temptation, with Two Negatives. Now I would venture a small wager upon it, take England round, and

301. Gaule, J., *Select Cases of Conscience Touching Witches and Witchcraftes*, at p.75.

302. Hutchinson, Francis, *Historical Essay on Witchcraft*, at p.139.

there are 3 Parts in 4 of the country People pronounce that Sentence generally after this manner."[303] Having tried this technique they also produced, from the store of rustic lore or custom: "... an infallible Secret of proving Jane Wenham a Witch, by putting some of Anne Thorn's [her alleged victim] urine into a stone Bottle, tying the cork down, and setting it over the fire."

In America, where, outside the untypical panic at Salem, the background to accusations of witchcraft was similar to that found in England, similar popular methods of "discovering" witches appear to have crossed the Atlantic from the mother country. Even at Salem, when a local physician opined that Abigail Williams and Betty Parris were "under an evil hand", neighbours, acting on the advice of Mary Sibley, encouraged John Indian and Tituba to bake a "witch cake" containing the two girls' urine. Their idea was to feed the cake to a dog to see if it, too, would start acting in a peculiar manner (like the girls) and thus confirm the presence of witchcraft. Although the Reverend Parris condemned such practices, in a sermon, as "going to the devil, for help against the devil", he realistically appreciated that Sibley had learnt this diagnostic tool from other "ignorant, or worse", people.[304] Looking back on various cases that he was personally familiar with, John Hale (a former "witch-monger" turned sceptic), writing in 1697, noted an American incident which was typically English. A woman from Charleston, in 1647 or 48, was suspected following a dispute with neighbours who had subsequently

303. Pamphlet 1712 at pp.17 and 18. It was allegedly written by a local physician in Hertfordshire.

304. Hill, Francis, *A Delusion of Satan*, at p.25.

suffered misfortune, and because "... some things supposed to be bewitched or have a Charm upon them, being burned, she came to the fire and seemed concerned."[305]

As this American case indicates, burning something, either belonging to the victim or the suspect, was at the root of many such tests. In 1586, Joan Cason of Faversham was implicated in bewitching a girl when a traveller, who stopped for a drink at the alehouse where the child's parents lived, suggested to the mother that the young girl was under a spell. He suggested that if she took a tile from the lodging of the person suspected of bewitching the infant, and placed it in a fire the tile would "sparkle and fly round about the cradle where the child lieth". Cason already being suspected (perhaps because of her eccentric and lewd behaviour), a tile was taken from her home and burnt, and the sparks duly flew. Similarly, a century later, in Northamptonshire, in 1674, neighbours of a farmer who believed his animals had been killed by witchcraft, told him to burn one of his flock of dead sheep and that "upon doing so the witch would appear". When he followed their advice (a fairly common practice) an old woman from the neighbourhood, that he had crossed earlier, promptly turned up.[306]

Although commonly used informally by the populace, even some JPs appear to have employed these tests, to help determine whether an accused woman was a witch or to cure an alleged case of bewitchment. Occasionally, they used them just to satisfy popular demands or their own curiosity. John Stearne recalled one case from the Isle of Ely,

---

305. Hale, John, *A Modest Inquiry into the Nature of Witchcraft,* 1697 at pp.409-411.

306. Pamphlet 1674 at p.4.

in the 1640s, when a child was brought to the house of a local Justice who was examining a supposed witch. The Justice made the woman stand still while the child scratched her face.[307] As Sarah Morduck's experience in London, in 1702, showed, some magistrates were still doing this almost 70 years later.

Nevertheless, it was also widely recognised that many sceptical Justices did not ascribe much, if any, significance to such tests. In an incident from The Witch of Edmonton, based on the real exposure of Mother Sawyer for witchcraft in 1621, one character ("Hamluc") produced a handful of thatch he had plucked from the roof of Sawyer's hovel, and declared that "when 'tis burning, if she be a witch she'll come running in". Sawyer duly entered as the thatch was burnt. In the play, however, the local JP strongly warned the company not to threaten her, as it was "against law". He also gave his views about the absurdity of such a test: "... unless your proofs come better arm'd instead of turning her into a witch, you'll prove yourselves stark fools." Goodcole, in his "factual" pamphlet of the same year, makes it clear that Robinson, the Middlesex JP actually involved in the case, thought that it was a "ridiculous custom", although also noting that the apparently positive result to the test "settled a resolution" amongst local people to prosecute her.[308] JPs' attitudes towards popular methods of proving witchcraft clearly varied greatly.

As the views of Robinson indicate, some strong believers in witchcraft did not subscribe to such arcane tests.

307. Stearne, *Confirmation*, at p.37.
308. *The Witch of Edmonton*, Act 4, Scene I, and Pamphlet 1621(2) at p.2.

Similarly, in his search for a rational approach to witch trials (to modern eyes an oxymoron, but an enterprise in which he showed considerable sophistication and learning), John Cotta expressly dismissed these "imagined trials of Witches", such as: "... the burning of bewitched cattell, whereby it is sayd, that the Witch is miraculously compelled to present herself." He also rejected cures effected: "... by beating, scratching, drawing bloud from the supposed or suspected Witches, wherby it is sayd that the fits or diseases of the bewitched doe cease miraculously." Indeed, Cotta dismissed the need for any special techniques to determine witchcraft cases, feeling that the use of natural science and standard investigative methods were quite appropriate: "... there can be no other ordinarie tryall of Witch-craft, than that which is common unto all other detections of truth."[309]

Usually, these tests appear to have operated as methods to confirm existing suspicions. It is apparent that they were not carried out at random, like a modern mass screening of DNA in a rural area. Even before they were conducted there were only a small number of likely suspects, and often only one. Once those conducting such tests had someone firmly in mind, given the mass of potential indicators for a witch, one test was always likely to be satisfied. The negative results from any tests conducted could always be ignored or explained away; as Francis Bacon observed, generally: "Men mark when they hit, not when they miss."[310]

That some people fulfilled the popular stereotype for a witch is not enough to explain the incidence of persecution.

309. Cotta, John, *The Trial of Witch-Craft, Shewing the True and Right Methode of Discovery: With a Confusion of erroneous wayes,* at p.21.

310. Bacon, Francis, *De Augmentis Scientarum,* Vol. v, p.4.

Given the incidence of poor people, many of them ignorant, unattached, women, there was always a large supply of potential suspects available for the role, so that they were found wherever they were actively sought (as Hopkins's campaign in the 1640s demonstrated). Obviously, in many parts of Europe, and much of England, they were either almost never looked for by the authorities, or, if sought, it was only very intermittently. What then becomes significant is not the number of witch trials, but their rarity. Given the ordinary vicissitudes of life in early modern England, and the inability to diagnose and identify many of the natural phenomena that must have lain behind so many domestic disasters, the question that must be asked is why there were not many more trials and executions for witchcraft than actually occurred? The answer seems to be that there were a number of substantial barriers that such allegations had to pass through, before an indictment, conviction and subsequent hanging could occur. Any one of them could prevent matters reaching their conclusion. Firstly, there had to be a potential suspect of the appropriate type, and a convincing incident of witchcraft that could be attributed to them. Then there had to be villagers willing to make a complaint, and, if these were not themselves people of some standing, other local men of influence willing to facilitate and support such a formal allegation. A sympathetic (to the reality of witchcraft) examining JP, was needed as was a similarly sympathetic Grand Jury (or at least a majority on it) willing to find a true Bill. Even at this stage it was still necessary to have a croyant trial jury potentially willing to convict (unanimously), and a trial judge who was not both hostile to such actions and capable of leading the jurors away from conviction, and also unwilling or unable to effect a post-conviction reprieve.

Role of the Victim

As Foster's case suggests, although minor criminals might be presented to the Justices or the church courts by parish officers (such as the petty constables and churchwardens), those accused of a serious felony would normally be prosecuted at the instigation of the victims themselves. This appears to have applied as much to witchcraft as to housebreaking, the constable's involvement normally being limited to executing the warrant for the arrest of a suspected witch. This was issued by the JPs acting on information laid by the crime's victims. There was often considerable reluctance to prosecute for both practical (usually financial) and social reasons.

For ordinary people, unless there was outside help (as not infrequently occurred) initiating a witchcraft prosecution could be expensive, difficult and inconvenient, as it was for any other serious felony. It might necessitate a long journey to give evidence at the local Assizes town, and quite heavy court fees and incidental expenses. These might begin as soon as the victim took his/her complaint to a JP. They might have to pay for the subpoenas needed to have other witnesses summonsed to make a deposition, and for a warrant to have the accused brought in for examination. Additionally, he (or she), would have to pay fees for drawing up the recognisances by which potential witnesses were bound over to give evidence, if the magistrate committed the accused to trial (these would be sequestrated if they failed to appear to give evidence at the trial hearing).[311] Further fees might be payable to the clerk of the Assizes court for drawing up the indictment, as well as to the other minor court officers. The total cost could easily exceed £1; for many people this was several weeks wages. Typically, Elizabeth Field, when asked, at the trial of Jane Wenham in 1712, why she had not prosecuted nine years earlier, when she first believed that her daughter had been bewitched by the defendant, stated that it was because she was a "poor woman, and the child had no friends able to bear the cost of prosecution." (This remark prompted the trial judge, the noted sceptic Justice Powell, to ask her, sarcastically, whether she had become rich since that time.) As a result, a formal prosecution (unless supported by the authorities) would not be entered into lightly, usually being a "last resort", after other, informal, measures had been exhausted. It also goes some way to explaining why the "victims" of witchcraft, judging from the Assizes records, appear so often to have been relatively "well to do". Poorer people who felt that they were bewitched might be deterred from taking formal action. This factor should certainly be borne in mind when considering modern paradigms based on the differing social status commonly found between witch and victim.

Social resistance to prosecution is also not surprising. Witchcraft was primarily a rural phenomenon, though this was not inherent to the nature of the subject. The crime was also regularly found in England's towns and cities, including London and its immediate suburbs. Indeed, it was largely the London market for popular tracts on witchcraft

---

311. Beattie, J.M., *Crime and the Courts in England 1660-1800,* at p.41.

that fuelled their production. Also indicative of this metropolitan interest and concern were the cases of two notorious suburban witches, Elizabeth Sawyer, the 1621 witch of Edmonton, and Joan Peterson, the 1651 witch of Wapping. By this time, Wapping, in particular, bore very little relationship to a normal English country village. It was a hamlet dominated by artisans and sailors (mariners making up a third of the population) with small docks, bakeries, timber yards and a market, with very few resident members of the gentry.[312] The popular and official reaction to Sarah Morduck in the City of London itself, in 1702, also indicates that there was nothing necessarily rural in such beliefs.

However, throughout the early modern period England was a predominantly rural society. The early statistician, Gregory King, calculated (in 1688) that 80 per cent of English people lived in small villages or hamlets. Even the towns were extremely small, with the single, and notable, exception of London. As a result, most allegations of witchcraft occurred at a village, and thus highly intimate, level, with all the parties being well acquainted with each other. In such small communities, suspected witches were inevitably the close neighbours of ordinary people. Their accusers might have seen them, on a daily basis, for a period of years, or even a lifetime. They were women with whom it was usually impractical not to have some social intercourse, even long after they had acquired a local "reputation" for being a witch. They might be met at the

---

312. *The Population of Stepney in the Early Seventeenth Century, East London History Group,* in *East London Papers Journal,* Vol.11, Number 2, 1968, at p.83.

market, in the street, or at church. Sometimes, this social connection could be very close. Thus, Dorothy Durrant, whose evidence was to play a large part in the case against Amy Duny (her neighbour) in 1662, had asked Duny to look after her baby five years earlier (in 1657), while she went on an errand. This was despite the fact that, as Durrant freely conceded, she knew that Duny had "gone under the Reputation of a witch". This apparently accounted for her instructions to Duny, not to "dry suckle" the baby in her absence.[313] Such prolonged intimacy would have made many reluctant to take proceedings against such local women. It was one thing to gossip about, and even shun and fear a local crone, another to formally accuse her of witchcraft. Significantly, the (much more frequent) making of such accusations in Scotland was greatly facilitated by the system, specifically commended by Jean Bodin, and described by Reginald Scot, whereby a chest sealed with three locks (with separate keys) was placed in the local Kirk, into which anybody was at liberty to put an anonymous written allegation of witchcraft. Every 15 days this chest was opened by three officers of the church, each holding one key, so that: "... the accuser need not be knowne, nor shamed with the reproch of slander or malice to his poore neighbour."[314] This probably meant that in Scotland, social resistance to naming suspects was greatly reduced. It must also be remembered that, at least in England, it was believed that witches did not normally "malice" people without a reason, even if it was sometimes not a very good one. For

313. Geis, Gilbert and Bunn, Ivan, *A Trial of Witches: A Seventeenth-Century Witchcraft Prosecution,* at pp.40 and 41.
314. Scot, Reginald, *The Discovery of Witchcraft,* Book v, Chapter 9, at p.20.

many, politeness, and the occasional gift, might be thought to be enough to keep on the right side of them.

Except in the case of the most clear-cut and serious felonies (such as murder), justice, in early modern England, was a negotiated commodity. The decision to invoke the formal control agencies of the State was not necessarily made as soon as a *prima facie* case existed. There were numerous recorded instances of thefts being dealt with informally. The thief might make restitution, be given a community beating and a warning about his future conduct, or both. The formal requirements of the law, contained in statutes and precedent (the more exact imposition of which was frequently demanded by the Privy Council and JPs), could be interpreted flexibly, to accommodate the feelings of other villagers. There is little reason to believe that this did not also apply to witchcraft, a serious, but certainly not clear cut, crime, and one which by its very nature produced only tenuous evidence. Most villagers, including parish office-holders, would be reluctant to act precipitately. This local tolerance for witches, and resistance to making formal accusations against them, was expressly touched on by the author of a pamphlet relating to the discovery of a group of witches at Windsor, in 1579. He felt that although: "... the justices be severe in executing of the laws in that behalf, yet such is the foolish pity, or slackness, or both, of the multitude and under-officers that they most commonly are winked at, and so escape unpunished."[315] The JPs were dependent on a number of much more ordinary men to enforce the law, so that parish politics and power structures

315. Rosen, Barbara (Ed.), *Witchcraft in England 1558-1618*, at p.84.

were crucial in deciding who, if anyone, would be formally accused of the felony.

The Village Decision Makers

The crucial determinant in such matters was not necessarily suspicion (or the lack of it) on the part of villagers generally, but probably only of a small section of them. It is possible to reconstruct the general social background to village witchcraft accusations. Fortuitously, Hatfield Peverel in Essex, which in the latter part of the sixteenth century experienced several major witch cases that resulted in formal action (whether before the secular or ecclesiastical courts), including a major case in 1566, lies adjacent to the parish of Terling. This has been the subject of a detailed and recent social micro-history for that period (though, interestingly, Terling itself appears not to have produced any formal accusations of witchcraft). It is clear from this, and a variety of other social studies of early modern England, that throughout the period, village life was dominated by a small élite. These men, invariably yeomen and the wealthier tradesmen, had a near monopoly of the major parish offices, such as sessions juryman and vestry man. In addition, their members also controlled the allocation of the lesser parish offices, such as constable and sidesman, which would normally go to villagers of a middling status (husbandmen and craftsmen). By contrast, the ordinary labouring poor in the parish were almost totally excluded from such offices. As a result, in Terling, at any one time, parish life was controlled by an oligarchy of men ranging in numbers from c.15-30 over the period.[316] There is little reason to imagine that a mile or two away, in Hatfield Peverel, the situation was significantly different. It is likely that in witchcraft cases this group of men, perhaps influenced by the local parson or a resident squire, would play a major role in deciding when a history of suspicion had reached the point at which a formal accusation, invoking the criminal justice system, could, and should, be made. Their support and encouragement would be vital if the matter was to be successfully prosecuted, as they would ensure that a range of reputable witnesses might attend to give evidence to the examining JPs and subsequently at trial. Quite often one of their number would have been the witch's alleged victim (at least in the precipitating incident), and some of them would normally be expected to give evidence at trial.

The potential importance of this group for the trial itself, can be seen in the manner in which the social status of witnesses was often carefully recorded by the pamphlet writers. This was probably also a reflection of the respective weight likely to be put on their evidence by the jury. Thus, John Soam, whose evidence was called to bolster the case against the witches at Bury St Edmunds in 1662, was noted as being a "yeoman, a sufficient person".[317] By contrast, one of the reasons that the initial allegations made in 1586 against Joan Cason at Faversham, by her neighbours, were not believed, was that they were "all very poor people". Mathew Hale, discussing the benefit of oral rather than

316. Wrightson, K. and Levine D., *Poverty and Piety in an English Village: Terling, 1525-1700,* at p.106.

317. Pamphlet 1662 at p.15.

written testimony, was quite open in stressing the manner in which it allowed jurors to assess the "Quality, carriage, age, condition [and] education" of the witnesses.[318] It is possible to imagine discussions amongst huddled groups in taverns, after church, or at meetings of the manorial court, and the gradual emergence of a consensus, that something had to be done. Such a consensus would only need a serious incident to result in action. By the late sixteenth century many of this important social group would be literate (a century later nearly all would be). Consequently, they would also have been influenced by the popular tracts that were increasingly available on the subject of witchcraft.

This process of developing and long-standing suspicion explains why, when formal allegations eventually were made, they could include accusations of malefic witchcraft that were many years old. These could appear either as charges on the indictment, or as general background evidence. In more conventional crimes, they would have been disregarded as hopelessly stale. This was important as, although English witches were accused of specific acts, proceedings were as much against the quality of the individuals, as any act they were indicted for. Once a crisis had precipitated a formal allegation, other incidents could be remembered, or reinterpreted if they had originally been given an innocent explanation. Thus, when Duny was formally accused in 1662, witnesses came forward to bolster the case against her and reported strange incidents associated with her over a period of years. One testified that

---

318. Hale, Mathew, *The History of the Common Law of England ... Written by a Learned Hand*, at p.258.

seven years earlier a child had fallen ill after its mother had scolded Duny. Others spoke of carts overturning shortly after damaging her fences, apparently prancing pigs and outbreaks of lice of "extraordinary bigness" (and thus possibly supernatural in origin), after some connection with the accused woman.[319]

In many places, however, these village élites also seem to have been subject to a degree of supervision, if not control, by local elements of the political nation. These sometimes operated as an early "filter", by which allegations might be weeded out. To take a typical scenario, if a yeoman felt that he was the victim of witchcraft by someone long suspected of the crime he might be expected to consult the local parson, or, perhaps less likely, the village squire. If he met an immediate rebuff, and his allegations were ridiculed, it would be less easy for him to summon the local constables or to lay an information.

The attitude of the local clergyman was often vital. He would normally be the most educated man in the parish "especially after the Elizabethan period", and usually familiar with both legal processes and witchcraft, as he would have the duty of presenting cases to the "bawdy courts", the local ecclesiastical courts (whose caseload largely consisted of illegitimacy, a failure to attend church, immorality, recourse to "white" magic etc.). The great

---

319. This was a common feature of witchcraft accusations throughout Europe. Allegations that would have been considered impossibly stale for conventional crimes were regularly adjudicated on. Thus, Jeane Craig from East Lothian in Scotland, tried in 1643 for witchcraft, was accused of killing a baby by witchcraft "twentie two yeir since," and of another offence 12 years earlier. Irvine Smith, J., (Ed.), *Selected Judiciary Cases 1624-1650, Vol.3, at p.812.*

majority of villagers at this time would have been regular communicants, and clerics would have felt a responsibility to provide moral leadership in many areas to their "flocks". This would have included advice surrounding the upholding of the law (especially when the law was intended to deal with enemies of God). Typically, the Reverend George Herbert (1593-1633), the celebrated poet and writer, was also preoccupied with the role of the clergy in administering justice in their villages on a range of matters not strictly relevant to the care of souls. In *The Countrey Parson*, he even suggested that a good vicar was: "... not onely a Pastour, but a Lawyer also." To fulfil this duty, he recommended that they read "some initiatory treatises in the Law", such as Michael Dalton's *Countrey Justice* (first published in 1618), although he accepted that "cases of an obscure and dark nature" should be left to professional lawyers. This interest in the law amongst the upper strata of clergyman is not surprising given their normal social backgrounds. Typically, many of Herbert's relatives, including his grandfather, father and brother had served as JPs. As a result, Herbert appears to have considered that parsons were under a special duty to involve themselves in local legal matters, something that St Paul (in his Letter to the Corinthians) also appears to have enjoined.[320] As late as 1712 the attitude of the Reverend Strut, appears to have been a moving force behind the prosecution of Jane Wenham for witchcraft.

Sometimes, it is apparent that an accused person

---

320. *See* generally, Powers-Beck, Jeffrey, *"Not Only a Pastour, but a Lawyer also." George Herbert's Vision of Stuart Magistracy.*

hastened the stage of a formal complaint by their own foolish behaviour, usually by not "lying low" at a time when suspicion was on the cusp of giving way to action. This can be seen in Ann Foster's case in 1674. An aggrieved farmer had attempted to draw her blood, by cutting her with a knife, the small wound produced was neglected and became infected, so that it "wrankled and swell'd extreamly". Consequently, Foster went to the farmer, threatening to have him arrested for wounding her. The farmer was apparently nervous enough, and sufficiently uncertain of his legal position, to attempt to buy her off. Despite believing that she had earlier killed 30 of his sheep, he offered her 20s. towards her 'cure' (a significant sum of money for the time). However, as soon as he did so she allegedly declared that it was the "devil's money", giving her power to punish him by supernatural means. Later, when his house and barn were set on fire she manifested a continuing inability or unwillingness to keep out of sight. She came to watch the blaze, apparently telling the neighbours attempting to put out the flames that: "... they shoulde never be able to quench the fire, whereupon they were more and more confirmed in the former strong presumptions they had, that all this mischief was done by her devilish Art." Even allowing for exaggeration and fabrication, it would appear that Foster had failed to appreciate that long-standing village rumour was about to give way to formal allegation, which it promptly did: "... thereupon laying hands on this suspected witch, [they] carried her before the next Justice of the peace", where she was formally charged.[321] If she had had the prudence to accept the money, and keep out of sight for a few weeks, the crisis might have passed.

Arrest

As Foster's case indicates, laymen could make a citizen's arrest. Officers of the law (such as village constables) could arrest pursuant either to the general duties imposed by their office, or a warrant issued by a Justice of the Peace. In Mathew Hale's words: "Who may Arrest or Imprison? This is either 1. By a private person. 2. By a publick Officer."[322] However, as today, the law (10 Ed.4. c.6) also provided that: "If a private Person arrest another ... knowing one to have committed Felony ... he ought to carry and deliver the Offender to a constable, Headborough or Tithingman, and they are bound to secure the Party arrested."[323] Alternatively, in sudden and apparently clearcut cases, a suspected witch might be seized by her neighbours and marched straight in front of a JP (as Foster was). Sometimes, in the delay before delivery to the JP, informal interrogations and "tests", such as swimming might be effected by local people (this appears to have been especially common in East Anglia in 1645). However, it would appear that the most common scenario was for a formal complaint to be made to a Justice of the Peace, who would then issue

321. Pamphlet 1674 at p.5.
322. Hale, Mathew, *Pleas of The Crown: Or a Methodical Summary of the principal Matters relating to that Subject*, at p.89.
323. Jacob, Giles, *The Compleat Parish Officer*, 7th Edn., at p.11.

a warrant for the arrest of the accused. The individual concerned would then be brought before him for examination by the constables. Allowing for the differing circumstances of Massachusetts, the initiation of the Salem witch hunt was a classic illustration of the onset of judicial involvement. Four village leaders made a formal complaint to the magistrates at Salem Town, accusing Tituba (a Caribbean slave), Sarah Good and Sarah Osborne of injuring other villagers by witchcraft. The magistrates then issued warrants for the arrest of these women, who were subsequently detained by the local constables (as in England, the holders of part time, annual positions).

Role of the Constable

Constables were normally elected to their office for a year by the courts leet of their manors, though sometimes, especially later in the period, this body might merely confirm the nomination of the local parish vestry. In theory, at least, they were men of some, if modest, estate, and with a reputation for integrity: "As for persons qualified for this office, they ought to be honest, understanding, and able Men; to be Men of Substance, and not the meaner Sort."[324] The typical village constable was usually somewhat above the average of the village in both wealth and education, but below the top dozen or so men who dominated the major offices. However, although the Privy Council in London, and Justices of the Peace at a local level, repeatedly issued

324. *Ibid.*, at p.9.

edicts demanding that honest and substantial men be recruited, these were not always met with success.[325] Because of the onerous, unpaid and often unpopular nature of the job, there were exceptions, where poorer villagers would be encouraged or coerced into taking the position, or where it would be occupied by individuals of low reputation or intelligence. Thus, on the January 8, 1644 the Reverend Ralph Josselin could note that: "This day Court kept in towne the jury of Colne Comit chose for constables 2 men very unfitt to order the alehouses and loose people of the towne."[326] Many of those who were recruited, and who had the means, employed paid deputies to stand in for them during their year in office.

In theory, even without a warrant, constables had a duty *ex officio* to arrest Felons and then to: "... carry them before a Justice to be examin'd."[327] However, the reality of village life meant that discretion was often the better part of valour, and certainly of preserving good neighbourly relations. As "Blurt", the constable in Thomas Middleton's play by that name (1601-1602), remarked: "I have two voices in any company: one, as I am master constable; another, as I am Blurt."[328] Independent formal action by a constable in witchcraft cases would be particularly rare. Nevertheless, constables might take low level summary action on their own initiative against minor allegations of witchcraft,

---

325. *See* on this, Wrightson, Keith, *Two Concepts of Order: Justices, Constables and Jurymen in Seventeenth-Century England,* at p.26.
326. *The Diary of Ralph Josselin 1616-1683,* January 8, 1644, at p.31.
327. Jacob, Giles, *The Compleat Parish Officer,* 7th Edn., at p.18.
328. Middleton, Thomas, *Blurt, Master Constable: or The Spaniard's Night Walk,* Act 1, Scene ii.

especially when these involved troublesome or disruptive white witches. Thus, In Shakespeare's *The Merry Wives of Windsor* (1598) Falstaff, who had dressed up as a wise woman, with unfortunate results, noted that he was "... like to be apprehended for the witch of Brentford: but that my admirable dexterity of wit, my counterfeiting the action of an old woman, delivered me, the knave constable had set me i' the stocks, i' the common stocks, for a witch."[329] There were many cases where such summary punishment (probably of doubtful legality) was taken on women, believed to be guilty of (theoretically) the more serious offence of black witchcraft. This was probably done in the interests of preserving village harmony. However, just as carrying out a constable's duties involved potential physical risk inflicted by angry members of the public, so it was believed that where the constable was involved in apprehending a witch there could be supernatural dangers. According to Stearne, in the 1640s, Nicholas Hempstead of Creeting in Suffolke (a male witch): "killed a horse of one of the constables, because he pressed him for a soldier."[330] Village constables would have been as frightened of upsetting suspected witches as any one else.

---

329. *The Merry Wives of Windsor,* Act 4, Scene v.
330. Stearne, *Confirmation,* at p.18.

Chapter 9

The Role of JPs and the Examination

"Get a warrant first to examine her; then ship her to Newgate."
Banks in
The Witch of Edmonton (1621) Act 4, Scene I

"... a foolish magistrate may have power, though he has otherwise no esteem or authority."
The Commonwealth of Oceana
James Harrington (1656).

The JPs

JPs were appointed by the Lord Chancellor, constituted the élite of county society, and were inextricably linked with the wider political nation. Many of them were qualified lawyers, and others served as MPs for their counties and boroughs. Their numbers were relatively limited for the large amount of judicial and administrative work that they were entrusted with, especially as, in practice, a hard core of individuals would do a disproportionate amount of the duties involved. No more than 15,000 men held the office, in the whole of England, over the entire 80 years between the accession of Queen Elizabeth and the outbreak of the civil war, and this might well be a significant overestimate.[331] In

331. Gleason, J.H., *The Justices of the Peace in England 1558-1640,* at pp.15-16, and 122.

1584, in populous Kent, there were only 76 JPs (some of them semi-honorary). Of these, 55 were members of the Quorum (of legally trained or experienced JPs, a number of whom always had to be present at Quarter and Petty Sessions), and 29 had been enrolled at one of the four Inns of Court in London.[332] However, the numbers of JPs appointed did rise appreciably during the seventeenth century (especially those who were of the Quorum, membership of which became a slightly debased distinction, in turn encouraging the Privy Council to ask that serious felonies always be tried by qualified Assizes Judges).[333] Lists for each county published in 1660 indicate that their numbers varied depending on factors such as the size and population of the county in question and the number of men willing and able to carry out the office. Thus, in Berkshire, that year, there were 42 JPs, of whom 20 were also members of the Quorum, and Buckinghamshire had as many as 75 (57 being of the Quorum). Tiny Rutlandshire, however, had only 12 JPs (9 of them belonging to the Quorum).[334]

It was a mark of local distinction and importance to be a JP. George Herbert, an ardent admirer of the office, thought that for men of standing it was the proper summit of their local ambitions: "But if he may be of the Commission of Peace, there is nothing to that: No Commonwealth in the world hath a braver institution than that of Justices of the Peace." However, even Herbert was aware that criticisms

---

332. *Ibid.*, at pp.15-16, and 122.

333. Herrup, Cynthia B., *The Common Peace*, at p.44.

334. *A Perfect List of all Such Persons as by Commission under the Great Seal of England are now confirmed to be, custos Rotulorum, justices of Oyer and Terminer, justices of the peace and quorum, and justices of the peace*, at pp.2-6.

were sometimes made of the office: that at least a few JPs abused their position, by taking "petty Country bribes"; that in some backward shires it was given to lowly and unsuitable men, "meane persons", and that given the considerable amount of work involved for active JPs, good men were sometimes deterred by the inherent "trouble of it".[335] As the last indicates, the demands of the position, for those who took their responsibilities seriously, were never small, and could be quite onerous. There were also significant forensic and procedural technicalities that had to be mastered. Samuel Pepys noted in his diary for May 1, 1666, that his cousin Thomas Pepys had visited him: "... to consult about the business of his being a Justice of the peace, which he is much against." Among his reasons for this (several were personal), Samuel noted: "Nor do he understand Latin, and so is not capable of the place as formerly, now all warrants do run in Latin." (Nevertheless, he encouraged his cousin to become a JP, feeling that the prestige of the office meant that "there may be some repute" reflected on himself.)[336] Michael Dalton, too, considered that concern about a lack of detailed legal knowledge may have deterred some of the "Honourable and worthie" people in the counties from seeking the position, or resulted in their incompetence when in office if they did. (This encouraged him to write his great work on magistrates' duties, effectively replacing that of Lambard(e). That he felt it was necessary might be indicative of concern about the abilities of some JPs.)

---

335. Herbert, George, *A Priest to the Temple, or, The Country Parson, His Character, And Rule of Holy Life,* at p.102.

336. *The Concise Pepys,* at p.391.

However, generally, the educational and intellectual level of JPs would have been relatively high. Essex may have been the centre of English witch-hunting, but the magistrates who supervised the process there were certainly not ignorant or ill-informed men. They would have shared much the same education as JPs from the other counties. Indeed, their average educational levels were probably higher than those of magistrates from some of the more remote, poor and obscure shires. Many had been educated at Oxford, Cambridge, and, significantly, the Inns of Court in London. Of the JPs appointed in that county in the years 1562-1571, 47 per cent (21 in total) belonged to an Inn of Court. Even in 1592-1601, when the number so qualified fell, the figure was still 27 per cent (9). Several others had received a legal education in the civil law tradition; one, Sir Thomas Smythe, even had a doctorate in law from the University of Padua.

A few JPs would have belonged to the group that were appointed, almost automatically, because of their status as county dignitaries. These included local members of the aristocracy, Royal Judges and bishops, in contrast to the ordinary knights and squires who made up the bulk of working magistrates. However, even some of these dignitaries were as active as their less elevated brethren. Thus, some of the few Essex JPs who were Judges of the central Westminster courts attended Sessions regularly despite their commitments in London (the geographical proximity of the county facilitated this). These included men such as Sir Robert Ward, who attended 20 Quarter Sessions between 1582 and 1595, and was a Baron of Exchequer, as was Sir Thomas Gente, who was involved in 27 Sessions between 1572 and 1591. Two others were Justices of the

Court of Queen's Bench (though their attendance at Quarter Sessions was very infrequent).[337]

It must be constantly borne in mind that the examination and collection of evidence in witchcraft cases, singular though they were, was merely one (relatively unusual) aspect of the justices' judicial function. Nathaniel Bacon, a Norfolk JP, who was a JP from the mid-1570s to 1620 (by which time he was 73), can probably be taken as an example of the better sort of magistrate. In his investigations, he faced a huge range of diverse criminal matters. Amongst them, he took evidence against one Agnes Amies, who was accused of witchcraft, the allegation coming from her neighbour, Elizabeth Mower, who was "vexed and troubled in mind and became lame of body" after a quarrel arose between them. However, he also dealt with the full range of conventional crime, including inter-personal violence, rape, arson and theft. Additionally, he inspected prisons and carried out the huge range of administrative and local government duties placed on JPs, such as licensing ale houses and administering the Tudor poor relief (by 1600 they were responsible for enforcing 300 Acts of Parliament). Although Bacon appears to have been dedicated and painstaking in his work, it is unlikely that, unless he had a deep personal interest in witchcraft (and admittedly some JPs did) that he could have had a profound knowledge of the subject. Instead, he would probably have had recourse to the same techniques used to deal with evidence for conventional crimes, plus a number of rough and ready

---

337. Emmison, F.G., *Elizabethan Life: Disorder,* at pp.322-324. On the division between working JPs and Dignitaries, *see* Gleeson, J.H., *The Justices of the Peace in England 1558-1640,* at pp.15-16.

special methods for establishing witchcraft, that were part of the common store of wisdom of informed men.[338] Significantly, even Dalton's Country Justice, first published towards the end of Bacon's life, and destined to become the JPs' vade mecum, had no specific guidance on the subject until its fourth edition.

Role of the JP in Witchcraft Cases

The role of the JPs was crucial to the entire criminal justice system, because they were the law's permanent representatives in the counties. The visiting Assizes Judges, on their transient visits (usually spending not more than three days in each county), saw the evidence that was presented to them. They had almost no opportunity to control the preparation of the cases that they presided over, other than by retrospective criticism and comments from the Bench or in private, and were heavily dependent on the JPs for this service. This was of crucial significance in witch cases, and explains the apparently strange phenomenon whereby two counties, Essex and Sussex, one famous for being a centre of witch trials, and the other noted for their relative absence, could be in the same (home) circuit, and be judicially serviced by identical Royal Judges, with their Assizes hearings separated by only a few days. As a result, it can be said that JPs were the main legal variable in witchcraft trials.

---

338. Graves, M.A.R., and Silcock, R.H., *Revolution, Reaction and the Triumph of Conservatisn,* at pp.148-151.

In respect to their personal beliefs in witchcraft, and the desirability of its prosecution as a felony, JPs would have shown the full range of views, from that of incredulous sceptic to out and out enthusiast. In this respect their opinions were probably much less homogenous than those found amongst the judiciary (especially after the early 1600s). At such a personal level, an enthusiastic witch hunting JP, like Brian Darcy in 1580s' Essex, or Roger Nowell in early seventeenth century Lancashire, could clearly have a major influence in initiating or encouraging a major persecution. Indeed, in the post 1660 period, it is fairly safe to assume that most cases of witchcraft that came for trial had involved the influence of one or more highly placed enthusiasts in the local Commission of the Peace, members of a by then rapidly dwindling group. These included men such as Sir Edmund Bacon, the JP who examined Amy Duny and Rose Cullender in 1662, and who appears to have been very influential in their subsequent trial at Bury St Edmunds. Although the number of magistrates advocating the prosecution of witches was diminishing, they were still not extinct, even in the early years of the eighteenth century. Significantly, despite the public disturbance occasioned by Hathaway's allegations against Sarah Morduck in 1702, a magistrate in the City of London, Alderman Sir Thomas Lane, seemed to think Hathaway's conduct legitimate in the circumstances, and even "ordered the defendant Hathaway to scratch Morduck in his presence". This was also done in the presence of other Aldermen (ex officio JPs) from the City, who concurred after some initial resistance: "... Hearne opposed it; saying, she had been too much abused already; notwithstanding which, Sir Thomas ordered Hathaway to scratch her, and ordered her to be stript and searched by some women in his own house That Hearne seeing Sir Thomas's resolution, bid him satisfy himself." Afterwards, Sir Thomas committed Morduck to the Wood-Street compter (a notorious London prison), and, initially, refused an offer of £500 bail for her appearance. However, upon later application made to him by Doctors Barton and Martin, and the other Aldermen, he granted her bail. Inevitably, such a public approval of a popular belief by the authorities had widespread consequences. It was noted that: "... these matters being acted by public authority, gave the licentious mob such a confidence," that even after the woman (Morduck) was tried and acquitted of witchcraft they did not believe that she was innocent. This eventually necessitated the trial for fraud of Hathaway, Morduck's alleged victim, in an attempt to end such rumours.[339]

Conversely, of course, a JP who was sceptical about the whole issue of witchcraft could prevent matters proceeding any further at an early stage in the judicial process. Both Reginald Scot and Sir Robert Filmer were JPs in Kent. A classic example of such an early dismissal, from Scot's own experience, is provided by a case involving a 17-year-old girl in the village of Westwell in Kent, in 1574. Apparently possessed one night by Satan, the young woman, Alice Norrington, was examined by the local Minister, the Minister from another nearby parish, and several other men and women of good reputations (i.e. a mixture of the village élite and representatives of the lower rungs of the "political nation"). She was reported to declare in a strange voice, that she was possessed, and Satan then spoke to her questioners

339. *See* generally, Pamphlet 1702.

through her, "sathans voice did differ much from the maids voice". S/he named the person who had sent him as Old Alice, from the same village, and claimed to have killed a number of local people and effected much other mischief. However, when further examined by two local JPs, Thomas Wotton and George Darrell, both apparently sensible, worldly men of ability, she admitted her deception and "received condigne punishment" for it. Nevertheless, as Scot appreciated, if the matter, and the woman implicated, had gone to trial: "How could mother Alice escape condemnation and hanging being arreigned upon this evidence?"[340] Even JPs who were believers in witchcraft, did not necessarily accept all allegations made to them. Thus, the Middlesex Justice, Arthur Robinson, though suspecting Elizabeth Sawyer well before 1621, and consequently staying "watchfull over her" prior to her arrest, clearly dismissed a number of earlier complaints. According to Goodcole he had previously "often & divers times ... laboriously and carefully examined" her, following accusations by her neighbours.[341]

The personal biases of the examining JPs, may account for some differences between individual cases but do not fully explain the fairly consistent variations in the incidence of witchcraft prosecutions between different counties. Variation which often persisted over extended periods, at least in the years to the civil war. Given that individual JPs would have held a variety of views on the subject, ranging from sceptic to enthusiast, the question that has to be

---

340. Scot, Reginald, *The Discovery of Witchcraft,* at pp.130-131.
341. Pamphlet 1621(2) at pp. 1 and 6.

addressed is whether such variations were purely random, with more enthusiasts just happening to be in some counties, and sceptics in others. Here, the answer is probably "no".

Undoubtedly, one reason for this regional variation was cultural. Different regions of England did produce diverse social cultures. These might manifest themselves in local attitudes to witchcraft amongst both the ordinary people and the social élites. This was appreciated even at the time. John Aubrey (1626-1697), writing on the natural history of Wiltshire, contrasted the people of the two principal regions of that large county, namely the "chalk" and the "cheese" countries. In the North was the dairy farming "cheese" country, with its abundance of sour plants such as sorrel. This apparently produced "melancholy, contemplative, and malicious" inhabitants, who were likely to give credence to witchcraft beliefs, and were also prone to both Puritanism and litigation. The "clayy" Malmesbury Hundred of that area, in particular, produced people who had "ever been reputed witches". These people were in marked contrast to the inhabitants of the "chalk" country, set in the downs of the Southern part of the county. There, because of the hard tillage involved in their agriculture, people were too weary after their work to "read or contemplate of religion", or become involved in strange practices or allegations.[342] On a regional level, it has been plausibly argued that the campaign against witchcraft effected in the Eastern counties in the 1640s was merely a facet of a wider process of "moral cleansing" that was being actively pursued by groups of

342. Underdown, David, *Revel, Riot & Rebellion,* at p.73.

powerful local Puritans.[343]

Although there may well have been social factors explaining the differential emergence of these attitudes, factors which probably continued in existence over a long period, this is inadequate as a total explanation. For example, the Sussex Bench was as dominated by gentlemen with a notably Puritan turn of mind, as that of Essex, yet failed to produce similar results with regard to witch trials. This alone, then, does not explain the difference in witchcraft prosecution. Research into the operation of modern JPs (like their early modern predecessors, lay people, usually of some note in their immediate communities) provides a possible insight. Such research has indicated the existence of localised legal "cultures", within the different sessional areas into which such JPs are divided. Until very recently, these manifested themselves in, for example, widely differing sentencing practices for identical crimes. JPs in some areas might, almost as a matter of course, impose a sentence of imprisonment for a crime that in others would normally only be met by a fine or community service order. In an early study on this subject, from 1962, Roger Hood concluded that magistrates from some parts of the country were twice as likely to imprison those guilty of indictable offences as others.[344] Within these areas, no doubt, some JPs disagreed with the consensus view, and felt that the local practice was either too lenient or too harsh; nevertheless, they normally accepted and concurred with the local policy, even if with some

---

343. *See* on this Elmer, P., "Saints and Sorcerers", in *Witchcraft in Early Modern Europe,* at p.175.

344. Roger Hood, *Sentencing in Magistrates' Courts,* at pp.11 and 123.

reluctance.

Similarly, in the early modern period, in some areas, such as Sussex, a legal culture that was resistant to prosecution for witchcraft may well have developed. In others, such as Essex, the converse may have occurred. Undoubtedly, there would have been witch-hunting enthusiasts in Sussex who regretted the predominant local position of exercising great caution before initiating such cases. In Essex there would probably have been sceptics who lamented the local willingness to do so. Nevertheless, most probably did not feel so strongly about the issue to resign from, or refuse, a prestigious office, one that was an essential mark of local status. These small scale legal cultures would have been transmitted to each freshly appointed JP. A justice considering an allegation of witchcraft, in Essex, would know that it was viewed as a serious matter by his colleagues, one which could not be dismissed lightly. Those in Sussex might fear the raised eyebrows of their fellows if they failed to dismiss any but the clearest case at the examination stage. Given that JPs were also sometimes found on the panels for the Grand Jury, they might be expected to influence the deliberations of that body as well, in deciding whether an indictment was valid.

However, recourse to witchcraft prosecutions can also be considered within a wider legal cultural context. The JPs of Sussex (especially the Eastern half), appear to have been notably more reluctant to use the secular courts (whether Quarter Sessions or Assizes) to regulate general "immoral" behaviour than many other counties, especially Essex and Lancashire (both witch-hunting areas). Prosecutions for drunkenness, gaming, swearing, and Sabbath violation were all rarely instituted in Sussex compared with these counties. Additionally, they appear to have been much less interested in using the secular courts against their local poor. There were relatively few actions for vagrancy, the erection of unlicenced cottages and other regulatory offences.[345] Witches can be seen (as sometimes appears to have been the case) to have been one of the tips of a troubling early-modern underclass (to use a modern term), being poor, fractious and un-godly. If this is the case it is then possible to view some witchcraft prosecutions as, essentially, very extreme forms of regulatory action. Given this, if local men, whether constables or JPs, were reluctant to invoke the secular courts against local drunkards, might they not have been even more nervous about using them to deal with such old crones as were rumoured to be witches?

The Examination

The pre-trial examination of those accused of felony, and that of their accusers, with the attendant taking of formal depositions, was one of the most important aspects of a JP's duties. Indeed, arguably, it was the centrepiece of the entire felony prosecution process. It allowed him to determine whether a case should be sent for indictment, the offences to be charged, and also to shape the evidence adduced at the subsequent trial (and thus its likely outcome). It was a particularly important aspect of witch cases.

Under the Marian Statute of 1555 (1 & 2 Philip & Mary

---

345. Herrup, Cynthia, B., *The Common Peace,* at pp.32-34.

c 13), the JP was required to observe certain procedures, as the Lincoln's Inn barrister Michael Dalton noted in his classic *The Country Justice* (first published in 1618; it went through many subsequent editions). When a person was brought before the JP accused of felony, before the justice committed him/her to prison, he had to take, firstly, "The examination of such offendor," and, secondly, "The Information of Such as bring him [i.e. potential prosecution witnesses]; viz. He shall take their examination, & information of the fact, and circumstances thereof; And so much thereof, as shall be material to prove the felony, he shall put in writing within two dayes after the said examination." He was also required to bind over any person likely to be able to give material evidence in the case, to appear at the next Assizes. Petty larcenies and "small felonies", however, could safely be remitted for hearing to the following Quarter Sessions. Having taken a written deposition, it would have to be duly produced: "... the said Ju. Or justices of P. [depending if it was taken by one or more] shall certifie at the next general Gaole delievry [i.e. Assizes] such examination, information, recog. & bailement." Defendants would not be examined on oath (they would "subscribe" to their examination), but their accusers normally would be. Advice to JPs was: "... that all Justices of the Peace do take examinations both of the Felons without oath, and the informers and witnesses against them upon oath in writing before they commit the Offenders to the Goal, and certifie the same the first day of the sessions, that they may be ready upon the Tryal of the felons."[346] As

346. Kelyng, Sir John, Knt. Late Lord Chief Justice of his Majestys Court of

the above cited works suggest, the Marian Statutes did not require that a note of the evidence given in front of the examining justice be written up contemporaneously, only that it be made within two days of the evidence being taken; nor did it have to be a verbatim transcript, a summary of the salient points was sufficient (and much more common). Thus, according to Lambard(e), every Justice of the Peace taking the examination of a prisoner, and that of any potential prosecution witnesses, should put it, or: "... so much therof, as shall be material to prove the felony in writing within two daies after."[347] This might allow favourable interpretations to be placed on statements (especially as most of those questioned were illiterate, and could not check what was recorded), although, despite the extended time limit, it was frequently written up either at the time of the examination, or immediately afterwards.

However, practice in such matters differed widely, especially in the sixteenth century. It was noted in 1619 that some JPs did not administer oaths even to prosecution witnesses under examination (although many others did). Indeed, it was the lack of standardised legal procedures regulating the office that, in part, moved William Lambard(e) (a barrister, JP, legal historian and Kentish gentleman) to write his classic text on the law and obligations of a Justice of the Peace, in 1581. This was exacerbated by the plethora of new statutes and duties

---

Kings Bench *A Report of Divers Cases in Pleas of the Crown, Adjudged and determined; in the Reign of the late King Charles II With Directions for Justices of the Peace and others.*, at p.2.

347. Lambard(e), William, *Eirenarcha, or of the Office of the Justices of Peace, in four bookes*, at p.212.

placed on JPs in the sixteenth century, which had made most older works hopelessly out of date. The speed with which it sold out, and then went into numerous print-runs and editions (these continuing long after his death) indicate that it filled a pressing need, as is the publication only three years later of Sir Anthony Fitzherbert and Richard Crompton's *L'Office et Aucthoritie De Justices De Peace* (1584).

In carrying out examinations, justices probably employed an array of the same techniques for suspected witches, as those used in ordinary felony cases. Michael Dalton enjoined that upon the examination of felons generally, certain "circumstances are to be considered". In particular, were the accused person's parents known to have been "wicked" (though given the age of many accused witches this would have to be by report). Was the person idle or a vagrant? Importantly for suspected witches, was he or she of "evill fame, or report"? How did the suspect answer questions, were they straightforward or evasive in their replies? In this context, justices should be particularly alert to: "The change of his countenance, his blushing, looking downewards, silence, trembling." In his work of 1627, specifically on witchcraft, Bernard, too, expressly identified these standard felony indicators as being potentially indicative of a witch under questioning. He enjoined those conducting the examination: "... to marke his or her down-cast lookes, feare, doubtfull answer, varying speeches, contradictions, cunning evasions, their lying, or defending of this or that speech and deede, or excusing the same, also to observe, if any words fall from him or her, tending to some confession, as to say, if you will be good unto me, I will tell you, & c."[348]

In later editions of his work, Dalton, like Bernard, addressed himself specifically to the issue of witchcraft. Along with witches' marks and familiars, he listed 13 other matters that might also be significant, depending on the case. These included: the accused woman taking an excessive personal interest in the apparently bewitched party; the confession of the examined witch herself (something, he considered, that "exceeds all other evidence" in importance); a dying declaration by the bewitched party as to the source of his or her misfortune; the evidence taken from the children and servants (if any) of the suspected woman; the discovery of materials for sympathetic magic, such as wax images and other suspicious material at the suspect's residence; any blood relationship with another convicted witch; and the "common report" of her neighbours as to whether she was involved in such activity. He appears to have extrapolated many of these principles directly from the earlier work by Bernard.

There was no necessary requirement for impartiality on the part of the examiner. Thus, the examination of Ann Baker, a spinster from Bottesford in Leicestershire, which was taken on March 1, 1618, was conducted by Francis Earle of Rutland whose family had allegedly been bewitched by the group of women to which she belonged, although, in this instance, he was assisted by Sir George Manners, a local Knight (both were Justices of the Peace for the county of Lincoln), and Samuel Fleming. The latter was, helpfully in a witchcraft case, a Doctor of Divinity and also a Justice of

---

348. Bernard, Richard, *A Guide to Grand Jury Men*, Second Edn., at p.235.

the Peace for the county of Leicester (the examination could be conducted by one or several JPs).

However, normally the examining JP would not be personally involved. Cases in which examinants had their statements totally fabricated were probably quite rare, the JPs usually having insufficient personal motive to do so. Nevertheless, the sort of interviewing standards thought appropriate in the modern era (and laid down in the Police and Criminal Evidence Act of 1984) were notably absent for all felonies. Some magistrates appear to have viewed their function as being to secure admissions, rather than to make a neutral examination. Dubious questioning techniques that have elicited admissions throughout history, were periodically employed. Thus, John Selden could note of felony cases generally: "Some men before they come to their tryall are cousen'd to confesse upon Examination by this Trick, they are made to believe somebody has confess'd before them, & then they thinke it a peece of honour to bee clear & ingenious & that destroys them."[349] Even by the standards of the age, the techniques employed to question witches were often particularly unfair. Where questioners were witch-mongers, and those interrogated of poor intelligence or generally overborne by the experience, the eventual deposition could be substantially the work of the questioner, as words were put into the mouths of those accused, albeit that they notionally assented to them. As one observer noted of the examination of Jane Wenham, in 1712, the questions asked about her familiar, were highly: "... ensnaring, she not knowing the meaning of the Term, or the

349. Pollock, Sir Frederick, (Ed.) *The Table Talk of John Seldon*, fo. 74, at p.133.

Use a Familiar is put to; [nevertheless] The parson help'd her out with a leading Question." He felt that Wenham was, in reality, nothing more than a poor, stupid, ignorant "Wretch", who had been: "... harrrassed out of her senses, threatend by all the parish, Brow-beaten by the justice, [and] loaded with 20 hard-mouthed Depositions."[350]

The disorientation, induced by isolation and the disruption of normal life, was clearly a psychological component that was often critical in making people co-operate in producing such confessions. Thus, John Stearne realised that it was necessary to keep suspected witches apart from "idle persons" of their own society, during their examination, as this would prompt them not to make admissions. This had been made manifest to him at the large trial held at Bury St Edmunds in 1647, after which numerous witches were executed. On this occasion, with 18 people awaiting execution, most of them were detained together in a barn. Stearne was convinced that, while in this improvised prison, they had made a "covenant amongst themselves not to confess a word next day at the gallows, when they were to be hanged, notwithstanding that they had formerly confessed." Most likely, a comparison of their experiences, and the support of each other while held in the barn, had restored their sense of reality, and an appreciation of the terrible injustice that they were to experience. As a result, at the gallows next day they refused to admit their guilt, and, in Stearne's words, they died "very Desperately". Significantly, the one exception to this group, "one penitent woman", who informed the authorities about her fellow

350. Pamphlet 1712(2) at p.33.

King James VI and I (1566-1625): Self-professed expert and author on witchcraft who became increasingly sceptical as he grew older

William Lambard(e): Kentish barrister and JP who became influential Elizabethan legal author

Sir Nathaniel Bacon: Experienced Elizabethan and Jacobean JP in Norfolk whose heavy case-load included allegations of witchcraft

Roger North (1653-1734): Lawyer and writer who witnessed trials for witchcraft on the Western Circuit in the 1680s

John Jewel (1522-1571): Bishop who pressed for draconian legal action against witches

Lord Chief Justice Sir John Holt (1642-1710): Eminent judge and noted legal sceptic about the existence of witchcraft

Lord Chief Justice Sir Matthew Hale (1609-1676): Influential and pious judge who helped preserve witch trials into the Restoration period

Lord Chief Justice Sir Edmund Anderson (1530-1605): Judicial scourge of witches

detainees agreement, acknowledged herself that they "had sang a psalm after making it". This was not, in itself, an obviously diabolical way of cementing a pact. Stearne appreciated that under the correct circumstances, people could be infinitely malleable to suggestion and inducements, something that usually meant that active mistreatment and violence were unnecessary. Thus: "... if honest godly people discourse with them, laying the hainousnesse of their sins to them, and in what condition they are in without Repentance, and telling them the subtilties of the devill, and the mercies of God, these wayes will bring them to Confession without extremity, it will make them breake into confession hoping for mercy."[351] Stearne's candour in providing these details, suggests that he genuinely did not appreciate the effect of their social and physical isolation on the veracity of his examinants. This is, perhaps, not surprising in an era when knowledge of human psychology was so much more basic than it is today. In the modern period, admissions produced when disorientated and confused suspects begin to doubt their personal memory of events, and eventually come to believe in their own guilt, have been regularly recorded, sometimes being referred to as "coerced-internalised" confessions. Such a process can be greatly facilitated where the suspect is of low IQ, infirm, frightened, or inherently mentally unstable, all of which might make them vulnerable to interrogative suggestibility.[352] Many witch suspects would have produced such character profiles. Even then, some jurors appear to

---

351. Sterane, *Confirmation,* at p.14.
352. *See* on this Sanders A. and Young R. *Criminal Justice* (1994) at pp.185-187.

have been doubtful about the value of confessions made to the justices. In 1645, Rebecca West was acquitted by her trial jury, despite making full admissions in her examination.[353]

The influence that a committed enthusiast taking the examination could have on the outcome can also be seen in the work of Brian Darcy, an Essex JP, and an enthusiastic Elizabethan persecutor of local witches. He went as far as adopting continental methods of interrogation, such as those suggested by the French jurist, Jean Bodin. Bodin had published *De la Démonomanie des Sorciers*, a little earlier, in 1580. His work was well known in England, which country he had also visited. Bodin advocated extremely robust measures against suspected witches. He considered that it was imperative to interrogate any detained witch quickly as she would confess freely immediately after arrest feeling that Satan had abandoned her: "But if she is left in prison for some time, there is no doubt that Satan will give her instruction." (This might equally refer to the initial process of disorientation that arrest commonly produces, especially in the ignorant, and a subsequent recovery of critical faculties.) Some of the techniques Darcy employed were, to modern eyes, grossly improper. Thus he used inducements to encourage admissions (as suggested by Bodin): "The said Brian Darcy then promising to the said Ursula that if she would deal plainly and confess the truth, that she should have favour; and so by giving her fair speeches she confessed as followeth ..."[354] Some of Bodin's other ploys,

353. Pamphlet 1645(5) at p.12.

354. W.W., *A true and just Recorde, of the Information, examination and Confession of all the Witches, taken at S. Oses in the countie of Essex* ... Reproduced in Rosen, Barbara (Ed.) *Witchcraft in England 1558-1618*, at pp.114-115.

which so influenced Darcy in Essex, included suggesting that: "If they [witches] are afraid to speak the truth in front of several people, the judge must have two or three people hide behind a tapestry, and hear the depositions without writing them down; then get the confessions and write them down."[355] Similarly, Bernard was well aware (and envious) of the efficacy of foreign systems of torture in securing confessions to witchcraft (though, sadly, he does not appear to have considered how the value of any ensuing admissions might be reduced as a result). Indeed, he appears to suggest that, even in England, pretending that such techniques were available might be a legitimate ruse for an examining justice: "If none of these will work to bring them to confesse, then such as have authority to examine, should begin to use sharp speeches, and then threaten with imprisonment and death. And if the presumptions be strong, then if the law will permit (as it doth in other countries in this case) to use torture, or to make a shew therof at least, to make them confess as many have done hereupon in other countries." Almost certainly some JPs did induce their confessions to witchcraft by issuing the threats contained in such sharp speeches.[356]

In this investigative environment, the psychological pressure to make admissions to the examining justice must have been enormous. Some women accused of witchcraft appear to have directly alluded to this process in their evidence at trial. Thus, two women accused of witchcraft at Worcester Assizes in 1647, accepted that they had made out

---

355. Bodin, *Demonomanie*, at p.177.
356. Bernard, Richard, *A Guide to Grand Jury Men*, Second Edn., at pp.235-236.

of court admissions to the JPs. These were made after teats for the use of their familiars were allegedly found by a midwife and other women who "Deposed in Court" that they were for the devil's imps. However, at trial, the women retracted their confessions "alledging that they were not then in their Sences".

Physical Mistreatment of Witch Suspects

At certain times (especially during the civil war) straightforward physical coercion was employed to extract admissions. Francis Hutchinson asserted that in Hoxne, in Suffolk, one woman from the village was questioned with brutality in the 1640s, after "witchfinders" came into that neighbourhood. She was "kept long fasting, and without sleep, [so] she confess'd". Fortunately, an influential local gentleman took charge of the situation and "put the People out of Doors [her house] and gave the poor woman some Meat, and let her go to bed, and when she had slept, and was come to herself, she knew not what she had confess'd."[357] Similarly, the Reverend John Gaule was convinced, in 1646 at least, that the manner in which accused witches were being detained was decisive in prompting admissions. He observed that often the suspected Witch was: "... placed in the middle of a room upon a stool, or table, crosse legg'd, or in some other uneasie posture, to which if she submits not, she is then bound with cords, there is she wacht & kept without meat or sleep for the space of 24

357. Hutchinson, Francis, *Historical Essay on Witchcraft*, at p.64.

hours." A hole was left in the wall for her "imp" to enter, any spiders or flies coming in being killed as suspected familiars.[358] When the septuagenarian Reverend Lowes was investigated by Hopkins and Stearne, in 1645, the local Lord of the Manor recorded the circumstances that had accompanied the investigation (albeit that this was based on hearsay). For such an old man, he appears to have been treated exceptionally harshly, with acute sleep deprivation and other disorientating techniques: "I have heard it from them that watched with him that they kept him awake several Nights together and ran him backwards and forwards about the Room, until he [was] out of breath. Then they rested him a little, and then ran him again; and thus they did for several Days and nights together, till he was weary of his life, and was scarce sensible of what he said or did." In about 1646 such practices were largely forbidden (at least in theory) by Judges and Magistrates.

Similar, unofficial violence used to extract confessions, appears to have occurred at Salem. In a letter of the July 23, 1692, sent by John Proctor, from the local gaol, to Increase Mather, Allen, Moody and Willard, he proclaimed the innocence of the prisoners, and noted that they were held on the evidence of five self-confessed witches who had named them guilty of the same crime. Of these: "Two of the five are (Carrier's Sons) young men, who would not confess any thing till they tied them neck and heels, till the blood was ready to come out of their noses; and it is credibly believed and reported this was the occasion of making them confess

358. Gaule, John, *Select Cases of Conscience Touching Witches and Witchcraftes*, at p.78.

what they never did." He alleged that his own son, William Proctor, had received similar treatment, after declaring his innocence when examined: "... they tied him neck and heels till the blood gushed out at his nose, and would have kept him so twenty-four hours, if one, more merciful than the rest, had not taken pity on him, and caused him to be unbound." He felt this treatment was comparable to the most infamous "popish cruelties".[359]

Mathew Hopkins's Methods of Interrogation

When it comes to methods of questioning in witch cases, those adopted by Mathew Hopkins, the self-styled Witchfinder General would probably constitute worst practice in the field. However, it is very important to note that Hopkins, Stearne et al were not themselves JPs, and conducted most of their work independently of the justices. Their (temporary) power was largely the result of the civil war, which had gravely affected the normal legal administration in England. As Edward Hyde observed, legally, the events of that time were unprecedented. Between February 1643 and the middle of 1646, Parliament authorised no circuits to be held in the country. Although Royalist Judges continued riding out of Oxford (their headquarters), and covered some counties in 1643, the number of these fell swiftly as their fortunes in the war

359. Calef, Robert, *More Wonders of the Invisible World,* at p.257. Drawing its title from Cotton Mather's work, and apparently written in 1697, it could not find a publisher in Boston and was first published in England in 1700.

waned. In much of the country, the functions (both judicial and administrative) that were previously administered by the Judges on circuit, were taken over by the county committees and local magistrates. Even at Westminster, between November 1642 and July 1644, the Inns of Court effectively ceased to function, admissions fell greatly, call to the Bar was virtually suspended, and few lawyers remained in residence.[360] The resulting situation was partly remedied by making large numbers of new, and often quite inexperienced, judicial appointments to fill the gaps that had accrued, something that was to bring its own problems. Many witch trials of the late 1640s and early 1650s were to be conducted by such marginal Judges.

Hopkins was acutely aware that his methods were controversial. This was not surprising, given the widespread appreciation that his activities against witches were in marked contrast to the situation prevailing in the 1630s, when such trials had become extremely rare. As a result, he took time to justify his actions in a short book, *The Discovery of Witches*. This was largely written in reply to Gaule's condemnation of his allegedly cruel methods of interrogation, and was based on a simple question and answer format. It was published shortly before Hopkins's own premature death, from consumption, at the age of 25, in 1647 (a susceptibility to the disease apparently ran in his family, and Essex was low lying and damp). According to his colleague, John Stearne, Hopkins was the son of a "Godly minister". Nevertheless, writing the year after his

---

360. Black, S.F., *The Courts and Judges of Westminster Hall During the Great Rebellion, 1640-1660*, in *The Journal of Legal History*, Vol. 7, May 1986, Number 1, at pp.30-32.

death, Stearne too, was sufficiently aware of public criticism to stress that Hopkins died "without any trouble of conscience for what he had done."[361]

In his work Hopkins dealt with the various complaints that had been made against him: "Certain queries [are] answered, which have been and are likely to be objected against Mathew Hopkins, in his way of finding out witches."[362] He fully appreciated that his methods of deep interrogation had come in for particularly heavy criticism, and that people had argued that he and his colleagues had used "unlawfull courses of torture to make them [suspected witches] say any thing for ease and quiet, as Who would not do?" To rebut these criticisms, he stressed two things. Firstly, he emphasised that the original suggestion for this method of investigation had actually come from a JP; indeed, sleep deprivation was specifically "enjoyned in Essex and Suffolk by the magistrates." Secondly, he emphasised that the motivation behind it was not primarily to gain a confession, but rather to put the witch in extremis and so force her into calling her familiars for assistance, and, perhaps, also to suckle from her: "So upon command from the justice, they were to keep her from sleep two or three nights, expecting in that time to see her familiars, which the fourth night she called in by their severall names." According to Hopkins, in one such case, four familiars duly came in, one "like a white Kitling", another arrived as a legless spaniel, a third came as a rabbit, etc. Perhaps not surprisingly, "all these vanished away in a little time."

361. Stearne, *Confirmation,* at p.61.
362. Hopkins, *Discovery,* at p.1.

Gratifyingly, her own involvement established, this witch (as was common on the continent, and perhaps for similar reasons) promptly implicated others and "confessed severall other witches". Allowing a modicum of good faith to Hopkins and his followers (and it is, perhaps, sometimes too swiftly withheld), it is possible that her questioners were as tired as the witch, and thus prone to hallucinations and mutual suggestion. Another possibility is that Hopkins and his fellows perpetrated what, in modern police forces, has been termed noble cause perjury. Being convinced that the people they questioned genuinely were guilty, they chose to fabricate extra details to secure their conviction, or at least trial. In other cases, any vermin, such as house mice or domestic rats (which abounded in early modern buildings), that came near the accused woman, might pass muster as a familiar. Sometimes, even spiders or insects were identified as familiars.

The denial of sleep was not the only form of coercion used against witches. It was widely alleged that: "Beside that unreasonable watching, they were extraordinarily walked, till their feet blistered, and so forced through that cruelty to confesse & c." Hopkins did accept that some of his local assistants, being "rusticall people", and acting "contrary to the true meaning" of their instructions, had "mis-used, spoiled, and abused" captives. However, he stressed that this had had nothing to do with him, it: "... could never be proved against this Discoverer to have a hand in it, or consent to it; and have likewise been unused by him and others."[363]

---

363. Stearne, *Confirmation,* at p.19.

In a remarkably precocious (for the era) analysis of the potential weaknesses of confession evidence, Hopkins utterly denied that an admission induced by duress, "drawn from her by any threat or violence whatsoever," was of any validity. Additionally, he claimed that he rejected any confessions secured by inducements: "... drawn from her by flattery, viz., if you will confesse you shall go home, you shall not go to goale, nor be hanged &c." He also stressed that he had rejected confessions to anything that was inherently improbable or impossible, such as "flying in the ayre, riding on a broom. & c." Hopkins also claimed that he was well aware of the potential risks of asking leading questions: "He utterly denyes a confession of a Witch, when it is interrogated to her, and words put into her mouth, to be of any force or effect." By this he included questions such as "you have foure imps have you not?" where the alleged witch answered "affirmatively".

It has sometimes been suggested that Hopkins, Stearne and their immediate followers were primarily motivated by a desire for money, as they were paid for their witch-finding services. However, there is no obvious reason to disbelieve Stearne when he stressed that: "Now whosoever thou beest that thinkest I ever made such gain of the way, or Favoured any, and persecuted others, or took bribes, I call God to witnesse, that considering the charge of going to several places, and Assizes, and Gaol deliveries, and the time I expended therabouts, I never, one time with another, got so much as I did by my calling and practice, towards the maintenance of my family." As for taking any money, or goods, as a bribe or gift, he stressed: "I never did, to the value of one penny, neither one way or the other, but what I openly took in view of the townsmen where I came." In many places Stearne claimed he was not paid at all, despite rendering his services, nor would he ever be "except I should sue".[364] Hopkins, too, was adamant that allegations that witch-finders merely sought remunerative employment, so that they could "fleece the country of their money", were absurd. It was the towns themselves that initiated the process, and first sent for him, while he normally only asked for 20s for his services. This was a sum of money which had to "maintaine his companie with three horses" (presumably being enough for Stearne and Phillips as well), and for which sum he might have to ride 20 miles, and discover three or four witches (he felt that even if he had only found one, the price would be "cheap enough", given the valuable service he was providing).[365] There is little reason to doubt their sincerity in this issue, it does not appear to have been a financially lucrative trade, even allowing for the value of money compared to the modern period. Perhaps a more likely ulterior motive was the sense of power their work may have provided, something that might have been highly attractive to otherwise obscure yeomen, barely on the fringes of political society.

John Stearne was to make his own literary contribution to the debate on witchcraft, though by the time it came out, in 1648, his colleague, and (to an extent) leader, Mathew Hopkins was dead. Stearne's aim, like that of Hopkins, was to defend witch-finders from allegations of fraud. His work shows a marked religious faith, with a particularly detailed biblical knowledge (more so than that demonstrated in

364. *Ibid.*, at p.60.
365. Hopkins, *Discovery*, at p.10.

Hopkins's writings). He may have been a Puritan, one who viewed his work as a religious duty. (He survived the Restoration, and in the 1660s was apparently living quietly in Manningtree in Essex; Hopkins's former hometown). The tenor of his work suggests that the witch-finders channelled/exploited (depending on perspective) existing fears amongst the towns and villages of East Anglia, rather than creating them where they had not previously been. Stearne, not surprisingly, totally concurred with Hopkins's analysis of their methods of examination during the East Anglian persecution of 1644 to 1647. Like Hopkins, Stearne readily accepted that many people considered that the witch-finders' confessions were obtained through duress, that they: "... watched them, and kept them from meat, drink, or rest, and So made them say what you would." However, like Hopkins, he was adamant that suspects were always well treated, and that he knew of no cases where examinants were deprived of food or water. He claimed that they always: "... had what was fitting till they were carried before some justice of Peace to be examined, and had provision to rest upon, as bolsters, pillows, or cushions, and such like, if they were kept where no beds were." Nevertheless, he did accept that, at least in the early days, there had been excessive delays in bringing some of them before a JP, albeit for justifiable reasons: "... but at first, some were kept two, three, or foure dayes ... but then it have been, either when no justice of Peace was neere, or when the witnesses against them could not goe sooner." He felt that suspects in this situation had fared better for comforts and provisions than they had in their own homes (given that many were poor this is not totally impossible). Nevertheless, this contains a significant admission. Even in the civil war period, it seems extraordinary that it was ever not possible to find a JP within such a period of time. There were dozens in Essex and Suffolk alone. (It would be interesting to know how far this situation applied, if at all, other than in the unusual circumstances of the 1640s.) Like Hopkins, Stearne stressed that watching was not to induce admissions: "... not to use violence, or extremity to force them to confess." Its (theoretical) aim was to make them call their familiars, spirits or imps. These would be either "visible or [conveniently] invisible"; the former could be seen by the watchers, the latter inferred by the subjects reaction to the unseen spirit.[366]

Professional witch-hunters, like Mathew Hopkins and John Stearne, appear to have been exceptionally rare, though they were not unique, at least in the 1640s. In 1649, in Berwick upon Tweed, the Mayor and Aldermen ordered that "the man that tryeth the witches in Scotland shall be sent for, and satisfaction to be given him by the Towne in defraying his charges." John Gaule speaks of them in the plural for East Anglia, possibly indicating the presence of more than the Stearne/Hopkins group in the 1640s, but also noting, significantly, that the profession of "witch-searchers, or witch-seekers" was "a trade never taken up in England till this [period]". This scarcity is not, perhaps, surprising. It was not an occupation with an obvious career path. Hopkins himself stated that he got his "skill" not from books or "learned authors" (of which there were many by 1644), but from "experience, which though it be meanly esteemed of, is yet the surest and safest way to judge by." Nevertheless,

366. Stearne, *Confirmation,* at p.13.

his work shows enough continental features to suggest that he was somewhat better read on the subject than he was willing to admit. He claimed that his (brief) career only came about by chance. In 1644, he discovered, to his horror, that the house in which he lived, in Manningtree in Essex, was close to the place where some seven or eight of that "horrible sect of witches", occasionally supplemented by witches from adjacent but more distant parts, met every six weeks for their sacrifices.[367]

Such ill treatment does not appear to have been a universal or even regular practice during interrogations, especially those conducted by JPs. It was rather something that might occur during panics, such as those of 1645 and 1692, or as a result of individual enthusiasts. Nevertheless, it is probably safe to assume that there were many unrecorded cases of it occurring, even during quiet times, especially where there was inadequate judicial supervision or control (for example by an Assizes judge subsequently failing to criticise what had occurred). The detailed confessions produced by examined witches often have a schematic quality that encourages scepticism about the role of the interrogator, many being broadly the same in content. Sometimes, the questioner was clearly hectoring and bullying, and, occasionally, brutal. Nevertheless, it is wrong to imagine that such admissions were always the result of leading questioning combined with intimidation, whether tacit or express. In many cases, the details provided by those being questioned are so bizarre, idiosyncratic, or personal, that it appears unlikely that they could all have been placed

367. Hopkins, *Discovery*, at p.1.

in the mouths of the suspected women by examiners following a set formula. In reality, as Christina Larner noted of Scottish witch trials, they often seem to have constituted an "agreed story", between both witch and inquisitor. The alleged witch herself drawing on a common store of fantasy, myth, popular fears and nightmares to respond to the questions put before her.

There could be several examinations of a suspect, these sometimes being continued while the accused was in gaol (the gaoler often being present, and sometimes participating in the questioning). This probably facilitated the embellishment of stories by the examinant, as hope was finally abandoned. The completed depositions would be signed by their makers, or, more commonly for defendants, marked. Thus, the examination of one Dorothy Ellis, from the Isle of Ely, for witchcraft, conducted by Thomas Castell on the May 30, 1647, followed the summary of her admissions with, "Dorethy X Ellis. hir marke".

Sometimes, it was believed, there might be special problems for examining JPs in witchcraft cases. Thus, when the children, the alleged victims of Edmund Hartley, were called in for questioning as potential prosecution witnesses in Lancashire, in the 1590s, Hartley apparently stopped them from giving their evidence to the magistrate by enchantment: "... when Maister Hopwood a justice of Peace came of purpose to take their testimony against Edmund Hartley to Lancaster Assizes and had them before him to that end, they were speachlesse, and that daye he gott no answer of them, being called out of one chamber into another, they sank down by the way speachlesse, when they spake they complayned that Edmond [Hartley] would not suffer them to speake against hym."[368]

The examining JP not usually being a professional lawyer, and the hearing not being a formal trial, proceedings were extremely flexible. Some indication of this, and the screening tests that might be employed for witchcraft generally, can be seen in the examination carried out by the JP investigating Edward Fairfax's case in 1621: "A justice of peace here desired that my daughter and Thorp's wife [a suspected witch] might be personally together before him; so they confronted, as he appointed, and the Wench fell in trance, and was senseless to all persons present, but to Thorp's wife she talked, and the woman (against her will, but enforced therunto by the justice) interrogated her of all these circumstances ..." This same JP apparently told Fairfax, in private, in the Church at Fuystone, that he would try to establish if this woman was a witch, by using the widespread test of: "... causing her to say the Lord's prayer; for if she were a Witch, he said that [in] the repetition of that prayer she could not say the words 'Forgive us our trespasses'." Fairfax was present when this test was conducted: "The woman, being put to it, could not say those words by any means. At first she repeated the prayer, and wholly omitted them; and then, being admonished therof, and urged to the point, she stood amazed, and finally could not at all utter them."[369] (Almost a century later this same test was still being employed, for example in Jane Wenham's case.)

A similar situation prevailed in the American colonies. After arrest, the first people questioned at Salem were taken

---

368. Pamphlet 1660 at p.4.
369. Pamphlet 1621(1), at pp.159-160.

for examination by the magistrates to the Salem Village Meeting house. The justices, John Hathorne and Jonathan Corwin, were from nearby Salem Town, both being prominent merchants. A full note was taken by Ezekiel Cheever, a local tailor, who acted as their clerk (this was not necessary, JPs could, and frequently did, make their own notes, as Roger Nowell had for his Lancashire examinations of 1612). The magistrates at Salem also prepared a report themselves, but, as was common in England, this was a summary, not a verbatim record of what was said. As was often the case in the mother country, the examination was not impartial, being characterised by overtly leading questions, and, at times, an aggressive approach. It may have been this which prompted the Caribbean slave, Tituba, to embark on the lengthy and detailed confession that played such a role in subsequent proceedings.

The Use of Depositions

The Assizes Judges would normally see the examinations taken by the JPs before the matter came for trial. This gave them the outline of the prosecution case, and was something that might influence their conduct of the trial itself. In the early sixteenth century, Judges appear to have been open about the prejudices that they might excite, even before the hearing. Thus, in the case of the Flowers in 1619: "These Examinations and Some others were taken and charily prefered for the contriving of sufficent evidences against them, and when the Judges of Assize came downe to Lincolne about the first weeke of March ... they were presented unto them, who not only wondred at the wickednesse of these persons, but were amazed at their practices and horrible contracts with the Divel to damne their own Soules."[370] These depositions would also, to a considerable extent, be the basis on which the Grand Jury would decide whether to indict (though it could, and regularly did, also hear oral evidence, unlike the situation in Ireland, where the depositions alone were normally used in this period). The JPs' depositions had many other valuable uses for the prosecution. They were extremely useful in co-ordinating the prosecution case. Witnesses giving evidence in open court might be examined on the basis of their earlier depositions, which could be used to prompt their memories. It was also thought that the existence of an earlier sworn statement, made by a potential prosecution witness, prevented them from resiling on their evidence at trial, having made an out of court bargain with the defendant, as a result of which a witness would "speake coldly against a felon before the face of the justice."[371] In the case of witchcraft, it may also have meant that formal accusations, made in the heat of the moment, were much harder to retract after time had allowed proper reflection to set in.

The Evidential Status of the Examination

Clearly, depositions had important practical uses. However, it must also be asked whether the written statement taken by

---

370. Pamphlet 1619 at p.G1.
371. Lambard(e), William, *Eirenarcha, or of the Office of the Justices of Peace, in four bookes,* at p.215.

the examining justice, and held by the clerk to the Assizes, had any formal evidential status at the subsequent felony trial? The principle of orality of evidence was very important to the common law criminal trial. According to Mathew Hale, this emphasis of English law on "personal and open Examination" provided the "Opportunity for all Persons concern'd, viz. The Judge, or any of the jury, or Parties ... to propound occasional Questions." This was, he felt, something that "beats and boults out the Truth" much better than other systems. It allowed the opportunity to confront adverse witnesses, and also to observe the "Contradiction of Witnesses", and so better provided for the discovery of the truth. He felt that this was far superior to the civil (and ecclesiastical) law systems, such as those found in continental Europe (and the Church courts), with their greater emphasis on formal statements being given into evidence.[372] However, more deposition evidence was received than these comments might indicate. This was especially common in treason and Chancery cases, but not unheard of in felony trials.

It is clear that, as with modern confessions to the police, admissions to the examining justice by an accused person her/himself could always be subsequently adduced as evidence in their own right. According to "T.W.", writing in 1660 about the traditional practice in such matters, the clerk: "... that keepeth the Goale Book, looketh out every examination of every prisoner as his cause is in hearing, and if it be evidence for the King [ie, prosecution evidence] he

372. Hale, Mathew, *The History of the Common Law of England ... Written by a Learned Hand*, at p.258.

readeth it to the jury."[373] Thus, in the trial of the Lancashire witches in 1612, a male witch, James Device, had his out-of-court examination adduced, as it apparently amounted to a confession. In this, the position was the same as for informal admissions made to any other person. Thus, for example, Rebecca West allegedly confessed to being a witch to a neighbour, one John Edes, who was subsequently "call'd as an Evidence against her" at the Assizes held at Worcester in 1647.[374] Nevertheless, even if the accused person had made full admissions to the JP, it did not preclude a subsequent "not guilty" plea at trial (any more than a modern confession to the police does). It was, in theory: "... no conviction of the offendor, except he shall after confesse the same againe upon his triall or arraignment [ie, formally plead guilty], or be found guilty by verdict of 12 men &c." It was this provision that allowed a number of witches who had made extensive incriminating replies as examinants to enter a "not guilty" plea. However, in this situation, their earlier admissions would always be adduced and read to the jury.[375] An example of this occurred at a trial for witchcraft at Chelmsford Assizes in 1589. Several women apparently refused to admit the offences alleged against them, in court, even though their extensive admissions to the examining justices were read out after arraignment: "When their indictments were read, and their examinations

---

373. cf., Preface to T.W. *The Clark of Assize, Judges-Marshall, and Cryer: Being The True Manner and form of the proceedings at the Assizes and General Goale-Delivery, both in the Crown Courts, and Nisi Prius Court,* at p.14.

374. Pamphlet 1670 at p.4.

375. Dalton, Michael, *The Country, Justice, Containing The practise of the Justices of the Peace out of their Sessions,* Third Edn., at pp.269-277.

also, they stood upon their terms to prolong life." At this point, the depositions were supplemented by oral testimony: "... to make the matters more apparent, sundry witnesses were produced to give evidence against them." However, in some cases, hearing these admissions repeated seems to have prompted a change of heart, or a recognition of the hopelessness of their position. Such an acceptance of the prosecution evidence, after an apparent "not-guilty" plea, can be seen in the case of Rebecca West. Having listened to cogent confession evidence from a variety of sources (including, it appears, Mathew Hopkins) she made little real effort to defend herself: "Upon which being asked by the Court what she could say for herself, she only alleged that her great Poverty had occasion'd all this, and pleaded guilty, desiring Mercy, but the jury after having received their charge, immediately brought her in guilty of Murther and Witch-craft." (Then, as now, once there had been evidence adduced, the jury had to return a formal verdict.) Whether these women were simply overawed by the occasion, or had come to believe the allegations made by such, often reputable, people, is hard to establish.[376] In the, possibly rare, situation in which the very fact that such admissions had been made to an examining JP was denied by the defendant, the JP concerned, or, if he had one, his clerk (who would sometimes have acted as scribe during the examination) could be called to prove them in court, on oath.

For most of the witch-hunting period, there was only the most rudimentary law against hearsay in criminal cases. As

---

376. Pamphlet 1670 at pp.2-3.

a result, not only could these examinations be adduced as confessions, but sometimes, it appears, they could also be brought in at trial as evidence against others implicated in them. Thus, the examination of the strangely named woman, Phillip Flower, the sister of Margaret, and daughter of Joan, which took place before Sir William Pelham, and a Mr Butler (both being JPs), on February 4, 1618, was later "brought in at the Assizes as evidence against her sister Margaret," who was referred to in her confession. By the 1660s the courts were increasingly doubtful about this practice, resolving before one treason trial: "But such confession so proved is only Evidence against the Party himself who made the confession, but cannot be made use of as Evidence against any others whom on his Examination he confessed to be in the Treason."[377] This was to become a well established principle of English Common law.[378]

Basic though the law against hearsay was at this time, the trial status of the depositions of the prosecution witnesses, such as any surviving victims of the witchcraft or the witch's neighbours, was viewed differently to admissions by the defendant. For most of the period, such documentary evidence was not *prima facie* admissible, in its own right, at trial, but rather had to be substantiated by the witness in question being called live, to give oral testimony on oath. In theory, by 1660 at least, prosecution witnesses nearly always had to testify personally at trial, regardless of the strength of his/her earlier deposition to the examining JP, because these documents had no evidential status in their

377. Dalton, Michael, *The Country Justice, Containing The practice of the Justices of the Peace out of their Sessions*, Third Edn., at p.23.

378. *See*, for example, *R. v. Gunewardene* [1951] 2 KB 600.

own right. However, as Mathew Hale acknowledged, there were two exceptions to this general rule. These were where the deponent had died or become gravely ill and unable to attend court after the deposition was taken.[379] Hale's views on this matter were reflected at a meeting, held in Serjeant's Inn, in April 1666, at which all the senior Judges of England, Hale, Tyrell, Kelyng etc., came together to determine evidential matters in advance of the major felony trial of an aristocrat before the House of Lords: "... to consider such things as might in point of law, fall out in the trial of the Lord Morly, who was on Monday to be tryed by his peers for a Murder." Agreement was reached on several matters, amongst them the circumstances in which pre-trial statements to an examining coroner (analagous to those to a JP) were to be admitted. They unanimously resolved that :"... in case any of the Witnesses which were examined before the coroner, were dead or unable to travel, and Oath made therof, that then the examinations of such Witnesses, so dead or unable to travel might be read, the coroner first making Oath that such Examinations are the same which he took upon oath, without any Addition or alteration whatsoever." Additionally, it was decided that a witness's sworn statement to a coroner could be read to the jury where it was declared on oath that that witness, who was absent: "... was detained by the means or procurement of the Prisoner." This issue was to be determined by the trial Judges. However, witnesses who simply disappeared, at their own behest, and who could not be found later, could

379. Hale, Mathew, in *History of the Pleas of the Crown*, 2: at pp.284-285. See also Green, A.G., *Verdict According to Conscience*, at pp.111-112 and 137.

not have their statements read: "... if a witness who was examined by the Coroner be absent, and Oath is made that they have used all their endeavours to find him and cannot find him, that is not sufficient to authorize the reading of such Examination."[380]

It is clear that the Judges' decisions on these issues were not particularly novel. Rather, they reflected existing good Assizes practice for the time, as this appears to have been a long-standing approach to such depositions even in 1666. Thus, later editions of Lambard(e)'s work suggest that the admissibility into evidence at trial of depositions by witnesses who failed to attend was usually confined to dead or sick examinants/deponents (some limited the former word to the questioning of the defendant), even in the early seventeenth century. As a result, he disapproved of magistrates failing to swear potential prosecution witnesses during their pre-trial examination (a practice that was still followed by a few JPs in the first decades of the century). He fully concurred with those who argued that if these: "... informers be examined upon oath, then although it should happen them to die before the prisoner have his triall, yet may their information be given in evidence, as a matter of good credit: wheras otherwise, it would be of little or no weight at all, and thereby offendors should the more easily escape."[381] In this situation, it was suggested that if the

---

380. Kelyng, Sir John, Knt. Late Lord Chief Justice of his Majesty's Court of Kings Bench *A Report of Divers Cases in Pleas of the Crown, Adjudged and determined; in the Reign of the late King Charles II With Directions for Justices of the Peace and others.*, at pp.54-55.

381. Lambard(e), William, *Eirenarcha, or of the Office of the Justices of Peace, in four bookes*, at p.215.

deposition of a party that was "dead or absent" was given in evidence, by being read to the jury at trial, it was only: "Prudence to have the justice or his Clerk sworn to the truth of the Examinations."[382] The adduction of such depositions in criminal cases was limited to felonies, the terms of the Marian statutes not extending to misdemeanours, as Lord Chief Justice Holt was to make clear.[383]

Nevertheless, in reality, the theoretical legal limitations on the use of felony depositions may not always have been observed, or even been universally acknowledged, in the late sixteenth and early seventeenth centuries. Some authorities spoke merely of a witness being absent, without defining what reasons, if any, would be acceptable for such an absence. There also appear to have been some hearings, especially in witch cases, in the earlier period, in which the trial jury was made aware of the contents of such depositions, without their makers being called to testify. Whatever their later theoretical status, or normal practice, such depositions were received as evidence, occasionally, up until the civil war, though the trial judge would normally expect to see them bolstered by at least some testimony given by "live" witnesses. Sir Edward Bromley, the Pendle trial judge in 1612, appears to have felt there was some indulgence by the court in calling several of the prosecution witnesses whose examinations had been taken, to give evidence to bolster the case against James Device, their depositions having apparently already been read to the jury. The court clerk at that trial, Thomas Potts, noted

382. *Ibid.*, at p.263.

383. *A Report of all the Cases Delivered by Sir John Holt*, London (1738) at pp.294-295.

(uncontroversially) that Device's confession to the examining JP had initially been admitted and read to the jury: "This voluntary confession and Examination of his owne, containing in itself matter sufficient in law to charge him, and to prove his offences, contained in the two severall Indictments, was sufficent to satisfie the Gentlemen of the jury of life and death [of his guilt]." However, he then went on to observe that Bromley: "... commanded, for their better satisfaction, that the Witnesses present in Court against any of the Prisoners, should be examined openly, viva voce, that the Prisoner might both heare and answere to every particular point of their evidence; notwithstanding any of their examinations taken before any of his majestie Justices of Peace within the same countie."[384] This suggests that not only were the depositions first read to the jury, but, it appears, that not all of them were backed up by oral evidence by the maker, given in court. Writing shortly afterwards, in 1618, Michael Dalton clearly thought that the use of the depositions in this case had been noteworthy. Citing Potts's account, and observing that the son and daughter of Elizabeth Device (also one of the accused witches): "... were not onely examined by the justices of P. against their said mother, and the said Examinations certified and openly read upon the arraignment and triall; But the daughter also was commaunded, and did give open evidence against her mother then prisoner at the Barre."[385]

---

384. Potts, Thomas. *The Tryall of Ralph Hall and Mary his wife upon suspicion of witchcraft* at p.H4.

385. Dalton, Michael, *The Country Justice, Containing The practise of the Justices of the Peace out of their Sessions*, Third Edn., at p.271. Strangely, although he had read Potts' book, it was only in the later editions of his own

Similarly, at the trial for witchcraft of Jennet Preston, at the York Assizes of July 1612: "... were diverse Examinations taken and read openly against her, to induce and satisfie the Gentlemen of the Jurie of Life and Death, to find she was a Witch," though this was bolstered by the "live" evidence of Anne Robinson and others: "... who upon their oaths declared against her."[386] When Sir Thomas Bowes, an examining JP, was called to give testimony at trial of Anne West in Chelmsford in 1645, he repeated the evidence ("affirmed unto him") of a glover by the name of Goff from Manningtree, who reported seeing familiars at the defendant's house (skipping black rabbits). Although Bowes declared that Goff was a "very honest man", who would not lie, the reason (if any) for his evidence being reported is not clear.[387] Nevertheless, by the latter part of the seventeenth century, it appears that the occasional practice of reading unsupported prosecution depositions had been firmly rejected, witnesses invariably being called to give their evidence in person, even if it meant replicating their examinations (unless sick or dead).

A similar degree of confusion about the use of such depositions, at least in witch cases, appears to have occurred, in America. In New York, at the Court of Assizes held on October 2, in 1655, Ralph and Mary Hall, from Seatallcott in Long Island were presented by the "Constable and Overseers" of the town for bewitching to death a child

---

work, a decade or so later, that he incorporated specific advice for JPs on detecting witches, by which time the number of trials was waning.

386. Potts, Thomas, *The Arraignment And Trial of Jennet Preston, of Gisborne in Craven*, at p.168.

387. Pamphlet 1645(5) at p.5.

of one Anne Pearce. The trial apparently proceeded despite the absence of live testimony: "Several Depositions, accusing the Prisoners of the fact for which they were indicted were read, but no witness appeared to give testimony in court vive voce." The jury was clearly not impressed by this "... we finde that there are some suspicions by the Evidence, of what the woman is Charged with, but nothing considerable of value to take away her life. But in reference to the man we find nothing considerable to charge him with." Ralph was bound over for his wife's good behaviour.[388]

Assessing the situation is not helped by the fact that oral testimony given at trial was seldom recorded. Accounts of witch trials, like that of Thomas Potts, often use the depositions to provide the facts of the case, rather than the trial testimony. This was probably for largely practical reasons. Trials were conducted very rapidly, and shorthand skills were rare or non-existent at most Assizes. The clerk to the court was already in physical possession of the written statements. Unless there was a radical departure from these, there would be little reason to attempt to make a close record of any verbal testimony given.

Absence of Torture in England

Torture was generally unknown to the common law. Its absence in England was not simply the result of a greater degree of humanity on the part of the English, but rather

---

388. *The Tryall of Ralph Hall and Mary his wife upon suspicion of witchcraft,* in Jameson, Franklin, *Narratives of the Witchcraft cases 1648-1706,* at pp.46-47.

due to the ramifications of the country's unique legal system. The lack of formal rules as to what degree of evidence was necessary to secure a conviction at common law meant that there was no need to bolster cases with forced confessions, unlike some civil law jurisdictions. Nevertheless, torture did appear in England in Tudor times, albeit to a modest degree, and always outside the common law courts, being an extra judicial use of the King's inherent executive power. Indeed, in Felton's case, in 1628, when the King had asked the Lord Chief Justice of Common Pleas whether the assassin of the Duke of Buckingham might be tortured, it had been unanimously held by the judiciary that "no such punishment is known or allowed by our [common] law." It appears largely to have been manifest through the prerogative courts, such as that of Star Chamber. This was noted by John Selden, who thought that: "The Racke is us'd no where as in England. In other Countries tis us'd in judicature, when there is semi-plena probatio, a halfe proofe ag[ains]t a man, then to see if they cann make it full, the[y] rake him to try if hee will Confess. But here in England, they take a man & rack him I doe not know why, nor when. Not in time of judicature, but when some body bidds."[389] Although not made explicit, by "some body bidds" Selden was referring to what was always a royal order, usually made in the Privy Council. Strangely, however, William Perkins, in 1608, had identified two ways of carrying out examinations of witches "either by simple question, or by Torture." Torture meant that besides the "enquiry by words", the Magistrate "useth the rack, or some other

389. Pollock, Sir Frederick, (Ed.) *The Table Talk of John Seldon*, fo. 74, at p.133.

violent meanes to urge Confession". Exhibiting an ignorance of common law procedure, Perkins felt that this could be lawfully used in some carefully regulated situations: "... howbeit not in every case, but onely upon strong, and great presumptions, and when the party is obstinate," though he was also aware that this was not normally the case in England. Sir Robert Filmer was firmly (and rightly) of the opinion that this was wrong, a justice had no power formally to order torture neither did members of the public have the right to resort to it if they thought they were living near a witch. However, he too, thought (again incorrectly) that a member of the judiciary could have recourse to it: "... it is not lawfull for any person, but the judge onely to allow torture, suspicious neighbours may not of their own heads use either threats, terrors, or Tortures; I know not any one of those presumptions before cited to be sufficient to warrant a magistrate to use Torture, or whether when the party constantly denies the Fact, it must be counted obstinacy."[390] Filmer believed that the only exceptions to this principle were treason cases: "Sometimes, when the maine Fact has beene either confessed, or by some infallible proofs manifested, the magistrate for a farther discovery of some circumstance of the time, the place, and the Person, or the like, have made use of the rack." His allusion to treason suggests that Filmer was confusing the prerogative courts with the normal common law courts. Englishmen were very aware of the differences between their own system and that of continental countries in this regard. John Hawles was to note, in 1680, that not only were foreigners judged by

390. Filmer, *Advertisement,* at p.10.

"strangers", who, he felt, were often corrupt, but they were subjected to the "tortures of the rack, which often make an innocent man confess himself guilty merely to get out of present pain."[391] Similarly, a judge, Baron Weston, also in 1680, observed to a woman who claimed that a potential witness had been tortured into refusing to give evidence: "But you must first know the laws of the land do not admit a torture, and since Queen Elizabeth's time there hath been nothing of that kind ever done." (Though he acknowledged that the recusant Edmund Campion and a few others had been "lightly racked" in Tudor times.)

However, although a stranger to common law, torture was present in other courts. The court of Star Chamber, which was operative during the Tudor and early Stuart period had been notorious for the method of its interrogations, and its subsequent punishments (which included facial mutilation, such as the cutting off of ears). It was made up of a mixture of privy councillors and legally trained Judges, in particular the two Lord Chief Justices from the Westminster courts (King's Bench and Common Pleas), because it had both a civil and criminal jurisdiction that overlapped with those courts. In 81 special cases from 1540 to 1640, torture warrants were issued by the Privy Council authorising its use. Most of these occurred in the Elizabethan period, for example the racking of the Jesuit Priest John Gerard. Of these 81 cases, the great majority (71), were conducted in London (68 of them in the Tower of London and the Bridewell prison), the rack and "manacles"

---

391. Hawles, John, *The Englishman's Right: A Dialogue inRelation to Trial by Jury*, at p.17.

(effectively the English term for the strappado) being the usual methods employed. Although the majority of cases involved State or quasi-state offences, such as treason, religious matters or sedition, 25 per cent of cases dealt with conventional felony, mainly murder and theft, albeit that in such cases prominent people or premises were the targets (amongst them Windsor Castle). The last case in which torture was used in England for an ordinary felony occurred in 1597. The last instance of its use for any offence took place in 1640, when Charles I issued a warrant for the torture of John Archer, to force him to name his accomplices in an attack on Archbishop Laud's palace. Only one case involving torture appears to have had clear overtones of sorcery, that of a schoolmaster named Peacock. He was incarcerated in the Tower of London in 1620, for plotting to influence James I by witchcraft, and appears to have been tortured during questioning.[392]

Nevertheless, occasional incidents of torture, apparently without proper legal foundation, do appear to have occurred even after 1640, and especially during the interregnum. Thus, in 1651, the diarist John Evelyn was present when two suspected felons were tortured in prison. One had been identified by the victim of a robbery, and it was decided that the "question or torture" should be given to him. This was administered by the local executioner, with the questioner and a scribe also being present. They initially subjected the prisoner to what amounted to an improvised rack. This appears to have "severed the fellow's joynts in

---

392. Langbein, John, *Torture and the Law of Proof,* at pp.77 and 135, Sharpe, J., *Instruments of Darkness,* at p.49.

miserable sort", but he refused to make any admissions. A horn or funnel was then placed into his mouth, and two buckets of water poured down his throat, causing his features to become bloated and distended, so that he appeared "dead with pain". Evelyn was not able to stomach the sight of the second torture and left.[393] It is impossible to know how frequently such cases might have taken place, and whether witches, many of whom were prosecuted during this period, were also on the receiving end of such treatment. Whatever the theory, it is clear from the debate between Filmer and Perkins that not only were suspected witches being subjected to ad hoc violence from other villagers but that they at least believed that some examining justices may have been ordering such procedures (something impliedly supported by Thomas Cooper in 1617). However, it is very difficult to establish cases where this did in fact occur, and such cases were probably extremely rare or non-existent. The significance that this general absence of torture had for English witch trials, can only be gaged by contrasting it with the situation that prevailed in much of the rest of Europe.

Foreign Tortures

Many continental legal systems placed a high importance on securing admissions from an accused person. Thus, it was widely believed in Germany that: "... common justice demands that a witch should not be condemned to death

393. De le Bedegere, Guy, (Ed.) *The Diary of John Evelyn*, entry for March 11, 1651, at p.76.

unless she is convicted by her own confession." However, such a confession was quite acceptable even if obtained by torture. The situation was made worse by the widespread belief that a witch, if aided by the devil, was "so insensible to the pains of torture that she will sooner be torn limb from limb than confess any of the truth," in turn necessitating its especially robust application.[394] (The prevalence of such an attitude towards a witch's fortitude also partly accounts for the harshness of much of the questioning in England in the 1640s.) Despite their willingness to entertain the use of torture, many continental jurisdictions also had well established rules to prevent the adduction of false confessions, elicited by leading questions during its application. Thus, in some countries, testimony made while being tortured was not admissible unless repeated freely, away from the torture chamber, within a day. Judges were often required to corroborate details of such confessions, and pregnant women and children were exempt from torture. There also had to be a *prima facie* case before torture could be employed. However, these rules were increasingly suspended for crimes like witchcraft, which were difficult to prosecute and prove by other means. Sometimes, they were even formally abolished. Leading questions became routine, and there was often no need, in such cases, to establish that a crime had actually been committed before embarking on torture. The severity and duration of torture was extended, and it was sometimes repeated indefinitely, where previously it had necessarily to be completed within

394. Sprenger, Jacob and Krämer, Heinrich, *Malleus Maleficarum* (1486), Translated by Montague Summers at pp.222-223.

a day. Thus, in 1621, a French Court in Bazuel noted of witchcraft that, contrary to normal practice: "One can repeat torture, because this crime of witchcraft is so extraordinary and so hidden and so secret." A French judge also observed, in a book published in Amsterdam in 1682, and entitled *Si la torture est un moyen seur a verifier les crimes secrets* that the reality of the imposition of torture often differed markedly from the theory. The judge supervising it could easily become caught up in the prosecutorial role of trying to convict the prisoner, and was not exempt from passion, and the fear of being outwitted by a criminal.[395] Not surprisingly, in these circumstances, conviction rates in the areas where it was used on a regular basis for witchcraft could reach more than 95 per cent (compared with less than 50 per cent in common law England).[396]

The tortures that were used outside England appear to have been fairly standardised. They were not supposed to kill the suspect being interrogated, so that most courts ordered forms that stretched and damaged the limbs and other bodily extremities, rather than the vital organs. Thus the "gresilons" (which corresponded to the "pennywinks" in Scotland), crushed fingers and toes in a vice. The thumbscrews worked in a similar way, with the benefit of easy portability.[397] The "strappado" was a pulley which jerked the body violently upwards, the feet having been

395. Cited in Langein, John H., *Torture and the Law of Proof,* at p.148.
396. Levack, Brian P., *The Witch-Hunt in Early Modern Europe,* at pp.78-83 and 174.
397. After two hours treatment with the "thumbingkins" in Scotland, in 1690, an attendant surgeon noted that the Jacobite Neville Paine's thumbs became as thin as the "back of Ane ordinarie Knife And both of them Becam as whyte as any member is Without lyfe."

attached to weights of between 40 and 660 pounds, something that could dislocate arms from their sockets. The "echelle" (or "ladder"), was a type of rack that progressively stretched the body, allowing a fine gradation of pain. The leg screw, or "Spanish boot" (especially favoured in Germany and Scotland) pressured the calf and eventually broke the shin-bone. Less commonly used tortures included the "lift", which violently raised the arms of its victim behind their back, and the "witch-chair", a seat made of spikes, heated from below. Particularly popular in Scotland, and some other continental countries, was the use of the "turkas" or pincers, to pull out finger nails. Less common (though also occasionally used in Scotland) was the "witches' bridle", made of iron, which had four sharpened prongs. These were forced into the victim's mouth, and against her cheeks and tongue. There were numerous others in regular use. Nevertheless, in many cases, simple sleep deprivation (for up to two days) or other low-level physical maltreatment might be enough to secure admissions, without the need for recourse to such extreme measures.[398]

Once an initial confession had been obtained, further threats, or the use, of torture could be employed to secure the incrimination of other alleged witches, producing a "snow-ball" effect. This was something that was much more modest in its extent in England, because of the absence of such institutional violence. It was to be a crucial aspect of many of the large scale anti-witch campaigns mounted in continental Europe. To take extreme illustrations, in Trier,

---

398. Trevor-Roper, R.H., *The European Witch-Craze of the Sixteenth and Seventeenth Centuries*, at p.46.

306 witches implicated about 1,500 accomplices, while at Rouen, in 1670, nine people apparently produced 525 indictments. These cases are also indicative of the manner in which earlier safeguards on the use of torture steadily became eroded in witch cases.

Clear examples of the potential results of such investigative torture can be seen in the experiences of those accused in some of the small Prince Bishoprics of Germany, where the methods of interrogation in witch cases could be particularly savage and devious. A secret letter written by the former burgomaster (mayor) of Bamberg, Johannes Junius, and smuggled from prison to his daughter, in 1628, just before his execution for witchcraft, gives an indication of the type of treatment that could be applied to anyone reluctant to confess to the crime. The small Catholic state of Bamberg witnessed a major witch persecution from 1628 to 1631. It was typical of the minor backwaters (compared with the larger German states), where small groups of witch hunting enthusiasts, often clerics, could gain a temporary political dominance. Often, as matters escalated out of hand, such persecutions were brought to an end by the spread of a personal fear for their own safety amongst their ruling élites (Junius had been a very important municipal officer). He began by telling his daughter that although innocent, he necessarily was bound to die: "For whoever comes into the witch prison must become a witch or be tortured until he invents something out of his head." At first he was asked if he would confess voluntarily, and warned of the consequences of failing to do so. Others who had succumbed to such tortures, and incriminated him, were placed before him to repeat their ridiculous allegations, but, initially, he resolutely refused to admit that he was a witch (before their own deaths these perjured witnesses apparently begged for his forgiveness). The public executioner, who also administered torture, was then called in, and placed thumb screws on him, and both his hands were bound together: "... so that the blood ran out at the nails and everywhere." Worse was to follow: "Thereafter they first stripped me, bound my hands behind me, and drew me up in the torture. Then I thought heaven and earth were at an end; eight times did they draw me up and let me fall again, so that I suffered terrible agony." This latter punishment was probably the "strappado". He was also subjected to the leg screws. So extreme were his agonies that even the executioner, who led him back to the prison, mercifully (or, alternatively, slyly) urged him to make admissions, and pointed out the futility of resistance: "Sir, I beg you, for God's sake confess something, for you cannot endure the torture which you will be put to; and even if you bear it all, yet you will not escape, not even if you were an earl, but one torture will follow after another until you say you are a witch." He observed that everyone so tortured, eventually made admissions. In the light of this, the former burgomaster asked for a day's respite to think, and then decided to make a confession: "... in order to escape the great anguish and bitter torture, which it was impossible for me longer to bear." However, implicating himself was not enough for his interrogators. He was then asked to name others he had seen at the witches' Sabbath, or who were known to be witches, and identify their addresses in the various streets of the city. He initially claimed not to have recognised them, and was then threatened with more torture. When he failed to implicate others in sufficient numbers, he was given back to the executioner who was told to strip, shave and torture him. He then made further allegations against other townsfolk and was forced to admit to acts of maleficium, including the killing of a horse and the desecration of a sacred wafer, at which point they finally left him in peace.[399] He was later burnt at the stake.

The potential for a chain of incrimination was always present where those detained were subjected to brutal treatment, even in England. Thus, according to John Stearne, Elizabeth Clark from Manningtree was held (arguably illegally) for three days and nights by the town's people; though he claimed he was unaware of the conditions in which she was detained, they were probably quite brutal. Her subsequent confession implicated several others, and: "... the Townes men desired me to goe with her confession taken in writing by another, to the justices of the Peace for a warrant for those she accused."[400] Nevertheless, generally, the English authorities were resistant to such a process of chain incriminations; foreign jurisdictions could be blatant about encouraging it. Thus, James VI noted, in 1597, that although witches should always be put to death as a punishment, their executions might sometimes be delayed, so as to get information "for further tryals cause". It is clear that, although harshly, and often brutally, treated by modern standards, by those of many contemporary European countries, people accused of witchcraft in England, where the majority escaped death one way or another, and almost none were tortured, were dealt with

399. Letter dated July 24, 1628, taken from and translated by Monter, E.W., *European Witchcraft*, at page 85. *See* also Kors, A.C., and Peters, E., *Witchcraft in Europe 1100-1700*, at pp.254-255.

400. Stearne, *Confirmation*, at p.14.

comparatively leniently. A comparison of the English situation with that prevailing in Scotland is particularly instructive.

Torture in Scotland

In Scotland, witchcraft prosecutions would often commence with a build up of local accusations at the Kirk's Sessions, citing acts of maleficium by the suspected person, these culminating in the instigation of formal proceedings. In Scotland, as in England, confession was of great importance in proving witchcraft. However, very importantly, and unlike England, torture was often used to secure it. Additionally, sub-torture techniques, such as sleep deprivation (known in Scotland as "waking the witch") were also more regularly used north of the Border. Perhaps not surprisingly, far more witches were executed there (at least 1,000, possibly as many as 1,500) than in England, in a population that was considerably smaller than that of its Southern neighbour. These figures do not include those who died in custody in Scottish prisons, which were no more pleasant than their English counterparts.[401]

An extreme illustration is provided by the famous tract *Newes from Scotland*, published in England in 1591 and supposedly taken from a Scottish original, though this has not been discovered, and it has been speculated that it might not have existed (a considerable English market was to develop for witchcraft "exotica" from Scotland).

401. Larner, Christina, *Enemies of God: the Witch-hunt in Scotland*, at pp.28-31.

Nevertheless, its accuracy has largely been confirmed by other records. In this tract, it was recorded that the Lothian witches who had attempted to kill James VI (and who were the subjects of a major campaign in 1590-1591), were initially identified by a servant maid. This girl had suddenly demonstrated miraculous powers, as a result of which she was suspected of witchcraft, leading her master and some others to "torment her with the torture of the pilliewinks [thumbscrew] upon her fingers, which is a grievous torture, and binding or wrenching her head with a cord or rope." Amongst those she then implicated, was one Agnes Sampson, the eldest of the large group. She was taken to Holyrood House and examined before the King (at this time still eager to demonstrate his learning in daemonologie). Initially, she strongly denied everything. However, despite this, she was "conveyed away to prison, there to receive such torture as hath been lately provided for witches in that country." She had her "head thrawen with a rope according to the custom of that country, being a pain most grievous which she continued almost an hour." Another alleged witch, detained on the word of the maidservant was one Doctor Fian, alias John Cunningham. Despite being "persuaded by fair means", and then by the "thrawing of his head" with a rope, he refused to admit anything, at which he was "put to the most severe and cruel pain in the world, called the boots."[402] After this terrible experience,

402. This torture involved the prisoner's legs being held in iron tubes, which then had wedges driven in between the tube wall and limbs; when, a century later, the Jacobite Neville Paine was subjected to the boots, his "external Malleol [the ankle bone] was made Smooth and equall with the Shinbone" as a result.

Fian was taken back before the King and promptly confessed. However, he subsequently managed to escape, and when recaptured withdrew his earlier admissions. At this he was given a "most strange torment", in which: "His nails upon all his fingers were riven and pulled off with an instrument called in Scottish a Turkas, which in England we call a pair of pincers, and under every nail there was thrust in two needles over even up to the heads." Despite this he maintained his innocence, so that he was put back in the boots where he suffered: "... so many blows in them, that his legs were crushed and beaten as small as might be, and the bones and flesh so bruised that the blood and marrow spouted forth in great abundance, wherby they were made unservicable forever." His defiance merely convinced his interrogators that the devil had gone deep into his heart. Evidently a man of great courage and fortitude, Doctor Fian was convicted and went to his death still denying his guilt, being strangled and burnt in Edinburgh in January 1591. Although by then employed less frequently, the use of torture in Scotland was only formally abandoned in 1708.

Chapter 10

Special Techniques to Establish Witchcraft

Special Techniques

The unusual nature of witch trials encouraged unusual methods of proof. In some cases this went well beyond ignoring the rather flexible evidential rules of the period, and entailed recourse to the supernatural. Over a period of time, two special, and highly esteemed, empirical tests, going beyond admissions and purely circumstantial evidence, developed to identify a witch. These were the presence of the witches' mark or teats, and the tendency of a witch to float when thrown into water. Thus, in James VI's words, besides confessions, there were: "... two other good helpes that may be used for their [witches'] trials: the one is the finding of their marke ... the other is their fleeting on the water."[403] Both were important pre-trial procedures, though their evidential status at the trial itself (at least in England) was, in the first case, initially debatable, in the second, nearly always non-existent. Strange though these tests may seem in the modern era, witchcraft was not quite unique in having supernatural signs to denote its presence, "conventional" crimes were not totally devoid of such a quasi-magical input. Thus, James VI considered that the supernatural operation of the "swimming" test could be properly compared to the way in which, it was widely believed, if a secret murder victim's "carcase" was touched by their killer, it would immediately gush blood. In the

403. James V1 and 1, *Daemonologie,* at p.80.

same way, "God having appoynted that secret super-naturall signe, for tryll of that secrete unnaturall crime" of witchcraft, the water would refuse to "receive them in her bosom, that have shaken off them the sacred Water of Baptisme, and wilfullie refused the benefite thereof."[404] Royal support certainly lent the swimming test credibility, Mathew Hopkins was to point out to his critics in the 1640s that King James had supported its use in his *Daemonologie* (in reply, Francis Hutchinson was to stress that James had been quite young when he did so).

Swimming

As James VI's words indicate, the pre-trial procedure of swimming was special to witchcraft. Suspected witches would be thrown into ponds or rivers to see if the water, also the medium of baptism, would reject them (ie, they floated), or accept them so that they sank (they would then be recovered by watchers). Although ordeal by water (effectively swimming), had been used in the Middle Ages in some parts of Europe, for example, in Bavaria in the 1090s, ordeal by hot iron had been preferred in the later medieval period. Nevertheless, legal commentators in seventeenth century England were well aware of the earlier existence of trial by cold water ordeal (as opposed to the separate trial by boiling water) as a determinant for crimes during the Saxon period and beyond. Thus, William

---

404. *Ibid.*, at p.81. The bleeding corpse was also applied to homicides effected by witchcraft. Jennet Preston's victim, Thomas Lister, was alleged to have bled when touched by her in 1607.

Dugdale observed that in such cases, after exorcisms had been pronounced the accused person might be cast into the water, being freed if he sank and condemned if he floated. However, he also noted that this had been abolished in England as early as the reign of Henry III.[405] Thus, the reappearance and use of the technique in the sixteenth century appears to have been a revival, rather than a survival from earlier periods, though its earlier uses lent it some intellectual weight.

One of the first mentions of swimming, in the sixteenth century, is by the Flemish sceptic, Johan Weyer, in his work of 1563 (the first edition) *De Praestigiis Daemonum.* He complained that such a test was not treated in many jurisdictions as being "fallacious evidence", but was often rather considered as conclusive on the issue. By 1583, in the last edition of his work issued in his lifetime (and thus under his personal supervision), he could observe that: "In many districts the magistrate and the executioners regard as certain proof and an infallible sign of guilt the fact that Lamiae guilty of maleficum never sink but float atop the water."[406] At much the same time, in 1584, a German writer considered the swimming of accused witches to be a relatively new custom (*neuer gebrauch*), one that was particularly associated with Westphalia. Interestingly, Sir Robert Filmer, writing 70 years later, in 1653, also associated the origins of the test with Germany, and gave another of the popular explanations as to why it should operate: "... the Germans used this triall by cold water, and it was imagined

405. Dugdale, William, *Origines Juridiales or Historical Memorials of The English Laws*, at p.87.

406. Weyer, Johan, *De Praestigiis Daemonum*, Bk.6, at p.500.

that the Devill being most light, as participating more of aire than of water, would hold them up above the water." By the middle of the 1580s, it appears to have spread from Germany to adjacent areas of Europe. Cases were occurring in parts of Northern France, and may have taken place in England, on an occasional basis, in the 1590s, though it did not become common there until the following century. Reginald Scot's massive work on witchcraft does not mention swimming, though he does mention many other popular tests for witchcraft. Thus, it would seem safe to assume that it was not in use, in South East England, in 1584. It was expressly referred to by James VI in his work of 1597, and it is sometimes suggested that it first arrived in the north of England from across the Scottish border. This is supported by several English manuscript sources. However, proven Scottish cases appear quite rare.[407] Nevertheless, it does appear to have been witnessed in the northern counties of England in the very early seventeenth century, before spreading to other parts further south. From a tract written in 1613 it is evident that the test was used in that year to identify witches near Bedford, at the suggestion of a passing traveller from the north, who declared: "I have seen it often tried in the north country."[408]

Sometimes, the use of swimming was specifically ordered by examining JPs, in both England and America. However, often it was carried out informally by those associated with the accusers, and the details of the result reported later (if at all) to the JP when the accused was

---

407. Bartlett, Robert, *Trial by Fire and Water: the Medieval Judicial Ordeal,* at pp.146-147.

408. Rosen, Barbara (Ed.), *Witchcraft in England 1558-1618* at p.342.

committed to his custody. Its legal status at trial, as admissible evidence, was, at least in theory, virtually non-existent, and this was freely conceded even by many of the test's proponents. Thus, to those who argued that the swimming test, was "a tryall not allowable by Law or conscience", Mathew Hopkins tartly replied that "It was never brought in against any of them at their tryals as any evidence." This suggests that it was employed to confirm existing suspicions about a suspected witch, rather than to convict them. He was supported in this by his colleague John Stearne, in such specific terms that there is little reason to suspect that they were not telling the truth. Stearne freely admitted that he "swome" some of the people accused by Hopkins and himself, early on in their campaign. However, he also pointed out that it was in the summer, when the water and weather would be warm, so that "none tooke any harm by it." He further claimed that many had requested it themselves, "thinking thereby to cleare themselves, wheras it fell out otherwise." This, apparently strange request to be swum, might appear unlikely, however, it is well supported by evidence from many other cases in both England and the Americas (such as that of Grace Sherwood in Virginia in 1706). Stearne, too, stressed that swimming had been abandoned after judicial warnings, and had never been adduced as formal evidence at the actual trials of those accused: "... neither was it ever given in or taken, that I know, as an evidence against any, nor used by any of us but the first summer, from March, or May 1645, to about the middle of August next following; when Judge Corbolt that now is, forwarned it."

Like the modern lie detector, the test was primarily viewed as indicative. Even witch-finders appear to have appreciated that there could be "false positives", while there were other cases in which a negative result did not absolve the accused person from suspicion. According to Francis Hutchinson, this was witnessed by the Lord of the Manor where the elderly Reverend Lowes was investigated for witchcraft: "They swam him at Framlingham, but that was no true Rule to try him by; for they put in honest People at the same time, and they swam as well as he." Nevertheless, despite these reservations, Stearne still maintained that it was true that witches, when thrown into a river or pond "lye topling on the water, straining to get their heads, or themselves under the water, but cannot."[409] At the very least, if an accused person floated, it would justify further close examination, for example a search for the witches' mark: "Then if she swim, take her up and cause some women to search her ..." Thus, Mary Sutton, the Bedford witch of 1613, having "floated upon the water like a plank" on two occasions, despite the alleged efforts of the men holding the rope to force her under the water "tossing her up and down to make her sink", was found to have a "kind of teat", under her left thigh, for her familiars. These tests having proved positive, she was "carried towards a Justice", where the formal accusation and examination was made.[410] Having been told that further denial was pointless, she made full admissions and was subsequently executed.

To some purists, in the late sixteenth and early seventeenth centuries, swimming was supposed to be conducted with the right thumb tied to the left big toe, and

409. Stearne, *Confirmation,* at p.19.

410. Reproduced in Rosen, Barbara (Ed.), *Witchcraft in England 1558-1618,* at p.343.

the left thumb connected to the right big toe, so that the limbs made a cross over the body.[411] However, in many cases, especially when the test was conducted informally (rather than under the supervision of a JP), the witch was simply heaved into the water, though she was often connected to a rope to prevent her drowning if she sank ("lest they should not be witches ... they may draw her up and preserve her").[412] On this last point, the popular (and mistaken) modern belief that suspected witches could only prove their innocence by drowning appears to have taken root fairly early on, being mentioned in a journal from 1736.[413]

As the judicial warnings to Hopkins make clear, the swimming of witches, though often popular at the lower levels of local administration, was widely, and consistently, disapproved of by the higher authorities. This despite their otherwise sceptical or enthusiastic approaches to identifying and punishing witches. One obvious reason for this was that it appeared to be using magic itself to establish the presence of witchcraft, or, as Louis Servin observed in France in 1629, employing "diabolic art to pursue the devil." More humorously, Sir Robert Filmer caught the legal absurdity of calling on the devil to prove his own presence when he pointed out that if: "Satan useth all meanes to discover a witch; which how it can be well done, except the devill be

---

411. *See* on this Weyer, Johan, *De Praestigiis Daemonum.*, Bk. 6 at p.500. Supported by English tract from 1613 in Rosen, Barbara (Ed.), *Witchcraft in England 1558-1618,* at p.341. *See* also Summers, Montague, *The Discovery of Witchcraft: a Study of Master Mathew Hopkins,* at p.40.

412. Rosen, Barbara (Ed.), *Witchcraft in England 1558-1618,* at p.342.

413. *See The Gentleman's Magazine* 1736, Vol. vi, at p.137.

bound over to give in evidence against the Witch, cannot be understood."[414] In 1692, the clergy of Connecticut, a colony where swimming was sometimes employed, observed: "We cannot but give concurrence with the generality of divines that endeavour of conviction of witchcraft by Swimming is unlawful and sinful." This was a view that was also regularly expounded in European law faculties, and by many eminent continental jurists. As early as 1591, Godalman observed that the test was commonly held to be wrong amongst both the university Doctors and "all the faculties of laws in the German Universities." Shortly afterwards, the Paris Parlement quashed the convictions of two witches in Champagne, citing their swimming as a "strange procedure", and in 1601 it issued a decree forbidding its use by inferior courts (though this was not always observed).

However, almost from its first appearance swimming moved from being employed at a low grade official level, to being used on a popular basis by the general public, an illustration of the symbiotic relationship between élite and mass cultures on the issue of witchcraft. Thus, in Burgundy, in 1644, it was observed that the: "... peasants raised themselves up as magistrates ... they banished all the formalities of justice and wished to rely upon trial by water." Clearly, implementation of the test was not confined to those who had made a study of witchcraft, but appears to have made a deep impression on the popular consciousness, one that lasted well into the eighteenth century. For the Widow Coman, suspected of being a witch in Coggeshall in

414. Filmer, *Advertisement*, at p.18.

Essex in 1699, this popular reliance on swimming was to prove fatal. The local vicar, having prudently retired from the scene, noted: "But the mob ... would swim her, which they did several times: and she always swam like a cork (as hundreds can testifie upon Oath)." Even if the accused person was roped and recovered from the water, there were considerable dangers in such operations, especially in winter. Coman was well over 60, the water bitterly cold at that time of year, and the villagers continued swimming her long after they had established their point, and despite her admissions. The crowd was: "... so troublesome to her she said (when she was swimming) 'Yee see what I am what need you swim me any more'." Perhaps not totally surprisingly: "... soon after whether by the cold she got in the water or by some other means, she fell very ill, and dyd."[415]

The popular use of swimming lingered in some places, long after witches had ceased to be actively persecuted by the authorities. Francis Hutchinson could note in 1718 that: "... our Countrey-People are still as fond of it, as they are of Baiting a Bear or bull."[416] Even in London, as late as 1701, Sarah Morduck, while walking in Newgate-market, was identified by a boy who called out, saying "there goes the old witch." At this, a "great company of people, in a riotous manner flocked about her, and threatened to throw her into a horse pond." She was escorted into an ale-house with the assistance of some women, and thus "avoided the fury of the rabble, otherwise she had been murdered." There were

415. Pamphlet 1712(1) at p.21.
416. Hutchinson, Francis *Historical Essay on Witchcraft*, at p.135.

recorded cases of witches being swum in Norfolk in 1748, Cambridgeshire in 1769, Leicestershire in 1776, and in Suffolk in 1795. In an effort to deter such popular tests, when presiding at the Essex Assizes, held at Brentwood, in 1712, Lord Chief Justice Parker warned that: "... if any dare for the future to make use of that experiment, and the party lose her life by it, all they that are the cause of it are guilty of Wilful murder."[417] The courts also tried to bring the practice under control by imposing sentences for assault where it had been employed. Thus, at the Quarter Sessions held in Leicester in 1760, two men were convicted of ducking "all the poor old women" in Glen and Burton. They were sentenced to be pilloried and jailed for a month. Similarly, in 1769, at the Cambridge Quarter Sessions, a husband and wife were ordered to pay five guineas compensation to their victim, fined, and severely reprimanded for the same offence.[418] Yet, as late as 1864, two people were convicted of assault at the Chelmsford Assizes in Essex, for swimming a suspected local witch.[419]

Even after 1712, however, such tests were not exclusively the preserve of the peasantry. In 1716, a JP in Hertfordshire was removed from the Bench, for, *inter alia,* misconduct while present at a test for witchcraft. The accused woman had been thrown into a sluice, to see if she would sink. After she was pulled out, the magistrate, John Dineley, apparently stripped his own clothes off, jumped

---

417. *Ibid.,* at p.140.
418. *The Gentleman's Magazine,* Vol.30 (1760) at p.346 and Vol.39 (1769) at p.506.
419. Bartlett, Robert, *Trial by Fire and Water: the Medieval Judicial Ordeal,* at pp.146-151.

into the water, and swam about it on his back "exposing his nakedness to the Men and Women that were present." When he got out of the sluice, he also used lewd language to the women who were there. Dineley may well have been slightly unbalanced, however, his presence at the test, four years after that county had witnessed the Wenham case, is indicative of a continuing judicial interest and involvement in such matters.[420] Nevertheless, most educated people, by this period, would have had little time for such practices. In one typical case, long after abolition, in December 1762, a number of enraged villagers surrounded the home of John Pritchers at West Langdon in Kent. They proceeded to drag out his wife (a suspected witch) with violence, "scratched her arms and face in a most cruel manner", and proposed to swim her. She was, however, saved when "some people of condition interpos[ed]", and she was taken by them to the protection of a local JP.[421]

Swimming was also widely practised in the American colonies, often on a quasi-official basis, until quite late (in England, though the JPs had occasionally ordered such a test, it appears to have been quite a rare occurrence for it to be judicially employed after 1660). Thus, as a result of an unsuccessful attempt to establish whether there were grounds for sending Grace Sherwood to trial for witchcraft, the local court in Virginia, where the complaint against her had been made, was forced to think again. The solution presented itself when the accused woman sportingly offered to be swum or, as the court termed it, "tried in the water by

---

420. Landau, Norma, *The Justices of the Peace 1679-1760,* at p.596.
421. *The Gentleman's Magazine,* Vol.32 (1762) at p.346.

Ducking." However, this was something that was initially frustrated by the threat posed by inclement weather, it: "... being very Rainy and bad soe that possibly it might endanger her health." The test had to be deferred until the following July, when she was taken to a plantation and ordered by the court to be thrown in: "... above Man's Depth and try her how She swims Therein, alwayes having care of her life to preserve her from Drowning." Unfortunately for Sherwood, though tied securely, in the "judgment of all the spectators" she swam, and even worse, afterwards, being searched by "Five antient women", proved to have "two things like titts on her private parts of a black coller." As a result, it was decided that she should be committed to the county gaol with orders that she be secured "by irons", and then sent to Williamsburg for trial. (What happened there is uncertain, however, she evidently survived because her will was proved in 1740; Virginia appears to have been less strict about such matters than Puritan New England.)[422]

Even some of the most enthusiastic writers on witchcraft had doubts about the validity, and not simply the legal admissibility, of the procedure. William Perkins accepted that it was not sufficient evidence; as Filmer observed of his work: "Hereby hee condemnes point blanke King Jame's judgement as favouring of Witch-craft in allowing of the triall of a Witch by swimming as a principall proofe." As early as 1616, the physician, John Cotta, attempting (rather fruitlessly) to introduce a more scientific method into the discovery of witchcraft, and to put paid to techniques that

---

422. Jameson, Franklin, (Ed.), *Narratives of the Witchcraft cases 1648-1706*, at pp.441 and 442.

he found unscientific or absurd, was very dismissive of swimming: "It is vulgarly credited, that the casting of supposed Witches bound into the water, and the water refusing or not suffering them to sinke within her bosom or bowels, is an infallible detection that such are Witches." The method was, he felt, ridiculous, as: "... nature cannot take notice, or distinguish a wicked man no not a Devill, and therefore much lesse a Witch."[423]

Many others needed little persuasion as to its inherent absurdity. Thomas Ady was ready to provide a plausible explanation for different levels of individual buoyancy, something, he felt, that anyone "used to the Art of swimming may know." Most importantly, he appreciated that, at least in a small space of time, few people being "tied hand and feet together can sink quite away till they be drowned." A lot would depend on physical variables, such as whether they went into the water when their bodies were "full of breath." Additionally, if, as was likely, they had been on the bank for some time before going into the water, they might have wind in their bowels through fear, also conducive to making them float more readily. Many suspected witches were clothed for the sake of "modesty", even when they were in the water, and their garments might encourage buoyancy (though some exponents of swimming enjoined that those tested should be stripped "into their smocks"). Perhaps more controversially, he thought that women who had had many children "always after remain spongiously hollow", again encouraging them to float. Even

---

423. Cotta, John, *The Trial of Witch-Craft, Shewing the True and Right Methode of Discovery: With a Confusion of erroneous wayes.*, At Ch. XIII, p.104.

in an age when swimming was not a regular pastime, this natural buoyancy on the part of some people was hardly esoteric knowledge. John Aubrey was to record of the celebrated soldier and traveller, Captain Thomas Stump, who was captured by the "wild People" of Guyana in 1632, that, rather than living with cannibals indefinitely, he determined to kill himself, and: "... threw himself into the River (Oronoque) to have drowned himself, but could not sinke; [since] he is very full chested." More sinisterly, Francis Hutchinson, writing in 1718, pointed out that one reason that so many suspected witches floated was due to the very manner in which their tests were conducted. In particular, he felt that the tension placed on the supporting ropes could explain their failure to sink: "... a rope being tied about the Suppos'd Witch, one End is held by some Man on one Side the River, and the other by others on the other, whereby a little pulling may keep her above water." He also accepted the explanations advanced by Ady 60 years earlier as to natural buoyancy, such as the inherent lightness of some bodies and the clothes that such people commonly wore: "... half of the Old Women in the Nation might swim, if they were try'd this Way in Woollen and sweaty Petticoats." Like Ady, he appreciated that there were questions as to natural "fatness and leanness", the presence of wind in the body, and that the very manner of tying the women up, and then putting them in the water trunk up, meant that the lightest part of the body was at the surface, this being conducive to flotation. He, too, noted, that in any event human beings immersed in water were in a state of near equilibrium, as evidenced by bodies floating after death.[424]

The Witches' Teat and Mark

A distinction must be made between the witches mark and the witches teat, though it was one that was liable to be confused by contemporaries, as much as modern scholars. The witches' teat, an extra nipple or nipples, was primarily for the suckling and nourishment of witches' familiars. Thomas Cooper felt that the mark was "usually raw" so that the spirit (familiar) could draw blood.[425] Given that familiars were heavily associated with England, being much rarer in continental Europe, so was the teat primarily an English (and American) phenomenon. Margaret Johnson from Marsden in Lancashire, accused in 1634, was adamant that the number of teats matched the number of familiars, so that "if a witch hath but one mark, she hath but one spirit." She felt that the devil "when sucking", usually in the form of a cat, could make a "pap or dug" in a very short time, and that "the matter which he sucks is blood." By contrast, the witches' mark, an insensible spot on the witches body, denoting her diabolical allegiance, was a widespread phenomenon throughout Europe, including England. Because of their similarity, some of the English mythology pertaining to marks and teats became confused.

Alexander Roberts discussed the origins of the mark in 1616. He believed that it was a relic of the sealing in blood

---

424. Hutchinson, Francis *Historical Essay on Witchcraft*, at p.138.
425. Cooper, Thomas, *The Mystery of Witch-Craft*, at p.275.

of the diabolical covenant between witch and Satan: "The Divell when hee hath once made the contract betweene himselfe and the Witch, and agreed upon the conditions, what they shall doe, the one for the other, giveth her some scratch, which remaneth full of paine and anguish untill his returne againe: at which time hee doth so benumme the same, that though it be pierced with any sharpe instrument, yet is without any sense of feeling, and will not yeelde one droppe of bloud at all: a matter knowne by Just, often, and due triall."[426] This lack of sensation appears to have been an almost universal phenomenon. Thus one of the Maidstone witches of 1652, had such a mark, of which it was noted that: "A Pin being thrust to the head into one of their arms, the party did not feele it, neither did it draw bloud from her."[427] To Bernard as well, the classic sign of the witches' mark was that it was: "... insensible, and being pricked will not bleede." To establish a genuine lack of sensitivity in the mark, when a suspected witch was being examined, and to prevent the suspect feigning discomfort, he felt it was advisable to take her by surprise with a sharp instrument and: "... prick it suddenly and secretly so the witch could not dissemble."[428] This feature even gave rise to specialist witch prickers in some parts of Europe.

As a sign that could establish the presence of a witch, the witches' mark/teat was only gradually accepted. However, as early as 1566, it appears to have existed in proto form in some areas, as, at the Chelmsford Assizes that year, the Queen's Attorney asked of one Mother Waterhouse "when

---

426. Roberts, Alexander, *A Treatise of Witchcraft,* at p.15.
427. Pamphlet 1652(2), at p.6.
428. Bernard, Richard, *A Guide to Grand Jury Men,* Second Edn., at p.215.

did thy cat suck of thy blood?." When she replied "never" he demanded "let me see". And then the jailer lifted up the kerchief on her head and there were spots on her face and one on her nose. The Queen's Attorney repeated his question, and she changed her answer, merely denying that it had sucked her blood in the last fortnight.[429] Obviously, at this point, the marks were not heavily associated with female genitalia (or proper teats), as they were to be later. Another early judicial record of it being used in England came in the demand of a leet jury in Southampton, in 1579, that one Widow Walker should be examined for bloody marks: "which is a common token to know all witches by." Three years later it was employed by Brian Darcy, the notorious Essex JP in his campaign. It was also used by Derbyshire JPs in 1597. Nevertheless, such an examination was not invariably carried out in the late sixteenth century. Thus, Mother Samuel, in 1593, only had her mark exposed after her execution in 1593. In 1617, Thomas Cooper still believed that a witch's mark (by then, often in some "privy place"), assuming that any "other reason in nature" for it could be eliminated, merely created a "shrewd presumption" justifying further examination, rather than conviction in its own right.[430] As late as 1621, Elizabeth Sawyer, the celebrated Witch of Edmonton, was only searched, in a very ad hoc manner, because one JP had vigorously pressed this course of action on his reluctant colleagues on the Middlesex Bench. Eventually, when it was agreed that this should be carried out, two of the three

---

429. Rosen, Barbara (Ed.), *Witchcraft in England 1558-1618*, at p.81.
430. Cooper, Thomas, *The Mystery of Witch-Craft*, at p.275.

women who effected the search had to be "broughte in by the Officers out of the streete, passing there by chance." (Sawyer apparently resisted the attempt to search her in a most "sluttish" manner). Not entirely encouragingly, one of the women brought in, Margaret Weaver, was the keeper of the Sessions House, and thus, perhaps, not a completely disinterested party.[431] A considerable boost was given to the practice of searching for such marks, especially in the genital area, by the fourth and later editions of the Cambridgeshire JP and lawyer, Michael Dalton's classic work *The Countrey Justice.*[432] As a result of Dalton's prestige, the search for such marks increasingly became a routine aspect of pre-trial procedure in witchcraft cases. Usually, it was ordered by the examining justice, who would nominate a group of women (alternatively the local constable would be authorised to arrange this), who would then visit the accused woman. Thus, in the case at Lowestoft in 1662, the examining JP, Sir Nicholas Bacon, appointed six women to visit Rose Cullender, who, with her reluctant consent, they stripped and searched, and then asked to explain several unusual marks found on her body. After the search the JP would take formal depositions from some of the women present (one would normally have had the effective role of forewoman) and they might be called to testify at the Assizes trial.[433] Thus, unlike swimming, which was viewed

431. Pamphlet 1621(2) at p.7.

432. This edition was published in 1630, Dalton had not addressed witchcraft at all in the first edition of his book, in 1618. It was directly influenced by Bernard's recent *Guide to Grand Jury Men* written in 1627 and Potts's earlier work on the Lancashire witches of 1612.

433. Holmes, Clive, *Women: Witnesses And Witches,* in *Past and Present* Number 140 at pp.70-72.

primarily as a screening test for the presence of a witch, by the early to mid-seventeenth century, the possession of marks and teats was of important evidential significance at the Assize trial itself.

One of the early recorded instances in which such evidence appears to have been received at the trial proper (poor records mean that there may well have been earlier ones) occurred at the Lancaster Assizes of 1634, when 20 people (including four men) were accused of the crime. There appears to have been an officially sanctioned search for the witch's mark, the results of which were then received at the trial as evidence. It was thought that 13 of the women examined had teats or marks (11 of them in their genital area). However, the ensuing convictions, troubling the authorities, their executions were respited, and further investigations ordered in London. These were carried out by 10 eminent midwives, supervised by the famous (and broadminded) physician William Harvey. The midwives made a "diligent search and inspeccion" of a selection of the women. Without the benefit of local prejudice, and with expert assistance, they could approach their task with relatively dispassionate minds. They found that in most cases, there was "nothing unnaturall neyther in the secrets or any other partes of theire bodyes, nor any such thing lyke a teate or mark, nor any signe that any suche thinge had ever beene." One woman did have apparently strange marks, but even these could be explained by a natural process.[434]

The mark or teat could be found anywhere on the body,

---

434. *Ibid.*, at p.66.

but especially "under the eyebrows, within the lips, under arme-pits, on the right shoulders, thigh, flanke, in the secret parts, and seate." The genital area became steadily more popular as a site for such marks as the seventeenth century advanced. Of course, in the early modern period, when medicine and hygiene were at a much more basic level than in the modern era, many people were likely to have marks and spots about them. That there could be such a difference of opinion over all 11 women in the tests of 1634 speaks volumes as to the test's subjectivity. Even then, it was appreciated that there was a constant danger that quite natural blemishes could be mistaken for the devil's mark. As John Gaule observed in 1646, simple ulcers and boils were being made into witches' marks.[435] Similarly, Francis Hutchinson noted that some of these marks were simply "Scurvy-Spots", "mortified or withered parts", piles, warts, moles or scars.[436] Nevertheless, contemporary observers who supported the existence of the test, stressed that they attempted to exclude such alternative possibilities. Mathew Hopkins himself addressed the popular argument (his "querie 5"), that natural spots were being wrongly attributed to sorcery, and that: "Many poore people are condemend for having a Pap, or teat about them, wheras many People (especially ancient People) are, and have been a long time troubled with naturall wartts on Severall parts of their bodies." However, like other believers in the witch's mark, he felt that these could be distinguished from the genuine article, and that those employed to judge these things were

---

435. Gaule, John, *Select Cases of Conscience Touching Witches and Witchcraftes*, at pp.4-6.

436. Hutchinson, Francis, *Historical Essay on Witchcraft*, at p.140.

highly skilled in this. If a man was involved, the inspection was assisted by a dozen of the "ablest men" in the parish (male witches as much as female ones could have such marks), if a woman was accused, by the same number of "ancient skillful matrons and midwives."[437] According to Hopkins, the women that he employed to search for marks were greatly experienced in the practice (this does not fully accord with what is known about the apparently modest level of witch trials in the 1630s, perhaps reflecting the presence of informal examinations in that decade). Thus, one suspected woman was: "... searched by women who had for many years known the devils marks, and found to have three teats about her, which honest women have not."[438] Similarly, over 50 years later, after the widow Coman's death in Essex in 1699, the local Vicar asked for a midwife to search her body "in the presence of some sober women." In Coman's "fundament" were found two "long buggs", which, being pressed, produced blood. The midwife emphasised that they were "neither Piles nor Emrods (for she knew both) but excressencies like to biggs with nipples; which seemed as if they had been frequently sucked."[439] In reality, however, despite all precautions, as was observed in 1712, just as: "The Water Experiment to try witches, is the most fallacious of any, so is the Marks about the Body: A mole or a wart, or any excrecancy, passing current for the stamp of the devil."[440]

The test was also widely used in the American colonies.

---

437. Hopkins, *Discovery*, at p.3.
438. *Ibid.*, at p.2.
439. Pamphlet 1712(1) at p.21.
440. Pamphlet 1712(2) at p.42.

John Hale, in 1697, and equating the two physical signs (marks and teats), noted that in such cases, as in England: "There was searching of the bodies of the suspected for such like teats, or spots (which writers speak of) called the devils marks."[441] In Virginia, as late as 1706, Grace Sherwood who was: "... a Long time suspected of witchcraft", was also subject to a careful physical examination. A sheriff was ordered to summon a "Jury of Women" to search her body for the witch's mark. As a result they "found Two things like Titts with Severall other Spotts." However, the first examination proving somewhat inconclusive, it became necessary for her to be examined de novo. Perhaps significantly, the women summoned to provide the jury of matrons for this purpose "refused and did not appear", possibly indicating a change in attitude towards such duties, and forcing the court to order that they be dealt with for contempt "to the utmost severity of the law."[442]

In any event, the lack of such marks did not necessarily denote innocence, they were not a *sine qua non* for witchcraft. Hopkins was clear that "there might be some witches who had not those marks." Furthermore, their absence might be the result of drastic steps taken by the accused person him/herself. According to Stearne, one suspected male witch from Huntingdonshire, named Cark, evidently a very robust individual, had prepared himself for a surprise examination. When he knew that he was coming under suspicion: "... expecting to have been searched

441. Jameson, Franklin, (Ed.), *Narratives of the Witchcraft cases 1648-1706*, at pp.409-411.

442. *Ibid*. at p.441. It forced the court to attempt the swimming test, *see* above at p.311.

another time, when he should not know of it, ... [he] confessed he had cut off his marks, saying that they were fools that were found with the marks."[443]

443. Stearne, *Confirmation*, at p.46.

Chapter 11

Detention and Witches in Gaol

"He that is taken and put into prison or chains is not conquered, though overcome; for he is still an enemy". Thomas Hobbes, *Leviathan* (1651).

Comparative Rarity of Bail

Those formally accused of witchcraft, being accused of a felony, were normally bound for trial at the bi-annual Assizes. They might, therefore, have to wait up to six months for their trials, depending on when in the court cycle they had been detained and examined. For those few accused witches whose trials were actually heard before Quarter Sessions (as was normal, it seems, in Sussex), things were better, as these were held at least every three months, meaning shorter periods of detention. Thus, to consider three women from the same batch of Elizabethan witches, two of them, Joan Cunny of Stisted, and Joan Prentice of Sidle Hedingham (both in Essex), were examined in late March 1589 by Anthony Mildmay JP. Joan Upney of Dagenham, however, was accused and examined later, in early May, by Sir Henry Gray JP. All were tried together at (and executed after) the Assizes held in Chelmsford on July 5, 1589. While awaiting trial they had all been kept in the local gaol, Upney consequently experiencing six weeks less confinement. Occasionally, for a variety of reasons, a defendant would not be listed for the next Assizes, and would have to wait considerably longer. If they were not granted bail, this could mean being lodged in the appalling conditions of a town or county prison for over a year. An example of this can be seen in the case of Elizabeth Pratt, who was committed to Bedford prison in 1666, accused of witchcraft. She was examined before the justices in April, and made some admissions to the offence. She was also examined for the devil's mark by a group of women who deposed that she "was not as other women are, but hath a piece of flesh which grow upon her privities." However, for reasons that are not clear, Pratt was detained in the prison for a year without receiving trial. Her case was finally listed to be heard in the Lent Assizes of 1667, but like so many, she succumbed to the rigours of the prison regime, and died before this could take place. As a result, marked against her name in the Assizes calendar for that Session are the words "Mortua est".[444]

Bail was readily available for misdemeanour offences, such as assault, but those accused of a serious felony (such as witchcraft) were only allowed bail in, theoretically, very restricted circumstances. Justices were encouraged to be cautious in granting it, and, usually, could not do so on their own, requiring a second JP to be present (at least one of them being of the Quorum). A single JP examining a witch who decided that there was a case for the Assizes, would normally remand the accused in custody. There were, sometimes, cases where bail was granted after application to the local Quarter Sessions, especially where the evidence was weak, and the accused articulate enough to petition for it. Thus, in 1615, Alice Stevens in Buckinghamshire, was

---

444. Stockdale, Eric, *A Study of Bedford Prison*, at p.16.

committed to the common gaol for four days, but fortunately arranged bail at the General (Quarter) Sessions of the Peace. She was bound over (entered into a recognisance), on forfeit of a sum of money, to appear at the next Assizes to be held in Aylesbury.[445]

However, an examination of the Assizes records for Hertfordshire and some other counties, in the reign of James I, indicates that whatever the theory, the reality was often very different. A significant number of alleged witches were granted bail, especially if they could find recognisances to ensure their appearance at trial.[446] JPs appear to have made a rough personal assessment, early on, as to whether an allegation of witchcraft was primarily a dressed up neighbours' dispute, unlikely to lead to a conviction, or rather more serious and well founded. Significantly, in those cases where bail was granted, an acquittal nearly always followed, those where it was refused, usually (though not always) witnessed a conviction. Perhaps the very fact that someone of substance was willing to guarantee the accused person's appearance was itself an indication that a woman did not fall into the class of marginalised individuals who were so often convicted of the crime.

---

445. L'Estrange Ewen, C., *Witchcraft in the Star Chamber,* at p.43. On bail for felons, *see* Dalton, Michael, *The Country Justice, Containing The practise of the Justices of the Peace out of their Sessions,* First Edition, 1618 (1619 printing) at p.276.

446. The frequency with which this happened in felony cases generally, might explain the repeated injunctions to JPs from central government not to be lax in granting bail. Dalton, Michael, *The Country Justice, Containing The practise of the Justices of the Peace out of their Sessions,* at p.2. "Directions for Justices of the Peace". A JP who gave bail improperly "to be complained of to the Lord chancellor, that he may be turned out of his Commission."

At the Hertford Assizes held on July 24, 1618, and presided over by Robert Houghton J., and Serjeant Ranulph Crewe (Serjeants making up the numbers of Assizes Judges where necessary), two women appeared before the court, accused of murder by witchcraft. One was a widow, one married, and both were from the village of Barkway. Alice Nashe was accused of bewitching one Margaret Bishopp of the same village on January 12, 1618, so that she languished until February 5, that year, and then died. On June 22, 1618, before a local magistrate (Sir Robert Chester JP) a group of men from Barkway, Thomas Fitch, a bricklayer, John Kinge a maltster, Henry Michaell a blacksmith, and William Bishopp, a roper, entered into recognisances to give evidence against Nashe. Despite this, however, she was bailed by Thomas Moyses, a fuller, and Richard Hullett, a blacksmith, from Barkway, who entered into recognisances for her appearance. She was found not guilty of the charge against her. At the same Assize session, Margery Hullett, another resident of Barkway, the wife of Richard Hullett, was also indicted for murder by witchcraft. It was alleged that on the September 7, 1616, in the same village, she had bewitched one Henry Braie, so that he languished until 12th September and then died. She appeared on 6th July 1618, in front of the same JP, Sir Robert Chester. Two men, John Osland and Richard Dewe, both of them labourers, and Agnes Bray a widow of Barkway (spelt differently, in the record, but probably the deceased's wife) entered recognisances to give evidence against Hullett. On June 22, 1618, Edward Walleys, a weaver, on behalf of Catherine his wife and William Newenham, a collarmaker, on behalf of his wife Agnes entered recognisances to give evidence against Hullett. However, Richard Hullet her husband and

Richard Downeham, both from Barkway, entered recognisances for her appearance. She, too, was found not guilty.[447]

Of course, those on bail also had the advantage of being returned to their communities, to live normally until the next Assizes. They would thus be seen by those who could, or might, testify against them, and such people would have time to dwell on the eventual human implications of their testimony. Those in custody, removed from sight, could be demonized much more easily in the months prior to their trial.

As with a modern court, those who were fortunate enough to be on bail would be summoned at the start of proceedings to answer to their bail. In the seventeenth century, this was done by the Court Cryer shouting: "... come forth, save thee and thy baile, or else thou forfeit thy recognisance."[448]

The Journey to Prison

In theory at least, when a Constable carried a Felon, or someone suspected of Felony, to Gaol, the Gaoler was obliged to receive him.[449] Thus, while awaiting transfer to the local county Gaol, a suspected witch would be put in the charge of a local constable. This might necessitate being held

---

447. *Calendar of Assizes Records Hertfordshire Indictments James 1*, at p.204.
448. T.W., *The Clerk of Assizure, Judges-Marshall, and Cryer: Being The True Manner and form of the proceedings at the Assizes and General Goale-Delivery, both in the Crown Courts, and Nisi Prius Court*, at p.8.
449. Jacob, Giles, *The Compleat Parish Office*, 7th Edn., "Of Constables" at p.21.

in his, or another's, house until transportation could be arranged to the prison, especially if the Examining Justice wished to re-examine the accused person (some were examined up to three times). For example, after her first examination by Robert Darcy, in Essex, in 1582, Ursula Kemp was committed to the "ward and keeping of the constable that night", being returned for a second examination the following day.

Appropriately, given that the early Quakers were sometimes mistakenly accused of witchcraft, the experiences of George Fox (1624-91), provide a vivid illustration of the haphazard measures that were sometimes used to transport suspected felons to the custody of their local gaol (though in his case it was usually for failing to swear oaths or for holding meetings). This is especially the case, as Fox took a keen interest in legal niceties. He, and several other Quakers, were arrested for holding an illegal meeting in 1662 at Swannington, and were ordered to be detained in Leicester gaol, by a JP, and to be conveyed there by the constables in Swannington. The magistrate prepared the "mittimus" for this (the appropriate legal document to commit someone to gaol, it was addressed by the examining JP to the gaoler of the prison in question, and contained details of the prisoner and the nature of his/her offence). However, when the constables had brought the Quakers back to Swannington: "... it being harvest-time, it was hard to get anybody to go with us. The people were loth to take their neighbors to prison, especially in such a busy time." They even offered to let them hand themselves in to the prison, carrying their own *mittimuses*, as had occurred on several occasions in the past with Quakers. However, in this case, Fox refused to be so accommodating, and, in the end:

"... they hired a poor labouring man, who was loth to go, though hired", to accompany them.[450] Although witches would not have been trusted, in the way that Quakers were, to commit themselves without escort, typically, their age, gender, resources and educational profiles probably meant that security was fairly rudimentary after arrest. For some of those accused, the journey to gaol and the Assize town may have been the longest of their lives. Amy Duny would have travelled 40 miles by road to get from Lowestoft to Bury St Edmunds for her detention and trial.

Almost throughout the time that witchcraft was a felony in England, there were two types of prison in the country, despite the fact that imprisonment *per se* was rarely used as a punishment. For vagrants, there were houses of correction, or bridewells where they were sent for both punishment (incarceration and whipping) and also for supervised work. The second type of institution was the local gaol. These were used for the detention of those awaiting trial for felony, or sentence after conviction, and for the imprisonment of debtors. In England, there were numerous such institutions, many being very small, often little more than a gatehouse. Of these the most important were the designated county gaols. These would normally be close to the local Assizes courts to facilitate the delivery of prisoners to the bi-annual trials. Quite frequently, where there was no purpose built gaol, they would be housed in an abandoned castle. It was to these institutions that most of those accused of witchcraft were sent pending the determination of their cases. Thus typically, Margaret Moore and the other witches from

---

450. Fox, George, *The Autobiography of George Fox from his Journal* at p.209.

Sutton, in 1647, were committed to Ely gaol to await their trials in the same city. The Samuels were detained at Huntingdon gaol in 1592, the Flowers in Lincoln gaol, in 1618, and the Suttons were held in that of Bedford in 1613.

This immediately raises questions as to the conditions in which they were kept, and how these might have differed from other prisoners, some of whom may have been wary of any intimacy with a potential witch. The prison authorities, too, probably had special apprehensions about detaining such felons. As a result, although for all prisoners, life in a sixteenth or seventeenth century English gaol was grim, for those accused of witchcraft, it appears to have been particularly unpleasant.

Early Modern Gaols

Although prisoners arrived in the seventeenth century gaol in the custody of the constable, from then onwards they were in the custody of the gaoler. This included those times when they were going to and from their Assizes hearings. As already noted, further examinations of the accused might be carried out in prison, and gaolers frequently took an active part in this process, sometimes on their own, sometimes with visiting magistrates. Elizabeth Stile, having been apprehended for witchcraft at Windsor and examined by Sir Henry Neville, was held in Reading gaol pending the next Assize. While there, she was approached by Thomas Rowe, the gaoler, who urged her to turn herself to God, and "therewithal urged in sign of her repentance to confess her former follies and facts." As a result of his encouragement she "desired to have some talk" with him, and, in the presence of a local constable and two other men, made full admissions also implicating numerous other witches.[451] Sometimes, of course, a gaoler might have a mercenary motive when called to testify against the detained woman as a witness. Ady described one "who also wanted vails [perquisites], and thought the more prisoners were executed, the more he should gain", and so gave testimony against them.[452]

Early modern prisons were squalid places. Although detailed information is often scarce, it is clear that they were laxly organised, overcrowded institutions in which segregation of prisoners (according to sex and offence) was minimal, conditions often filthy and staff corrupt. One pamphlet describing the detention and execution of Mary Barber, a Northamptonshire witch, in 1612, who was held in Northampton gaol pending the Assizes there, observed: the prison made "men be fellows and chambermates with thieves and murderers (the common guests of such despised inns)." Obviously, most of those accused of witchcraft, would have been of a different age and sex to the typical gaol inmate.[453] Except for those with the money to pay for superior accommodation (nearly always available to those wealthy enough) prisons were cramped and verminous. Inmates were crammed together in communal cells, and were dependent on a small bread allowance and charity for their survival. Indicative of the lack of hygiene was the so-called Black Assize, held at Oxford in 1577, where

451. Rosen, Barbara (Ed.), *Witchcraft in England 1558-1618,* at p.85.
452. Ady, *Candle,* at p.102.
453. Reproduced in Rosen, Barbara (Ed.), *Witchcraft in England 1558-1618,* at p.354.

assorted Judges, jurors, and witnesses, died after contracting "gaol fever" (a form of typhus) from the defendants brought up from the local gaol for trial. George Fox's account of the jail in Leicester, in 1662, would have been typical of such institutions. The chief gaoler there was, apparently, a "very wicked, cruel man." He was notorious for putting the Quakers into the dungeon "amongst the felons" (the part of the prison where detained witches would normally be held) where there was "hardly room for them to lie down." According to Fox, they were even refused straw to sleep on. His earlier custody in gaol at Nottingham had been equally unpleasant. It was a: "... nasty, stinking prison; the smell whereof got so into my nose and throat that it very much annoyed me."[454] The dangers were clear. In Yorkshire alone, half a dozen Quakers, imprisoned for non-payment of tithes in Pickering Castle, died while in custody, probably of disease.

The horrors of prison were as well known to those facing witchcraft accusations (even before their committal) as to anyone else. Thus, when Jane Wenham fell down before one of her accuser's feet "begging her not to swear against her, using many expressions of fear, least she be sent to gaol", it was treated as a "discovery of her own Guilt." However, a local physician pointed out the absurdity of drawing such an inference. He observed that there was nobody without "dismal Apprehensions of a Gaol", and no-one "Who thinks of Confinement without Horror?" This was especially the case for an accused witch, usually "an abandoned wretch, without friends or money", and

---

454. Fox, George, *The Autobiography of George Fox from his Journal,* at p.209.

"detested by the whole parish." As this last passage indicates, one of the primary reasons that witches would find custodial life so unpleasant, even by the standards of the times, was their social isolation and poverty. On the whole they had no money to buy the luxuries or better conditions that could be secured, for a price, in the entrepreneurial gaols of early-modern England,[455] and no friends to bring in supplies of food and drink. There would be few outsiders prepared to provide charity for a witch, as sometimes occurred for other inmates. Additionally she could expect to make few friends amongst the other prisoners, who would look upon her with fear and loathing. As was noted, of Wenham, her lack of money meant that in gaol "under her circumstances, she could expect nothing less than a Course of misery and Hardship worse than death."[456] Coroners' inquisitions on the deaths of inmates at Colchester gaol in Essex, suggest that no fewer than 21 women accused of witchcraft died while in custody there, between 1560 and 1603.[457] This was not unusual; when the Lancashire witches of 1612, were held in Lancaster castle, the local gaol, the octogenarian Elizabeth Sowtherns, swiftly "dyed in the castle before she came to her Tryall."

The harsh treatment was exacerbated by a widespread fear, on the part of both the keepers and other inmates, that the imprisoned witch might use her powers to effect diabolical schemes. This was despite the fact that many commentators believed that witches were rendered

---

455. Significantly, the gaoler at Bedford prison in the 1680s, Richard Freeborne, was also an Innkeeper.
456. Pamphlet 1712, at p.20.
457. Macfarlane, Alan, *Witchcraft in Tudor and Stuart England*, at p.60.

powerless once brought before a Justice (Satan apparently respecting the office!) or taken into custody. One physician writing in 1712, thought that it was "a received Opinion, that Witches had no power over a person after being in the hands of a Justice." This was merely a late manifestation of an already long-standing belief. According to some, two of the seven recognised "cures" for witchcraft were linked to the criminal justice process itself. The first was to "punish the witch", and the other lay in the belief held by James VI, that "If the witch is imprisoned, she is void of hurt, and Satan leaves her."[458] Interestingly, King James was convinced that Satan only lost his power if a witch was held lawfully, a view that might have discouraged mob action. If the "forme of their detention" was irregular, for example, if they were apprehended and detained by any "... private person, upon other private respectes, their power no doubt either in escaping or in doing hurte, is no lesse nor ever it was before." By contrast if their apprehension and detention was carried out by a: "... lawfull Magistrate, upon the just respectes of their guiltinesse in that craft, their power is then no greater then before that ever they medled with the matter. For where God beginnes justlie to strike by his lawfull Lieutenentes, it is not in the Devilles power to defraude or bereave him of the office, or effect of his powerful and revenging Scepter."[459] William Drage, a

---

458. *Daimonomageia* at pp.5-7. The others were to "call upon GOD", "Use special medicines, antipathetical to Demons," "Use, or make the witch use the Ceremonie of ridding the sickness;" make her take the disease herself; find charms hidden about [her] house. The special medicines might have included rosemary and birch bark, which were believed to have anti-witch properties.

459. James VI & I, *Daemonologie*, at p.51.

physician who, despite his calling, still believed in the power of enchantment to make men ill (even in 1666), was slightly more cautious about the effects of custody. He felt that once imprisoned a witch was "void of hurt and Satan leaves her." However, although this prevented fresh cases of bewitchment, it did not automatically cure those already afflicted by a spell. This was dependent on how the Devil chose to address the situation: "... sometimes she then acquits those she hath bewitched, if Satan will give leave."[460] The origin of this popular belief might have lain in the *Malleus Maleficarum* itself. According to this classic work, one of the three classes of men who could not be injured by witches (the other two being exorcists and those "specially blessed" by the angels) were "those who administer public justice against them [witches] or who prosecute them in any public official capacity." According to Krämer and Sprenger, some German witches had even bourne witness to the fact that "merely because they have been taken by the officials of public justice, they have immediately lost all their powers of witchcraft." The rationale for this was that, as all power ultimately came from God, avengers of wickedness against God would themselves be protected. It also, of course, provided a ready explanation as to why such allegedly powerful people could be brought to judgment without either escaping or killing the court officers.[461]

Nevertheless, this belief was clearly not universal (or even widely held). In an unusual case from 1574, one "Mother Arnold" was convicted and executed at Barking

460. Drage, William, *A Treatise of Diseases from Witchcraft* at p.24.

461. Sprenger, Jacob and Krämer, Heinrich, *Malleus Maleficarum* (1486), Translated by Montague Summers at pp.89 and 90.

Assizes for witchcraft. Clement Sisley, the JP who examined her prior to trial, and who had warned her that he was about to commit her to prison, promptly became one of her victims. When he "tooke paper in his hand to make his warrant [of committal] suddainly both his feete were taken from him", causing him to collapse and putting his thigh bone out of joint. This meant that he could not move for three weeks, and was dependent on crutches for a long time afterwards.[462] Similarly Jane Wenham was supposed to have appeared to her victim, Anne Thorn, from gaol.[463] Many were obviously terrified that the power of witches survived even when they were detained, and used this to justify stricter confinement than normal. This might include the permanent, and heavy, shackling of such (often feeble) prisoners. Accused witches were much more likely than others (especially of their gender and age) to be kept chained up. Thus, a 1612 pamphlet noted that the "jangling of irons" in the Northampton prison that held Anne Barber failed to make her mindful of the chains that she was likely to wear for eternity (suggesting that she had herself been held in irons).[464] Similarly, in 1674, the elderly Ann Foster, also held in Northampton Gaol, was confined in the same way: "No sooner was she brought in, but the Keepers of the Gaol caused her to be chained close to a Post that was in the Gaol." Not surprisingly, the effect of binding her aged limbs so tightly produced drastic consequences, and her body

---

462. Gibson, Marion, *Mother Arnold: A Lost Witchcraft Pamphlet Rediscovered* in *Notes and Queries*. September (1998), pp.296-300 at p.297.

463. Pamphlet 1712(2), at p.40.

464. Reproduced in Rosen, Barbara (Ed.), *Witchcraft in England 1558-1618*, at p.354.

began to swell. This caused her to cry out in a "most lamentable manner" so that they were forced to unchain her again. Unfortunately, the result of this charitable indulgence was apparently only: "... to give her more liberty that the devil might come to fuck her, the which he usually did, coming constantly in the dead time of the Night in the likeness of a Rat, which at his coming made a most lamentable and hideous noise which affrighted the people that did belong to the Gaol." That such gaols were usually overrun with vermin made discovering an appropriate familiar easy. The many visitors who came to see Foster during her incarceration: "... could see nothing but things like rats, and heard a most terrible noise."[465]

Another illustration of the belief that a witch's power could survive incarceration involved those at Warboys in 1593. After they were imprisoned, they apparently added the gaoler's son to the people they had afflicted. However, in this situation, at least, the gaoler had the advantage of physical control over them, something which allowed him to bring Mother Samuel, their alleged principal, to his son's bedside, where he held her physically until his son scratched her, and thus "drew her blood". This ended her power over him, and led to the boy's recovery.

Whether or not they lost their powers after lawful detention, it was believed that the Devil could still visit his own in gaol, unless they were "penitent and confesse", in which case God would "not permit him to trouble them anie more with his presence and allurementes." Satan could still

465. Pamphlet 1674, at p.6. If the keepers were sufficiently tipped many prisons were periodically opened to the public so that they could view the inmates for entertainment.

appear to incarcerated yet unrepentant witches, encouraging them to kill themselves to avoid trial, or, alternatively, holding out hopes for their survival. On these occasion he might appear in "divers forms" to the imprisoned witches, and their fellow prisoners (there for ordinary crimes) might even see these visits, but, conveniently, would not always do so: "... some-times they will, and some-times not, as it pleases God."[466]

A policy of special restrictions was also justified by reported cases of supernatural escape. One boy, of less than nine years of age, who was detained as a witch in the mid to late 1640s, his mother having earlier been executed for the same crime in 1645, was supposed to have a familiar who appeared in the form of a mare. It was believed that he had used this supernatural horse to facilitate the escape of a fellow prisoner: "But after he was in Burie Goale, not long before the Assizes, the first since these warres [English civil war] the Goaler questioned this boy, and upon some threatening speeches, the boy confessed, that he was gone home on his mare over the walls, and shewed where, and told him he should finde him with his wife." This was given general credence when the man was discovered 12 miles away, still shackled, with his spouse.

Supernatural interference not withstanding, security in most early modern gaols was fairly lax, as can be seen in the relative ease with which Charles Courtney, a "gentleman" burglar, twice escaped from London's Newgate prison when he was confined there in 1612 (less than a decade before the Edmonton witch, Elizabeth Sawyers, was incarcerated there

---

466. James VI and I, *Daemonologie* at pp.51-53.

in 1621). This was despite the fact that Newgate would certainly have been superior to the average county gaol in its level of security. In the second attempt, both he, and his accomplice "Sly", managed to get clean away. By Courtney's account, having carefully examined the prison and its warders for weaknesses: "I had searching eies touching the strength of the prison, the condition and humor of the officers", he acted to avoid his appointment with the executioner. The escape was effected by means of a rope ladder, improvised from cords and sticks, which he used to get into an outer yard, having fastened it to the battlements on the roof of the prison. Once in the yard: "... by means of a ladder, which by chaunce we found there, got into the streete", and escaped into the City. (He was subsequently recaptured, executed, and his body "begd by thee Barbar surgeons for an anatomie".)[467] At Salem, in America, a significant number of those detained for witchcraft also managed to effect escapes from the local gaols they were held in, prisons that would have been similar to their English counterparts. As a result, they saved their lives, though their estates were seized by the authorities, as was common in such cases. Thus, Robert Calef noted: "Edward Bishop and his wife having made their escape out of prison, this day Mr.Corwin, the sheriff, came and seized his goods and chattels." Later, "Mr. Philip English, and his wife having made their escape out of prison, Mr.Corwin, the sheriff, seized his estate, to the value of about fifteen hundred pound, which was wholly lost to him, except about three

467. Pamphlet 1612 at p.16.

hundred pound value (which was afterward restored)."[468]

It might be wondered why more witches in England did not escape? Undoubtedly, a few who were hale and hearty must have done so. Certainly several others were recorded as being fugitives from justice having avoided arrest after a warrant had been issued, such as Mother Saunder of Muche Bardwell in Essex in 1591. Nonetheless the number of escapees was comparatively small. However, a brief comparison with America probably explains this. The unusual profile of many of those detained at Salem: younger, more often married or male, better educated, and more articulate, in a vast, but still English speaking land like the Americas, and often with recourse to outside assistance, meant that they were in a much better position than those normally detained for the crime in England. The main deterrent to escape, for most of the simple, confused and often elderly, women accused, was that they had nowhere else to go. They were often familiar only with their own villages, places in which they had spent their whole lives, and to which they evidently could not return.

For much of the witch trial period, modern notions of *habeas corpus*, although in the process of development, were largely absent (especially for impoverished women). Although it built on a disputed interpretation of rather ambiguous words in Magna Carta, the Habeas Corpus Act was only passed in 1679. It obliged a Judge to issue, upon request, a writ directing a gaoler to produce a prisoner and show cause for his or her imprisonment. It also provided that a prisoner should be indicted in the first term of his

---

468. Calef, Robert, *More Wonders of the Invisible World*, at pp.265 and 266.

commitment, tried no later than the second term, and once set free by court order should not be imprisoned again for the same offence. Prior to the Act, when a witch was acquitted at Salisbury in 1676, a local Knight and JP, Sir James Long, was apparently "extremely concerned" at her being at liberty, fearing that she would drive people away from his lands. As a result, to "save the poor gentleman's estate", Mr Justice Rainsford "ordered the woman to be kept in gaol", and that the town should allow her 2s.6d. per week. The Knight's initial thanks, however, soon turned to dismay as he became alarmed at the excessive cost of keeping her in prison. At the very next Assize he came back to the Judge: "... to desire his lordship would let her come back to the town. and why? They could keep her for 1s. 6d. there; and in gaol, she cost them a shilling more."[469]

Prison Fees

For those detained before their trial, even acquittal did not necessarily bring immediate release, as it was normal to pay the gaoler fees for time spent in prison. In default of payment by the accused (or another on his or her behalf) he could keep the person in custody, even though their innocence had been established (though, in many cases, the trouble of doing so if the prisoner was obviously impoverished may have led to this being waived). In one Quaker tract, from 1659, it was noted that when one George Whitehead was discharged at the Sessions, the keeper of

469. North, Roger, *The Lives of the Right Hon. Francis North ...* at p.269. Long is also mentioned by John Aubrey as an examiner of witches.

Norwich gaol, where he had been in custody: "... brought his action against him for 4d. a night; and although he had layn on the floor most part of the time, yet was by him unjustly detained."[470] This provision, which applied to alleged witches as much as to any other type of acquitted felon, was a constant source of grievance for all defendants who were found "not guilty." It was something that was manifest in the unprecedented degree of criticism of the judicial system that was voiced in popular tracts, as censorship became less effective during the early part of the Interregnum. England's prisons, and the conditions in which people were detained in them, were especially unpopular, and the fees that had to be paid aroused the bitterest feelings. One commentator noted that it was a common course to keep "poore creatures sometimes two or three years in prison, upon this account merely for their Fees; nay in every County Hell in England the villainous Jaylors have some miserable soules, whom they chaine, begging there meerly for money to pay their fees the Hellhounds doe exact of them."[471]

Many of those eventually released at Salem, in America, also remained in custody afterwards, living in the atrocious conditions of the local gaols, and awaiting payment of their prison fees. Thus, the elderly Sarah Dustin, although acquitted at the trials of oyer and terminer, could not meet the expenses of the local prison where she had been detained, and : "was remanded in prison for her fees, and there in a short time expired."[472] Another prisoner at Salem,

---

470. Pamphlet 1659 at p.81.
471. Pamphlet 1653(2) at p.36.
472. Calef, Robert, *More Wonders of the Invisible World*, at p.334.

Margaret Jacobs, was only let out after a stranger paid them on her behalf (though he later sued her for the cost, which she eventually repaid).

Chapter 12

The Trial Process

"Who is so deaf or so blind as he
That wilfully will neither hear nor see?"
English Proverb. Collected in: J. Heywood's
Dialogue of Proverbs (1546).

Sources of Information

Our knowledge of the details of early-modern witch trials is necessarily incomplete. English court records, even where they survive, are normally extremely thin for this period. Indictments provided the nature of each offence, the date that it was alleged to have occurred, and the parish of residence of the accused person (though this latter point is sometimes unreliable). The plea, verdict and sentence are also usually recorded on the indictment. However, details as to the defendant's age, and the evidence adduced against them are usually absent. Until 1731, such information as there was, was normally written in court Latin, with numerous conventional abbreviations (again, apart from a brief period in the Interregnum). If the prisoner admitted the charge against him/her (something that was judicially discouraged and much rarer than today), the indictment was simply marked *cognovit* (he acknowledged), and the matter was put back for sentence until after the other trials in the session had been completed. If he, or she, pleaded "not guilty," the clerk would mark the indictment *po se*, an abbreviation of *ponit se sper patriam* (puts himself upon his country). A death sentence was recorded by the entry *sus per coll*, being short for *suspendatur per collum*.[473] Apart from the records for the home circuit, which survive from 1559, most available indictments date from the seventeenth century. Occasionally, the sworn written deposition of a witness, originally taken before the examining Justice of the Peace also survives, and has been appended to the papers on the case. Along with these records, the Judges' commissions, and their "calendars" (lists of prisoners to be tried), also sometime survive.

However, supplementing these official sources are large numbers of pamphlets and tracts, ranging in degrees of reliability from the highly accurate to the extremely fanciful and unreliable. There are also a number of published books from the era. Many of these cover felony trials generally, and are essential in reconstructing the forensic environment for such hearings. Some of them comment directly on witch trials, others touch on them tangentially. Amongst the most important is that of Thomas Potts, published in 1613, and based on his personal experience as the court clerk during the major witch trials that occurred in Lancashire in 1612. The number of trials, and crimes of witchcraft alleged there, was "knowen to exceed all others at any time heretofore." Nineteen men and women were tried, and seven executed.[474] Potts considered his publication was necessary

---

473. Stockdale, Eric, *A Study of Bedford Prison*, at p.22.

474. Potts, Thomas, *The Wonderful Discoverie of Witches in the Countie of Lancaster. With the arraignement and Triall of Nineteene notorious Witches, at the Assizes and generall Gaole deliverie, holden at the Castle of Lancaster, upon Munday, the seventeenth of August last 1612. Before Sir James Altham, and Sir Edward Bromley, Knights; Barons of his Majesties Court of Exchequer: and justices of Assizes ...* at p.B1.

to explain why some of the accused had been acquitted, something which apparently caused several prosecution witnesses to "rest very discontented." He also intended it to stand as a general warning to the nation about the danger of witchcraft. As a clerk, his legal expertise meant that his work provided a rare professional insight into a Jacobean witch trial (though he was clearly not an impartial observer). It also influenced many subsequent writers on the subject, and thus later trials for witchcraft.

The Court Building

A building would be set aside for the Assizes hearings, though it would have other uses when the courts were not sitting (ie, for most of the year). Thus, the Assizes Sessions for 1662, at Bury St Edmunds (the borough having been a regular venue for such hearings from 1187), was held in the Shirehall, near the centre of the town. This building contained two large rooms, one for civil cases (those heard nisi prius) and a slightly bigger one for the Crown side (ie, criminal matters including cases of witchcraft). These rooms were overlooked by a public gallery for spectators. There were also smaller, separate, rooms for the Grand Jury to meet before the Assizes to determine if there was a case to answer, and for witnesses to wait in, before giving their evidence.[475]

475. Geis, Gilbert and Bunn, Ivan, *A Trial of Witches: A Seventeenth-Century Witchcraft Prosecution*, at pp.30 and 31.

Conviction Rates for Witchcraft

A conviction, followed by execution, was by no means a certainty, or often even likely, in witch cases. The most extensive statistical research into such trials, that carried out by C. L'Estrange Ewen in the late 1920s, determined that, on the home circuit at least, comparatively few accused witches actually suffered death when brought before the normal Assizes courts. Allowing for acquittals and post-conviction reprieves by the trial judge (a situation in which a convicted witch would usually be returned to prison for a year or more pending her release back into the community), 81 out of 100 escaped the rope. However, levels of conviction and execution fluctuated significantly within this period. During its peak, in the last six years of Elizabeth's reign, and the first four of that of James I, 41 per cent of those tried went to the gallows, and trials were relatively frequent.[476]

Surviving gaol calendars suggest that if the numbers of those found "not guilty" by the petty jury, are combined with those whose Bills were marked ignoramus, by the Grand Jury, at least one half of all who were indicted for witchcraft on the home circuit, between 1560 and 1680, were ultimately acquitted.[477] This pattern of acquittal (and, if there was a conviction, reprieve) does not appear to have been untypical for the remainder of the country, and also seems to have applied in New England. Thus, when, in 1670, Katherine Harrison was imprisoned for 12 months and then tried at Hartford, Connecticut, she was "found guilty by the

476. L'Estrange Ewen, C., *Witch Hunting and Witch Trials*, at p.31.
477. Cockburn, J.S., *A History of English Assizes*, 1558-1714, at pp.120-127.

jury, but acquit by the Bench, and released out of prison, [though with an encouragement to leave the town] putting her in minde of her promise to remove."[478]

An acquittal was still possible, even where there was strong suspicion against the accused, supported by apparently tangible evidence. Edward Bromley was clearly convinced that some of those acquitted in 1612 were guilty of the crimes for which they had stood trial (and over which he had presided). He went so far as to give a homily to them, urging them to: "... presume no further of your Innocencie than you have just cause: for although it pleased God out of his Mercie, to spare you at this time, yet without question there are amongst you, that are as deepe in this action, as any of them that are condemned to die for their offences." He exhorted them to forsake the devil as a matter of urgency.[479] His address was very similar to that given to the acquitted Sarah Dustin at one of the final Salem trials, by Judge Danforth. He admonished her, saying: "Woman, woman, repent; there are shrewd things come against you."[480]

The Grand Jury

Before a witch could even come for trial, the Grand Jury would have to have been satisfied that there was a case to answer. There were two Grand Juries, one for Quarter

---

478. Jameson, Franklin, (Ed.), *Narratives of the Witchcraft cases 2648-1706*, at p.47.
479. Davies, Peter, *The Trial of the Lancaster Witches*, at p.v4.
480. Calef, Robert, *More Wonders of the Invisible World*, at p.33.

Sessions, and one, socially by far the more prestigious, for the Assizes. The latter body attracted quite substantial men, usually of significantly greater social and economic standing than those who would preside over the trial itself. As Giles Jacob was to note at the beginning of the eighteenth century: "The Qualifications are £80 per Ann. Freehold, for a Grand Juryman; and £10 per Ann. Freehold or Copyhold, for a Petty Juryman." This meant that most villagers were not sufficiently wealthy to serve on either jury involved in the Assizes, and the overwhelming majority failed to qualify for the Grand Jury. [481]

As a result, members of the Assize Grand Jury were frequently gentlemen, so that the Grand Jury that presided over the decision to send for trial six witches in Kent, in 1652, could be described as "consisting of persons of good integrity, and estates." Because of their status, these men were also charged with making General recommendations about law breaking in their own localities. However, their main judicial function was to exercise a supervisory role. Although the JPs committed the accused to trial, the Grand Jury decided whether they should be indicted to stand that trial. It sat privately at the start of each Assizes, to decide whether there was a case that should go for trial by the Judge and "petty" jury; this meant that: "... no Man's Life is to be tried but by the Oaths of Twelve Men, and by the Preparatory Accusation or Indictment by Twelve Men or more precedent to his Trial."[482] Decisions were reached by a simple majority (unlike the trial, or "petty" jury, which had

---

481. Jacob, Giles, *The Compleat Parish Officer*, 7th Edn. at p.24.
482. Hale, Mathew, *The History of the Common Law of England ... Written by a Learned Hand*, at p.264.

to be unanimous), so that an odd number was usual, with up to 23 men being selected, and 15 or 17 being common. If the Grand Jury found no case to answer, it would return a finding of *ignoramus*; if it thought that trial was warranted, it would return a *Billa vera* or "true Bill". Because of its generally higher social and educational level, something that often put it at some distance from the tensions in the locality in which an allegation had arisen, it provided a potentially vital judicial function in giving a cool consideration to accusations. Thus it could prevent undeserving but emotive cases, such as those involving witchcraft, going before the trial jury, a body that was likely to show significantly less detachment and sophistication. This responsibility to provide an independent scrutiny of the strength of the cases against those committed for trial, was reflected in the oath that their foreman had to take. He was asked to declare that he would: "... present no man for envy, hatred or malice, neither shall you leave any man unpresented for love, fear, favour or affection."[483] Significantly, Bernard specifically addressed his major work on witchcraft of 1627 to the Grand Jury, perhaps because he knew that they would be less prejudiced and more capable of rational argument. As Bernard remarked, it was incumbent on Grand Jurors not to leave trial jurors (a "Jury of Simple men") to determine a difficult allegation of witchcraft, unless the evidence in the case was "very Cleere."

For normal felonies, the Grand Jury does appear to have infused the law with common sense notions of prudence.

483. T.W., *The Clerk of Assize, Judges-Marshall, and Cryer: Being The True Manner and form of the proceedings at the Assizes and General Goale-Delivery, both in the Crown Courts, and Nisi Prius Court*, at p.5.

Most of the cases that they rejected in Sussex (up to a fifth of all cases that came before them) were returned ignoramus because of perceived deficiencies in the evidence underlying them, rather than for purely technical reasons (though there were regular cases of this as well). In particular, they searched for a cohesive charge, one that connected criminal with crime. They appear to have disliked cases based only on slender circumstantial evidence, such as opportunity, and charges that appeared to be founded in malice. In routine criminal cases Grand Juries appear to have preferred cases that were founded on sound witness detection, and searched for supporting witnesses, and for allegations that were made neither without proper thought, nor late after the evidence had become known.[484] If this was typical of early modern Grand Juries in England generally, and there is no reason to believe it was not, it can be seen what problems witchcraft cases were likely to pose to this body.

Perhaps not surprisingly, surviving gaol calendars suggest that during the seventeenth century about 12 per cent of all Assizes Bills in witchcraft cases were returned ignoramus and so thrown out without going to trial.[485] A classic illustration of this occurred in the January of 1615, in Buckinghamshire, when Alice Stevens, a widow, was accused by one Elizabeth Mason, of bewitching her baby to death. Stevens said that this accusation was made to avoid repaying a debt of £12, owed by Mason to her. She stated that Mason had obtained a warrant for her arrest (for witchcraft) and then offered not to execute it on condition

484. *See* on this generally, Herrup, Cynthia, *The Common Peace*, at pp.68 and 114.

485. Cockburn, J.S., *A History of English Assizes, 1558-1714*, at p.127.

that Alice released her from her debt and also "gave a further recompense of 20l." Significantly, there had been a substantial delay, five months, between the death of the baby and Mason obtaining the warrant used as blackmail. As the warrant was being executed by two local constables, Stevens was scratched by Mason until blood flowed, Mason, perhaps a natural actor, vowing to prosecute her to her death: "This blood shall not serve our turne, we will have hart blood." However, on March 1, at Aylesbury, at the start of the Assizes, the Grand Jury returned the Bill of indictment ignoramus, and Stevens walked free. She subsequently took proceedings against Mason in the Star Chamber.[486]

The Grand Jury's decision was substantially based on the depositions taken by the justices in their initial examination, though they could, and frequently did, also receive oral evidence. Thus, the Grand Jury that sat to consider the case against the six women accused by Edward Fairfax at the Assizes in York in August 1622, called Fairfax and all the other prosecution witnesses live to give testimony before them, which they did: "... upon our oaths before the Grand Jury, who were all of them gentlemen of such wisdom and discretion ... Six of them were justices of peace." Having questioned all the witnesses, they found every indictment to be Billa vera.[487] Nevertheless, the Grand Jury was not totally detached from outside influences. Members of the judiciary could certainly make their views known to them. Thus, in Fairfax's case the Grand Jury had

---

486. L'Estrange Ewen, C., *Witchcraft in the Star Chamber,* at p.43.
487. Pamphlet 1621(1), at p.234.

been warned by the trial Judge of the need for special caution before finding a true Bill: "... they received also a good caveat, by a message from the Judge to be very careful in the matter of Witches; which message was delivered to them in my hearing."[488]

The Judges

One feature of early modern Assizes trials, on which all observers agree, was their high level of judicial involvement (or interference). The Judge was a dominant presence in the courtroom, even by modern standards. (They would often be accompanied by local dignitaries on the Bench, such as the Lord Lieutenant and High Sheriff of the county, but these served an ornamental rather than functional purpose.) Because of this, judicial attitudes to witchcraft generally were potentially crucial to the outcome of the trial. A sceptical Judge might encourage a jury to find a reason to acquit by pouring scorn on such evidence as was admitted, or, refusing to admit evidence that might encourage a conviction. Thus, it was widely believed that Lord Chief Justice Holt, who, as part of his Assizes duties, was required to preside over the trials of at least 11 witches, helped ensure their acquittals on every occasion by his overt scepticism.[489] Conversely, an enthusiast might encourage

488. *Ibid.*, at p.234.

489. According to Francis Hutchinson, Holt acquitted witches on 11 occasions, so he certainly had more experience than did Hale, who appears only to have presided over three witch trials. In March 1669 Isabel Rigby of Lancaster was sentenced to death by Hale for the bewitching of two neighbours at Hindley.

conviction. In reality, however, as will be seen, whatever their personal views, they were often heavily circumscribed by the need to preserve good relations with the trial jury.

Origins of the Assizes Judges

Who were the Assizes Judges who presided over these witch trials? If Thomas Potts is to be believed, they were men of whom it could be said that: "GOD Almightie, hath singled them out, and set them on his seat, for the Defence of Justice." More mundanely, Judges in England developed from the twelfth century members of the Curia Regis. As the English legal profession emerged, the practice developed of appointing Judges to the Westminster courts from amongst the most eminent of these lawyers, in turn, these men went on Assizes duty round the circuits.[490] As a result, Mathew Hale could observe (in a manuscript written before his death in 1676, though not published until 1713), that the Assizes, were tried by people: "... well acquainted with the Common Law, and for the most Part are Two of those Twelve ordinary Justices who are appointed for the Common Dispensation of Justice in the Three great courts at Westminster."[491]

Invariably, they would have started their careers as lawyer-advocates before being raised to the Bench. As a result of the barristers' swift emergence during the 1500s, by the late sixteenth and seventeenth centuries, there were two

490. Baker, J.H., *An Introduction to English Legal History*, at p.178.
491. Hale, Matthew, *The History of the Common Law of England ... Written by a Learned Hand*, at p.255.

types of senior lawyer fulfilling the advocacy function in England, in Blackstone's words "advocates or (as we Generally call them) counsel [fall into] ... two species or degrees, barristers and sergeants."[492] Both professions produced Judges. An effective monopoly of judicial appointments to the courts of King's Bench, Common Pleas and Exchequer had been held for centuries by the Serjeants at Law. However, this was ended by the increasing practice (observed by John Stow to be well established by 1598), of making barristers Serjeants, as a purely formal and procedural measure, before promoting them (often on the very same day) to the Bench (the need for this was only abolished by the Judicature Act of 1873). This ended the monopoly on judicial posts held by "real" (ie, formerly practising) Serjeants. Many famous Judges from the seventeenth century, such as Edward Coke, were appointed in this way. Typically, Edward Bromley, who presided over the trial of the Pendle witches in 1612, had been made a Serjeant on February 5, 1610, and a Baron of the Exchequer in the same month. Socially, both groups of lawyer would be largely recruited from the traditional gentry families, but with a very significant admixture from the sons of successful merchants, clerics etc.

Increasing Judicial Professionalism and its Consequences for Witch Trials

England's Judges were becoming progressively more

---

492. Blackstone, William, *Commentaries on the Laws of England*, Vol.3, at p.26.

"professional" throughout the witch-hunting period. From the middle of the seventeenth century judicial standards appear to have improved especially rapidly. This was most obviously manifest in hardening attitudes towards judicial corruption, something that had been widespread at the start of the era. In 1604, Sir William Wentworth could still openly advise his son to procure a Judge's "opinion with discretion and gifts", suggesting satin doublets and horses as appropriate douceurs. Even in 1638, Richard Braithwaite, a student at Gray's Inn, prayed that God might deal with Judges so that He would: "Remove from them covetousness ... [and] revenge in their hearts." Francis Bacon was surprised when he was impeached and dismissed as Lord Chancellor, in 1621, for taking bribes. However, significantly, and indicative of future reforms, Sir Henry Montagu, when he became Chief Justice of the court of King's Bench in 1616, promised that "no man shall justly tax me ... [with] corruption." Sir Edward Coke in his celebrated *Institutes* also lambasted judicial corruption. Gradually, such attitudes became more widespread, especially after the mid-seventeenth century.

It has been argued that, after 1688, and especially after the Act of Settlement of 1701, the reduction in monarchical interference with the judiciary, contributed to a growing judicial self-confidence and public-standing.[493] They were, increasingly, seen to be professional men exercising a special calling, rather than place-men. It may be that as this occurred they also became increasingly reluctant to tolerate the travesty of due process that witch trials so often were. It

---

493. *See* on this Grest, W., *Judicial Corruption in Early Modern England.*

is almost inconceivable that by 1692, a series of trials as extensive as that seen at Salem, and resulting in so many executions, could have occurred in England. The judiciary would have prevented it from happening. By contrast, at Salem, the Judges, though not totally inexperienced in the law, were still amateurs, at best approximating in their degree of legal knowledge to the better JPs that sat in English Quarter Sessions. They were certainly devoid of the learning and experience that characterised the typical Assize Judge by this time.

Somewhat incongruously, although the Interregnum was to see a revival in levels of witch persecution in some parts of England, English lawyers sent into Scotland were also to show the potential power of a sceptical judiciary to prevent such local witch hunts. After the Rump Parliament abolished the monarchy in England, the Scots, unwilling to limit the Stuart Crown to their own country, proclaimed and crowned Charles II King of Great Britain (and thus England too). This prompted an English invasion, with the conquest and subsequent incorporation of Scotland into an expanded English state. As part of this process, not only was Scotland's parliament abolished, and the power of its nobility greatly reduced, but English Judges were sent north of the border to promote the integration of the two countries' legal systems. Faced with a plethora of witchcraft cases, they tended to be overtly sceptical. The advanced scepticism of the English Judges arriving in Scotland, when compared with their more superstitious Scottish predecessors, produced a near eradication of witch hunting during the early period of Cromwell's rule in that country. In 1652, the Cromwellian Commissioners for the Administration of Justice in Scotland were faced with 60 cases of alleged witchcraft. However, they found "so much malice and so little proof against them that none were condemend." They were also shocked at the Scottish use of torture, and demanded that the "tormentors" involved be found out. The revelations of mistreatment suffered by witches held in custody, such as being forced to wear "hair shirts dipp'd in vinegar put on them to fetch off the skin", or being starved and forced to lie on cold stones, were considered "enough for reasonable men to lament on." As a result, witch cases were reduced to a trickle, at least until 1657, when they increased sharply again. Whether this increase was due to the English Judges adopting native attitudes towards the crime, or whether it was as a result of domestic pressure within Scotland, in areas such as Alloa and Ayr, is not clear. However, there were 40 executions for witchcraft in Scotland in the years 1658 and 1659.[494]

Ironically, one of the best examples of the new ethical and professional breed of Judge, Mathew Hale, was also a firm (and very late) believer in the reality of witchcraft. As a Judge he did much to preserve trials for the crime into the Post-Restoration period. Hale had a well deserved reputation for outstanding integrity. Shortly after being appointed a Judge, in 1654, he had established 18 cardinal Rules for a Judge, whereby he should conduct his own judicial business, stressing the need for fairness, compassion, honesty, lack of prejudice, and an absence of personal bias. He seems to have conducted himself according to these lights for the remainder of his career. At first sight, this makes his decisions in the witch trial at Bury St Edmunds in 1662 appear so strange. However, he was

494. Larner, Christina, *Enemies of God: the Witch-hunt in Scotland,* at p.75.

also a firm believer in the scriptural foundation for witchcraft, and the menace that it posed to society, and was convinced, more generally, that Judges necessarily had to make hard decisions to preserve the social fabric. Illustrative of his attitude to the law was the diary he kept while on circuit in the early autumn of 1668. He felt that the proper administration of justice was essential to society, without it a people would "soon become a heap of confusion and disorder, a forest of wild beasts." The office of Judge, if properly conducted, was "full of labor and pains" and required a mind not only "constantly possessed with a love of justice", but one that was also permanently "awed with the fear of almighty God." He accepted that in such a position, a man was certain to displease some, and often all, parties. He also, realistically, accepted that mistakes would occur, even in a trial process in which the presiding Judge would rather acquit 10 guilty people, than let one innocent man be convicted. That these would include convictions in felony cases made it inevitable that, "many an innocent man has suffered even death itself." Being a Judge was not for the faint-hearted. Nevertheless, the inherent problem in witchcraft cases lay in the nature of the evidence admitted to prove them. By 1668, this was often evidence of a type that Hale himself had concluded was generally unsafe to found a conviction on. He believed that: "In cases especially of life it is ordinarily a safe rule not to condemn a person as guilty upon such evidence as might befall the most innocent person living; it is a great adventure in any Judge that out of the abhorrence he has of a crime imputed barely upon circumstances to conclude a person guilty, which circumstances may nevertheless befall a person innocent." Whether his development of this view was linked to his experiences in Bury St Edmunds in 1662 is hard to say.[495] However, given that in March 1669, Isabel Rigby of Lancaster was sentenced to death by Hale for bewitching two neighbours at Hindley, it may be that his opinions on the issue had not changed greatly.

It is, perhaps, salutary to remember that Assizes Judges, when sitting in the Westminster courts, or dealing with other types of case on circuit, would address problems and issues that are readily familiar to modern lawyers, often in a highly sophisticated manner. In doing so they established principles that are still fundamental to present-day common law. Thus, Lord Chief Justice Holt was highly influential in the development of the distinction between warranties and conditions, and also notions of "executory consideration", in

495. Diary reproduced in Jansson, M., *Mathew Hale on Judges and Judging,* at pp.201-213. Mathew Hale was born in 1609. After his father's death, his education was supervised by a noted Puritan, Anthony Kingland, and by a local Vicar. This undoubtedly shaped his future beliefs. He went up to Oxford where he was influenced in the direction of the law by Serjeant Glanville. As a result, he entered Lincoln's Inn when he was 20, and there, apparently, spent up to 16 hours a day studying; he also read widely in the classics and theology. Hale was certainly a deeply religious man (he attended church twice every Sunday), something that heavily influenced his legal thought. Perhaps significantly, only his religious works, and not his extensive, and very important, legal ones, were published during his own lifetime. According to his friend, Richard Baxter, on one occasion, when a horse that Hale was riding on the Sabbath became lame, he took this as a sign of divine anger, and never profaned the holy day in such a way again. However, although twice married it has also been argued that Hale was a misogynist, though the evidence for this is slender. His first wife had been very extravagant, and he was, perhaps as a result, a strong critic of vain women (though this was a common enough theme in the period). Whether this influenced his views on witches, most of whom were female, is hard to assess.

the law of contract.[496] In his case, it is safe to assume that he found all allegations of bewitchment ridiculous, as did most of his brother Judges by the early 1700s. However, some equally able and significant members of the judiciary, only a few decades earlier, had been firm believers in witchcraft.

Interventionist Judges

As previously noted, and unlike a present-day trial, the presiding Judge took a very active role in the early modern hearing, often being the only man present with a legal training. He would ask questions of the witnesses, and usually make his opinion on the merits of the case clear to the jurors. It was axiomatic that a trial Judge should provide them with: "... a great Light and Assistance by his weighing the Evidence before them, and observing where the Question and Knot of the Business lies, and by shewing them his Opinion even in Matter of Fact, which is a great Advantage and Light to Lay-Men."[497] As in the modern period, if the evidence did not appear remotely credible, the presiding Judge could halt proceedings on his own initiative, though this was rare. Nevertheless, it occurred in Edward Fairfax's witchcraft case in Yorkshire, in 1622, to his evident chagrin: "... but the Judge, upon what occasion moved I know not, after some good plausible hearing of the evidence for a time, at last told the jury that that evidence

---

496. In cases such as *Thorpe v. Thorpe* (1701) Vol. 12. Mod. Rep. 455 and *Coggs v. Barnard* (1703) 2 Ld. Raym. 909.

497. Hale, Mathew, *The History of the Common Law of England ... Written by a Learned Hand*, at p.259.

reached not to the point of the statute, and so withdrew the offenders from their trial by the jury of life and death."[498] For most of the time, it seems, this interventionism did not occasion too many problems, and Judge and jury worked closely together, though there were celebrated exceptions to the contrary.

Nevertheless, the heavy handed (and sometimes bullying) involvement of Judges at Assize trials generally, and the manner in which they indicated their opinions in particular, did not pass without objection. It was periodically the subject of fierce criticism by those who considered that it was used to prevent defendants putting their cases properly. One commentator in 1653 observed (albeit with considerable exaggeration) that prospects of acquittal at such trials were remote as it was almost impossible to find a Judge that would: "... suffer a Prisoner to speak for himself, nor any one else for him, but he'll daunt them, vilifie & threaten them with his great menacing words and big looks, as if the very name of being a prisoner were sufficent enough to argue him guilty, without any further evidence or testimony; this practice has cost many an innocent man's life."[499] Bunyan's caricature, Judge "Hategood", was clearly such a Judge. When "Faithful" asked to speak a few words in his own defence, the Judge was annoyed (though he did acceed to the request): "Sirrah, sirrah, thou deservest to live no longer, but to be slain immediately upon the place; yet that all men may see our gentleness towards thee, let us see what thou hast to say." In a trial for witchcraft, this high level of judicial activism

498. Pamphlet 1621(1), at p.238.
499. Pamphlet 1653(2) at p.37.

could have obvious and important ramifications. A Judge who was sceptical about the very existence of such a phenomenon would, inevitably, take a different approach to one who was an enthusiastic believer. Nevertheless, even in this situation, many would temper any personal doubts with a realistic appraisal of the mood of the public, especially if they (members of the judiciary) were of a personally timid disposition. Witch trials could arouse strong, often hostile, feelings, something that meant that both Judge and jury (trial and Grand) would be making their decisions in an emotionally charged atmosphere. This could influence some Judges to act against their own beliefs. Sceptical Judges could have an important effect on the process, as witnessed by the career of Sir Francis North, but this was not invariably the case, especially if they were not subtle.

Conversely, of course, a trial Judge who was a "witch-monger" could direct in a manner that encouraged the conviction of an accused woman. There were some cases of this occurring, especially at the turn of the sixteenth century, though such enthusiasts became rarer as the seventeenth century advanced. Even Hale's directions to the jury in 1662 were not nearly as damning as those delivered by Lord Anderson, in 1603, during the trial of Elizabeth Jackson for bewitching Mary Glover. A vigorous persecutor of Puritan dissenters on the Western circuit in his early judicial career, he was, according to Lord North: "... the hottest man that I did ever see in judgment." This was bourne out by his attitude to alleged witches. He apparently told the jurors presiding over Jackson's trial that England was full of witches, and that he had convicted and hanged 26 of them himself. Anderson then went on to remind them that witches had "divers strange marks" on their bodies, and, expressly encouraging a conviction, that: "This woman hath the like marks on sundry places of her body as you see testified under the hands of the women that were appointed to search her."[500] His views are especially interesting, as, having been born in 1530, and admitted to the Inner Temple in 1550, he was well embarked on his legal career before witchcraft was effectively criminalised (he would have been too young to have practised during the time of the little used Henrician statute that was repealed in 1547). Perhaps not surprisingly, given the tenor of his summing up, Jackson was swiftly convicted and sentenced to prison and the pillory (she was fortunate not to have been tried after the 1604 Act came into force, when she might have faced execution). Even stranger, was the case of Elizabeth Sawyer, tried in 1621 at the Old Bailey, before the Recorder of that court, Heneage Finch (ironically, the office was as close as England came to a Judge specialising in criminal law). Accused of three counts of witchcraft, including using it to murder a neighbour, the jury at her trial was clearly very confused. After retiring to consider their verdict, the foreman returned to court to ask for Finch's (further) "direction, and advice" on the case. Not deigning to descend into details of the evidence adduced, and how it might be weighed, the Judge apparently simply advised them to: "Doe in it as God shall put in your hearts." Perhaps revealing their continued uncertainty, despite such an appeal to divine assistance, the jury convicted of the count involving Sawyer's neighbour (for which she was hanged), and acquitted on the other two.[501]

500. Pamphlet 1603 at pp. 313-315.
501. Pamphlet 1621(2) at p.6.

Although Hale's conduct of the Assizes at Bury St Edmunds in 1662 makes a flattering comparison with that of Anderson 60 years earlier, given the marked increase in judicial professionalism between 1580 and 1700, it reflects little credit on him. Moreover, even at the start of the seventeenth century, Anderson's views were certainly not typical of all Judges. Sir David Williams, a Judge of the court of King's Bench (1604-1613), appears to have actively contributed to the acquittal of two women who came before him in 1605. Quite unusually, he even appointed three sceptical JPs to the trial jury, one of whom became its foreman.[502]

By 1660, most members of the judiciary were more sceptical, at least about the individual cases that came before them, than the local men who appeared on the trial juries. Consequently, an interventionist Judge, who was also sceptical would appear to have had considerable scope to discourage a conviction. Nevertheless, interventionist or not, as Hawles was to observe, the verdict was still a matter for the jurors: "As a discreet and lawful assistant to the jury, they [Judges] do often recapitulate and sum up the heads of the evidence; but the jurors are still to consider whether it be done truly, fully and impartially."[503] Moreover, it is clear that, in practice, the Judge's ability to pressure jurors in such cases was exercised sparingly. There were two potential reasons for this. The first was a realistic one, namely that in emotive cases of felony (not simply those involving

---

502. Brian Levack, *Possession, Witchcraft, and the Law in Jacobean England*, at p.1625.

503. Hawles, Sir John, *The Englishman's Right: A Dialogue in Relation to Trial by Jury*, at p.20.

witchcraft), members of the jury were often annoyed and consequently prepared to defy the Judges' directions, if they lent too heavily in favour of an acquittal. The second was that the Judges themselves were afraid of the adverse publicity that being seen to be soft on (for example) witchcraft, would excite. This was, probably, especially the case as many accused witches were from a strata of society where there would be little downside to sacrificing them. Both these reasons were alluded to by the Judge Sir Francis North, Baron Guilford, in the 1680s (by which time educated people, such as lawyers, were usually sceptical about the subject). He observed that if a Judge was so clear and open as to "declare against that impious vulgar opinion, that the devil himself has power to torment and kill innocent children, or that he is pleased to divert himself with the good people's cheese, butter, pigs, and geese, and the like errors of the ignorant and foolish rabble, the countryman (the triers) cry, this Judge hath no religion, for he doth not believe witches; and so, to show they have some, hang the poor wretches."[504] Some insight into the consequences of this can be gleaned from an experience in the life of Sir Francis North himself.[505] He was advanced to the Bench in 1675,

---

504. North, Roger, *The Lives of the Right Hon. Francis North ...*, at p.269.

505. North was born in 1637. He was educated in Cambridge, and admitted to the Middle Temple in 1655, being called to the Bar in 1661. He had a meteoric legal career, being made a King's Counsel in 1668, and a Judge of the Royal Franchise of Ely in 1670. By 1671, he was Solicitor General and had been knighted, and in 1673 he was made Attorney General. He appears to have been adroit at securing Royal support throughout his career, but had a violent personal dislike for Mathew Hale, then the Chief Justice of the Court of King's Bench. This apparently led him to switch the bulk of his legal practice to the Court of Exchequer, in order to avoid him. North was also the M.P. for Kings Lynn in Norfolk.

when he became, almost immediately, Chief Justice of the court of Common Pleas. In this capacity, he took his turn attending Assizes on the Western circuit, until his death in 1685. North was apparently "somewhat more thoughtful upon this subject" (witchcraft prosecutions) than many other Judges, as a result of sitting as co-adjutor with Mr Justice Raymond, at hearings in Exeter. There, the normal division between nisi prius civil cases and the Crown/criminal side was followed. North heard the civil cases, and Raymond took the Crown side, so that he presided over the trial of Temperence Lloyd and another woman accused of witchcraft. It was clear to North that these two old women had been "hurried out of the country" to be tried for the felony, in an atmosphere of acute excitement, something that was itself extremely unhelpful to the measured conduct desirable in a criminal trial. In the case of Temperence Lloyd and her fellow accused, Exeter apparently "rang with tales" of their occult powers. Many people even thought that the Judges' own horses had even been bewitched, en route, by the accused women so that they could not carry them up Castle Lane (a steep road in the city) to their lodgings.

Though not personally presiding, North took a close interest in this case (not surprisingly, given its comparative rarity by the 1680s),and was greatly concerned at what occurred at the hearing. This was that: "... brother Raymond's passive behaviour should let those poor women die." *Prima facie*, this was easily done, as the women had openly confessed in court that they were witches.[506] However, it was evident to North, at least, that in reality:

506. North, Roger, *The Lives of the Right Hon, Francis North ...* at p.268.

"These were two miserable old creatures, that, one may say, as to sense or understanding, were scarce alive; but were overwhelmed with melancholy, and waking dreams, and so stupid as no one could suppose they knew either the construction or consequence of what they said." The evidence against them, other than their admissions, was apparently "trifling", and (significantly) the JPs' depositions were also feeble. However, in his directions and summing up to the jury, Raymond failed to vigorously expose their delusions, and followed a path that was, in some ways, similar to that taken by Mathew Hale at Bury St Edmunds almost 20 years earlier. Although he didn't attempt to promote the concept of witchcraft, he left the issues to the jury without firm guidance on how they should return their verdict.[507] In particular, Raymond made no "nice distinctions", as to how it was possible for old women suffering from a "melancholy madness" to: "... contract an opinion of themselves that was false; [so] that their confession ought not to be taken against themselves, without a plain evidence that it was rational and sensible, no more than that of a lunatic, or distracted person; but he left the point upon the evidence fairly (as they call it) to the jury, and they convicted them both."[508]

It is clear from North's observations that by this period

507. Sir Thomas Raymond (1627-1683) had followed a standard path in the law. He attended Cambridge University, followed by further study at Gray's Inn, became a Serjeant-at-law in 1677, and was called to the Bench in the court of Exchequer in 1679, shortly afterwards transferring to the court of King's Bench. His son, a more eminent lawyer (England produced a number of outstanding legal "families" at this time), was to prosecute the fraudulent "witch-monger," Richard Hathaway, in 1702.

508. North, Roger, *The Lives of the Right Hon. Francis North ...* at p.269.

(*post* 1670), Judges did not directly encourage juries to convict witches as they sometimes had a century earlier, and as they frequently still did with other "conventional" felonies which they felt to be obviously proved. Rather, they committed sins of omission, in not adequately attempting to discourage jurors from returning a guilty verdict. However, even had they done so, an acquittal would not automatically have resulted. Jurors did not always follow the direction in which the judiciary might try to steer them. The landmark cases in the history of the constitution in which jurors resisted judicial encouragement to convict, such as *Bushell's Case* of 1670 (acquittal of the Quaker leaders William Penn and William Mead for conspiracy) are well known and celebrated. However, jurors might equally refuse to follow judicial encouragement to acquit. Of course, in many cases jurymen would listen to such exhortations. Indeed, the barrister John Hawles felt that "Such a slavish fear attends many jurors, that let but the court direct to find Guilty or not Guilty ... as the court sums it up."[509] However, this was not always the case, especially where witchcraft was concerned. Robert Filmer aimed his book specifically at trial jurors, in part, because he was aware that they were usually ignorant of a subject on which they made the ultimate decision. This meant that: "It concerns the People of this Nation to be more diligently instructed in the Doctrine of Witch-craft, than those of forraigne Countries."[510] Significantly, in the last case to produce a conviction at Assizes, that of Jane Wenham in 1712, the trial Judge, John

509. Hawles, Sir John, *The Englishman's Right: A Dialogue in Relation to Trial by Jury,* at p.50.

510. Filmer, *Advertisement,* at pp.A1-3.

Powell, appears to have made his scepticism about the case quite overt, not surprisingly, given that his disbelief in witches, ghosts and fairies was notorious.[511] However, despite Powell's views and patent hostility to the prosecution, Wenham was duly convicted. Fortunately for her, Assizes Judges also had the power to recommend a reprieve from execution, which he immediately did. Even North appreciated that the popular "tendency to mistake" on the subject of witches required a very "prudent and moderate carriage" in a presiding Judge. The best approach was not to ridicule witchcraft beliefs generally, but rather to focus on the facts of a particular case, and to convince: "... rather by detecting of the fraud, than by denying authoritatively such power to be given old women." He believed that jurors would not follow judicial guidance on their verdicts (especially in witch cases), if it was laid on too heavily (Powell's case supports this). Generally, North was "infinitely scrutinous" of all "doubtful" cases, especially if they were capital felonies. He was especially cautious where there was a popular outcry over a case, for in such trials: "...

511. Foss, Edward, *Foss's Judges of England*, Vol.7, at pp.399-401. John Powell became a Justice of the Common Pleas in 1692, and of the Queen's Bench in 1702. During 22 years as a Judge, his conduct on the bench was apparently without reproach, and he was considered a profound lawyer, one who ably seconded Lord Chief Justice Holt's efficient judicial rule in the first decade of the eighteenth century. Powell's scepticism led him to play a celebrated trick on the Bishop of Gloucester (an equally strong believer in witches and the demons). In a conversation with that cleric, he painted a vivid picture of a spectre that appeared by his bed at midnight, agitating the bishop by telling him of its fearful aspect, and then flatly concluded his story by telling him that it was only the old watchman who had come into his bedroom, to inform him that the street door of his house was open.

he had the jury to deal with, and if he did not tread upon eggs, they would conclude sinistourly, and be apt to find against his opinion." It was best in such cases, for the trial Judge to use his intelligence to coax the jury into acquitting, rather than attempting to coerce them to the same result. An illustration of this was provided by North's conduct of the trial of a Taunton "wizard". The man was accused on the word of a young girl, who had strange and unaccountable fits, and: "... used to cry out upon him, and spit out of her mouth straight pins." This last feature was unusual, crooked pins being a more normal sign of witchcraft. It particularly surprised North, who appreciated that the straight pins could not be so easily "couched in the mouth as crooked ones." As a result of his suspicions, he examined the witch in court "very tenderly and carefully", but at the same time conducted his questioning "so as none could collect what his opinion was; for he was fearful of the jurymen's precipitancy, if he gave them any offence." When the accused man was told he must "answer for himself" (ie, give his version of events to the court, albeit unsworn), he apparently made a defence as "orderly and well expressed as [North] ever heard spoke by any man, counsel or other." The defendant asserted that the accusations were based on personal malice and imposture on the part of the girl, and called other witnesses to support his account, whose evidence was also heard. This done, however, the Judge was still not satisfied that it was safe to sum up, feeling that though the imposture was clear to him, it was still not "fully declared" to the jurors. Fearing a conviction if he was premature in this, he stonewalled for a while by questioning the witnesses, he: "... studied, and beat the bush awhile, asking sometimes one and then another, questions as he thought proper." At length, however, he turned to the JP who had originally examined and committed the defendant for trial, and called him to give evidence, asking: "... will you ingenuously declare your thoughts, if you have any, touching these straight pins which the girl spit; for you saw her in her fit?" He struck gold. The JP replied that he had not expected that he would have to give evidence at the trial having taken the examination, and committed the defendant. However, since his opinion was asked, he declared that he thought that the girl: "... doubling herself in her fit, as being convulsed, bent her head down close to her stomach, and with her mouth, took pins out of the edge of that, and then, righting herself a little, spit them into some by-standers' hands." This very plausible explanation "cast a universal satisfaction" on the jury as to the lack of merit in the case, and they speedily acquitted.[512]

Nevertheless, pressure on the judiciary not to discourage conviction in such cases did not always come only from the "vulgar multitude" or even the middling elements of society. On the first occasion that North went on the Western circuit for Assizes, his brother Judge was the experienced circuiteer, Mr Justice Rainsford. Rainsford told him that the year before, a witch had been brought to Salisbury, and tried before him (this was probably in 1676). However, a local dignitary (and JP), Sir James Long, came to his chamber and "made a heavy complaint of this witch, and said that if she escaped, his estate would not be worth any thing; for all the people would go away."[513]

---

512. North, Roger, *The Lives of the Right Hon. Francis North* ... at pp.269-271.
513. North, Roger, *The Lives of the Right Hon. Francis North* ... at p.269.

Legal Representation

The same decade that saw witchcraft abolished as a crime (the 1730s) witnessed some early signs of major changes in the English criminal trial, changes that by the end of the century had substantially produced the modern form of trial on indictment. However, for most of the crime's history, many modern legal niceties were rare or non-existent. In particular, there was no right to active legal representation (as opposed to advice and arguments on points of pure law) for the defendant. In any event, the cost of hiring counsel would have been prohibitive for most of those accused, though, in exceptional situations, a Judge's special interest in a case appears to have led them to assign counsel to advise a defendant. For those accused of witchcraft, an inherently difficult crime to defend against (because of its strange nature), this may not have been without serious consequence. Christina Larner noted that in Scotland, where such representation was not automatically forbidden, cases appearing before the High court in Edinburgh, in which the accused person normally did have legal representation, had a significantly higher rate of acquittal than those which were tried by local commissions, where the defendant was usually unrepresented (though, of course, other factors could also have been relevant).[514] Legal advice might also have helped to reduce the disorientation experienced by many accused women. At Bury St Edmunds, in 1662, Cullender and Duny: "... replyed, nothing material to any thing that was proved against them." However, they clearly

514. Larner, Christian, *Enemies of God: the Witch-hunt in Scotland,* at p.175.

felt themselves to be innocent of the allegations, because, after sentence of death was passed against them: "They were much urged to confess, but would not."

There was no formal reason why the prosecution should not be legally represented in felony cases; however, this was unusual (though normal in state trials for treason). Nevertheless, in witchcraft cases the Crown was sometimes represented by counsel. The fact that the supposed victim of the witchcraft might well be dead, put it in a class where the state sometimes would be willing to provide assistance in the form of a prosecuting lawyer at trial. It was also a crime that, at least in its early days, could be perceived as a threat to the wider commonwealth. Indicative of the degree of concern over witchcraft prevalent in the early years was the involvement of the Attorney-General in the case of Agnes Waterhouse. She was tried at the Assizes held in Chelmsford on July 27 1566, before Justice Southcote (a Judge of the Queen's Bench from 1563 to 1584), and "Master Gerard the Queen's Attorney." This latter individual appears to have been Gilbert Gerard, the Attorney-General from 1559 to 1681. He acted as the prosecutor at Waterhouse's trial, Waterhouse herself being unrepresented (as was normal in felony trials). Even with Gerard present, the order of questioning appears to have been very fluid. Waterhouse was arraigned and promptly "confessed that she was guilty." However, Agnes Brown, a 12-year-old girl, and the alleged victim of her witchcraft was still called to give evidence: "The said Agnes Brown was then demanded and called for ... and then the Queen's Attorney asked her what she could say." She gave an account of a horned dog that threatened to kill her and indicated by gesture that it came from Waterhouse (he "wagged his head to [her] house").

Gerard then sought the defendant's reply to this accusation, and asked Agnes Waterhouse "what she said to it." Although not disputing the more pertinent facts, she took issue with some of the peripheral details, in particular that the type of knife that the horned dog had carried, described as a dagger by Brown, had existed: "There thou liest ... she saith it is a dagger knife and I have none such in my house but a great knife, and therin she lieth." Her daughter, Joan, a co-defendant, also questioned the visual appearance of the fiendish hound, though to what purpose is not clear: "... she lieth in that she saith that it had a face like an ape, for this that came to me was like a dog." The Queen's Attorney was prepared to offer "deals" in his in-court questioning that would be considered highly improper today, even asking Agnes Waterhouse whether she could make the dog appear in court and declaring that: "... if ye can, we will despatch you out of prison by and by."[515]

The Course of the Trial

In the seventeenth century, it was common for felony defendants to be tried in batches of anything from one to almost a dozen, hearings being conducted swiftly, one after the other. Cases might last only a few minutes, and rarely more than an hour or two. The verdicts would often be given together, at the end of the batch of trials. However, in witch trials, probably because they were usually longer, and their evidence more complicated, a sole trial, with the jury

515. Rosen, Barbara (Ed.), Witchcraft in England 1558-1618, at p.81.

considering the case before them on its own, was quite common. Alternatively, they might be tried in sequential groups of witches, if there were multiple accused, as occurred in Lancashire in 1612. The trial of the two witches at Bury St Edmunds, in 1662 was recorded as "a long Tryal from Seven or Eight in the Morning till seven or Eight at night." This was partly because of the number of "physicians and other learned men" who had been called to advise or give evidence.[516] Similarly, the trial of the two witches accused by the Gunters at the Lent Assizes held at Abington, Oxfordshire, in 1605, lasted at least eight hours, with the jury not retiring to consider its verdict until 10.00 pm (they acquitted).[517]

In theory there were quite a few safeguards in the trial process, such as the right to peremptory challenge (without cause) of up to 36 jurors. In reality, such was the speed and complexity of the process, and the unassisted ignorance of those being processed, that few would have been aware of what was occurring or any of their rights. Nevertheless, this does not mean that a conviction was pre-ordained, except in the clearest cases; as the statistics indicate, it was not.

The Indictment

The indictment was the main court document, being the

516. Hale, Mathew, Preface to *A Discourse concerning the Great Mercy of God, in Preserving us from the Power and Malice of Evil Angels,* Unfinished Manuscript by Mathew Hale, written at Cambridge on March 26, 1661.

517. Levack, Brian, *Possession, Witchcraft, and the Law in Jacobean England,* at p.1623.

formal allegation of felony, and the details thereof, on which the defendant would be tried. They were usually less precisely drafted than modern ones, and, apart from a period in the Interregnum, were always in (legal) Latin, something that persisted for all felonies until 1731. However, the accused person, and the jury, would be given an oral translation so that they knew what the allegations against them were, and for which they would be tried. Each individual offence of maleficium would normally be specified as a separate count, unlike Scotland, where more general non-specific allegations of witchcraft were fairly common, and probably made running an effective defence more difficult. A (modern) translation of a typical indictment for witchcraft, for the Assizes held at Witham in Essex, in August of 1583, runs: "The jurors for our lady the Queen do present that Margery Barnes, late of the parish of St Osyth in the county aforesaid, spinster, on 1 July, 25 eliz., in her possession did entertain, govern and maintain three imps otherwise called spirits named or called by the name or names: Pygine, resembling a mole; Russoll resembling a grey cat; and the other called Dunsott resembling a Dun dog with intent that she might enchant and bewitch as well men as beasts and other things, to the grievous damage of the entire people of the said lady the Queen Elizabeth. And against the peace and her crown. And against the form of the statute in this case made and provided."[518]

Defendants would be arraigned and enter a plea of guilty or not guilty to the counts in the indictment. Generally, guilty pleas were discouraged in felony trials.

---

518. L'Estrange Ewen, C.L (Ed.), *Witch Hunting and Witch Trials*, at pp.83-84.

However, some accused witches do appear to have "put their hands up" in court without too much opposition from the Bench, Judges perhaps appreciating that proving such cases might be difficult. Thus, when Joane Williford in Kent in 1645: "... being brought to the Barre, was asked Guilty or Not guilty, she answered guilty."[519] Similarly Mistress Moores, a widow of Isle of Ely admitted being a witch for 20 years, "wept at her tryall, and confessed her selfe guilty before the Judge, Bench and Country."[520] Others might change their pleas or make only token defences. Those accused of the felony often appear to have appreciated that they had a "role" to play in the proceedings. Once hope of escape had been abandoned, they would sometimes conform to the part that society expected of them, confessing their crimes freely and in the appropriate terms. Thus, when the Assizes in Northampton in 1674 were held, and Ann Foster was called to the bar, she at first pleaded not guilty to the indictment: "... but it being so evidently proved that she was the person that had committed all those things before mentioned, she then confessed, and said that the devil did provoke her to do all those Mischiefs." Seeing that sentence of death was passed upon her, she also prayed to God to forgive her and asked for forgiveness from her victim, especially as she could in "no way make amends."

The consequences of refusing to plead at all (ie, standing "mute of malice") for an accused witch would have been appalling, as they were for any other felony defendant. It would have resulted in the imposition of the *peine forte et*

---

519. Pamphlet 1645(3) at p.4.
520. Stearne, *Confirmation* at p.22.

dure. This ancient custom required that the defendant be taken back to prison and tied down with a wooden board, placed on his (or her) chest, which was then progressively loaded with iron weights (or stones), until they died (or asked and were permitted to enter a plea). Virtually no witches failed to enter a plea; and it only occurred in other cases on very rare occasions. At Salem, however, one man, Giles Cory, having seen how the trials were being conducted, would not put himself to trial by the jury, probably because he knew he would have no chance of acquittal. He chose instead an agonising manner of dying: "In pressing, his tongue being prest out of his mouth, the Sheriff with his cane forced it in again when he was dying. He was the first in New-England that was ever prest to death."[521]

The English system of criminal justice at this time, was largely an accusatory and (albeit to a much smaller degree than today) adversarial one. The prosecution of witches as much as other types of felon, was, therefore, heavily dependant on the action of the injured party, usually the victim of the spell.[522] The normal Assize procedure was not totally dissimilar to that of a modern Crown court. The prosecution would call its witnesses first, these giving their evidence on oath. At the end of the prosecution case the Judge normally asked the defendant(s) what they had to say about the allegations against them, at which they would give their version of events.[523] Trials were rather more flexible than in the modern period. Typically, Bunyan's

---

521. Calef, Robert, *More Wonders of the Invisible World*, at p.261.
522. *See* Sharpe, J., *Women, Witchcraft and the legal process*, at p.107.
523. Beattie, J.M., *Crime and the Courts in England 160-1800*, at p.343.

"Envy," in *The Pilgrim's Progress* (1678), when giving evidence against "Faithful," offered to say more than he had done initially, but rather than boring the court, suggested that he let the other prosecution witnesses give their own evidence first, and then, if necessary, return to fill in any gaps ("enlarge my testimony"). This proposal was accepted by the court and he was asked to "stand by." Given that Bunyan had personal experience of the criminal process, this may well have been a true reflection of the relatively informal conduct of a normal Assizes hearing. It also appears to be borne out by records of actual witch trials. In one trial at Worcester Assizes, Susan Cock and Rose Hallbread, were jointly tried amongst a batch of four witches (ie, both were in the dock together) for witchcraft and the resultant murder of children. A, to modern eyes unpardonable, degree of informality is indicated by the fact that, initially, the two chief prosecution witnesses (Abraham Chad and a man called Shearcraft) were called together to give their evidence. They testified that they were present when the two defendants first bewitched the children concerned. However, it should be noted that the court itself quickly found this method of receiving testimony irregular, as, while: "... they both were jointly declaring the whole matter, ... the court caused them to be examined, apart and separate from one another, to find whether their evidence agreed."[524]

---

524. Pamphlet 1670, at p.6.

Trial Juries

To Mathew Hale, the jury trial was the clearest evidence of the "Excellency of the Laws of England above those of other Nations." It provided the "best Trial in the World", and was something that distinguished England from the continental European countries. However, although overtly similar, it was, in many ways, very different to its modern equivalent. The jury was made up of 12 men who for "Estate and Quality" were appropriate to the office, these being selected from the county where the trial was to take place. Although only 12 in number, they were drawn from a larger panel of 24 men, the greater number being needed in case some failed to attend or there were challenges to individuals who were selected to be among the 12 (though this was rare). For the Assizes, the jury was to be ready at the Bar of the court on the first day of the Return of the Writ (the start of the hearings).[525] Not everyone could serve, even on a trial jury. At Michaelmas Sessions each year, constables were supposed to hand in to the JPs a list of the names and addresses of every man qualified to serve on a jury (of either type), who was between the age of 21 and 70.[526] The property requirement precluded any below the middle orders of society from performing this office. Typically, they would be yeomen farmers, merchants and tradesmen. Aliens, apothecaries, butchers, clergymen, infants, and those convicted of a serious crime could not serve on juries

---

525. Hale, Mathew, *The History of the Common Law of England ... Written by a Learned Hand*, at p.253.
526. Jacob, Giles, *The Compleat Parish Officer*, 7th Edn., at p.24.

(though, interestingly, clergymen could be JPs).[527] As Sir Edward Coke observed in his classic legal work of 1628 if a potential juror was: "... attainted or convicted of treason, or felony, or for any offence to life or member, or in attaint for a false verdict, or for perjury as a witnesse", he could not serve. By this time it was also recognised that a juryman should not be personally biased against one of the parties, so it was one of the sheriff's functions to ensure that he: "... returne[d] indifferent juries for the triall of mens lives."[528] They could not be connected (of "Kindred or Alliance") to any of the parties to the trial, so that they were "prejudiced" before hearing the evidence in the case.[529] However, although by the early modern period jurors were not supposed to be intimately involved with the parties, or to have a personal axe to grind in the case, modern notions of juror detachment were also not present (and probably often not practicable). John Hawles, writing in 1680, was, realistically, of the opinion that because the trial jurors would come from the defendant's neighbours they "... consequently cannot be presumed to be unacquainted either with the matters charged, the prisoners course of life, or the credit of the evidence."[530]

Irrespective of whether they had independent knowledge or not, jurors' attitudes towards those accused of witchcraft could be very prejudiced. This was alluded to by

---

527. *Ibid.*, at p.24.
528. Coke, Sir Edward, *The First Part of the Institutes of the Laws of England*, Sections 158 and 16.
529. Hale, Mathew, *History of the Common Law, See* generally Chapter XII. *Touching Trials by Jury*.
530. Hawles, John, *The Englishman's Right: A Dialogue in Relation to Trial by Jury*, at p.17.

Reginald Scot, as early as 1584, when he observed that: "... the name of a witch is so odious, and hir power so feared among the common people, that if the honestest bodie living chance to be arraigned therupon, she shall hardlie escape condemnation."[531] Nevertheless, this was not always the case, and Scot may have been exaggerating. To imagine that jurors were invariably seething with such hostility towards those accused of witchcraft that they would not consider the apparent merits of individual cases, is not borne out by acquittal rates. Indeed, Thomas Potts, in publishing his pamphlet account of the trial of Jennet Preston in 1612, was partly motivated by a desire that potential jurors might not let their "connivance, or rather foolish pittie, spare such as these."[532]

Service on the trial jury (also known as the petty jury, or the jury of life and death to distinguish it from the Grand Jury) was often not a popular duty. This can be seen in the objections raised in John Hawles's "dialogue" between a barrister and juryman, the latter observing: "I am summoned to appear upon a jury, and was just going to try if I could get off [service]." His reasons for this decision (still a constant problem with modern jurors) being the inherent trouble involved in sitting, the loss of time, and the fact that he was reluctant to burden his conscience with making decisions in such "weighty matters."[533] The special difficulties faced by juries determining witch cases, and

---

531. Scot, Reginald, *The Discovery of Witchcraft,* at pp. 5-6.
532. Potts, Thomas, *The Arraignment And Triall of Jennet Preston, of Gisborne in Craven,* published anonymously, at pp. 163-174, and at p.173.
533. Hawles, John, *The Englishman's Right: A Dialogue in Relation to Trial by Jury,* at p.9.

their likely aftermath, were well caught by the jurymen, including their foreman Thomas Fisk, who sat at the Salem trials. Writing a few years afterwards, when passions had cooled, these men expressed grave doubts, and remorse, about their decisions in convicting the accused. The admission to which they put their signatures shows, all too clearly, the problems faced by a jury in such trials: "We confess that we ourselves were not capable to understand nor able to withstand the mysterious delusions of the powers of darkness, and prince of the air; but were, for want of knowledge on ourselves, and better information from others, prevailed with to take up with such evidence against the accused, as, on further consideration and better information, we justly fear was insufficient for the touching the lives of any."[534]

Commentators on the modern jury trial have sometimes speculated on the possibility that jurors, in the artificial forensic environment of the court-room, might abandon commonsense, and their experience of everyday life, and attribute significance to matters that are really mundane and insignificant. Arguably, this is particularly applicable to the retrospective importance that was so often placed on earlier routine inter-personal abuse and cursing in witch cases.

The jury had to be unanimous in reaching a decision (unlike in Scotland, where a simple majority sufficed), as Mathew Hale noted: "... all ought to agree, and any one dissenting, no Verdict can be given." This was potentially important in witch trials, as there was likely to be at least one sceptic amongst the dozen, though obviously much

---

534. Calef, Robert, *More Wonders of the Invisible World,* at p.339.

might depend on the individual's strength of character. A classic example of this, in Reginald Scot's experience, concerned the case of Margaret Simons of Brenchlie in Kent. She was accused and tried at the Assizes held in Rochester in 1581, after falling foul of the local Vicar, an ignorant man by the name of John Ferral. Although the case against her was weak in the extreme, she only narrowly escaped being convicted at trial. Ferral's son, an "ungratious boie", had been barked at by Simons' small dog. The boy became annoyed and pursued the animal to her door, where she rebuked him "with some such words as the boy disdained." Five days later he fell ill, and the Vicar, who could not accept that the Lord might "visit his children with sicknes" remembered the altercation, and also apparently (despite his cloth) consulted some wise women or cunning men ("other witches"). This led him to conclude that his son was bewitched. His son was supposedly cured by one of the "white" witches. However, not content with this, the Vicar made further accusations against Simons, amongst them that when he was reading in Church his "voice so failed him" that he was almost inaudible, something he attributed to the woman's magic. However, many of his neighbours were convinced that it was a symptom of nothing more diabolical than the "French pox." The Vicar was forced to produce a letter from a London doctor, which he had stuck up in his Church, so that he was "excused the shame of the disease." Even so, despite the apparent malice and self serving nature behind his complaint, most of the trial jurors still appear to have been willing to convict Simons: "... if one of the Jurie had not beene wiser than the other." This one stalwart man saved her from execution.[535]

Juries that could not reach a unanimous decision were rare. Faced by confusing evidence, and an arcane subject, many must have taken their lead from the judiciary and the more significant witnesses, or their more confident colleagues. As with any jury system, their deliberations were probably not the result of a genuine equality of influence and debate. Even Mathew Hale expressly recognised that: "... an ignorant Parcel of Men are sometimes governed by a few that are more knowing, or of greater Interest or Reputation than the rest." Similarly, John Hawles, although a great exponent of the jury system, worried that when jurors retired to consider their verdict, they forgot their individual oaths, and allowed one or two strong personalities, usually including the foreman and other "old hands", men who called themselves "antient jurymen", to dominate the discussion. He feared that "to avoid the trouble of disputing the point, or to prevent the spoiling of dinner by delay ... [they] forthwith agree blindfold." (This has remained a concern to the present day.) In an area like witchcraft, one that was inherently perplexing, this factor probably gave considerable scope to both sceptics and enthusiasts, with strong opinions, or to anyone who could claim a special knowledge of such an esoteric subject, perhaps adding greater unpredictability to verdicts.

Jurors were not so in awe of the trial Judge that they were mere passive observers of the trial. Witnesses, according to Hawles, were "always ordered to direct their speech to the jury", and, much more than modern juries,

---

535. Scot, Reginald, *The Discovery of Witchcraft*, at pp. 5 and 6.

they were willing to take an active, and sometimes interventionist approach to the cases that were heard before them.[536] As the acquittal rates for witchcraft indicate, if the evidence was not persuasive, they were very ready to return a verdict of "not guilty." Even in the late fifteenth century, Sir John Fortescue, a former Chief Justice of the King's Bench, when eulogising the English method of trial by jury, had clearly been well aware that it did not produce as many convictions as the methods employed in the rest of Europe.[537] A classic (and perhaps extreme) illustration of jury interventionism can be seen in the trial of the fraudulent witch-monger Hathaway. Sergeant Jenner, on behalf of the defendant, argued that a proposed piece of evidence was hearsay, in a sotto voce conversation with the Judge. A juryman, concerned at Jenner's adoption of what, in modern American procedure, might be termed a "side-bar," intervened in the conversation between Judge and counsel: "Mr Sergeant, if you have any thing to object, we desire to hear what you say, for you speak so low we cannot hear you." To which Serjeant Jenner replied: "I object to what the doctor says by hearsay only." At this (and contrary to all modern practice), the argument on a point of pure law was concluded by the juryman replying: "I believe that will be little considered by the jury."

536. Hawles, John, *The Englishman's Right: A Dialogue in Relation to Trial by Jury*, at pp.49 and 19.

537. Bellamy, John, *Crime and Public Order in England in the Later Middle Ages*, at p.156.

Judicial Directions to the Jury

Because Judges made their views on the merits of the case plain to the jury, and because the trials were so brief (even witch cases would be completed within a day, and were often much shorter), a lengthy summing up was usually unnecessary. Directions were often fairly brief. A typical one in the early modern period might be: "Ye have heard what these men say against the prisoner. You have also heard what the prisoner can say for himself. Have an eye to your oath and to your duty, and do that which God shall put in your minds to the discharge of your consciences, and mark well what is said."[538] There would have been little variation for cases involving witchcraft. Thus the presiding Judge at the trial of one of the witches held at the Worcester Assizes in 1647, "having explain'd and Sum'd up the Evidence, told the jury, that as they ought to beware of Condemning the innocent, yet if they thought the Credit of the evidence Sufficient in what they had deposed, their Eyes ought not to spare her, adding that the Holy Scripture declares, that we must not suffer a Witch to Live, Especially, when guilty of Murther Tortures, & c. Wherupon the jury after an Hour's Consultation brought her in guilty."[539] Mathew Hale has been criticised for the brevity of his summing up at Bury St Edmunds, and his lack of discouragement to the jury to convict. However his directions were in keeping with the traditional approach; more controversially however, and certainly more damningly, he delivered a brief, but probably highly influential exposition on the reality of

---

538. Cockburn, J.S., *A History of English Assizes, 1558-1714,* at p.122.
539. Pamphlet 1670, at p.4.

witchcraft, something which may have encouraged a conviction.

Court Room Uproar

Witch trials were *causes celebres*, and often seem to have occasioned considerable noise from the spectators present in the public gallery. John Aubrey noted this when a "cabal of witches detected at Malmesbury" were tried at Salisbury Assizes. The strange allegations made against them included "flying in the air on a staffe" (a rare example of the aerial properties of the witch's broom). At their trial: "The crowd of spectators made such a noise that the Judge could not heare the Prisoner, nor the Prisoner the Judge; but the words were handed from one to the other by Mr R.Chandler, and sometimes not truly reported." (It was this trial that was observed, according to Aubrey, by his friend Anthony Ettrick, a "very judicious" Middle Temple barrister, who was "not satisfied" by it.)[540] Such commotion does not appear to have been confined to the spectators. Histrionics and in court possession were also seen amongst the witnesses (as Salem illustrates). Even the accused could behave in an extraordinary manner in court, perhaps caught up in the emotion of the moment. Thus, one of the women tried at Maidstone in 1652, Anne Ashby, who was allegedly the ringleader or "chief Actresse" in the drama, freely admitted her crimes at the Assizes. She then "fell into an extasie before the Bench, and swll'd into a monstous bigness, screching and crying out very dolefully."[541]

---

540. Dick, O.L. (Ed.), *Aubrey's Brief Lives,* at p.54.
541. Pamphlet 1652(2) at p.4.

Chapter 13

The Evidence Adduced at Trial

> "We may hence see ground to fear, that there hath been a great deal of innocent blood shed in the Christian world, by proceeding upon unsafe principles, in condemning persons for Malefick Witchcraft."
> *A Modest Inquiry into the Nature of Witchcraft*, John Hale (1697).

Proving witchcraft cases was inherently difficult. To rational modern people the reason for this is obvious, there can be no real evidence for the non-existent. However, to many in the early modern period, the lack of clear evidence in such cases had an equally obvious, but very different, explanation. By its very nature witchcraft was secret and frequently carried out at night, therefore it made sense that, in Bodin's words, its "investigation and proof are difficult." The problem was succinctly summed up by Lord Anderson in his address to a jury in 1603, though the conclusions he drew from it (effectively, the need to accept inferior levels of proof), were obviously flawed: "The Devil is a spirit of darkness, he deals closely and cunningly; you shall hardly find any direct proofs in such a case, but by many presumptions and circumstances you may gather it." This was to be a regular judicial theme. It was the secret aspect of the crime that was sometimes advanced as a justification for using supernatural techniques to establish guilt. Given its inherent nature, witchcraft was not susceptible to conventional proof. As John Cotta noted: "It may be objected, the Art of Witch-craft, being supernaturall, and the practice thereof sustained by an extraordinary power; that therefore the meanes and waies of discoverie must be likewise more than ordinary and supernaturall." As a result, conventional techniques could appear inadequate: "It may bee and is objected, that it is a hard and difficult matter to detect Witch-craft, by the former and ordinary courses, as is often Seene and found apparent." Of course, as Cotta also appreciated, the converse problem was that the innocent found it equally difficult to defend themselves in such cases, it was: "... as hard by the same meanes of times, for many a just man to prove and cleere his opposed innocency."[542]

Because it was not amenable to normal methods of proof, many lawyers in early-modern Europe considered witchcraft to be *crimen exceptum*. It was a crime that necessitated the use of supernatural techniques of proof, torture and the admitting of testimony from parties, such as convicted felons, whose evidence would often be excluded for other types of serious crime. Just as excommunicates, heretics, notorious evil doers, the wife and children of the accused and criminals could give evidence in cases involving heresy, so they could in witchcraft cases (as could another accused witch). This was contrary to the general practice in many courts. Even worse, such evidence could often: "... only be admitted for the prosecution and not for the defence."[543] Consequently, the conduct of witch trials went against developments emphasising rationalisation and

---

542. Cota, John, *The Triall of Witch-Craft, Shewing the True and Right Methode of Discovery: With a Confusion of erroneous wayes*, at pp.20 and 21.

543. Sprenger, Jacob and Kramer, Heinrich, *Malleus Maleficarum* (1486), Translated by Montague Summers at p.209.

depersonalisation in the rest of the criminal law, at a time when, for conventional crimes, standards and methods of proof were coming closer to those accepted as normal today.[544] In England, by the sixteenth and seventeenth centuries, modern notions of the legal constituents of a crime, a combination of external actions, sometimes termed the *actus reus*, with an appropriate mental state, sometimes termed the *mens rea*, were becoming established. As Blackstone was to comment in the following century: "In all temporal jurisdictions an overt act or some evidence of an intended crime is necessary to demonstrate the depravity of the will ... [similarly] ... an unwarrantable act without a vicious will is no crime at all."[545] A similar process was occurring in much of continental Europe. Witchcraft, however, did not readily lend itself to such an analysis. As a result, it was accepted that its trial could not be fettered by the rules and restrictions that were increasingly present for conventional crimes.

This process was most obviously noticeable in the continental civil law systems, with their more technical prerequisites for proof (compared with those found in the common law tradition). However, although less obvious, it also applied, to an extent, in common law England. Much of the evidence accepted in English witch trials would have been ignored in routine felonies, making it, effectively, a "crime apart", with its own special regime of proof. As early as 1584, this was apparent to Reginald Scot. Given that "none that be honest are able to detect them", evidence was

---

544. Larner, Christina, *Witchcraft and Religion: The Politics of Popular Belief,* at pp. 44-45.
545. Blackstone, William, *Commentaries on the Laws of England,* Vol iv, at p.20.

received that would normally be considered of little value (though only for the prosecution, not the defence, of the accused witch). This included the testimony of "infamous persons" and infants,[546] despite the normal position in English trials, that if a witness was "infamous, he shall not be sworn" as a prosecution witness (such a reputation would usually be gained by being convicted of felony, pilloried, or excommunicated etc.).[547] Similarly, one (rather out of date) commentator, in 1712, lamenting the absurdity that in Germany, if alleged witches denied their guilt, they were "put to the torture", while if they admitted it "they pronounce their own sentence", opined that the situation in England, was not that much better. The quality of the prosecution evidence was often highly defective: "... proof against the Criminals of this kind amongst us, is for the most part very precarious, the chief evidence against them being generally taken from Persons said to be betwitch'd by them, who are for the most part distemper'd in Mind."[548] By then, however, he was following a very long tradition in harbouring doubts about the process. Sixty years earlier, Ady had remarked that it was clear that witch cases were subject to a very different evidential regime. In one section, specifically aimed at lawyers, he asked them to appreciate that opinions that rendered the ordinary working of the law absurd were of no value. As he pointed out, most ordinary criminal cases did not even entertain the possibility of magic. Thus, it was normal to acquit a man accused of murder, even if he had a personal enmity towards the

546. *Ibid.*, at p.19.
547. Nelson, *The Law of Evidence*, at p.18.
548. Pamphlet 1712(2), at p.40.

deceased individual, if he had an alibi and was shown to have been 100 miles away from the victim. However, if the reality of witchcraft was accepted, there was no reason why the murder should not have been effected by devilish imps or some other form of magic so as to "to witch him to death at that time." Similarly, if two men had a fight, and one died, the other would normally be "questioned for his life." But in such situations, how could it be possible to ensure that the crime was not actually committed by a witch, rather than the accused combatant? [549]

For jurors, there was a marked difference between assessing evidence at trials for normal crimes, where much of the evidence might be direct testimony of the facts in issue, something which merely left a question of credibility to be determined, and witch trials, where so much was speculation and supposition of a type not normally heard. This was a problem expressly identified by George Gifford, who noted that normally: "If witnesses doe sweare directly that in their knowledge a matter was so or so, and sweare falsely, the jurie is cleare which proceedeth according to their evidence, unlesse the Jurie do perceive that their oath can not be true. But what is that to make the testimonie sufficent where men doe but thinke, and can shewe no necessarie reason to ground their thought upon." In such trials, witnesses might give evidence of their personal beliefs about the accused, of occurrences such as being awakened from dreams and seeing spectral faces in front of them, of dying declarations made by victims as to the cause of their

---

549. Ady, Thomas, *An Instruction for Lawyers*, appended to Ady, *Discovery*, at p.172.

fatal sicknesses, of their opinion that they had been harmed by someone suspected of being a witch.[550] Mere coincidence was often enough. According to Lord Anderson, in 1603 "When they are full of cursing, use their tongue to speak mischievously, and it falls out accordingly, what greater presumption can you have of a witch." The problem was that there could also be natural explanations for such occurrences. This was even appreciated, towards the end of his life, by Mathew Hale, in his classic treatise *Pleas of the Crown*, published (as with so much of his legal work) after his death. He observed that witchcraft, like rape, was especially difficult to prove, with those who were guilty of the crime being particularly hard to convict. This was because "such an evidence, as is satisfactory to prove it, can hardly be found", while, conversely, the innocent might be "entangled under such presumptions, that carry great probabilities of guilt."

There was also a widespread feeling, amongst many sceptical commentators, that the standard of proof in trials for witchcraft was often watered down from the generally high standard that was becoming common, for other felonies, in the late sixteenth century. Although Gifford was a believer in the reality of witches, he was very sceptical about many individual cases of alleged witchcraft, and considered that only the very highest standards of proof were appropriate. Most "proved" cases fell woefully short of this. As he noted in 1593, the correct situation would be one in which if it was suspected that a defendant was a witch, but there was, even so: "... no proofe, the jury doeth more

550. Gifford, *Dialogue*, at pp.L3-4.

rightly in acquitting than in condemning, for what warrant have they upon their oath to goe by gesse, or to find that which they know not?" He was very aware that in this regard, witchcraft was not treated in the same way as other crimes, where a strong suspicion, which still left room for reasonable doubt ("the likelihoods are great he is guiltie of the same, but yet it may bee he is cleere"), would normally result in an acquittal. A willingness to accept such lower degrees of proof was closely linked to judicial perception of the threat they posed to the wider society. Judges were likely to incline to such procedures if they believed, like Lord Anderson, that: "... if we shall not convince [convict] them without their own confession, or direct proofs, where the presumptions are so great, and the circumstances so apparent, they will in short time over-run the whole land."[551] As this statement also makes clear, in witchcraft cases, unlike other forms of felony, the courts were forced to place an unprecedented degree of significance on purely circumstantial evidence, something that was normally considered with suspicion in conventional cases. Anderson, though a particularly strong believer in witchcraft, was not exceptional in holding such attitudes at this time. A few years later, James Altham, presiding over the trial of Janet Preston for witchcraft in York, in 1612, appears, according to the court clerk, to have given a similar direction: "... expect not, as this reverend and learned Judge saith, such apparent proofe against them, as against others, since all their workes, are the works of darknesse."[552]

551. Pamphlet 1603, at pp. 313-315.
552. Potts, Thomas, *The Arraignment And Triall of Jennet Preston, of Gisborne in Craven*, at pp. 163-174, at p.173.

Distinction Between Grounds for Suspicion and Conviction

Nevertheless, although *crimen exceptum*, there were firm limits to the judicial willingness to allow unusual methods of proof at witch trials. It is important to appreciate that many of the popular examinations for the presence of witchcraft were not legally admissible as evidence at trial. This was not always made clear by the sceptics. Thus, Francis Hutchinson, in his polemical work, was to remark that the methods used to convict witches were "thrown, with scorn, out of all other tryals", so that the courts did not, for example, use the "sieve and shears" technique to convict thieves.[553] This is very misleading, such tests were not admissible to convict witches either. Indeed, as Hopkins and Stearne make clear in their literary work, even the well regarded swimming test was not received in evidence by the restored Assize Judges in East Anglia in 1645-1647. However, although, theoretically, such arcane tests had no evidential validity for the trial proper, there were undoubtedly cases where the jury were well aware that they had been carried out (and produced a positive result) and probably some where the formal results of such tests were expressly revealed to the jurors. Indeed, one such (quite bizarre) incident involved Judge John Archer, of the court of Common Pleas, trying a septuagenarian woman by the unusual name of Julian Cox at the Summer Assizes at Taunton in Somerset, in 1663. He announced to the jury that he had heard that witches could not repeat the words of the

---

553. Hutchinson, Francis *Historical Essay on Witchcraft*, at p.55.

Petition in the Lord's Prayer (a common belief), "And Lead us not into Temptation", and had decided to try this experiment in open court. However, being a legally correct (!) man, he told the jury that : "... whether she could or not, they were not in the least measure to guide their Verdict according to it, because it was not Legal Evidence, but that they must be guided in their Verdict by the former Evidences given in upon Oath only." Despite this acknowledgment of the legal inadmissibility of the test, the defendant was called upon to attempt the petition, but repeatedly failed to include the negative in the sentence, though she tried it "near half a score times in open court." Not surprisingly, perhaps, the jury convicted her, and she was executed.[554] This perhaps confirms Roger North's description of the Judge as a man of "whose abilities time hath kept no record, unless in a sinister way." In fairness, he was not typical of the judiciary by this time, and was forbidden from sitting after 1672.

In most witchcraft cases, there was a bifurcation between matters that were considered to be merely evidential "make weights", only of value when bolstering other types of evidence, and evidence that justified a conviction in its own right. William Perkins, though a strong believer in witches, was well aware that the evidence that would justify their conviction had to "proceed from just and sufficient proofs" and not from "mere presumptions." Such "presumptions" provided grounds for a vigorous examination by the JPs, but not (on their own) a guilty

---

554. Glanvil, Joseph, *Sadducismus Triumphatus*, part II, at p.105. Kors, A.C., and Peters, E., *Witchcraft in Europe 1100-1700*, at p.296.

verdict at trial. Many of these have been referred to already, including misfortune following an argument or curses made by the accused witch, her previous reputation, and her being implicated in the confession of another witch (Perkins was especially adamant that this was "not sufficent for conviction or condemnation"). To found a conviction, Perkins believed that there must also be either a reliable confession by the accused, following such "pregnant presumptions", or evidence of at least two witnesses (unlike the normal situation in English criminal trials). These witnesses must have either seen her familiars or other illustrations of her diabolical status, or, more controversially, seen the accused invoking the assistance of the devil.[555] As Sir Robert Filmer tartly noted of this: "But if every man that hath invocated the Devill, or desired his helpe must have formerly made a league with him, then nations are every Man of them Witches, which I thinke none will say."[556] This division, between grounds for suspicion and those for conviction, was a common one amongst authorities on the subject, though there was not always agreement on where the line was to be drawn between the two categories. Writing a few years after Perkins, in 1617, Thomas Cooper, also made it clear that the sort of evidence that justified examination by a JP (again "weightie Presumptions"), were very different from the "sufficient proofes" that justified "manifest convictions" at trial. Among the former he identified many matters stressed by Perkins (whose work had clearly influenced him), such as "Notorious" reputation for the crime amongst the "better

---

555. Perkins, William, *A Disclosure of the Damned Art of Witchcraft*, at pp. 587-609 at pp. 602-604.
556. Filmer, *Advertisement*, at p.14.

sort" of the accused person's neighbours, an allegation by another witch, or a death bed accusation by an alleged victim. Among the latter "proofs," many of which, like Perkins, he felt would have to be supported by two witnesses, were confessions or witnessed acts of witchcraft, producing faces in glass vessels etc.[557] Similarly, Michael Dalton, in later editions of his book, also challenged by the problems of proving a crime where JPs might not "always expect direct evidence, seeing all their workes are the workes of darkness", accorded different weight to varying types of evidence. Although Dalton identified many secondary indicators that might provoke suspicion, he stressed the importance of identifying the witch's mark and the presence of a familiar, in whatever form, as the two "maine points to discover and convict these witches."

This bifurcation clearly survived the extraordinary events at Salem, albeit in an attenuated form. As Robert Calef noted, even there, coincidences of misfortune and reputation were not enough to convict, on their own. In the trial of the elderly Sarah Dustin, who was reputed to have been a witch for 20 or 30 years, a multitude of witnesses were produced against her. However, their testimony: "... seemed wholly foreign, as of accidents, illness, &c., befalling them, or theirs after some quarrel; what these testified was much of it actions said to be done 20 years before that time, the spectre evidence was not made use of ... so that the jury soon brought her in not guilty."[558] As this indicates, and despite popular belief to the contrary, no one was convicted

---

557. Cooper, Thomas, *The Mystery of Witch-Craft*, at p.276.
558. Calef, Robert, *More Wonders of the Invisible World*, at p.333.

purely on "spectral evidence". Cotton Mather dealt with this when he wrote *The Wonders of the Invisible World* in the autumn of 1692 (finishing a little under a month after the last of the Salem trials had been completed). He intended to produce a defence of the court of oyer and terminer to counteract the mounting criticism over the conduct of the trials. In particular, he sought to justify the procedures employed to determine the truth. In doing so, and relying heavily on the works of three English authors, William Perkins, John Gaule and Richard Bernard, he produced what has been referred to as the most thorough discussion available on the subject.[559] Although a total of 156 people were investigated and indicted by the justices during the life of the special court only 28 came to trial, and only 20 were executed. There were three types of evidence admitted at the trials, confession evidence, acts of malefic witchcraft and spectral evidence. Underlying spectral evidence was the belief that a person having made a covenant with the devil could assume spectral form to carry out his will. A special group of accusers developed at Salem, mainly children, claiming that they could see the alleged spectres, by virtue of a "special sight" that was not generally possessed. Malefic evidence appears to have been, as usual, simply the misfortunes of life with a supernatural explanation imposed, often prompted by a grudge or personal animosity. The allegations of spectral evidence were made first, at which point others from the community stepped forward to reinforce these, claiming that they had been bewitched by

---

559. *See* on this Cracker, Wendel D., *Spectral Evidence, Non-Spectral Acts of Witchcraft, And Confession at Salem in 1692*, at p.335.

those accused. None of the 156 accused were called for trial on purely spectral evidence. Indeed, some Judges were uneasy about the very admissibility of such evidence. The trials were suspended while this was considered and resumed only after several leading Ministers advised the court that such evidence might be used, but only with "exquisite caution." All defendants who had made a pre-trial confession, were also convicted. Where their confessions appear to have been decisive, and where the manifestly unjust system broke down, was in the post-trial decision to recommend a reprieve, which those who had confessed were granted. Those who had not made a confession were refused.[560]

Judicial and Juror Attitudes to Evidence

Sir Edward Bromley, who presided over the trial of the Lancashire witches in 1612, provides some insight into what evidence influenced Judges and, presumably, jurors (the experience of this trial must have been useful, as Bromley was also to be one of the Assizes Judges present at the trial of the Flowers in 1619). Born of a legal family, he had been made Baron of the Exchequer in 1610, in which capacity he conducted the Crown Side of the Lancaster Assizes two years later. At the conclusion of the case, when passing sentence on the large number of people condemned, Bromley indicated a degree of judicial defensiveness (given their numbers, this is not surprising), and remarked on the

---

560. *Ibid.*, at pp.331-358.

high quality of the evidence on which the witches had been convicted. He showed a, perhaps surprising, degree of caution about the value of unsupported confessions, and observed that they had no: "... cause to complaine: since in the Triall of your lives there hath beene great care and paines taken, and much time spent: and very few or none of you, but stand convicted upon your owne voluntarie confessions and examinations." He stressed, instead, the "direct", rather than circumstantial, nature of much of the witness evidence. Most of the witnesses called, or whose depositions had been read, had been people intimately involved with the accused, being "present, and parties in your assemblies." As a result, Bromley was convinced that nobody of their "nature and condition, ever were Arraigned and Tried with more solemnitie, had more libertie given to pleade or answere to everie particular point of evidence." He also felt that they must acknowledge that "extraordinarie meanes" had been used to test the prosecution evidence, and to discover any malicious intention amongst any of the Crown's witnesses to "touch your lives unjustly."[561]

Jurors, too, did not totally abandon commonsense in such cases. Although the cursing/misfortune scenario was an important piece of evidence (though usually not enough for a conviction on its own), the coincidence of misfortune would lose its evidential significance if a rational explanation for it could be found, and juries appear to have

561. Potts, Thomas, *the Wonderful Discoverie of Witches in the Countie of Lancaster. With the arraignement and Triall of Nineteene notorious Witches ...*, at p.V3. Having instructed them in the justness and exemplary conduct of the proceedings, he also urged them to use their remaining time on earth to repent of their sins.

been receptive to such explanations. Thus, one allegation made in 1600, arose out of a long-standing dispute between two Norfolk families, the Cremers and the Stockdales. It was asserted that one of the Stockdales had bewitched sheep, belonging to the Cremers, which had suddenly fallen ill. Although the Grand Jury found a true Bill in the case, the petty jury acquitted, upon hearing proof that the sheep, having been put in a freshly mowed barley pasture, had gorged themselves and "were burst with feeding" (the shepherd tending them had managed to save them).[562]

Nature of Oral Testimony at Trial

Although Mathew Hale noted that exception could sometimes be taken to physical evidence or oral testimony, the rules of evidence were still very flexible at this period. The first major text on the Law of Evidence, that of William Nelson, only appeared in 1717. Hearsay evidence was regularly being admitted up to the beginning of the eighteenth century, though with some reservations as to its weight. Witness testimony was also largely ungoverned by rules of admissibility. Because of the lack of accurate records of in-court testimony, firm conclusions are difficult. However, assuming (as is reasonable) that the deposition drawn up by an examining JP of the evidence to be adduced by a potential prosecution witness would not dwell on matters to which s/he could not give oral evidence at trial (and remembering that some such depositions were

---

562. L'Estrange Ewen, C., *Witchcraft in the Star Chamber*, at p.20.

themselves adduced in evidence), it is clear that for much of the period, and especially in the sixteenth century, testimony was almost unregulated. When Brian Darcy was examining Margery Sammon in February 1582 about the St Osyth witches, she gave evidence that constituted an acute form of multiple hearsay: "The said Margery ... saith, that the said Widow Hunt did tell her that she hath heard the said Joan Pechey, very often to chide."[563] Nevertheless, by the close of the witch trial period, a stricter, more regulated use of such evidence was developing (in 1717 Nelson could firmly declare that "Hearsay from others is not to be applied immediately to the Prisoner").

Interestingly, this emerging strictness was evident at the trial of the fraudulent witch-monger Richard Hathaway, in 1702. In particular, it can be seen in the lengthy debate that took place between Sergeant Jenner (this was a rare example of the defendant being legally represented) and Lord Holt (the trial Judge) over the ambit of the hearsay rule. The two lawyers were vexed by the distinction between reported statements that were adduced for a purpose other than their testimonial effect (sometimes called "original" evidence by modern English lawyers) and hearsay. This was a foretaste of a problem that has continued to trouble generations of law students and barristers for the last three centuries (Nelson accepted that in treason cases, at least, it could be admitted to "shew the temper of the prisoner").[564]

---

563. Rosen, Barbara (Ed.), *Witchcraft in England 1558-1618,* at p.111.

564. Cobbett, William, *Cobbett's State Trials,* Vol. 14, at p.654; Nelson, *The Law of Evidence,* at p.232. Holt CJ had shown sensitivity towards hearsay evidence, albeit allowing its admission as part of the emerging *res gestae* exception to the exclusionary rule, in *Thompson v. Trevanion* (1693) Skin,

If witnesses were called to testify that out of court confessions to acts of witchcraft had been made by the accused, or that they had personally seen the defendant perform such acts, the most obvious defence available was that such witnesses were motivated by personal antipathy towards the accused (as may often have been the case). Margaret Landis, when speaking in her own defence, at Worcester in 1647, was faced with this situation. The prosecution called several witnesses, including one who had alleged that Landis had confessed her involvement, and had also tried to entice her (the witness) into becoming a witch. She elaborated on this by saying that she even went with Landis to a witches' Sabbath, or, as she termed it, a "witches Meeting", where she saw the devil in the likeness of a "tall black man" (a typical description by the 1640s), but was so frightened by the sight that she refused to go there again. Faced with these accusations: "The prisoner in her own defence, said that they were all Malicious people and denied that she had Confessed any thing to the evidence, insinuating as if they had formerly an old grudge against her." This plausible, and coherent, defence was somewhat marred, when, to the "great disturbance of the whole bench" she made a "strange howling" in the courtroom (perhaps simply distress, or, alternatively, a sign of some mental disturbance). Nevertheless, before finding her guilty, the jury was out, considering their verdict, for an hour, a lengthy period by the standards of the time (though not uncommon in witchcraft cases).[565] Jurors, clearly, were very

---

402. For an indication of the perceived undesirability of hearsay generally, see *R. v. Charnock* (1699) 12 St Tr 1377, cols 1454.

565. Pamphlet 1670, at p.4.

alert to the fact that allegations of witchcraft could be malicious.

Defence Witnesses

Reputation and character were crucial to anyone accused of any type of felony, the trial being as much concerned with the individual as the act. Thus, typically, one Robert Hallam, who killed his pregnant wife in a domestic row, by throwing her out of a window in his house, when speaking in his defence at the Hampshire Assizes: "... denied the charge, and called several witnesses, who gave him a good character."[566] The same applied to witchcraft cases. Not only were village rumour and social or blood connection with other witches grounds for examination, but if someone accused of witchcraft could establish good character, it might tell heavily in deciding whether they should be formally indicted, and, if they were, convicted. Thus, character witnesses might be called (and be decisive) by all who could do so. However, by their very nature, this was something that many of the marginalised women who made up the bulk of such defendants, could not do. Typically, it was noted of two convicted witches at the Worcester Assizes in 1647 that "none appear[d] on their Behalfs" to give evidence in their support. Nevertheless, an example of a case where such character evidence was successfully adduced to defeat a witchcraft allegation, can be seen in Wiltshire in 1613. There, in the village of Wylye, one John

566. Pamphlet 1795 at pp.3-8.

Potticarie accused John Monday, a married village labourer who was also dependent on parish alms, of bewitching his child. Although the child recovered, Potticarrie subsequently brought charges against Monday at the Quarter Sessions. However, after a testimonial was provided on the defendant's behalf, signed by 13 villagers, amongst them the Rector of the parish, the case was dismissed.[567]

Expert Evidence

The arcane nature of witchcraft meant that expert evidence on the subject might be called at trial, especially for the Crown. In this, a witch trial was no different to any other case. As early as the 1550s, English law had recognised that expert opinion evidence might be received at trial in all matters where it was required. In the words of Judge Saunders: "If matters arise in our law which concern other sciences or faculties we commonly apply for aid of that science or faculty which it concerns."[568] Thus, in the case of the two witches accused before Mathew Hale, in 1662, the prosecution called a "Dr Brown" of Norwich. The man referred to was no ordinary doctor; Sir Thomas Browne (1605-1682), was a prolific writer, thinker and scholar, one who had travelled extensively in Europe and studied medicine in England, France and Italy. He combined a large medical practice with writing books, in a highly idiomatic

567. Ingram, M. *Church Courts, Sex and Marriage in England 1570-1640*, Cambridge University Press (1987) at p.114.

568. *Buckley v. Rice-Thomas (1554)* 1 Plowd 118 at 124.

style, such as the *Garden of Cyrus* (1658) and works on the mystery of death. Like James VI 80 years earlier, he had been heavily influenced by the continental, and more particularly Danish, experience, of witch offences. He stated to the court, by way of comparison with the "facts" of the case before them: "That in Denmark there had been lately a great discovery of witches, who used the very same way of afflicting persons, by conveying pins into them, and crooked as these pins were, with needles and nails." Less eminent experts were called by the Crown in the case of Margaret Landis, one of four witches tried at Worcester Assizes in 1647. She was indicted as a result of an incident in which she had been publicly accused of witchcraft by a child in the street; she had turned round at this allegation, and said to the girl involved that she would "smart for it." Unfortunately, the child fell sick that night and died three weeks later, again accusing Landis of bewitching her as she lay ill (always considered a significant sign in such cases). Medical evidence was adduced in court to support this juvenile analysis: "... the Child's doctor also deposed that she dyed of a Distemper, which was more than meerly Natural, and that she was under the Torture of some Diabolical Agent."[569]

Although most experts appeared for the prosecution, their evidence could also be received on behalf of the defence, something that applied as much in witchcraft cases as any other. In the celebrated case of Mary Glover, in 1602, Edward Jorden, a noted physician, who had been educated in both Cambridge and Italy, gave evidence in London for

---

569. Pamphlet 1670, at pp.2-3.

the defendant. Glover, a 14-year-old girl alleged that a common cleaning woman, Elizabeth Jackson, had bewitched her, causing her to suffer fits and episodes of blindness and muteness. Jorden, however, opined that Glover was suffering from a form of hysteria. He asserted that she was not a deliberate "counterfeit," one who was consciously dissembling, but rather suffering from some form of mental disturbance (such hysterical but sincere fantasy would be readily familiar to a modern psychologist). Unfortunately, the elderly Lord Chief Justice Anderson, a scourge of witches, presided over the trial, and was not impressed by so vague a diagnosis. In directing the jury, he took the opportunity to reveal his opinion of such experts, and declared to the professional witnesses present in court: "Divines, Physicians I know they are learned and wise, but to say this natural and tell me neither the cause nor the cure of it I care not for your judgment; give me a natural reason and a natural remedy, or a rush for your physic."[570]

Unlike "experts," ordinary witnesses were, as a general rule, not supposed to give opinion as opposed to evidence of facts. Nelson was to note in the first text devoted exclusively to the law of evidence in 1717, witnesses were sworn to tell the truth: "... not what they believe, for they are to swear nothing but what they have heard or seen."[571] However, this necessarily became attenuated in witch trials. Gifford produced an incisive analysis of the danger of non-expert opinion evidence being adduced in such cases, rather than that of hard facts (the latter being necessarily

570. Rosen, Barbara (Ed.), *Witchcraft in England 1558-1618,* at p.315.

571. Nelson, *The Law of Evidence,* at p.7.

very rare, and the former widespread). Thus, "Daniel", his imaginary interrogator, says to "Samuel" a countryman: "If others take their oath that in their conscience they think so, is that sufficient to warrant me upon mine oath to say it is so?" There was an inherent lack of certainty in this type of evidence, something that he considered should lead witnesses to ask themselves whether: "... upon matters which induce you to think so, present upon your oath that you know it is so."[572]

The Evidence of Children

Children played a notable, if sometimes exaggerated, role in many witch cases. According to Robbins in his *Encyclopaedia of Witchcraft and Demonology* (1959) during the witch hunting period hundreds went to their executions because of the "wanton mischief" of "undisciplined youngsters", with England and America being especially afflicted with such "little monsters".[573] The best known example of this occurred at Salem in America in 1692, when allegations made by young girls initiated, and largely sustained, the whole proceedings. However, this was merely the most notorious in a long series of such cases that had occurred earlier throughout Europe. A recurring theme of English witchcraft was the possession by, or infliction of disease on, such young people. Such allegations were frequently accompanied by fits or convulsions in the children concerned, often enacted in the courtroom itself. Although

572. Giiford, *Dialogue* at p.159.
573. at p.94.

not confined to any one sex, this was especially notable in girls. These fits would often occur when the witch entered the court, or was in close physical proximity to the child.[574]

However, a closer examination of the evidence, such as Macfarlane's Essex study, suggests that in reality most cases did not involve children's evidence, and even where they did, it was usually supplemental to that of adults. Nevertheless, there were a number of high profile English and Scottish *causes célèbres* where the direct testimony of children, or that of adults narrating their symptoms, was crucial to the outcome of the case. In Leicester, in 1619, nine women were hanged for witchcraft on the evidence of a single child. In Scotland, as late as 1697, seven people appear to have been executed on the evidence of an 11-year-old girl. Children played a crucial role in the trial of Duny and Cullender in 1662 at Bury St Edmunds. This phenomenon was not confined to the British Isles, there was a late outbreak of witch-hunting in the Swedish town of Mora towards the end of the seventeenth century, based on the evidence and widespread incriminations of children, something which resulted in 85 people being burnt. There were many others that are less well known. Amongst them was the trial of Joan Cunny, a widow of about 80 years of age, in Chelmsford, in 1589. Her grandchildren, the eldest being "about 10 or 12 years" old, were called against her, and, and rather chillingly, "gave in great evidence" for the prosecution. The Assize Judge apparently first encouraged them as to the form that their evidence should take, and "commended them greatly for telling the truth of that which

574. *See* Sharpe, J.A., *Women, Witchcraft and the Legal Process*, at p.115.

he should ask them concerning their grandam and their mothers." The potential susceptibility of children to suggestion or deliberate fabrication appears to have been totally ignored in this case, and several others.

Even in the sixteenth and early seventeenth centuries, there were many sceptics, such as the Reverend George Gifford, from Maldon in Essex, who doubted the value of juvenile evidence. Although they may not have had access to modern research on the deficiencies inherent in some children's testimony, their ordinary experience of life was enough to warn them about its risks. As Gifford noted: "Yea sundry times the evidence of children is taken accusing their own mothers, that they did see them give milk unto little things which they kept in wool. The children coming to years of discretion confess they were enticed to accuse." Significantly, the status of children in witchcraft cases was different to that in most other types of felony.

Although the defendant was not allowed to give evidence on oath throughout the witch trial period, for fear of facilitating perjury (nor were other defence witnesses, until 1702) they were allowed to make unsworn statements to the jury. In the minds of the 12 jurymen these were probably treated in the same way as ordinary sworn testimony. However, all prosecution witnesses normally had to be sworn if they were to give evidence. This meant that they had to understand the nature and significance of the oath, that is, properly appreciate that their souls would be damned if they lied. Thus, in the case of *Braddon,*[575] Judge Jeffreys questioned a 13-year-old boy as to his competence

575. Reported at [1684] 9 St Tr, 1127 at pp. 1148-9.

to give evidence, in the following terms:

J.J.: Suppose you should tell a lie, do you know who is the father of liars?
Boy: Yes.
J.J.: Who is it?
Boy: The devil.
J.J.: If you should tell a lie, do you know what will become of you?
Boy: Yes.
J.J.: What if you should swear to a lie? If you should call God to witness to a lie, what would become of you then?
Boy: I should go to hell fire.[576]

If this procedure had been followed universally, it might have acted as a powerful safeguard in such cases. However, witchcraft appears to have been in a small sub-class of cases, where the normal rules did not apply. In his *History of the Pleas of the Crown*, Sir Mathew Hale felt that in cases like "buggery, witchcraft, and such crimes which are practiced upon children", if the children in question did not have the "sense and understanding" to appreciate the obligation imposed by an oath (an issue that, he believed, would have to be considered carefully for those under the age of 12), they: .". ought to be heard without oath to give the court information." Hale believed that because such crimes were often committed secretly, it would often be impossible to

---

576. Spencer R., and Flin, R., *The Evidence of Children: The Law and the Psychology*, 2nd Edn., at pp.45-49.

find sufficient evidence to convict the guilty without such relaxation of normal practice. He pointed out that allowing the mother to repeat what the child had said to her, rather than calling the child in person, would be no superior to hearing from the child itself, being merely "narrative" (though he does not identify such evidence as being inadmissible simply because of its hearsay nature). This allowed the evidence of children as young as nine to be adduced (for example, those of Elizabeth Device at Pendle in 1612). Even so, whether children were sworn or not, he felt that some form of corroboration of their testimony was desirable: "... it is necessary to render their evidence credible, that there should be concurrent evidence to make out the fact, and not to ground a conviction singly upon such an accusation."[577] However, in witchcraft cases, the "supporting" evidence required could be found quite readily, and might be of the flimsiest type.[578]

Before attributing too much malice to juvenile witnesses, it is pertinent to remember that in many cases adults had expressly encouraged and cajoled them into giving their evidence. Many were quite overt (to modern eyes) about the stratagems they employed to do this, suggesting that a genuine lack of appreciation of the fallibility of such evidence. Thus, Bodin was quite explicit about the way in

---

577. Oldys, William (Ed.), *History of the Pleas of the Crown*, at pp.634-5.

578. This category of exceptions seems to have only been rejected in 1779, when, in the case of *Brasier* (East PC, 445) the Judges in London, assembled together, determined that: "... a child of whatever age cannot be examined unless sworn," though given the abolition of witchcraft as a felony in 1736, this then only applied to sexual cases.

which at their "tender age it [was] easy by promises of immunity to persuade and re-educate" them, so that they provided evidence against their mothers and others who had been involved in witchcraft.[579] The same situation undoubtedly applied in England. In 1584, Reginald Scot deplored the fact that little children, if "craftilie handled", might "confesse against their own mothers." Gifford, too, observed in 1593 that: "Many go so farre, that if they can intice children to accuse their parents, they thinke it a good worke."Technically, there was no law against calling children to give evidence against their parents (indeed they were legally compellable), as numerous witch trials showed (such as the Lancashire trial of 1612), unlike spouses, who, even then, could not be made to testify against their husbands or wives.[580] Doubtless, many children, flattered or frightened by such adult attention, or not appreciating its full implications, would readily provide evidence of the type desired. Others were probably intoxicated by the power over adults, and the public sympathy, that was provided to them by such accusations. The capacity of children to deceive deliberately, and, alternatively, their powers of auto-suggestion, were often seriously underestimated throughout the period, especially when there was no motive that would appear obvious to an adult (though many that a modern child psychologist could probably identify). Additionally, the potential sophistication of their stories was not fully appreciated. Thus, it was felt of the juvenile witnesses at Bury St Edmunds in 1662, that it

579. Bodin, *Demonomanie*, at p.L1.

580. Lambard(e), William, *Eirenarcha, or of the Office of the Justices of the Peace, in four bookes*, at p.271.

was: "... not possible that any should counterfeit such distempers, being accompanied with such various circumstances, much less children; and for so long time, and yet undiscoverd by their parents and relations." Furthermore, it was doubted that so many children could conspire together, although drawn from several families, and "as they affirm, no way related one to another, and scarce of familiar acquintance", to do an: "... act of this nature whereby no benefit or advantage could redound to any of the parties, but a guilty conscience for perjuring themselves in taking the lives of two poor simple women away, and there appears no malice in the case."[581] Even so, several people present in court had grave reservations about the prosecution case, and especially the child evidence. In particular, there was an "ingenious person" (possibly Kelyng) who felt there was a "great fallacy" in the experiment, so that no importance should be placed on it to convict the women, because the children: "... might counterfeit this their distemper, and perceiving what was done to them, they might in such manner suddenly alter the motion and gesture of their bodies, on purpose to induce persons to believe that they were not natural, but wrought strangely by the touch of the prisoners." This disconcerting (and not particularly arcane) possibility apparently put the court and everyone present "into a Stand." An experiment was conducted, and the result was, not surprisingly, negative. To a modern reader the fear is obvious, and does

581. *A Trial of Witches, at the Assizes held at Bury St Edmund's, for the County of Suffolk ... Taken by a Person then attending the Court, London: Printed for William Shrewsbury, at the Bible in Duck-Lane'*, In *Cobbett's State Trials*, Vol. 6 at p.699.

not require an "ingenious" observer to notice it.

It was a recurrent problem in such cases that a firm believer in witchcraft could always find a supernatural (rather than the obvious), explanation for results or conduct that did not conform with expectations. Thus, in the case of a family whose children and their friends were allegedly bewitched by one Edmund Hartlay in the 1590s, it was noted: "... in the 5 youngest, that when they gave themselves to any sporte, they had rest [from their demonic symptoms] & were pleasant though the time was longe." It was observed that they were quiet, and "fit-free" all the time when at play in a neighbour's house, however, "as soone as the[y] went about any godly exercise they were troubled." That work, prayer or Bible study might have been less pleasant to such infants, rather than more irksome to the devil, was not, apparently, considered.[582]

There could also be straightforward practical explanations for juvenile fabrication. Sometimes children might simply invent stories about witchcraft to cover up their own misdemeanours, these stories then taking on a life of their own, and becoming progressively harder to retract. Thus, the large-scale Lancashire witch trial of 1634 appears to have started when a boy, playing truant, made up a bizarre story rather than face being whipped for failing to bring home his father's cattle.[583]

---

582. Pamphlet 1660, at p.5.
583. *See* on this Spencer, R., and Flin, R., *The Evidence of Children: The Law and the Psychology*, at pp.309-311.

Chapter 14

The Execution of Witches

Even after a conviction for capital witchcraft, there was a possibility of escaping death. There might be a judicial reprieve, if the case was of lesser gravity, or, as Hale was to note in his *Pleas of the Crown*, if for some reason the trial Judge was not satisfied with the correctness of the jury's verdict, or thought that the evidence on which it was founded was uncertain. Another stratagem available for women (ie, most witches) to escape execution was by "pleading their bellies", that is asserting that they were pregnant. A woman believed to be in this condition would secure a temporary reprieve until the delivery of the child. As "T.W." noted, in 1660, of female prisoners convicted of felony: "If she say she is with child, then must the sheriff return a jury of women who must be sworn, and charged to try whether the Prisoner be quick with child or not." This provision was aimed at protecting an innocent life from the consequences of its mother's sin. In these situations the Judge had to: "... direct a jury of twelve matrons or discreet women to try the fact."[584] The "jury of matrons" was made up of worldly women, familiar with the tell-tale signs of pregnancy, which they normally established by intimately examining the convicted woman (in the same way that they might search for the witches' mark or teat). An oath was administered to the leader of these women: "... you as forematron of this jury, shall true swear that you shall search and try the prisoner at the bar, whether she be quick

---

584. Blackstone, William, *Commentaries on the Laws of England*, Vol.iv, at p.388.

with child, and thereof a true verdict shall return, so God help you."[585] The provision applied as much to witches as to any other type of female felon.

After the birth of a child (or a woman proving not to be pregnant from the passage of time), her sentence would, in theory, be carried out, and she would be hanged. However, in this situation, for most felonies, a considerable proportion were not, the woman often being released after a year or so in prison.[586] Thus, one witch, in Elizabethan Kent, Alice Daye, was sentenced to hang at the Dartford Assizes in March 1574, having been convicted of murdering three people by witchcraft, in her home village of Boxley, the previous year. However, she was reprieved when the jury of matrons found her to be pregnant. It appears that the original sentence of death was never carried out and that she was released fairly speedily from custody, as her name comes up a few years later at the July Assizes of 1578, held in Maidstone, for another, similar, accusation (killing two heifers and making one John Collyns ill by witchcraft). Unfortunately for her, on this second occasion, Collyns died shortly after her conviction for making him ill, she was kept in prison, and retried for murder by witchcraft at the next Assizes (held the following March); this time she was sentenced to hang, and, it appears, executed (the concept of *autrefois* convict and the double jeopardy rule not being well developed at this time).[587] Nevertheless, although some

585. Preface to T.W., *The Clerk of Assize, Judges-Marshall, and Cryer: Being The True Manner and form of the proceedings at the Assizes and General Goale-Delivery, both in the Crown Courts, and Nisi Prius Court* at p.36.

586. Beattie, J.M., *Crime and the Courts in England 1660-1800,* at p.431.

587. Cockburn, J.S. (Ed.) *Kent Indictments: Elizabeth 1,* at pp.127, 158 and 161.

convicted witches were permanently reprieved, they appear to have fared slightly worse in this respect than other pregnant female felons. This is probably because they were often convicted of murdering via witchcraft. Thus, Agnes Crockford, of Chertsey, was hanged in 1575 for murdering a six-year-old child by witchcraft, her sentence having been postponed for a year after conviction due to suspected pregnancy. Much might also depend on whether a woman was ultimately found to be genuinely pregnant or merely pretending (as many were). In this respect, some women accused of witchcraft failed the "examination of matrons" straight away, such as Jane Wallys of Stebbing in Essex. She was convicted in 1592, at the summer Assizes in Chelmsford, and was found not to be pregnant by the matrons, despite her plea, and swiftly hanged. Her indictment was marked simply "tri non pgn" to denote this. Nevertheless, Wallys was unlucky. Where there is a record of the determination of this issue on the Home circuit (and some records are missing) it appears that there were two not-pregnant verdicts for five pregnant ones in witchcraft cases, suggesting that the benefit of the doubt was normally given to the defendant.[588] The same or a similar provision applied in America and several other parts of Europe. Thus, at the Salem trials, in 1692, both Elizabeth Proctor and Abigail Falkner were spared execution because they were believed to be pregnant.

Bizarrely, at Maidstone, in 1652, it was alleged that three of the six condemned witches: "... Anne Ashby, Anne

---

588. L'Estrange Ewen, C., *Witchcraft in the Star Chamber,* at pp. 104-105, 132 and 174.

Martyn, and one other of their associates, after they were cast, and upon the pronunciation of judgment against them, pleaded that they were with child pregnant, but confessed it was not by any man, but by the Divell."[589] There had been considerable academic debate in the early-modern period as to whether the devil could father a child, with most opinion tending towards the negative. The sceptic Johan Weyer was certain that such a thing was impossible, not least because the Devil was a: "... spirit and does not have the flesh and bone required for the sexual act. The organs are lacking - specifically, the penis and testacles" (let alone the ability to produce seed). However, even if he could be the successful subject of a paternity suit, it was probably unlikely to result in the courts indulgence, and all three women were promptly executed!

Absence of Burning for English Witches

English witches that were executed, were almost invariably hanged. This was the normal penalty for felony (though aristocrats might be beheaded), and its use as the means of execution in England was, according to William Dugdale, "very antient" (though he noted that in some parts of the country, in the medieval period, other ways of putting people to death had sometimes been employed).[590] Additionally, if the jury found a defendant guilty of felony, the court had also to ask the jurors what lands, tenements,

589. Pamphlet 1652 (2) at p.5.
590. Dugdale, William, *Origines Juridiales or Historical Memorials of The English Laws*, at p.88.

goods and chattels the convicted person had, these being recorded, and, in theory, potentially forfeit. As Sir Edward Coke noted in 1628: "... the Judgement against a man for felonie is, that he be hanged by the neck untill he be dead ... [and] that he shall forfeit all his lands and tenements ... [and] all his goods and chattels."[591] However, almost invariably, and regardless of the true situation, the jury gave a formal answer to this question, "their common answer is, none to our knowledge."[592] In any event, most of the women convicted of the offence probably owned very little, though there were exceptions, such as the apparently prosperous Witch of Wapping.

The only situation in which a convicted witch in England would have been executed by burning, rather than being hanged, would have been where a deceased victim of her witchcraft had previously been the master or husband of the accused. In this case, like any other such murder, it would also have been classified as petty treason, for which burning was the normal penalty (albeit that the condemned woman was often first strangled with ropes after 1660). An example of this occurring was the execution of a Suffolk witch, Mother Lakeland, who was burnt at Ipswich on September 9, 1645. Amongst her victims had been her husband, who died after a lingering illness induced by her familiars: "... for all which she was by Law condemned to die, and in particular to be burned to death, because she was

---

591. Coke, Sir Edward, The First Part of the *Institutes of the Laws of England.*

592. T.W., The *Clerk of Assize, Judges-Marshall, and Cryer: Being The True Manner and form of the proceedings at the Assizes and General Goale-Delivery, both in the Crown Courts, and Nisi Prius Court,* at p.16.

the death of her husband."[593] A graphic illustration as to how this was effected, in England, can be seen in the case of Prudence Lee, who was burnt on April 10, 1652, at Smithfield, for stabbing her husband during a heated argument, the executioner set her: "... in a pitch barrel, bound her to the stake, and placed the straw and Faggots about her ... and after the fire was kindled she was heard to shriek out terribly some five or six times."[594]

The lack of differentiation between the manner of execution for witchcraft and that for ordinary felonies was something that annoyed some "enthusiasts", among them Brian Darcy, the notorious witch-hunting Essex JP. He noted that: "An ordinary felon ... is throttled: a sorcerer, a witch ... defying the Lord God to his face ... is [also] stifled." Given that the latter's trespass was so much greater than that committed by an ordinary felon, he felt that this produced an "inequality of justice", and that the convicted witch deserved a death that was "much the more horrible."[595]

Despite its rarity in England, the belief that witches were normally burnt appears to have been a well established part of popular folk lore, even in the early modern period (as it still is today), and one that was often subscribed to by the witches themselves. Thus, a witness giving evidence against Joan Flower said that Joane had told her: "... that her spirits [familiars, in her case an owl and a rat] did say that shee should neyther be hanged nor burnt." The reasons for this belief are not totally clear. Possibly, it was a folk remembrance of the rarely exercised power of the medieval

---

593. Pamphlet 1645(4), at p.8.
594. Pamphlet 1652(1), at p.8.
595. Rosen, Barbara (Ed.), *Witchcraft in England 1558-1618,* at p.106.

church courts to punish for all heresy, including witchcraft, in this manner. Statutes in England from 1400, 1414 and 1539 expressly stated that heretics should be burnt to death, and it was the fate met by noted men such as Latimer and Ridley. As Mathew Hale was to observe: "At Common Law Witchcraft [was] punished with death, as Heresy." Though this appears to have been imposed exceptionally rarely.[596] The last case (not one involving witchcraft) of this actually occurring in England appears to have been in April 1612, when an Anabaptist, William Wightman, was executed by burning at Lichfield. Such a popular belief might also have been a confused popular recollection of the burning of Protestants during the reign of Queen Mary. This may have been fostered by the graphic illustrations of immolations in John Foxe's Book of Martyrs (first published in 1563), perhaps the most widely read English book (other than the Bible) in that century.

There may have been other reasons, based on folk belief. After the conviction of six Kentish witches in 1652, a plea for such a disposal was apparently made by several of the condemned women. As the narrator of an account of their trials recalled: "Some there were that wished rather they might be burnt to Ashes; alledging, that it was a received opinion amongst many, that the body of a witch being burnt, her bloud is prevented thereby from becoming hereditary to her Progeny in the same evill, which by hanging is not; but whether this opinion be erroneous or not, I am not to dispute."[597] This may also explain why, in

---

596. Hale, Mathew, *Pleas of The Crown: Or a Methodical Summary of the principal Matters relating to that Subject*, at p.6.

597. Pamphlet 1652(2), at p.7.

the case of Ann Foster in 1674, having admitted the allegations against her in court and: "After Sentence of Death was past upon her, She mightily desired to be Burned; but the court would give no ear to that, but that she should be hanged at the Common place of Execution."

Such a belief might also have been encouraged by an awareness of foreign practice in such cases. Although the burning of witches was not carried out in England, it was common (indeed "normal") in most continental European countries and Scotland, albeit that it was customary in some of them for the witch to have been first put to death by some other means. Thus, in Scotland, Dr Fian, after conviction: "... was put into a cart, and being first strangled, hee was immediately put into a great fire, being readie provided for that purpose, and there burned in the Castle Hill of Edinburgh."[598] Scottish witch trials, often viewed in England as fascinating exotica, made very popular reading matter. It is also clear that in some parts of late medieval and early modern Europe, such burning was seen as a necessary prerequisite if a witch was to be safely executed and disposed of after death, so that she could not trouble her neighbours post-mortem. Thus, in the town of Lewin, in eastern Europe, it was believed that in the fourteenth century, when a reputed witch, after her death (from natural causes), was merely thrown into a ditch (because her pact with Satan prevented her from being interred in consecrated ground), rather than consigned to the flames, disaster ensued. She apparently walked the earth in a variety of forms, dealing out death to local people. This continued

---

598. *Newes from Scotland* at p.D.2.

even though her body was recovered from the ditch and a stake driven through her heart, to prevent her continued wandering (unfortunately she still persisted in walking the earth, and even used the stake as a weapon!). However, when her body was retrieved a second time and properly burnt, she immediately ceased troubling the locality.[599]

Nevertheless, in the early modern period, most of the authorities on witchcraft appear to have attributed little theoretical importance to immolation or post-death cremation, and burning does not usually appear to have been associated with any necessary function in dispatching witches. As James VI noted, although witches should always be put to death as a punishment the actual manner of effecting this was not important. The English departure from the norm in most of the rest of Europe (hanging rather than burning) did not have any import: "It is commonly used by fire, but that is an indifferent thing to be used in every cuntrie, according to the Law or custome thereof."[600] Strangely, however, it is recorded that the four witches convicted at the Worcester Assizes: "Received sentence to be burnt at the stake all four together."[601] Whether this was a minor local aberration, carried out under the impetus of the civil war (Mathew Hopkins apparently gave evidence at their trials), or a mistake in recording what actually occurred, and whether, if such a sentence really was passed, it was carried out, or commuted to hanging, is not clear.

---

599. Evans, E.P. *The Criminal Prosecution and Capital punishment of Animals,* at pp.196-197.
600. James VI and I, *Daemonologie,* at p.77.
601. Pamphlet 1670, at p.7.

Hanging of Witches

Provision for appeal against conviction or sentence being rudimentary, or non-existent, execution would usually be carried out very quickly after a guilty verdict, if the Judge did not first decide to reprieve the convicted defendant. Thus, at Bury St Edmunds, in 1662: "... the Judge and all the court were fully satisfied with the [jury] verdict, and thereupon gave Judgement against the witches, that they should be hanged. ...That morning we departed for Cambridge, but no reprieve was granted: And they were executed on Monday the 17th of March following." Similarly, the three Essex witches convicted in July 1589, in Chelmsford, were returned to prison for only two hours before being conducted to the local place of execution, where they were hanged. Even so, as with any other condemned prisoner, they were entitled to spiritual help, from an attendant clergyman, before sentence was carried out.

In early modern England, an essential part of public execution was the ritual and ceremony that accompanied it (more so, it appears, than in either the medieval period or the late eighteenth century). In this function, clerics appear to have played a major role in producing almost stereotyped patterns of behaviour at the gallows, manifest in features such as the last dying speeches of the condemned. Everyone present, the person to be executed, the hangman, the crowd (always substantial, especially when a witch was involved), and the Minister of religion had a role to play, were expected to play it, and usually did so. Socially, an expression of full contrition might even serve to re-integrate the witch into the community, while establishing a triumph over the devil, and providing a cautionary example of the dangers of witchcraft. It appears that the condemned person often co-operated in this process.[602] An obvious example of this was Mary Smith, who was executed for witchcraft in Norfolk in 1618: "... in particular manner confessed openly at the place of execution, in the audience of multitudes of people gathered together (as is usual at such times) to be beholders of her death. And made there also profession of her faith, and hope of a better life herafter; and the meanes hereby she trusted to obtaine the same, as before, hath beene specified. And being asked, if she would be contented to have a psalme sung, answered willingly that she desired the same, and apointed it herself, the Lamentation of a sinner."[603] Similarly, in the case of the Essex witches of 1589, spiritual guidance was provided by one Master Ward, a "learned divine." This cleric, having been exhorted by the Judges to encourage the three women to public repentance, managed to get most of them to say a few prayers. With Joan Upney, however, he had much more success, and she made a satisfying dying speech at the gallows, as was felt to be both customary and desirable for a condemned person. She was deemed to have died: "... very penitent, asking God and the world forgiveness even to the last gasp, for her wicked and detestable life." Even where a woman denied involvement in witchcraft, she might, like Elizabeth Cason in Faversham in 1589, repent for a previous immoral lifestyle. Indeed, some such women, though still pleading their innocence of witchcraft might accept their judgment as being deserved for other crimes that they had committed.

---

602. Sharpe, J.A. *Judicial Punishment in England,* at p.34.
603. *The case of Mary Smith for witchcraft'*, in *Cobbett's State Trials,* Vol.11, at p.1049.

Thus, around 1648, in America, a Dorchester woman who "utterly denyed her guilt of Witchcraft" to the very end, nevertheless "justifyed God for bringing her to that punishment: for she had when a single woman played the harlot, and being with Child used to destroy the fruit of her body to conceal her sin and shame."[604]

The pressure on some convicted witches to make public penance could be quite extreme. In 1651, the Ordinary of Newgate (the chaplain to the prison), exhorted Joan Paterson so often, at least nine times, to confess at Tyburn (the customary place for London executions) that even the hangman was moved to ask him whether he was not "ashamed to trouble a dying woman so much." His predecessor, Henry Goodcole, freely confessed that it was only after "great labour" that a pre-execution confession was "extorted" from Elizabeth Sawyer in 1621.[605] However, contrition was certainly not universal. In 1612, Jennet Preston had died "impenitent and void of all feare or grace." Even worse, not only were some witches at the scaffold not willing to die "well", but, a few, at least, would not even die in a dignified silence. According to the accepted tenets of decorum, Anne Bodenham, the Salisbury witch, certainly did not meet her death in a proper manner in 1653. She was apparently "desirous for drink", and demanded beer from houses on the route to the gallows, becoming annoyed on those occasions when it was refused. It was only through the undersheriff's intervention that she was not totally drunk by the time she mounted the scaffold. Her conduct continued

---

604. Hale, John, *A Modest Inquiry into the Nature of Witchcraft,* in Jameson, Franklin, *Narratives of the Witchcraft cases 1648-1706,* at p.409.
605. Pamphlet 1621(2) at p.8.

to be scandalous at the place of execution. First, she tried to jump off the scaffold prematurely, so to begin the process of strangulation, and then she refused to confess in public, ask for the prayers of the onlookers, or pardon the hangman for his necessary work. Nevertheless, she readily accepted that she could not lie in consecrated ground; after sentence was pronounced, she: "... shrik'd out with a most hideous noise, and desired to be buryed under the Gallows and coming to the place of execution, she ran up the ladder, and the rope being put about her neck, she went to turn herself off; but the executioner staid her, and desired her to forgive him: she replied, 'Forgive thee! A pox on thee, turn me off', which were the last words she said."[606]

Despite the importance of dying speeches, the crowds that assembled to watch a witch's execution often do not appear to have witnessed them in a respectful silence. The potential number of people present, and the volume of sound they could produce, was noted, in passing, by the author of a pamphlet on the three witches executed at Biddiford in Devon in 1682. He reproduced the "substance" of their last words, with the caveat that they were recorded as fully as could be done: "... in a case liable to so much noise and confusion, as is usual on such occasions." (The very complete questions and answers recorded a partial confession in which they admitted meeting the devil but denied acts of malignant witchcraft.)[607] If the condemned were articulate, and continued to deny involvement in the

---

606. Pamphlet 1653(1) at p.8.
607. *Proceeding against Temprance Lloyd, Mary Tremeles, and Susanna Edwards, for Witchcraft 1682 From a Pamphlet Entitled ... by D. Beare,* in Cobbett, William, *Cobbett's State Trials,* Vol. VIII, at p.1018.

crime of witchcraft, even at the gallows, it might, on occasion, raise concern in the crowd about the safety of their conviction. At Salem, some onlookers at the gallows tree, where those to be executed were hanged, were obviously disturbed by the repeated denials and pious conduct of some of the condemned.

It was customary for the prison gaoler to arrange disposal of the bodies after death, and he could, if he wished, claim their clothes and possessions for himself. He might also conduct a final search for supernatural signs on the body of the dead woman, to confirm their guilt. It was noted of the three members of the Samuel family, executed for witchcraft in Huntingdon, that after the execution was over and the three people were "thoroughly dead" (something that would take up to 15 minutes or more, as death was by strangulation rather than the garrotting occasioned by a modern hanging using a drop), the gaoler, "whose office it is to see them buried", stripped the bodies. He discovered a "teat to the length of half an inch" in the genital region of Alice Samuel.

Because of their crime executed witches would usually be buried in unconsecrated ground (especially if unrepentant), often in unmarked graves. Indeed, fear that he would not receive a Christian burial prompted Parson John Lowes to recite his own burial service on his way to execution, in 1645. However, this was not invariably the case (especially if a witch died of natural causes). The widow Coman, a self-confessed (if mentally deluded) Essex witch, having died as a result of being swum by her fellow villagers in mid-winter, was "carried to the grave in an ignominious manner and buried upon the north side of the churchyard, upon the 27th December 1699."

Chapter 15

Analysis and Conclusion

A Prosecution Model for Witchcraft

A possible model for English witch prosecutions, and an explanation for regionally differentiated levels of witch trials, might include the following sequence of events. In rural areas, there was an ongoing, centuries old, "steady state" of private allegations of witchcraft against, and suspicions about, certain people. These were largely, but not exclusively, old, poor, socially isolated and women. Such beliefs rose out of a peasant culture in which some of the finer ramifications of Christian theology (in whatever denominational form) were absent. Orthodox Christianity was obfuscated by a sub-culture of traditional beliefs and superstitions, supplemented by the more "eye-catching" new ideas transmitted in the popular literature on the subject. The presence of such rumours and allegations would be almost universal, but their precise level might depend on the wider religious and social culture of a particular region. Some of these suspicions would mature, over time, so that certain individuals would acquire a particularly strong local reputation as witches. A few of the people concerned might themselves reinforce this, by taking advantage of the special status that it gave them, if only to facilitate begging or to give them enhanced local standing. Eventually, this reputation might extend to a strata of villagers of significant, if localised, importance.

However, all villagers would be concerned at the potentially disruptive social effects of criminal litigation, and would have recourse to their natural leaders to avoid it where possible.[608] It is likely that mediation or appeasement would be attempted in many situations. Alternatively, low level informal sanctions might be imposed on the witch, and special "remedies" employed against her person. These might range from social isolation to drawing her blood. Periodically, however, a major "flash point" might occur, perhaps the result of coincidence, chance or folly, in which a serious and specific act of maleficium could be attributed to such a woman, prompting a demand for action. At this point, situational and legal cultural variables would be crucial. What was the attitude of the local parson, and, to a lesser extent, village squire, to such allegations? If they were hostile, these individuals might use their influence amongst the village élite to stop such an allegation becoming formalised. If, however, they were sympathetic, or, perhaps, simply not hostile or uninterested, the matter could progress to the conduct of other informal tests, if necessary, such as swimming, followed by an accusation to the local JP, the taking of formal depositions and the conduct of an examination. At this level (the examination by the Justice), immediate situational factors (was the local JP, personally, a sceptic or an enthusiast?), would still be very important. However, also very significant, would be the wider "legal culture" of that part of the county. Was there a tradition of judicial activism against witches in the area? The strength of this would be a crucial determinant, so that some JPs would send villagers asking for warrants, or producing witches without them, home with a suggestion that they should

608. Underdown, D., *Revel, Riot & Rebellion,* at p.16.

know better. Others would be sympathetic. This would combine with individual factors at the remaining three stages to decide the outcome of a case. How did the members of the Grand Jury and trial jury view witchcraft generally, and what evidence would the presiding Judge's interpretation of the law allow to be admitted? Even if they accepted the reality of witchcraft how would these "social actors" define it, given that it was a flexible concept? Would the Judge be personally minded, and if so brave enough, to order a post-conviction reprieve? Together, these multiple factors would decide who was accused, indicted, convicted and executed for the crime.

General Conclusions

It is fashionable in some modern works on Tudor and Stuart witchcraft to conclude by drawing wider social lessons from the whole process. Although witchcraft is unlikely to become a major popular concern in the modern period, one engendering criminal trials, the witch-hunting past is often brought up as an example of the dangers of wider forms of intolerance. In this context, McCarthyism is sometimes discussed as a more modern parallel, and a degree of (perhaps fairly synthetic) anger is expressed at these long ago miscarriages of justice, as if history does not have numerous more pressing and widespread cases of injustice than the fates of the few hundred wretched women (and few dozen men) who were executed for the crime in early modern England, tragic and awful though they were. Given this, it is, perhaps, salutary to remember that progress is not always forwards. The newly individualistic and rational society that emerged in the early eighteenth century had no place for anything so irrational as the prosecution and execution of a small number of witches. However, it was also the same society that had no place for the regulated grain prices of the "moral economy," although they arguably still had an important function in what was still a pre-modern state. More pertinently, some specific lessons can be extrapolated from the witch trial process, especially from its legal aspects.

At a very practical level, the prosecution of witches in early modern England may provide wider lessons for the modern criminal justice system than many might care to admit. At first sight this might seem ridiculous. Although witches continue to be actively persecuted in some parts of the developing world, such as southern and west Africa (where, in the mid-1990s, a number were lynched for shrinking their neighbours' penises) their prosecution in England is distant history. However, it must be remembered that although English law places great faith in the common sense of jurors, and has been reluctant to see "trial by expert", there are numerous, and increasing, areas of knowledge in which the jury is recognised as needing expert assistance in reaching its decisions. As a result, such forensic evidence has been received on hundreds of subjects, DNA evidence, pathology, ballistics, etc. This is an essential part of the modern trial process, but occasionally carries risks. Jurors are sometimes exposed to information and opinion as much beyond their understanding as the seventeenth century tests for witchcraft were to their ancestors, but on which they are invited, nevertheless, to place great reliance. Usually this is not a problem, such evidence being supported by scientifically valid empirical testing. Occasionally, however, it will, in retrospect, be seen to have been almost as unfounded and unscientific as that presented by Mathew Hopkins in the 1640s, or "Dr Brown of Norwich" at the trial of the Lowestoft witches in 1662. In recent years this problem has arisen with particular significance in connection with child abuse and recalled memory syndrome. Ironically, many allegations of large-scale child abuse in Britain, especially in the 1980s, took place amidst (apparently spurious) accusations of Satanism, in places such as Orkney and Rochdale. In these cases, numerous children were taken from their parents and placed in local council care. What exactly would Reginald Scot have had to say about the adults who, having seen psychotherapists, suddenly "remember" supposedly long forgotten incidents of incest and extreme sexual abuse engendered by their parents? Interestingly, in 1997, the British Royal College of Psychiatrists concluded in a report, that many such re-covered "memories" actually had "no basis in reality."[609] Other *causes celebres* in recent years have made people acutely aware of the extreme suggestibility of some, often rather ignorant, people, when held in custody, and their capacity to admit to whatever is put to them by their questioners, however untrue or absurd. This, too, is some-thing that many a convicted witch could no doubt have attested to. Also significantly, in 1989, the role of juvenile evidence at Salem, in 1692, was cited before an English court as an example of the need for caution in accepting the evidence of children as to sexual abuse.[610] To that extent, some of the lessons of the witch trial process are

---

609. *Abuse Claims may be false memories,* in *The Independent,* October 1, 1997.
610. *R. v. Norfolk County Council Social Services Department, ex parte M* [1989] QB 619.

still germane.

Judicial action against witches is also illustrative of the way in which the law, like any other human institution, is susceptible to the beliefs and fears of the wider society in which it exists and from which it draws its personnel. Early in the twentieth century, the great American legal scholar James Thayer observed that an examination of witch trials was particularly indicative of the manner in which the apparent security provided by existing legal forms, procedures and solemnities, established to regulate the investigation of facts, could nevertheless, break down when the: "... men who do the judging have their minds saturated with certain sorts of opinion."[611] Legal safeguards are only ever as strong as the people administering them, and men who are already persuaded about the existence of something often need very little evidence to find that it has been proved. Nevertheless, this should not be exaggerated. On witchcraft, the common law, and English judiciary generally, emerge with far more credit than many of their continental counterparts.

More generally, it is, perhaps, worth remembering that witch-hunting was, geographically, very localised, both within England and within Europe. Many Justices resisted the popular pressure to indict for the "crime," in doing so they provided an instructive example to their neighbours. Throughout its history, whenever part of Europe has fallen into misguided practices, another part has been moving slowly towards the light. This can truly be said of the

---

611. Quotation reproduced in Young, M., *The Salem Witch Trials 300 Years Later: How far has the American Legal system come? How Much Further does it Need to go?* at p.258.

persecution of witchcraft. The large parts of both England, and continental Europe, which did not indict witches to any appreciable extent, and which, nevertheless, managed to survive without meeting catastrophe, provided inspiration for many of the sceptics. Had there been a standard European-wide directive on witch-hunting, and the conduct of witch trials, the process might have become self-validating and self-perpetuating.

Finally, these trials (like the successively dominant themes in modern witchcraft studies) remind us that we are all children of our time. The most intelligent and able men can subscribe to the most absurd ideas, and thus ignore the glaringly obvious. In the face of the "condescension of history" towards them, the shades of Judges like Lord Chief Justice Anderson and Sir Edward Bromley might wonder how so many enlightened and rational twentieth century men could have made so many mistakes about their own era's political systems, at a far greater human cost than their errors over witchcraft. They might note that one of the (rightly) greatest modern scholars of their period, could observe, on the death of Joseph Stalin in 1953, that it was his (Stalin's) great happiness to have made a major contribution to the creation of a society characterised by human freedom, as a result of which humanity would "always be deeply in his debt." Absurd though this seems today, a significant number of highly intelligent and educated Englishmen in the early 1950s clearly subscribed to such an idea.[612] Anderson and Bromley might permit themselves a wry smile.

---

612. Hill, Christopher, *Stalin and the Science of History*, at p.212.

Select Bibliography

Abbreviated Citations for Commonly Occurring Texts

Ady, *Candle* - Ady, Thomas, *A Candle in the Dark: Or a treatise Concerning the nature of Witches And Witchcraft; Being Advice To Judges, Sheriffes, Justices Of The Peace And Grand-Jury-Men, What To Do, Before They Passe Sentence On Such as are Arraigned for their Lives As Witches*

Ady, *Discovery* - Ady, T., *A Perfect Discovery of Witches, shewing The Divine Cause of the Distractions of this Kingdom, and also of the Christian World*

Bodin, *Demonomanie* - Bodin, Jean, *De la demonomanie des sorciers* 1580 translated by Randy A. Scott

Bovet, *Pandaemonium* - Bovet, Richard, *Pandaemonium or the devils Cloyster*, 1684

Daimonomageia - *Daimonomageia a Small Treatise of Sicknese and Diseases From Witchcraft, And Supernatural Causes.* Published London, Printed by J. Dover, 1665

Filmer, *Advertisement* - Filmer, Sir Robert, *An Advertisement to the Jurymen of England Touching witches, together with the Difference between an English and Hebrew witch*

Gifford, *Dialogue* - Gifford, George, *A dialogue concerning Witches and Witchcraftes*

Gifford, *Discourse* - Gifford, George, *Discourse of the Subtill Practises of Devilles by Witches and Sorcerers*

Hopkins, *Discovery*, - Hopkins, Mathew, *The Discovery of Witches: In Answer to Severall Queries, Lately Delivered to the Judges of Assize for the county of Norfolk, and now Published By Mathew Hopkins, witchfinder, for the Benefit of the whole kingdom*

James, VI & I, *Daemonologie*, - James VI &1, *Daemonologie In Forme of a Dialogue*

Stearne, *Confirmation* - Stearne, John, *A Confirmation and Discovery of Witch Craft, Containing these severall particulars; That there are witches called bad Witches, and Witches untruly called good or white Witches ...*

Abbreviated Citations for Contemporary Pamphlets/Tracts

1599 *Discovery of the Fraudulent Practises of John Darrel*, Harsnett, John (1599)

1603 *Marie Glovers late woefull case, together with her joyfull delievrance written upon occasion of Doctor Jordens discourse of the Mother ... A defence of the truthe against D.J. His scandalous Impugnations.* Reproduced in Rosen, Barbara (Ed.), *Witchcraft in England 1558-1618*

1612 *The Life, Apprehension, Arraignment, and Execution of Charles Courtney, alias Holice, alias Worsley, and Clement Slie, Fencer: with their Escapes and Breaking of Prison.* Printed for Edward Marchant, London (1612)

1616 *The case of Mary Smith for witchcraft 1616*, at p.1049, in Vol. 11 *Cobbett's State Trials*, (1809) Taken from a "*Curious tract printed in 1616*"

1618 *A true and just Recorde, of the Information, examination and Confession of all the Witches, taken at S. Oses in the countie of Essex.: whereof some were executed and other some entreated according to the determination of lawe ...* By W.W. 1582, Reproduced in Rosen, B. (Ed.) *Witchcraft in England*, 1558-1618

1619 *The Wonderful Discoverie of The Witchcrafts of Margaret and Phillip Flower, daughters of Joan Flower neere Beuer Castle: Executed at Lincolne, March 11, 1618*, Printed by G. Eld for I. Barnes, dwelling in the long Walke neere Christ-Church, London (1619)

1621(1) Fairfax , Edward, *A Discourse of Witchcraft as it was acted in the Family of Mr. Edward Fairfax of Fuystone in the County of York, in the year of 1621* Reproduced in Miscellanies of the Philobiblon Society, Vol.V. London (1858-1859)

1621(2) *The Wonderfull Discoverie of Elizabeth Sawyer a Witch, late of Edmonton*, by Henry Goodcole, printed for William Butler, London (1621). Unpaginated in the original, page numbering by G. Durston

1645 (1) *The most Strange and Wonderfull apparition of blood in a poole at Garraton in Leicestershire*, Printed at London by I.H. (1645)

1645(2) *A True and Exact Relation, of the severall informations, Examinations, and Confessions of the Late Witches, arraigned and executed in the County of Essex who were arraigned and condemned at the Late sessions, Holden at Chelmsford Before the Right Honourable, Robert, Earle of Warwicke, and severall of his Majsties Justices of Peace, the 29th of July, 1645*, printed at Charles Clark's private press, Great Totham, Essex

1645(3) *The Examination Confession, Triall, and execution of Joane Williford, Joan Cardien and Jane Hott: who were executed at Faversham, in Kent, for being Witches, on Monday the 29 of September, 1645. Being a true Copy of their evill lives and wicked deeds, taken by the Major of Feversham and Jurors for the said Inquest*, Printed for J.G. London 1645

1645(4) *The lawes against Witches, and Conjuration and Some Brief Notes and Observations for the Discovery of Witches ... also the Confession of Mother Lakeland.* Published by Authority, Printed for R.W. London 1645

1645(5) *A true and exact Relation of the severall informations, examinations, and confessions of the late Witches, Arraigned and Executed in the county of Essex ... Before Robert Earl of Warwicke and several JPs.* By 'H.F.' London 1645

1649 *Serjeant Thorpe, judge of the Assize for the northern circuit, his charge; as it was delivered to the Judge at York Assizes, the twentieth of march 1648,* printed London 1649 in: Oldys, William (Ed.) *The Harleian miscellany a collection of scarce, Curious, and Entertaining pamphlets and extracts, vol.2,* at. pp. 1-13, London (1809)

1652(1) *The Witch of Wapping. Or, An exact and Perfect Relation, of the Life and Devilish Practises of Joan Peterson, that dwelt in Spruce Island, near Wapping',* Printed by Th. Spring (1652), Reprinted privately 1939, Joseph Foster (Ed.)

1652(2) *A Prodigious & Tragicall History of the Arraignment, Tryall, Confession, and Condemnation of six Witches at Maidstone, in Kent, at the Assizes there held in July, Friday 30, this present year, 1652, Collected from the Observations of E.G. Gent, a learned person, present at their Conviction and Condemnation, and digested by H.F. Gent.* Printed for Richard Harper, London (1652)

1653(1) *Doctor Lamb's Darling: Or, Strange and Terrible News from Salisbury; being A true, and exact, and perfect Relation, of the great and wonderful Contract and engagement made between the Devil, and Mistris Anne Bodenham; ...* by James Bower, Cleric London, Printed for G. Horton, London (1653)

1653(2) *Mercuriius Rhadamanthus: The Chief Judge of Hell. The fifth time discovering and delineating the villainies ... of all attorneys, clerks, Sheriffs, Bayliffs, Sargeants, catchpoles, Knaves in graine & c. From Munday July 18 to Munday July 25 1653.* London (1653)

1659 *A Word of Reproof, and Advice to my late Fellow-Souldiers and Officers of the English, Irish and Scotish Army ...* Printed for Thomas Simmons, London (1659)

1660 *A True Narration of the Strange And Grievous Vexation By the devil of 7 persons in Lancashire, and William Somers of Nottingham,* By John Darrell, minister, Reprinted (1660)

1662 *A Trial of Witches, at the Assizes held at Bury St. Edmond's, for the County of Suffolk ...Taken by a Person then attending the Court, London:* Printed for William Shrewsbery, at the Bible in Duck-Lane; in *Cobbett's State Trials* Vol. 6 at p.699

1664 *A Return of Prayer: or a faithful Relation of Some Remarkable Passages of Providence concerning Thomas Sawdie, A boy of twelve years of Age, Servant to John*

Roberts of Trebitian in the Parish of Lawrack, and County of Cornwall. Who was possest with an unclean Spirit, and through mercy by Prayer and Fasting, dispossest and delievered from the servitude and Jaws of Satan. (1664)

1670 *The Full Tryals, Examination and Condemnation of Four Notorious Witches, at the Assizes held at Worcester, on Tuesday the 4th March* (1647?) Printed by J.W., Fleet Street, London (1670 Edn.)

1674 *A Full and True Relation of the Tryal of Ann Foster,* Printed for D.M., London (1674)

1682 *Proceedings against Temprance Lloyd, Mary Tremeles, and Susanna Edwards, for Witchcraft 1682 From a Pamphlet Entitled ...* by D. Beare Reproduced in *Cobbett's State Trials* Vol.8, at p.1018

1686 *A Discourse Proving by Scripture and Reason And the Best Authors, Ancient and Modern, That there are Witches. Anon.* (John Brinley), Printed by J.M. London (1686)

1693 *A Relation of a Yarmouth Witch, who with Fifteen more Convicted upon their own Confession, was executed in 1644, published in A collection of Modern Relations of Matter of Fact, Concerning Witches and Witchcraft Upon The Persons of People.* Part 1, Printed for John Harris (1693)

1702 *A short Account of the Trial held at Surrey Assizes; in the Borough of Southwark: on an information, against Richard Hathaway ... for a Riot and Assault,* from *Cobbett's State Trials,* 1812

1712(1) *The case of Witchcraft at Coggeshall Essex, in the Year 1699,* Revd., J. Boys, *Being the Narrative from his Manuscript in the possession of the Publisher, penned down by him in 1712,* printed from his manuscript, A. Russell Smith, London (1901)

1712(2) *A full confutation of Witchcraft: More particularly of the Deposiytons against Jane Wenham, Lately condemned for a witch; at Hertford.* printed for J. Baker at the black-boy in pater-noster-row, London, (1712)

1795 *The Life, Trial, & Execution. of Robert Hallam, convicted at the last Hampshire Assizes, for the Wilful Murder of his wife,* published at Shepton Mallet (1795), Facsimile Edn. by The Toucan Press, Guernsey (1979)

Bibliography

A *Report of all the Cases Delivered by Sir John Holt* ... from materials by Thomas Farrelfly, Printed by E. & R. Nutt, London (1738)

Ady, Thomas, *A Candle in the Dark: Or a treatise Concerning the nature of Witches And Witchcraft; Being Advice To Judges, Sheriffes, Justices Of The Peace And Grand-Jury-Men, What To Do, Before They Passe Sentence On Such as are Arraigned for their Lives As Witches*, Printed for R.I., London (1656)

Ady, Thomas, *A Perfect Discovery of Witches, shewing The Divine Cause of the Distractions of this Kingdom, and also of the Christian World*, Printed for R.I., London (1661)

Aubrey, John, *Aubrey's Brief Lives*, O.L. Dick (Ed.) Penguin Books Edn., Harmondsworth (1962)

Baker, J.H., *Criminal Courts and Procedure in England*, in Cockburn, J.S. (Ed.), *Crime in England 1550-1800*, Methuen, London (1977)

Baker, J.H., *An Introduction to English Legal History*, 3rd. Edn., Butterworths, London (1990)

Barry, J. *et al* (Eds.), *Witchcraft in Early Modern Europe*, CUP, Cambridge (1996)

Bartlett, Robert, *Trial by Fire and Water: the Medieval Judicial Ordeal*, Clarendon Press, Oxford (1986)

Baxter, Richard, *The Certainty of the World of Spirits*, London (1691)

Beattie, J.M., *Crime and the Courts in England 1660-1800*, Clarendon Press, Oxford (1986)

Bellamy John, *Crime and Public Order in England in the Later Middle Ages*, Routledge and Kegan Paul, London (1973)

Bernard, Richard, *A Guide to Grand-Jury Men*, 2nd. Edn., printed by Felix Kingston, for Edw. Blackmore, London (1630)

Bilson, C.B., *The Jewel of Salisbury*, Published by the Dean and Chapter, Salisbury Cathedral (1996)

Black, S.F., *The Courts and Judges of Westminster Hall During the Great Rebellion, 1640-1660*, in *The Journal of Legal History*, Vol 7, Number 1, May 1986, at pp. 23-52

Blackstone, William, *Commentaries on the Laws of England*, First Edition, Vol. iv, *Of Public Wrongs*, London (1769)

Bodin, Jean, *De la demonomanie des sorciers*, 1580, Translated by Randy A. Scott, CRRS Publications, Toronto (1995)

Boulton, Reginald, *The Possibility and Reality of Magick, Sorcery and Witchcraft, demonstrated. Or a vindication of a complete History of Magic, sorcery and Witchcraft. In Answer to Dr. Hutchinson's Historical Essay*, Printed for J. Roberts, London (1722)

Bovet, Richard, *Pandaemonium or the devils Cloyster*, Printed for J. Walthoe, London (1684)

Briggs, J. *et al*, *Crime and Punishment in England*, UCL press, London (1996)

Briggs, R., *Witches and Neighbours*, Harper Collins, London (1996)

Briggs, R., *Many Reasons Why: Witchcraft and the problem of multiple explanation*, in Barry, J., *et al*, *Witchcraft in Early Modern Europe*, CUP, Cambridge (1996), at pp.49-63

Calef, Robert, *More Wonders of the Invisible World* (1700), reproduced in Fowler, Samuel (Ed.) *Salem Witchcraft*, Published by Whipple and Smith, Salem (1861)

Catlow, C., *The Pendle witches*, Hendon publishing, Burnley (1976)

Chaucer, Geoffrey, *The Canterbury Tales*, Wordsworth Edn., Ware (1995)

Clark, Stuart, *Inversion, Misrule and Witchcraft*, in *Past and Present* Number 87 (1980) at pp. 98-127

Cobbett, William (Ed.), Cobbett's *Complete Collection of State Trials,* Vols. 1-34, published 1809-1826, Printed by T.C. Hansard for Longmans and Co., London

Cockburn, J.S., *A History of English Assizes, 1558-1714*, CUP, Cambridge (1972)

Cockburn, J.S. (Ed.), *Calendar of Assizes Records: Hertfordshire Indictments James 1*, HMSO, London (1975)

Cockburn, J.S. (Ed.), *Crime in England 1550-1800*, Methuen, London (1977)

Cockburn, J.S (Ed.), *Essex Indictments Elizabeth*, HMSO, London (1978)

Cockburn, J.S. (Ed.), *Western Circuit Assizes Orders 1629-1648: A Calendar*, Royal History Society, London (1976)

Cohn, N., *Europe's Inner Demons* Paladin, St. Albans (1976)

Coke, Sir Edward, *The First Part of the Institutes of the Laws of England*, (1628), 1823 Edn., reproduced by Legal Classics Library, New York (1989)

Cotta, John, *The Triall of Witch-Craft, Shewing the True and Right Methode of Discovery: With a Confusion of erroneous wayes*, By John Cotta, Doctor in Physicke, Printed by George Purslowe for Samuel Rand, London (1616)

Cooper, Thomas, *The Mystery of Witch-Craft*, Printed by Nicholas Okes, London (1617)

Cracker, Wendel D., *Spectral Evidence, Non-Spectral Acts of Witchcraft, And Confession at Salem in 1692*, in *The Historical Journal*, Vol. 40, 2 June (1997)

Daimonomageia a Small Treatise of Sicknese and Diseases From Witchcraft, And Supernatural Causes, published anonymously, Printed by J. Dover, London (1665)

Dalton, Michael, *The Country Justice, Containing The practise of the Justices of the Peace out of their Sessions*, First Edn.1618, Printed for the Society of Stationers, London (1619)

Dalton, Michael, *The Country Justice, Containing The practise of the Justices of the Peace out of their Sessions*, 3rd Edition, London (1630)

Davies, Owen, *Methodism, the Clergy, and the Popular Belief in Witchcraft and Magic*, in *History*, Vol.82, No.266 (1997) at pp. 252-257

Davies, Peter, *The Trial of the Lancaster witches*, G.B. Harrison (Ed.) London (1929)

Dean, M., *Law-Making and Society in Late Elizabethan England: The Parliament of England 1584-1601*, CUP, Cambridge (1996)

Dekker, T., Rowley, W., & Ford, J., *The Witch of Edmonton*, first published 1621, London (1658 Edn.)

Directions for Justices of the Peace, Anon. 3rd Edn., Printed for Isaac Cleave, London (1708)

Drage, Dr. William, *A Treatise of Diseases from Witchcraft appended to Physical experiments: being a plain description of the causes, signes, and cures of most diseases incident to the body of man*, London (1666)

Dugdale, William, *Origines Juridiales or Historical Memorials of The English Laws*, printed by F. and T. Warren, London (1666)

Emmison, F.G., *Elizabethan Life: Disorder*, Chelmsford Essex County Council (1970)

Emsley, C., *Crime and Society in England: 1750-1900*, Longman, London (1987)

Englander, D. *et al* (Eds.), *Culture and Belief in Europe 1450-1600: An Anthology of Sources*, Basil Blackwell Pubs., Oxford (1990)

Evans, E.P., *The Criminal Prosecution and Capital punishment of Animals*, (1906), Faber and Faber Edn., London (1987)

Evelyn, John, *The Diary of John Evelyn*, Guy de le Bedegere (Ed.), Boydell Press, Woodbridge (1995)

Filmer, Sir Robert, *An Advertisement to the Jurymen of England Touching witches, together with the Difference between an English and Hebrew witch*, London, Printed by I.G. for Richard Royston (1653)

Foss, Edward, *Biographica Juridica*, John Murray, London (1870)

Foss, Edward, *Foss's Judges of England*, Vol.7, 1660-1714, John Murray, London (1864)

Fowler, Samuel (Ed.), *Salem Witchcraft*, Published by Whipple and Smith, Salem (1861)

Fox, George, *The Autobiography of George Fox from his Journal*, Newman, H.S. (Ed.), Partridge and Co., London (1886)

Gaule, John, *Select Cases of Conscience Touching Witches and Witchcraftes*, By John Gaule, Preacher of the Word of God at Great Staughton in the County of Huntingdon, Printed by W. Wilson, London (1646)

Geis, Gilbert & Bunn, Ivan, *A Trial of Witches: A Seventeenth-Century Witchcraft Prosecution*, Routledge, London (1997)

Gifford, George, *A dialogue concerning Witches and Witchcraftes*, Printed for John Windet, London (1593)

Gifford, George, *Discourse of the Subtill Practises of Devilles by Witches and Sorcerers*, Printed for Toby Cooke, London (1587)

Ginzburg, C., *The night battles, witchcraft and agrarian cults in the sixteenth & seventeenth centuries*, Routledge, London (1983)

Glanvil, Joseph, *Sadducismus Triumphatus*, part II, London (1700)

Gleason, J.H., *The Justices of The Peace in England: 1558 to 1640*, Clarendon Press, Oxford (1969)

Graves, M.A.R. & Silcock, R.H., *Revolution, Reaction and the Triumph of Conservatism*, Longman Paul (1994)

Green, A.G., *Verdict According to Conscience: Perspectives on the English Criminal Trial Jury, 1200-1800*, University of Chicago Press, Chicago (1985)

Gregory, Annabel, *Witchcraft, Politics And 'Good Neighbourhood' in Early Seventeenth-Century Rye*, from *Past and Present*, No.133 (1991) at pp.31-66

Hale, John, *A Modest Inquiry into the Nature of Witchcraft*, (1697) in Jameson, Franklin (Ed.), *Narratives of the Witchcraft cases 1648-1706*, Charles Scribner's Sons, New York (1914)

Hale, Sir Mathew, late Lord Chief Justice of the Kings Bench. *A Discourse touching Provision for the Poor,* London, Printed for William Shrowsbery, at the Bible in Duke-Lane, London (1683)

Hale, Sir Mathew, late Lord Chief Justice of the Kings Bench, *A Discourse concerning the Great Mercy of God, in Preserving us from the Power and Malice of Evil Angels,* published in *A collection of Modern Relations of Matter of Fact, Concerning Witches and Witchcraft Upon The Persons of People,* Part 1, Printed for John Harris (1693)

Hale, Sir Mathew, late Lord Chief Justice of the Kings-Bench, *The History of the Common Law of England ... Written by a Learned Hand,* Published Posthumously, by J. Walthoe, in the Savoy, London (1713)

Hale, Sir Mathew, late Lord Chief Justice of the Kings-Bench, *Pleas of The Crown: Or a Methodical Summary of the principal Matters relating to that Subject*, London (1678)

Hale, Sir Mathew, late Lord Chief Justice of the Kings-Bench, *History of the Pleas of The Crown*, first published posthumously, this edition in Oldys, William (Ed.), *The Harleian miscellany; a collection of scarce, Curious, and Entertaining pamphlets and extracts*, Vol. 2, at. pp.1-13, London (1809)

Harrison, G.B. (Ed.) *The Trial of the Lancaster witches*, Peter Davis Publishers, London (1929)

Hawles, Sir John, *The Englishman's Right: A dialogue In Relation to trial by Jury*, first pub. anon.1680, reprinted from the 1772 Edn., Rollins, Daniell (Ed.) Soule and Bugbee, Boston (1883)

Hay, D. & Rogers, N., *Eighteenth-Century English Society*, OUP, Oxford (1997)

Heal, F. & Holmes, C., *The Gentry in England and Wales, 1500-1700* Macmillan, London (1994)

Helmholz, R.H. (Ed.), *Select Cases on Defamation to 1600*, Selden Society, London (1985)

Herbert, George, *A Priest to the Temple, or, The Country Parson His Character, And Rule of Holy Life*, (1652), Wall J.N. (Ed), The Classics Of Western Spirituality, SPCK, London (1981)

Herrup, Cynthia B., *The Common Peace.* CUP, Cambridge (1987)

Hill, Christopher, *Stalin and the Science of History, in The Modern Quarterly*, Vol. 8, No.3, (1953) at pp.198-212

Hill, Francis, *A Delusion of Satan*, Penguin, London (1997)

Hobbes, Thomas, *Leviathan*, London (1651)

Holland, Henry, *A Treatise Against Witchcraft*, printed by John Legatt printer to the University, Cambridge (1590)

Holmes, Clive, *Women: Witnesses And Witches, in Past and Present*, Number 140 (1993) at pp.66-78

Hood, Roger, *Sentencing in Magistrates' Courts*, Stevens and Sons, London (1962)

Hopkins, Mathew, *The Discovery of Witches: In Answer to Severall Queries, Lately Delivered to the Judges of Assize for the county of Norfolk, and now Published By Mathew Hopkins, witchfinder, for the Benefit of the whole kingdom*, printed for R. Royton, at the angell in Ivie Lane, London (1647)

Hutchinson, Francis *Historical Essay on Witchcraft*, London (1718)

Ingram, M., *Church Courts, Sex and Marriage in England 1570-1640*, CUP, Cambridge (1987)

Irvine Smith, J., (Ed.), *Selected Justiciary Cases 1624-1650*, The Stair Society, Edinburgh (1974)

Jacob, Giles, *The Compleat Parish Officer*, 7th Edn. (1734), Republished by Wiltshire Family History Association (1996)

Jacobean and Caroline Comedies, Lawrence, R.G., (Ed.) Everyman's University Library, J.M. Dent, London (1973)

James VI & I, *Daemonologie, In Forme of a Dialogue*, Printed by Robert Walde-Grave, Edinburgh (1597), [Facsimile edn. Da Capo Press, Theatrum Orbis Terrarum Ltd. Amsterdam & New York (1969)]

Jameson, Franklin (Ed.) *Narratives of the Witchcraft cases 1648-1706*, Charles Scribner's Sons, New York (1914)

Jansson, M., *Mathew Hale on Judges and Judging*, in *Journal of Legal History*, Vol.9 (1988) at pp.201-213

Jorden, Edward, *A brief Discourse on Disease Called The Suffocation of the Mother*, London (1603)

Josselin, Ralph, *The Diary of Ralph Josselin 1616-1683*, Macfarlane, Alan (Ed.), OUP, Oxford (1976)

Kaye, J.M., *The Early History of Murder and Manslaughter*, (part 2), in *The Law Quarterly Review*, Vol.83 (1967) at pp.569-601

Kelyng, Sir John, Knt. Late Lord Chief Justice of his Majestys Court of Kings Bench *A Report of Divers Cases in Pleas of the Crown, Adjudged and determined; in the Reign of the late King Charles II With Directions for Justices of the Peace and others.*, 3rd Edn., Printed for Isaac Cleave, London (1708)

Kishlansky, M., *A Monarchy Transformed: Britain 1603-1714*, Allen Lane, London (1996)

Klaits, Joseph, *Servants of Satan*, Indiana University Press, Indiana (1985)

Kocher, Paul, *Science and Religion in Elizabethan England*, Octagon Books, New York (1969)

Kors, Alan & Peters, Edward, *Witchcraft in Europe 1100-1700: A Documental History*, University of Pennsylvania Press, Philadelphia (1972)

Lambarde, William, *Eirenarcha, or of the Office of the Justices of Peace, in four bookes*, (original edition published in 1579), corrected version, London (1619)

Landau, Norma, *The Justices of the Peace 1679-1760*, University of California Press, London (1984)

Langbein, John H., *Torture and the Law of Proof*, University of Chicago Press, Chicago (1977)

Lapoint, E. *Irish Immunity to Witch-Hunting*, in *Eire-Ireland* Vol.27 (1992) at pp.76-92

Larner, Christina, *Crimen Exceptum? The Crime of Witchcraft in Europe,* in Gatrell, V.A.C., *et al* (Eds.), *Crime and the Law: The social History of Crime in Western Europe since 1500,* Europa Press, London (1980)

Larner, Christina, *Enemies of God: the Witch-hunt in Scotland,* Chatto and Windus, London (1981)

Larner, Christina, *Witchcraft and Religion: The Politics of Popular Belief,* Basil Blackwell, Oxford (1984)

Lawson, P., *Property Crime and Hard Times in England, 1559-1624,* in *Law and History Review,* Vol 4., (1986)

L' Estrange Ewen, C., L. *Witchcraft in the Star Chamber,* Printed Privately for the Author (1938)

L' Estrange Ewen, C. L. (Ed.), *Witch Hunting and Witch Trials,* Kegan Paul, London (1929)

Levack, Brian, *The Civil Lawyers in England 1603-1641: a political study,* OUP, Oxford (1973)

Levack, Brian, *Possession Witchcraft and the Law in Jacobean England, in Washington and Lee Law Review,* No. 52 (1995) at pp.1613-1640

Levack, Brian *The Witch-Hunt in Early Modern Europe,* 2nd. Edn. Longmans, London (1995)

Llewellyn Barstow, A., *Witch-Craze: A New History of the European Witch Hunts* Pandora Publishing, London (1994)

McLachlan, H. and Swales, J., *Lord Hale, Witches and Rape: A Note, in British Journal of Law and Society,* (1978), Vol. 5 at pp.251-261

Mather, Cotton, *Wonders of the Invisible World,* reproduced in *Salem Witchcraft,* Fowler, Samuel (Ed.) Published by Whipple and Smith, Salem (1861)

Mather, Cotton, *Satans Invisible World Discovered,* (1685) Reproduced by Lea, H., (Ed.) in *Materials Towards a History of Witchcraft,* Vol. 3, University of Pennsylvania Press, Pennsylvania (1939)

Menninger, Karl, *The Crime of Punishment,* Penguin, Harmondsworth (1977)

Middleton, Thomas, *The Witch,* (c.1613), Edition of J. Nicholls, London (1778)

Middleton, Thomas, *Blurt, Master Constable: or The Spaniard's Night Walk,* (c.1602) Reproduced in *Miscellanies of the Philobiblon Society,* Printed by Charles Whittingham, London (1858-9)

Monter, E.W., *European Witchcraft,* Wiley, New York (1969)

Nelson, William, *The Law of Evidence,* London (1717)

Newes from Scotland, Declaring the Damnable Life and death of Doctor Fian, a notable sorcerer, etc., Anon, London (1591)

Nichols F.M., *Britton an English Translation and Notes*, John Byrne Publishers, Washington D.C. (1901)

North, Roger, *The Lives of the Right Hon. Francis North, Baron Guildford, ... The Hon. Sir Dudley North, ... and the Hon. and Rev. Dr. John North*, Vol. 1. First published 1740-1742, Published by Henry Colburn, London (1826)

Notestein, Wallace, *A History of Witchcraft in England from 1558 to 1718*, American Historical Association, Washington (1911)

Parry, L.A., *The History of Torture in England*, Samson Low, London (1933)

Pepys, Samuel, *the Diary of Samuel Pepys*, Vol. iii, R. Latham & W. Mathews (Eds.), Bell and Hyman Ltd., London (1972)

Pepys, Samuel, *The Concise Pepys*, Wordsworth Classics Edn., Ware (1997)

A Perfect List of all Such Persons as by Commission under the Great Seal of England are now confirmed to be, Custos Rotulorum, justices of Oyer and Terminer, justices of the peace and quorum, and justices of the peace, Printed by J. Leach, London (1660)

Perkins, William, *A Discourse of the Damned Art of Witchcraft* (1608) Reproduced in Breward, I. (Ed.), *The Work of William Perkins* in the Courtney Library of Reformation Classics, Abingdon (1970)

The Population of Stepney in the Early Seventeenth Century, East London History Group, in *East London Papers journal*, Vol.11, Number 2, (1968)

Pollock, Sir Frederick (Ed.), *The Table Talk of John Selden*, Quartich, London (1927)

Porter, Roy, *A Social History of Madness, Stories of the Insane*, Weidenfeld and Nicolson, London (1987)

Potts, Thomas, *The Arraignment And Triall of Jennet Preston, of Gisborne in Craven*, anon. (Thomas Potts) London (1612), Printed by W. Stansby for John Barnes, reproduced in Lumby, J.(Ed.), *The Lancashire Witch-Craze*, Carnegie Publishing (1995) at pp. 163-174

Potts, Thomas. *The Tryall of Ralph Hall and Mary his wife upon suspicion of witchcraft* (1613) Charles Scribner's Sons, New York (1914)

Powers-Beck, Jeffrey, "*Not Onely a Pastour, but a Lawyer also": George Herbert's Vision of Stuart Magistracy*, in *Early Modern Literary Studies* Volume 1, Number 2 (August 1995)

The Present State of Justice in the American Plantations, Anon, Possibly by Thomas Hodges, London (1704)

Prest, W., *Judicial Corruption in Early Modern England*, in *Past and Present*, No.133, (1991) at pp.67-93

Prothero, G.W. (Ed.), *Select Statutes and Other Constitutional Documents illustrative of the reigns of Elizabeth I and James I*, 4th Edn., Clarendon Press, Oxford (1913)

Pugh, Brian B., *Imprisonment in Medieval England*, CUP, Cambridge (1968)

Report on Court Procedures in the Colonies (1700), from the reports of Six colonies as a result of a request from the Lord Justices and Privy Council in England, Reproduced in *American Journal of Legal History*, Vol. 9 (1965)

Roberts, Alexander, B.D of Kings-Lynne, *A Treatise of Witchcraft*, printed by N.O. for Samuel Man, London (1616)

Rosen, Barbara (Ed.), *Witchcraft in England 1558-1618*, University of Massachusettes Press, Amhurst (1969 and 1991)

Rowley, William; Dekker, Thomas and Ford, John *The Witch of Edmonton* London (1621)

Sanders, A., and Young, R., *Criminal Justice*, Butterworths, London, (1994)

Scot, Reginald *The Discovery of Witchcraft*, London (1584) EP Publishing, Wakefield (1973)

Sharpe, J.A., *Early Modern England: A Social History 1550-1760*, Edward Arnold, London (1987)

Sharpe, J.A, *Women, Witchcraft and the Legal Process*, in Kermode, J., and Walker, G., (Eds.), *Women, Crime and the Courts in Early Modern England*, UCL Press, London (1994)

Sharpe, J.A, *Judicial Punishment in England*, Faber and Faber, London (1990)

Sharpe, J.A., *Instruments of Darkness: Witchcraft in England 1550-1750* Penguin, Harmondsworth (1997)

Sinclair, George, *Satan's Invisible World Discovered*, Edinburgh (1685), Reproduced in Lea, Henry (Ed.) *Materials Towards a History of Witchcraft*, Vol. 3, University of Pennsylvania Press, Philadelphia (1939)

Spencer, R. & Flin, R., *The Evidence of Children: The Law and the Psychology*, 2nd. Edn., Blackstone Press, London (1993)

Sprenger, Jacob and Krämer, Heinrich, *Malleus Maleficarum* (1486), Translated by Montague Summers (1928), Bracken Books Edn. (1996)

Stearne, John, *A Confirmation And discovery of Witch Craft, Containing these severall particulars; That there are witches called bad Witches, and Witches untruly called good or white Witches ...*, Printed by William Wilson, London (1648)

Stockdale, Eric, *A Study of Bedford Prison*, Philimore, London (1977)

Summers, Montague, *The History of Witchcraft*, (1925) Senate Edn., London (1995)

Summers, Montague, *The discovery of witchcraft a study of Master Mathew Hopkins*, Cayne Press, London (1928)

T.W. *The Clerk of Assize, Judges-Marshall, and Cryer: Being The True Manner and form of the proceedings at the Assizes and General Goale-Delivery, both in the Crown Courts, and Nisi Prius Court.* Published London (1660), Printed for Timothy Twyford

The Tatler, Vol. 1, D.F. Bond (Ed.), Clarendon, Oxford (1987)

Thomas, Keith, *Religion and the Decline of Magic*, Weidenfeld and Nicholson/Penguin, Harmondsworth (1971 &1991)

Trevor-Roper, H.R., *The European Witch-Craze of the Sixteenth and Seventeenth Centuries.* Penguin Edn., Harmondsworth (1990)

Underdown, David, Revel, *Riot & Rebellion*, OUP, Oxford, (1987)

Wesley, John, *The Journal of the Reverend J.W. Wesley* in 4 Vols. London (1827)

Weyer, Johan, *De Praestigiis Daemonum*, (6th. Edn.1583), Translated by John Shea (1991) Mora, G. (Ed.) Medieval and Renaissance texts and studies, Binghamton, New York (1991)

Willard, Samuel *A briefe account of a strange & unusuall Providence of God befallen to Elizabeth Knap of Groton*, Printed in the *Collections of the Massachusetts Historical Society*, Volume viii, Fourth series, at pp.555-570

Wormald, Jenny, *Court, Kirk, and Community: Scotland 1470-1625,* Edinburgh University Press, Edinburgh (1981)

Wrightson, Keith, *The Politics of the Parish in Early Modern England,* in Griffiths, T. P. *et al* (Eds.), *The Experience of Authority in Early Modern England,* Macmillan, London (1996)

Wrightson, Keith, *Two Concepts of Order: Justices, Constables and Jurymen in Seventeenth-Century England,* in Brewer, J. and Styles J. (Eds.), *An Ungovernable People,* Hutchinson, London (1980)

Wrightson, K. & Levine D., *Poverty and Piety in an English Village: Terling, 1525-1700,* Clarendon, Oxford (1995)

Young, M., *The Salem Witch Trials 300 Years Later: How Far has the American Legal System Come? How Much Further does it Need to go?* in *Tulane Law Review* (1989) Vol. 64 No.1 at pp.235-258

Contemporary Journals Cited

The Gentleman's Magazine
The Spectator
The Tatler

Index